The
Catcher
Was a Spy

The

THE MYSTERIOUS LIFE

Catcher

OF MOE BERG

Was a Spy

▼

Nicholas Dawidoff

PANTHEON BOOKS / NEW YORK

Library of Congress Cataloging-in-Publication Data
Dawidoff, Nicholas.
The catcher was a spy : the mysterious life of Moe Berg /
Nicholas Dawidoff.
p.   cm.
Includes index.
ISBN 0-679-41566-1
1. Berg, Morris, 1902–1972. 2. World War, 1939–1945—
Secret service—United States. 3. Spies—United States—
Biography.
I. Title.
D810.S8B4693   1994
940.54′8673—dc20   93-41324

BOOK DESIGN BY CHRIS WELCH

Manufactured in the United States of America

9 8 7 6 5 4

For my mother and
my grandmother

Contents

▼

The
Catcher
Was a Spy

Who Was
Moe Berg?

T he Headquarters Building at the Central Intelligence
Agency in Langley, Virginia, is a grim maze of identical
corridors flanked by blank, color-coded office doors
that are always shut tight. Only deep within the Headquarters
Building, in the CIA Exhibit Center, is there any evidence of
the dash, the violence, and the sangfroid of professional espionage. Displayed in glass cases like a collection of Han Dy-
nasty relics are devices for flattening automobile tires, a sensor
in the guise of a dung pile, a letter from Joseph Stalin's daughter requesting asylum in the West, an undetonated bomb discovered at a U.S. government facility in the Middle East, a
miniature camera masked as a box of matches, a battered
beacon used in the disastrous Cuban Bay of Pigs operation,
and a bust of Hermann Göring that the future CIA director
Allen Dulles hustled out of Germany at the end of World
War II.

There is as well a glass case devoted to the Office of Strategic Services (OSS), which preceded the CIA as America's first national intelligence agency. On a shelf above a pistol and silencer that once belonged to the OSS director "Wild" Bill Donovan are two worn cardboard baseball cards. Beside them is a placard that says,

MORRIS (MOE) BERG BASEBALL CARDS.

Following his 15-year career with five different major league teams, the Princeton-educated Berg served as a highly successful Office of Strategic Services (OSS) operative during World War II. Among his many missions on behalf of OSS, the former catcher was charged with learning all he could about Hitler's nuclear bomb project. . . .

Because of his intellect, Moe Berg is considered the "brainiest" man ever to have played the game. He spoke a dozen languages fluently and often autographed pictures in Japanese. These cards are from his playing days with the Washington Senators (1932–34) and Boston Red Sox (1935–39).

When Linda McCarthy, the CIA museum curator, talks about Moe Berg, her face flushes sanguine and her conversation comes in breathless, staccato surges. Moe Berg is her passion. "People think I'm making him up," she says. "I idolize Moe. He did it for the right reasons. He joined OSS with a purpose in mind. He knew he'd be useful to this country. He knew what the Germans were doing with the atomic bomb. That's what intelligence is all about. You have to know what the other side's doing.

"As a ballplayer he was a gentleman," continues McCarthy, who drives a utility vehicle—"for a utility catcher," she says—adorned with MOE BERG license plates. "I admire Renaissance men. I'd love to sit down and talk with him. In the evening when I close up my museum, I go over and say good night to Moe. I think his spirit is here. I think I do know him."

ALLAN SIEGAL IS an assistant managing editor at the *New York Times*. Over time, Siegal has developed correspondences with, as he puts it, "people who feel an obligation to police the language." Many of these are elderly readers, retirees with ample time on their watches, but others are simply grammar mavens, and they include—Siegal begins ticking them off— "prominent lawyers, a prominent real estate man who nobody would suspect was concerned with this sort of thing, a well-known Columbia professor; there are people who have been corresponding with me for ten or twenty years." In recent years, Siegal has received several letters on a variety of syntactical subjects from Moe Berg. There is never any return address, so Siegal hasn't been able to reply, but he has taken Berg's diffidence in stride.

Berg's latest piece of mail came in response to an article about the German physicist Werner Heisenberg, who American military staff feared was building an atomic bomb for Adolf Hitler during the Second World War. It was Berg's job to find out whether or not Heisenberg was really doing this. The offending sentences in the *Times* article describe Berg's only encounter with Heisenberg, at a lecture in Switzerland. "But if Heisenberg seemed to suggest that a Nazi atomic bomb was eminent, Berg was instructed to kill him on the spot. Berg watched and listened. He decided that Heisenberg's eyes were sinister." The *Times* writer had, of course, written "eminent" when he meant "imminent," and, sure enough, a few days later Siegal received a note that said, "If a German bomb were eminent, small wonder Heisenberg's eyes were sinister." It was signed "Moe Berg." Siegal thought it was nice that Moe Berg was monitoring his appearances in the newspapers, and he said as much to a colleague. As he did, a look of anxiety spread across the colleague's face. "Al," said the colleague, "I think Berg has been dead for a long time." Siegal checked, and it was true. Moe Berg died in 1972. The identity of whoever it is who thinks he—or she—is Moe Berg remains a mystery to Siegal. Moe Berg was always a very private man.

CHARLES OWEN IS a beer and Scotch drinker, but he has stocked his one-bedroom apartment in suburban Maryland with Pouilly-Fuissé, a white Burgundy. Pouilly-Fuissé was Moe Berg's favorite wine. On Owen's walls are three copies of Berg's life mask, two made of bronze, one in white ceramic. Owen has commissioned artists to paint Berg's portrait on the surface of baseballs. At holiday time he sends out Moe Berg greeting cards of his own design. For more casual correspondence, he relies upon the Moe Berg postcards he gets printed up by the hundreds. Moe Berg's baseball cards are worth as much as $150 apiece. Owen owns over one hundred of them. In his wallet, he carries a few of Berg's business cards. Berg was an avid reader of newspapers; he bought as many as ten a day. Whenever Owen visits an old Berg hangout—the Mayflower, say, which was Berg's favorite Washington hotel —Owen leaves a fresh copy of the day's *Washington Post* on a side table in the lobby.

Owen, fifty-eight, completed high school, did a stretch in the air force, and has since worked in a variety of jobs. He is a bachelor, so his spare time is his own, or, rather, it is Moe Berg's. During his weekends and vacations Owen travels the world learning all he can about Moe Berg. He does not consider himself a writer or a historian. He wants only to know. In this spirit he has been to England and to Florida, he has met former spies and faded lovers, ranking generals and retired ambassadors, old-time ballplayers and elderly Princetonians. Berg was a Princeton graduate, Class of 1923, and Owen refers to the university as "the place where the legend began."

Owen first heard about Berg a dozen years ago when he

read a brief article about him in the *Washington Post*. "I said to myself, 'No man could have done all this,' " he remembers. He began writing letters and making telephone calls. In time, he met Berg's older brother, Samuel, a Newark doctor. Berg lived in Newark with Samuel—who went by "Dr. Sam"—for nearly twenty years, until Dr. Sam threw him out in 1964. Dr. Sam took a liking to Owen. He gave him the run of Berg's papers, photographs, and possessions, which were stored in the attic, and then Owen says Sam presented them all to him before he died in 1990, at the age of ninety-two. "I've almost been compelled to try and understand this mysterious man," says Owen. "Moe opened up a new world to me. I did it because I wanted to know who Moe Berg was. A lot of people knew parts of Moe Berg. Moe was a different person to different people. He was complicated and he was simple." Owen shakes his head and smiles. "I don't know him now. I don't know if anybody knows Moe Berg. He kept secrets from everybody. Nobody'll ever know him."

In 1989, DURING his sophomore year at Princeton, Lou Jacobson, a writer for the *Daily Princetonian*, was driving back to school from a college newspaper convention in Washington, along with three other *Princetonian* writers. Seated behind him was Sharon Katz, whom he'd never met. "To kill the time," says Jacobson, "I told her the story of Moe. The long version. From Washington well past Delaware." Some time later, back on campus, he bumped into Katz again, and soon the conversation turned to Moe Berg. Jacobson remarked that he had some photographs of Berg up in his room, and wondered if Katz would like to come up and see them. Katz would, indeed. They have been together ever since.

Jacobson likes to tweak himself for what he calls "my obsessive interest in Moe Berg." So did his friends on the *Princetonian*, who tacked a sheet of paper to his door outlining the seven tenets of "Ritual for the Worship of Moe Berg (The

Moeslem Religion)." Jacobson wrote about Berg for a confirmation project, again for a Princeton seminar, and once more for the *Princetonian*, and he admits, "I'm still fascinated by him. So many unanswered questions in my mind. I try to be detached from the Moe mystique, because I just want to understand the guy. Why did he stay in baseball so long when he played so little? Why did he suddenly go into spying? What happened after he finished law school? Why did he never marry? Why did none of the Bergs ever marry? Why were their relations so strained?"

"MOE BERG WAS a fraud!" says George Allen, his voice rising as it always does when Berg is the subject. Allen is the proprietor of the William H. Allen antiquarian bookshop in Philadelphia. He met Berg in the late 1960s. Berg walked into the shop one day, asked to be directed to the linguistics section, and spent the day there, perched on a stool, reading. He refrained, even, from breaking for lunch. Berg returned for several more days of reading, always appearing to Allen as though "he had slept in the railroad station the previous night." Only once did Berg buy a book; it cost $1. "I never took him seriously," says Allen. "He wasn't a nice man. He was a professional liar, a layabout who lived on his brother, a lecher, a charlatan. Just why the OSS took him I can't see. He didn't speak any foreign language well enough to be a spy and he was rather the parody of a spy. Berg was a self-invented mystery, a charming chap, but an outright fraud. The mystery is that there is no mystery."

IRWIN BERG IS a Harvard-educated, New York City lawyer. He saw his first cousin once removed Berg only twice, but he thinks about him constantly. "In 1939, I wasn't yet six years old," he says. "My father took me to see the Yankees play the Red Sox. We went because Moe was playing for the Red Sox.

My father left a message for Moe, saying that we'd meet him by the players' entrance after the game. After the game my father took me and my cousin David there and then my father walked away halfway down the block. We waited forty minutes and then Moe walked out. He shook hands with me, said 'Hello,' and then he shook David's hand. Somebody in a car said, 'Hey, Moe! Come on!' He jumped into the car and that was it.

"The second time was in Sam Berg's house. Moe was living there, and Sam invited me and my mother to dinner. Sam told us to wait in his office. He had a few things to do, he said. In the meantime, I heard somebody walking back and forth upstairs. It wasn't Sam. Then the person came down and went outside. This was around 1955, I think. My mother said to me, 'That's Moe.' What was happening was that Sam was giving him time to get out of the house. Moe didn't want to meet anyone. Moe brought his mother to my grandmother's funeral. And then he sat outside, waiting for her on a bench with an open newspaper covering his face."

CHAPTER 1

The Public Berg: Professor Moe

John Kieran created the public Moe Berg. At heart, Kieran was a naturalist, happiest when crossing a rocky headland below a flock of migrating seabirds. But Kieran could also discourse at length upon Rossini's librettos, Jefferson's journals, Virgil's translators, or Manet's politics. Or Lou Gehrig's strength. For Kieran earned his living by writing "Sports of the Times," the *New York Times'* first signed daily column of any kind.

Kieran wrote "Sports of the Times" from 1927 to 1942, a period when the sports section was not yet a place for investigation, opinion, or quotation. Reporters covered the games, not the personalities, while columnists specialized in diversion rather than revelation. Most of the best early sports columnists—Lardner, Runyon, Kieran—were humorists, and much latitude was permitted them in the name of entertainment. They needed it, for the columnist's relentless obligation is to find something worth writing about when the news is dull. Kieran wrote a daily column for his newspaper, and whenever events, temperatures, or inspiration were wanting, "the most erudite sports writer of this, or any day," according to Runyon, simply turned to Moe Berg. Over time, Kieran all but invented a persona for Berg, spinning installments in the life of his beloved "Professor," the bookish ballplayer.

Kieran produced Berg columns at the slightest provocation. News out of Ohio that Cincinnati Reds pitcher Johnny Vander Meer had recently submitted to his third tonsillectomy, for instance. "As soon as Professor Moe Berg of the Boston Red Sox Department of Languages and Obscure Sciences can be located, this observer plans to consult him about an obscure item that popped up in the recent baseball news," Kieran begins on December 8, 1938. "It may be hard to catch the learned catcher. He moves mysteriously." Kieran alludes to the most recent Berg sighting, "in the audience down at Princeton University a week or so ago when Doctor Thomas Mann, the eminent exile, was delivering a lecture on Goethe's *Faust*." Berg is then trailed to an appointment in Princeton with Albert Einstein, with whom he discusses Professor Archibald Henderson's musings on the internal bisector problem in Euclidean geometry, which "Professor Berg has had on his mind since he read Professor Henderson's monograph in the bull pen during a doubleheader between the Red Sox and Detroit Tigers in Detroit one day late last summer." Vander Meer's third tonsillectomy is finally mentioned, in passing, as another conundrum suitable for Berg's consideration.

In a January 27, 1938, column, entitled "When the Bookworm Returned," "Catcher Moe Berg" is off for a visit to Princeton in the company of his bosom friend, the perpetually aggrieved Al Schacht, a Red Sox coach, better known to baseball enthusiasts as "The Clown Prince of Baseball." Berg intends to show students at his alma mater some movies of Russia and Japan that he made during a tour of those countries in 1934. Driving duties fall to an overwrought Schacht. "He

speaks eight languages—he has sixteen degrees from universities—and he can't drive a car," moans Schacht. "He can't
do anything in a car—refuses to touch a thing—wouldn't turn
on the radio—wouldn't turn on the lights—wouldn't put his
hand in his pocket for gasoline." The journey begins inaus-
piciously. Berg is an hour and a half late for their rendezvous
in New York, and when he finally does show up, he delays the
trip further by insisting that they make a stop at his house in
Newark. Schacht is awed by the Berg residence. He has never
seen so many books in so many languages. "The living room
is lined with shelves—French. The dining room is lined with
volumes—clear up to the ceiling—German. There's two other
rooms down there—one lined with Italian books—the other
with Spanish. So we go upstairs. There's nothing on the walls
but bookshelves filled with books—astronomy books in one
place—chemistry in another. . . . No wonder he can't hit a
curve ball! A guy who read half of those ought to be stone
blind."

Berg retrieves his films from the attic. They get back in the
car, and passing references are made to the time Berg spent
studying at the Sorbonne in Paris (Schacht calls it the "Sun-
burn"). Eventually they arrive at Princeton, Berg shows his
movies, slips off to purchase a few books—"seven big ones—
I can't even understand the titles," says Schacht—and then,
twenty miles down the road back to New York, Schacht is
forced to turn back. Berg has forgotten his films.

The mysterious Berg becomes Kieran's response to Ring
Lardner's fictional Jack Keefe, the solecistic Busher whose
streak of artless volubility is nearly as strong as his pitching
arm. Each Kieran column about Berg serves as another chapter
in the meandering comic adventures of baseball's erudite
eccentric.

For a 1937 column about the reluctance of ballplayers to
talk about their own team unless it is winning, Kieran places
Berg hurrying through Grand Central Terminal in New York
just after the Yankees have, as usual, smothered the Red Sox.

Berg is carrying "a bale of newspapers under his arm, foreign and domestic," and when he spots Kieran, he greets him in Japanese. Berg is prodded into joining Kieran for lunch, at which he orders applesauce, "no more, no less." Awaiting his applesauce, Berg settles his newspapers onto a chair beside him, whereupon a paperback copy of *An Enquiry Concerning Human Understanding*, "by a certain David Hume, not known in American League circles," falls to the floor. "It was a wonder he didn't come up at that dark moment with a volume of Schopenhauer," says Kieran, who then begins grilling Berg on the source of the Red Sox latest swoon. Kieran asks about pitching. Berg explains his ambition to own the *New York Times*. Kieran inquires about a particularly ineffective pitcher. Berg outlines the subtleties of ordering roast beef in a London restaurant. Kieran wants to know about the Boston outfield. Berg tells him about Japanese foreign policy. In desperation, Kieran asks about the Yankees. He hears about Al Schacht's latest comic skit, a pigeon act.

Berg is even summoned into service for a January 31, 1939, column about ice hockey. Kieran finds himself much confused following a disputed goal and "this puzzled observer determined to see a lawyer about it. Just by luck Professor Moe Berg was encountered in conversation with a literary gent, Mr. Percy Waxman. . . . It will be remembered that Professor Berg, the Red Sox catcher who officiates only in the second games of doubleheaders and not even then if it is a hot day, is a licensed barrister in this area."

Kieran summarizes the controversial goal problem. " 'It sounds like Sanskrit to me,' muttered Mr. Waxman.

" 'That reminds me,' said Professor Berg," who then launches lengthily into a discussion of the roots of Sanskrit, with attendant remarks upon the Rosetta Stone and Egyptian hieroglyphics until Kieran interrupts with another swipe at Berg's baseball skills.

"Very interesting, but it had nothing to do with the flowers that bloom in the Spring, tra-la, or the summary removal from office of a goal judge at a hockey game. Professor Berg was, allegedly, a big league ballplayer in the summertime. Anyway, he had a uniform and was allowed to travel with the team."

Undaunted, through the course of the next few paragraphs Berg offers up the fact that the word "league" is derived from the same Latin root that gives us the word "ligature," discusses the Basque, Magyar, and Finno-Ugric roots of modern diction, explains that the Canary Islands are not named after canaries but "are really the Dog Islands, from 'canis' in Latin," and drops in Jacob Grimm, the German philologist, as well. The controversial goal problem remains unresolved.

"Professor Berg" proved irresistible to many sportswriters, and while none gilded him with prose as witty as Kieran's, the Berg that appeared in columns and features around the country during his life and afterward was a consistent, recognizable character.

Berg was a voracious reader, and journalists, naturally, liked that, especially when they caught sight of the tomes he was hauling around the American League with him to complement his copy of their newspaper. "What's the book?" Berg was asked by a writer one day in the Washington Senators clubhouse. " 'Oh, just a little thing I picked up in England,' he answered nonchalantly, heaving the volume to an adjacent table. 'Not very deep reading, but it's interesting,' he added deprecatingly. The volume was titled *Ancient Law: Its Connection with the Early History of Society and Its Relation to Modern Ideas.*"

Berg also enjoyed talking, and in many tongues, another endless source of editorial delight. "Movius Berg Homo Eruditissimus Est / With a Gift of Languages He Is Blest" was the headline for John Drohan's May 23, 1935, column in the *Boston Traveler*, a mock screed charging Berg with "having too much education."

" 'Nobody can have too much,' replied the illustrious Berg, as he gently perspired in the Red Sox dugout." Drohan takes it upon himself to investigate how much is too much. "Having studied cologne bottles, we decided to try out our French on him.

" 'Comment vous portez-vous?'

" 'Ça va bien, merci,' rejoined Berg. (Maybe he was calling us names. We wouldn't know.)" After Berg passes a similarly taxing Spanish test, Drohan calls upon outfielder Edmund "Bing" Miller to "put a stop to this nonsense by giving him some of that Iowa German by gargling, 'Wie geht es Ihnen?'

"Without so much as the quiver of an eyelash, Berg replied, 'Sehr gut, mein Herr.' " Drohan adds Hungarian and Italian to Berg's tally before confiding that the player some of his teammates call "Lingwee" is now learning Gaelic. That won't take long, he thinks, if Berg's Japanese study is any indication; on his trip to Japan the previous year Berg "picked up the Japanese language so well in three weeks, he could speak it like a native." Other Drohan disclosures include Berg's conversational Greek—he's a marvel in coffee shops—his preference for baseball over his off-season job as a lawyer at "one of the largest firms in lower Manhattan," a fondness for movies, and a bug for travel; Berg has just been to Russia, where he was arrested six times in a matter of weeks for making films without permission.

Berg spent his summer afternoons at the ballpark, but at other times he could turn up anywhere. Frank Yeutter in the December 17, 1938, *Philadelphia Bulletin* portrays a Berg who is as comfortable with aristocrats as he is with infielders. "The other night in New York, while thousands waited to hear Anthony Eden, former British foreign minister, talk on foreign affairs, shortly after his arrival, the dapper British diplomat was chatting with a baseball player.

"The player was Morris Berg, of the Boston Red Sox, otherwise Moe, a graduate of Princeton who later studied at the Sorbonne in Paris and Heidelberg in Germany. Moe's forte is Oriental languages and he reads them as a hobby. While Mr. Eden was adjusting his white tie, Moe lounged in a chair in his room discussing certain Sanskrit verb forms." Just why he was in Eden's room to begin with is left unexplained.

In 1938, there was a new dimension. It was all Kieran's doing. Kieran was one of the regulars on the popular radio program "Information, Please!"—the intellectual's quiz show. *New Yorker* magazine literary critic Clifton Fadiman sought to stump a panel of learned experts—Kieran, Franklin P. Adams, Oscar Levant, and a special guest—with questions on arcane subjects sent in by the listening public. At Kieran's suggestion, Berg appeared as the guest panelist in early 1938. He performed superbly. The sporting press was ecstatic, and Berg spent much of the following summer seated in the dugout, answering trivia questions. The transcripts of those sessions, of course, became columns.

In 1942, Berg abruptly retired from the Red Sox and accepted a position offered him by Nelson Rockefeller, the coordinator of the Office of Inter-American Affairs. The OIAA was responsible for maintaining friendly relations between the U.S. and its Central and South American neighbors during the Second World War. Berg was to be a goodwill ambassador. Baseball and brains meshed triumphantly with jingoism on sports pages from Chattanooga to New York. In a column headlined "Dodgers Cheer As Their Brain Joins Uncle Sam," Joe Williams of the *New York World-Telegram* wrote that "this is no empty title, no empty assignment. It's a job Moe Berg, the veteran catcher, can perform as competently and diplomatically as any man in the country."

Berg spent the first part of 1943 working for Rockefeller before signing on with the OSS. He returned to Newark in 1946, and for the next twenty-five years was a habitué of New York ballparks, where he watched several dozen games each summer, often from a seat in the press box. What Berg was doing for a living was anyone's guess. For such a raconteur, he had always been extremely reserved. There was something forbidding about him. People sensed that this was a person you didn't push. Cajoling the "man in the black suit," as Francis Stann of the *Washington Star* called him, wouldn't have worked anyway. To those who wondered aloud about his work for the OSS or about his life after baseball, Berg only put a finger to his lips and issued a sibilant rebuke. Most didn't ask, though. There were rumors that Berg was a CIA agent, and any fool knew that discussing that kind of work was *verboten*.

Talking baseball was another matter. Berg never tired of that. And so he remained a popular subject for sportswriters for all the usual reasons. When, for instance, a United Press International reporter asked him about George Scott, a hulking Red Sox rookie in 1966, Berg replied, "I believe there are fortunes to be made by the contractors who replace the walls he will tear down by the force of the baseballs he will hit." Berg, said the UPI writer, knows Sanskrit but "he gets a bigger kick out of George (The Great) Scott."

It all did make for wonderful reading, and there were crumbs of truth in every story, yet the jolly world of Professor Berg was false at the center. This was not the man, it was caricature on a grand scale. Which didn't bother Berg. In fact, he encouraged the burlesque and guided the creation of this shimmering distortion. By cloaking himself in the quirky adventures of Professor Berg, he carefully obscured the real Moe Berg. Behind the prop stood something quite different. Berg's was a life of abiding strangeness. The secret world of Moe Berg was charming and seamy, vivid and unsettling, wonderful and sad. And unlike the caricature, it was resonant with ambiguity.

CHAPTER 2

Youth:
Runt Wolfe

W hen Bernard Berg left behind the tiny Ukrainian village of Kippinya in 1894, and headed west, no doubt he hoped for prosperity. But it's also true that he was on the run. It wasn't easy for the slim young accountant with the thick hedge of mustache and dark brown eyes to part from Rose Tashker. Rose came from a nearby town in the Kamenets-Podolski region of the Ukraine, along the Bug River not far from Romania. Her father worked as the accountant for a Prince Krapinsky, who had a vodka distillery and other holdings there. Rose was beautiful, she was mellow, and she had agreed to marry Bernard. All his life, however, Bernard Berg's ethical sensibilities attenuated any conflicting strains of sentiment, and leaving Kippinya was a moral decision. Kippinya was entirely populated by Jews, a place where the laws and superstitions of Eastern European Judaism permeated every moment of a man's day. Bernard Berg could not abide such complete deference to faith. What to others was a comfort and a fillip was to him a burden. And so, promising Rose he'd send for her when he was settled, he left Kippinya behind. Another of Rose's virtues was patience. It would be two years before she saw Bernard again.

He traveled first to the U.S., didn't like what he saw and went to England, where he'd heard that citizenship would be granted to anyone volunteering for service in the Boer War. Upon arrival in London, he was told he was too late. The offer had been rescinded four days earlier. So Bernard went down to the docks, found a New York–bound freighter, and shipped out, earning his passage back across the Atlantic by shoveling coal in the engine room.

In New York, Bernard took an ironing job in a Ludlow Street laundry on Manhattan's Lower East Side. Like most streets in the neighborhood, Ludlow was a narrow channel lined with walk-up tenement apartment buildings and stables. Small shops selling everything from fresh matzo to salt herring spilled onto the sidewalks, while a chaos of pushcarts, horses, and shoppers wheedling for bargains in plangent Yiddish clogged the street. It was New York, but it was also very familiar. Bernard had no intentions of staying in the Jewish ghetto and began to put away money. When Rose joined him in 1896, he was running his own laundry and taking evening classes at the New York College of Pharmacy. During the day, he propped open his textbooks on a washboard as he pushed the heavy black iron across shirts. Bernard learned without any apparent strain. Before reaching New York he had taught himself to read English, French, and German, which meant that, also including Yiddish, Hebrew, and Russian, he could now understand six languages. Once he was settled in New York, he learned very quickly to speak acceptable English. After that, he did his best never to speak Yiddish again, and banned it from his home.

Between 1898 and 1902, Rose and Bernard had three children. A son, Samuel, came first, born in a room at the back of the laundry. A daughter, Ethel, followed in 1900, and then another son, Morris, two years after that. By this time Bernard had sold the laundry and begun clerking at an uptown pharmacy. The family had moved north, to a cold-water tenement not far from the Polo Grounds on 121st Street in Harlem, by March 2, 1902, when Morris was born. He was immediately and forever called Moe, a slim appellation that from the start belied his husky stature: Moe Berg was a twelve-pound baby.

Rose Berg crocheted beautifully, spending days on pieces of handwork that were later exhibited in museums. Her youngest son hadn't the same patience and could be a capricious child. At three and a half, he begged his mother to let him start school, "like Sam and Eth." His aunt Sophie overheard. "Dress that boy and send him to school," Sophie told her sister-in-law. Moe wore a suit with short pants, a white shirt with a starched collar clasped high at the neck, stockings, and leather shoes laced well up the calf. The laces took his mother a while to fasten. When she was finished, off he went.

By 1906 Bernard had bought a pharmacy on Warren Street in West Newark, operated it there until 1910, and then purchased a building at 92 South Thirteenth Street, on the corner of Ninth Avenue; this was the Roseville section of Newark, not far from West Orange, and very close to Bernard Berg's notion of perfection. Roseville had good schools, middle-class residents, and very few Jews. He would work there, and the family would live in an apartment above the pharmacy, until he died.

When the Bergs arrived in Newark, it was a raucous place. "The city of Newark is undergoing the most astonishing changes in its history," said Newark mayor Henry M. Doremus in his 1907 address to the city. Between 1870 and 1910, 250,000 immigrants, including 40,000 Jews—or Hebrews, as the Board of Trade referred to them—poured into the self-described "Workshop of the Nation," leading the city's historian Frank John Urquhart to marvel in 1913 that "it is to be doubted if more than a few hundred who can trace their lineage back to the founders still remain in Newark." The Germans

▼

and the Irish had come first, followed by Italians, Hungarians, Romanians, Poles, and Russians. "Here the natives of every country under the sun have found and are finding a conjenial [*sic*] home," declared a pamphlet published by the city. If there was anything truly congenial about life in rough, hard-nosed immigrant neighborhoods, where the stench of the Passaic River floated over teeming streets, it was the abundant supply of jobs. Antebellum Newark, a city of not quite 350,000 people, had over 2,200 factories, 11 miles of industrial wharfs, 14 freight yards, and ambitious city fathers who sponsored a near surfeit of public works projects, including a railroad tunnel under the Hudson River to Manhattan, parks, hospitals, paved streets, gas lights, trolley lines, 19 new schools between 1908 and 1912, and even, in 1909, a Newark museum.

It was also a city of self-contained neighborhoods. Most of Newark's 21,000 recent Russian immigrants crowded onto and around Prince Street, the Newark version of New York's famous Hester Street, but Bernard Berg no longer required the whiff of the old country that kept many immigrants clinging to the slums. By moving to the Christian, middle-class neighborhood of Roseville, he was dispensing with his past and savoring the self-determination he'd come looking for in America. The Bergs weren't wealthy and they never would be, yet without question Bernard had elevated them.

Once known as Boiling Spring, Roseville was renamed for James Rowe, a stubborn Irish dairy farmer who refused to sell his land to the city until someone thought to grease his vanity with nomenclature. In the first decades of the twentieth century, Roseville was a pretty neighborhood. People went to their jobs, kept up their property, and sat on their stoops in the evening, talking with the family. As the owner of a pharmacy, Bernard was at once chemist and physician. Customers would come into the store and describe their own or their child's symptoms. If things sounded serious, they were told to see a doctor. Otherwise, Bernard treated the affliction himself. For constipation, he'd put a spoonful of castor oil in a root beer soda, with instructions to drink it up and go straight home without any stops. When a prescription was called for, he went to the rear of the store and ground up the compound in his mortar with a pestle. Over time, people came to trust him, and the drugstore prospered to the point where it became the locus of neighborhood activity. Women sat together gossiping on the long bench near the front door, teenagers ate banana splits and egg creams at the soda fountain, and children came in for penny candy, unlacing their high leather shoes to fish change from their socks. There was a scale where you could weigh yourself, cosmetics and school supplies for sale, and a wooden telephone booth.

Bernard worked fifteen hours a day, seven days a week. His family communicated with him from the upstairs apartment through a speaking tube. When she wasn't cooking, bringing down Bernard's meals from upstairs, washing laundry, or scrubbing her immaculate floors, Rose sat behind the store counter, making change and crocheting. General opinion had it that the Bergs were a little strange. Bernard was rumored to be a semi-Communist, and some people wondered about a Jewish family that never went to temple. Still, they were well liked. For one thing, Bernard often didn't charge poor families for prescriptions.

"They were so friendly and accommodating," remembers Eugenia O'Connor, who grew up buying two-cent ice-cream cones from the Bergs. "They were old world people from the other side who seemed so grateful to be here. They were trying to be Americans, to blend right in. They weren't greedy."

No, they weren't. They were ambitious. If Bernard had put his children to work for him, that might have suggested a man interested in swollen profits. Yet, he didn't do that. Instead, he encouraged them to study. The only times a Berg child was asked to spend any time in the pharmacy were the occasional interludes when Sam pulled out his harmonica. When that happened, he was sent downstairs to play inside the wooden telephone booth.

THE REPORT CARDS Berg brought home from the South Eighth Street public school complained that he sang off key. His parents could overlook this peccadillo, though, because otherwise he was a seamless student. Knowledge came easily and stayed with him, all of it. Moe Berg had a photographic memory. On days when they confronted an unresponsive class-room, Berg's teachers took to dealing with the languor by call-ing on him. "Moe, get up," they would say, and he could be relied upon to rise to his feet and hold forth on the subject of the moment in the low, deliberate way in which he spoke. With his large head, thatch of black hair, soft olive complexion, wistful eyes, and serious mien, he was the sort of child friends of his mother's would have referred to as "that wonderful little boy."

Even as a toddler, he loved a game of catch, badgering Sam to toss an apple or an orange with him. A few years later, another favorite companion was patrolman Hibler, who lived across the street from the Bergs in Newark and could some-times be diverted from his travels around the neighborhood. Hibler was brawny inside his brass-buttoned policeman's uni-form, and fastidious. Carefully he would set aside his derby and then sweat like a thresher as Berg, standing one man-hole—twenty feet—down the street, yelled, "Harder, Mr. Hibler! Harder!" When there was nobody around to play with, Berg collected the baseball cards that were sold in ciga-rette packages—he didn't ever smoke—and taught himself to juggle three apples. He tried juggling with raw eggs, too, but only once.

Frederick Law Olmsted's lush, winding Branch Brook Park, with its famous bust of Mendelssohn, wasn't far from Berg's house, but he preferred the sandlots. Roseville, still converting from farmland into a residential neighborhood, was full of open spaces. Although baseball players in Roseville had to compete for the grassy tracts with hurling and cricket matches, there was usually just baseball on the vacant lots at North Eleventh Street and Sixth Avenue. Boys would play all day there, and then sometimes set up a gypsy kettle over a fire to cook molasses candy. An empty lot on South Fifteenth Street was another popular makeshift diamond. The land had once belonged to an Italian farmer, and around the neighborhood, the word once the crocuses were purple was "Meet you at the Guinea Farm." Moe usually played there. Sure hands compensated for the fact that, growing up, he was small for his age. Berg was an excellent fielder always, and fearless. When anyone called him a "Christkiller," he wasn't slow with his fists, either.

From the first, baseball made him very happy. Berg couldn't get enough of the game. He would spend a generous share of his life inside ballparks. He felt comfortable, truly at ease, on the field or in the stands. The famous old New York Giants pitcher "Iron" Joe McGinnity ended his career with the Newark Indians of the International League, and some of the best days of Moe's childhood were spent seated beside Sam at Weidenmeyer Park, watching the Irishman, then in his early forties, try to nudge his faded fastball past a bunch of teenagers.

On many spring evenings, Moe would creep out of the house with his glove when Bernard would have preferred him to be studying. Over time, Moe grew brazen about it. His father, who knew nothing about American sports, wondered aloud to some of his neighbors whether baseball was a sordid influence on his son. Yet if he thought about it, Bernard had to admit that nothing kept Berg away from school. Once Berg challenged his father to a race from the front of the store to the rear. Bernard would go straight through, while Moe would run around the building. A coal chute had been left outside leaning against the side of the house, and Moe collided with it, tearing cuts up his leg. He insisted upon going to school the next day, and he did, in a wheelbarrow.

Founded in 1838, Barringer High School was the nation's third oldest free public high school, and probably Newark's best. By the time he graduated from high school, in 1918 at the age of sixteen, Berg had been awarded a stack of certificates for "attendance," "deportment," and "diligent attention to study." His classmates voted him "Brightest Boy." He studied Latin and Greek, was awarded a French medal, visited his friend John Jennings every day when Jennings had polio, worked a summer in the shipyards, played basketball, and made his first headlines as a baseball player.

In an article entitled "Here Are the Stars," the *Newark Star-Eagle* selected a nine-man "dream team" for 1918, drawn from the city's best prep and public high school baseball players. "Third base on the mythical team is taken care of by Berg of Barringer," said the newspaper. "If size were to count in choosing this team, Berg probably would have been overlooked when it came down to a choice for 'substitute water carrier.'

"But Berg, in spite of his four feet and some odd inches, is a crackerjack in scooping them up around the dangerous corner. He has an arm like a whip and is a steady batter." In the three years Berg played for Barringer varsity coach "Chief" Broadhead, Berg never once made a throwing error.

Yet for all his accomplishments, he was not a school sensation at Barringer. In part, this was a function of personality. In the high school yearbook, *The Acropolis*, under Berg's class photo, appeared a quatrain:

> There is a boy who is a star,
> Now this might seem quite queer;
> Though Morris Berg is smart, you know,
> It's not known when he's near.

It went further than being withdrawn, however. Barringer was the first of the series of institutions Moe Berg joined during his life where his religion made him unusual. At Barringer, most of his classmates were either poor East Side Italian Catholics or rich Protestants from Forest Hills. Moe saw wealth and he saw misery at Barringer, but he didn't see many Jews, and that's how Bernard wanted it.

There were no bar mitzvahs, no confirmations, no formal introduction to Judaism of any sort for Bernard Berg's children. But they *were* Jews, of course, and religion affected them in different ways. Sam was full of conflict. Following his father, he would write late in his life that "to be polite, religion is a bunch of equine droppings." A year before he died, he seemed to soften, writing, "Moe, as Ethel and I, returned to our Jewish faith always, though not to the extent of observing orthodox Judaism. We did not flaunt it, though we were proud of our heritage." As a grown woman, Ethel solicited advice from a local rabbi and developed an interest in Israel, which she visited. Moe Berg generally made it his policy to distance himself from the religion, a practice he began as a boy, when he adopted the slightly less ethnic pseudonym Runt Wolfe and joined the Roseville Methodist Episcopal Church baseball team. He also spent a lot of time with John Jennings, whose family was Catholic. The Jenningses annually invited Berg over to help trim their Christmas tree, and he sometimes accompanied them to Mass. He particularly liked the midnight service on Christmas Eve. Afterward, he went home with the Jenningses for a breakfast feast. All his life, Moe would enjoy attending an occasional Sunday service, but it was pleasure of an aesthetic or even recreational variety, rather than any stirrings of Christian faith.

His early interest in the Hebrew language was similarly secular. Moe liked languages, and one day he asked his father how he could learn some Hebrew. "Go see the rabbi," Bernard told him. Moe did so and reported back, "The rabbi's talking to me about religion. I want to learn Hebrew."

"Okay," said Bernard. "Sit down." And he taught Berg himself.

CHAPTER 3

The Stiff Collar

M ost of the 211 members of the Princeton Class of 1923 were the children of wealthy Christians, prep-school graduates who began a typical college morning reading the *New York Times*, later lunched at an eating club, and finished their day with tie loosened and sleeves folded to the elbow, puffing on a pipe and playing bridge. On weekends they went to football games, perhaps a dance in the evening, and definitely chapel every other Sunday. For Princeton students, attendance at services every other week was mandatory.

It was a little different to be the Newark-bred son of immigrants and "a Hebrew," as the Class of 1923 yearbook would describe Moe Berg beneath his senior photograph. Berg was never exactly sure how he felt about Princeton. Years later, as an adult, when he talked about college with his friend Ted

Sanger, also a Princeton graduate, his classmates were "all those conservative so and sos." Yet when Jimmy Breslin, a raffish young newspaperman with whom Berg drank Bloody Marys in blowsy New York City bars in the 1950s, would say "to hell with those stuffy bastards," Berg would be horrified and admonish him, exclaiming, "Oh, no! That's where you learn to be truly liberal." Berg found Princeton immensely appealing, but it made him wary as well.

The shortstop on a Princeton baseball team that won eighteen consecutive games during his senior year was also a scholar of distinction, a modern languages major who graduated twenty-fourth in his class. But his notoriety didn't go much beyond recognition. Nobody at Princeton could honestly claim that they knew him. They knew things *about* him, that he took copious notes, never carried any books but was always prepared for classes, wore hair tonic, maybe even that he sent his laundry home to his mother in Newark for washing. But he had no intimate friends or even close ones, and he divulged almost nothing about himself to anyone.

After graduating from Barringer High School in the spring of 1918, Berg had entered New York University the following fall at age sixteen. He spent two semesters there, and played basketball and baseball. His NYU transcript is unavailable, but it must have sparkled, because when Berg sent it along with his application to Princeton, he was accepted and enrolled as a freshman in September 1919. He didn't glance back, never mentioning his year at NYU in conversation or acknowledging that he'd been there on either job or government service applications. He presented himself exclusively as a Princeton man, and that is how the world knew him.

Princeton was a country village in 1920, known affectionately as the University in the Jungle. The isolation and the absence of women made the school's social institutions loom prominent for all but the most detached students. Bicker, the competition to be among the 60 percent of each class chosen

for membership in one of the eighteen eating clubs in the
sprawling mansions along Prospect Street, lent intrigue
and some hoopla to a sedate setting. This Princeton was
largely a hermetic society that thrived on pedigree and
rewarded reputations established at prep schools like Andover,
Choate, and Lawrenceville. It was a Princeton Berg never
penetrated.

He didn't really have any choice. At the school F. Scott
Fitzgerald fondly described as "lazy and good looking and
aristocratic," there were very few men with names that ended
in "berg" or "stein." "I'd say he was a loner," said Berg's
classmate and double play partner on the baseball team, Crossan Cooper. "He had very few intimate friends. There weren't
many Jewish people at Princeton. As a group they were kind
of looked down upon." Howard Baer, a Jewish member of the
Class of 1924, who joined the Cloister Inn, says he felt that
he "led a double life there. I was the only Jewish guy in my
class that made a club. I was living in two worlds, but it wasn't
easy." Religious discrimination at the college was so strong
that one of Berg's Jewish classmates pretended to be a Christian. After graduation, when he revealed the truth, "his standing suffered an eclipse," according to Don Griffin, Class of
1923.

Berg's situation was much like that of Robert Cohn, the
Jewish middleweight boxing champion in *The Sun Also Rises*,
of whom Hemingway writes, "No one had ever made him feel
he was a Jew, and hence any different from anybody else, until
he went to Princeton." Princeton, like Barringer, made Berg
aware that he was branded with the mark of a faith he had
been raised to resist. Yet Berg made no attempt to hide his
Jewishness. When a group of Jewish students decided to hold
Friday night services, Berg was asked to preside. Baer says
Berg readily agreed. It wasn't that prejudice was making a
believer of him, though. The services were a ruse. Mandatory
biweekly attendance at chapel and the absence of Sunday

morning rail service from New York and Philadelphia to Princeton meant that, half the time, it was impossible to flee campus for a weekend in the city. But for students who were not Christians, an exception was made. "The weekend problem," says Baer, "was solved!"

Berg *was* the rare Jew invited to join an eating club. Yet the offer came with a caveat: he was welcome so long as he did not press for the admission of any other Jews. Berg declined. His cousin Elizabeth Shames remembers Berg describing the situation. "When his name was coming up, he left campus and went home," she says. "I said, why? He said you had to be there for your name to come up. He said, 'I was too proud of being a Jew to allow them to bandy my name about.' He said this with intensity."

The Princeton where Berg felt comfortable was the Princeton that stood as one of the nation's best academic institutions. To other students, he seemed a little shy. "He was not unfriendly," says Griffin. "He had a certain reserve about him, but he was extremely courteous. There was never a time when he didn't regard traditions. But he was so devoted to scholarship and his interest in languages that he didn't have time for the life of the campus."

Berg was a superior student. Foreign languages were what interested him, and by the time he received his B.A. degree, magna cum laude in modern languages, he had studied seven of them at Princeton: Latin, Greek, French, Spanish, Italian, German, and Sanskrit. He did well with each, except during an unaccountably moribund second junior semester, when he nearly failed German and dropped Spanish. To that point, both had come easily to him, so perhaps his mind was elsewhere. He impressed some of the university's finest instructors— Christian Gauss, his adviser, who taught him the French romantics; J. Duncan Spaeth, the famous Shakespeare lecturer; the classics professor Edmund Robbins; and especially Harold Bender, the chairman of the Department of Oriental

▼

Languages and Literatures, who offered courses in German, Sanskrit, and linguistic science.

Developing his lifelong zest for eclectic knowledge, Berg found himself engaged by all manner of subjects, from the satires of Juvenal and Dryden to economic conditions in eighteenth-century France to Petrarch's sonnets to Boccaccio's *Decameron*, and mathematics, philosophy, and biology besides. He didn't enroll in the last, but he attended lectures on the side, because his brother, Sam, studying medicine in New York City, "told me to."

His moods varied. As a junior, during exams, he complained in a terse letter home that the work was "hard." He could also be testy with himself, writing elsewhere, "I am a great procrastinator and it will get me into trouble some day." At other times, however, he sounded pluckier. To his family he declared, "I'm feeling fine and rather ambitious now. My studies take up most of my time, but I find enough leisure moments to play ball." Berg's letters home were littered with descriptions of courses, critiques of professors, and classroom bon mots. He traveled to football games in New Haven, attended the Triangle cabaret show, occasionally went home to Newark for dinner with the family, joined the Whig Hall debating society, and played in the class baseball championships.

Bernard Berg still wasn't interested in baseball, and he thought it high time for his son to put away his childish things. But Moe Berg was more drawn to sports than ever, and couldn't resist saying so. Thus he regaled a man who'd grown up walking through the fields outside a small Ukrainian country village with tales of the Princeton football team's heartbreaking loss to Navy—"an example of how much our opponents like to beat us." Not only had Bernard raised a partisan Princetonian, his son was also developing into the best baseball player in the school's history.

Berg played basketball during his first three winters at Princeton. He was, of course, a fine athlete, and had grown.

He had filled out to a willowy six foot one, so he handled himself adequately, but it was in the spring that he excelled. As a freshman, he played first base on an undefeated team. The following spring he became the varsity shortstop, starting every game there for the Tigers over the next three years. The Princeton coach was Bill "Boileryard" Clarke, a witty, profane man who'd played with John McGraw and Wilbert Robinson on the hardscrabble Baltimore Oriole teams of the mid-1890s. Clarke told Berg that he ran so slowly that he'd "get to first base just as fast wearing snowshoes," and the coach was right; Berg was a hopeless plodder. He compensated in the field, though, with a strong, accurate throwing arm and with what can only be called sound baseball instincts. The best infielders sense the path of the ball before it is struck, and Berg did that. Howard Baer, a lifelong baseball enthusiast, remembers Berg in a game against Yale, floating into shallow left field, behind the third baseman, to spear a line drive as "one of the two greatest plays I've ever seen." The other was Enos Slaughter's famous sprint home from first on a single in the 1946 World Series.

Never a powerful hitter, at first Moe Berg was not even a particularly good one. He batted .235 as a sophomore, hit .230 the next year, and then, as a senior, he emerged as something special. His batting average was .337, and the more rigorous the competition, the better he played. In Princeton's five games that year against Harvard and Yale, he batted .611, including hitting a ringing home run against the Elis. When Princeton pitcher Charlie Caldwell took on Holy Cross and the future Detroit Tigers righthanded pitcher Ownie Carroll, Berg doubled and scored the game's only run, handing Carroll one of the two defeats he would suffer as a collegian. For one of the games against Harvard, Brooklyn Dodgers manager Wilbert Robinson sent his ace pitcher, the spitballer Burleigh Grimes, out to Princeton to look over a Princeton pitcher. Grimes returned to Brooklyn afterward to tell Robinson that

▼

the pitcher wasn't much, but that the Tigers had some shortstop.

Berg's happiest moments at Princeton were on the baseball field. In addition to the actual play itself, he tutored teammates struggling with their studies and, with Crossan Cooper, the Princeton second baseman during Berg's senior year, he devised a cunning system of communication. When an opposing runner was on second base, they disguised their intentions by yelling back and forth to each other in Latin. As he grew older, Berg was quick to tout baseball's democratic charms. To him baseball was "the great leveller," a green field in the spring where men of every height, breadth, shade, and creed were joined in harmonious competition. Skill and nothing else made you special. In this way as well, he resembled Robert Cohn. Success as a college athlete was crucial to both of them. Like Cohn, Berg found that sport helped him "to counteract the feeling of inferiority and shyness he had felt on being treated as a Jew at Princeton."

During vacations Berg took odd jobs, like delivering mail. His most satisfying employment experience came in the summer of 1921, when he went north to Bristol, New Hampshire, to be a counselor at Camp Wah-Kee-Nah on Lake Newfound.

Most of the boys at Wah-Kee-Nah were Jewish, and they adored their counselor, the Princeton shortstop—at least according to that counselor. "There isn't a boy in this camp who doesn't jump with glee to play ball with me and I make it a point to teach them something new every day," Berg wrote to his father in July. Some of these lessons were imparted during the Sunday morning games Berg and the other counselors played against the children. "Every Sunday morning I hit one, a long one, out in the left field bushes for the edification of the boys," he wrote. And then a sudden moment later, in the same letter, a fleeting moment of introspection unfurled like a breaker. "Pa," he continued. "I'm surely enjoying this, probably mostly because it's a novelty for me but mostly [sic] be-

cause it's what I like most of all, the open country air with
unprejudiced boys for real companions and none of the stiff-
collar conventions or proprieties of the city and especially because I'm being paid for what is easy for me and appreciated."
The "city" was a euphemism. It was at Princeton where he'd
met discrimination dressed up in a stiff collar.

Happy as he said he was, to others Berg appeared a dour
figure. Monroe Karasik, a camper when Berg worked at Wah-
Kee-Nah, remembers that Berg was the only counselor who
had an electric lamp installed over his bed. "The rumor was
that he had to memorize Dante's *Divine Comedy*," says Karasik. "Most campers said that was kind of peculiar, because
Moe rarely smiled." Whether he was reading Dante or not,
Berg was definitely studying Hebrew again. A Palestinian
Ph.D. named Dr. Bassan was on hand at the camp, and Berg
solicited lessons from him every day after lunch while the
campers were having their rest period.

Back at Princeton for his final year, he was more of a success
than ever. In the classroom, he received his highest marks, and
New Jersey sportswriters took note of his skill as a ballplayer.
"Berg to Pass Out of Princeton This Week with Fine Record
in Classes and Afield," headlined the *Newark News* in a story
that went on to applaud "one of the finest baseball careers in
collegiate ranks." On June 19, his graduation day, Berg was
photographed seated at the Princeton sundial. Dressed in a
well-cut suit, his trousers creased, shoes gleaming, and thick
hair combed smooth, he had matured into a dashing man. But
posed there at the sundial he looked glum. The truth was that
Berg's time at Princeton seemed to him to have been carpeted
with rejection. He'd been voted neither baseball captain nor
into Phi Beta Kappa, two honors that he might well have felt
he merited. His marginal standing amidst his peers was rein-
forced for him one more time with the publication of "The
Class and Its Opinions," a collection of senior plaudits. Berg
received 2 votes for "Most Brilliant" (the winner had 37), and
not a single tally in any of the 41 other categories, among them

"Best All-Around Athlete," "Most Scholarly," and, predictably, "Most Representative Princetonian."

While no student in the Class of 1923 thought Berg "Most Likely to Succeed," his professors were more optimistic. On June 26, despite a Berg single and double in four at bats to complement several marvelous plays at shortstop, Yale beat Princeton 5–1 at Yankee Stadium to win the Big Three title. Princeton finished the season 21–4. The next day Edmund Robbins, Berg's classics professor, addressed a brief note to him, which concluded, "I congratulate you on the [baseball] record you made—and your record in scholarship as well. You have had the finest spirit that Princeton can show—all the time—and I am proud of you." The modern languages department did that one better, offering him a teaching post. Berg thought not. He intended, eventually, to go to law school, his father's wish, but first, what he really hoped to do was to spend some time in the places where people spoke those many languages he'd been learning. He was best at French, and wanted badly to see Paris, Versailles, and Provence. It would cost money to cross the ocean and enroll in a foreign university but, fortunately, a high-salaried summer job was waiting for him in Brooklyn.

IN 1923, NEW York City's two National League baseball franchises were both managed by those illustrious former teammates of Princeton coach Clarke. John McGraw of the New York Giants and Wilbert Robinson of the Brooklyn Robins (soon to be called the Dodgers) both knew all about Berg, and both wanted him. They liked his elegant play at shortstop, and they liked his blood. New York City had a huge Jewish population, and the team that could sign on a talented Jewish ballplayer would have quite a drawing card on its hands.

McGraw was especially keen. Despite being a first-place team on its way toward winning the National League pennant,

the Giants weren't selling tickets. Attendance at the Polo
Grounds was off 130,000 from the previous season. The shrewd
manager began confiding his efforts to "land a prospect of
Jewish blood" to reporters. But McGraw, nicknamed "Little
Napoleon," was a domineering, abrasive man. Robinson was
the opposite, a jolly, rubicund sort known generally as "Uncle
Robbie." Robinson had one more thing besides temperament
going for him in Berg's mind: a mediocre team. Berg wanted
to play, and he thought the Robins would give him the chance
sooner. Brooklyn was thin at shortstop, while McGraw had two
future Hall of Famers at the position, Dave "Beauty" Bancroft,
the veteran team captain, and Travis Jackson, lean, quick, and
a year younger than Berg.

Berg was hesitant. Perhaps he ought to listen to his father,
dispense with games, and begin law school. But he loved baseball. Berg had met Dutch Carter, a former Yale pitcher who
spurned the big leagues for law school, and it was Carter who
made up his mind for him. "Take the baseball career," Carter
advised. "The law can wait. When I was your age, I had a
chance to pitch in the National League. But my family looked
down on professional sports and vehemently opposed my accepting. I've always been sorry I listened to them, because it's
made me a frustrated man. Don't you become frustrated. At
least give it a try."

On June 27, the day after his heroics at Yankee Stadium,
Berg exchanged his orange and black Princeton jersey and
knickers for the blue and white flannel of Brooklyn. "The check
they offered me for signing [$5,000] wasn't hard to take," Berg
would say years later. For three months' work, the check was
his independence. The money bought him his first trip abroad,
and it let him postpone decisions about his career.

During his life Berg would go back to Princeton at frequent
intervals to visit friends in the science community, to read
books and newspapers in Firestone Library, and to watch football games. He never once attended a Class of 1923 reunion,
but as an old man, he did like to settle himself under the

▼

afternoon sun in the bleachers during varsity baseball practice. Sometimes the players would invite him out for a meal afterward, and he would go, gladly, and regale them with baseball stories. Some of the younger players thought he sounded wistful.

CHAPTER 4

▼

Robin in Paris

On June 27, 1923, Brooklyn's newspapers were full of booze, betrayal, and Berg. Thousands of block parties in Brooklyn and Queens were exposed as "Carnivals at which bootleggers and gamblers reap a rich harvest and the morals of young girls put in peril." Mrs. Gladys Miller, a "Former Long Island Society Girl," was granted a divorce from her husband, who maintained a "Love Nest" near their home. And Moe Berg became a major league baseball player. "Brooklyn Club Signs Moe Berg" was the banner headline in the *Brooklyn Daily Eagle*. The *Brooklyn Citizen* was more subdued, with its one-column introduction: "Shortstop Berg of Princeton Joins Robins."

Berg had signed his Brooklyn contract at Yankee Stadium following the Yale game and then spent the night in a New York hotel. The next morning he took the team train to Philadelphia, where the Robins had an afternoon game at the

Baker Bowl against the Phillies. He checked into the Lorraine Hotel in the morning, worked out at shortstop after lunch, played three fine innings behind Dutch Ruether in Brooklyn's 15–5 victory in the late afternoon, and was fodder for the headline writers by nightfall. "Moe Berg Impresses as Superbas Swamp Phils," cried the *Eagle*. The *Citizen*, casting aside discretion, crowed, "Berg, Rah Rah Boy, Shows Real Class in Big League Debut."

With Brooklyn ahead 13–4 in the seventh inning, Robinson had decided to have a look at the college boy. Berg handled five chances flawlessly in his debut, including snaring Cy Williams's ninth-inning line drive, which he converted into a game-ending double play. At bat, although "plainly a little nervous" and handicapped by "a false shoulder movement," to the eyes of *Eagle* correspondent Thomas Rice, Berg managed to scratch a bouncing single up the middle past pitcher Clarence Mitchell and later scored in the eighth inning. In assessing Berg, Rice observed "that like many other baseball performers, and some of them the best, he is more agile than fast. He can bob around quickly in scooting after wide hit balls, but is rather a slow runner on the bases."

For his part, Berg told reporters that he had yet to decide upon a career, that he hoped to study abroad after the season, and that life with the Robins was "a good way to accumulate jack" toward tuition. "He has noted the number of college balltossers, stars on collegiate fields, who have joined big league camps only to warm the bench for a long while and then start through minor circuits," explained a *Newark News* reporter who had covered Berg at Princeton. "That is not to be his lot, he says. He will make good with Brooklyn or he will make his exit from the professional game." Berg's caution was prudent. Robinson wouldn't make him the regular Brooklyn shortstop until August, when the Robins were far out of pennant contention.

As the weeks stretched deep into July, most people, including John McGraw, forgot all about Berg. On July 27, the *Jewish Tribune* reported that the Giants manager was offering $100,000 for a good Jewish player. Musing on the subject, McGraw said, "Right at the moment, [Sammy] Bohne is the only Jew I can recall in either major league." McGraw revealed his theories on the paucity of Jews in the big leagues: "The parents . . . influence them not to let anything interfere with their mental training for the future," and cited the Jewish "love of combat" as his reason for dangling such a princely sum. The truth of it, of course, was in the declining attendance.

Although Brooklyn was 35 percent Jewish by 1927, Berg's presence on the Superbas roster did not send charges of excitation through Williamsburg, Brownsville, Bensonhurst, or the borough's other Jewish neighborhoods, probably because Robinson made no real effort to hype the rookie shortstop's religion. He may have sensed that Berg was touchy about his faith. During his long baseball career, Berg's reticence in regard to religion and the fact that he never played very much or very well usually kept the Jewish paparazzi at bay. Beyond this, something about Berg's manner held even zealots at a distance.

With Brooklyn wallowing in the National League's second division, Berg started a handful of games in August and September, pleasing his mother, who exulted over the progress of her son the ballplayer. "Oh, she loved it, she *loved* it," Sam Berg recalled years later. Throughout Berg's career, Rose would consult national weather forecasts in the newspaper. "Oh," she might say, "it's raining in Chicago." Relatives soon recognized that this meant Moe was scheduled to play a game that day in Chicago and Rose was worried that it would be postponed. On game days in Brooklyn, Rose gathered up friends and family members with the cry "Moe is playing with the Robins and we have to go!" Bernard always stayed home, and the Brooklyn baseball cognoscenti were likewise unimpressed. "I don't think he was much of a shortstop," says

Charlie Segar, then a young baseball writer for the *Citizen*. No, he wasn't. Berg was slow afoot, increasingly erratic with his throws, and overmatched as a hitter.

The poor throwing put him in headlines for the third and final time that summer, on August 17, when the *Eagle* fretted, "Berg Worried Over Queer Twist He Gets on Throw; Curving of Ball a Mystery." His throws, it seemed, veered and dipped suddenly, the way a pitcher's slider does. Rice, of the *Eagle*, explained that "Berg is essentially an overhand thrower, and he has a wonderful arm. Uncle Wilbert Robinson says it is one of the best arms he ever saw and it is certainly one of the best the present writer ever saw. He gets the ball away faster than most overhand throwers, his aim is true and his speed terrific, but in some unknown way he gives the ball a twist which interferes with his effectiveness."

Berg did play well in a September 17 loss to the Philadelphia Athletics. He had two hits in four times at bat and fielded ten chances at shortstop without incident. Unfortunately, the Athletics were an American League team and the game was an exhibition, so it didn't count. More typical was August 17, when Berg was 0–3 with an error. In all, Berg had played in 47 games for Brooklyn, batted .186, and made 22 errors. It was time to get out of town, and that's what he did. In early October, Berg left for Paris.

MOE BERG WAS an innocent on his first trip abroad, and what else could he have been? Thus far his compass had spread narrow; he had studied, he had played, but he hadn't *lived*. Now he was bound for postwar Paris, and the Left Bank at that, where ideas fresh and strange dusted the air like pollen.

When he sailed from New York, Berg hadn't been sure whether to enroll at a university in Paris or somewhere in Provence. Language study was his main concern, and the less than lilting varieties of provincial patois he heard aboard ship predisposed him toward the capital. He was certain as soon as he saw it. Within a week of his arrival in Paris, he had looked over the Sorbonne, found an apartment in the Latin Quarter, and written to his family, "I am settled, registered, and the happiest one in the universe."

France delighted him for the sheer difference of it all. Hot chocolate, private train compartments, seatless toilets, the book stalls along the Seine—quotidian Paris was a blissfully enervating experience for Berg. His French, he immediately discovered, "was fine," and it took him everywhere. Just to "walk for several hours," he told his family, "was exhilarating." He wandered through the Tuileries, the Louvre, and the sprawling produce market at Les Halles, stepped into a Mass at Notre-Dame—"I go in like I'm going to a show," he wrote, drank beer in cafés, spent the obligatory evening at the Folies-Bergère, and went to the theater as often as he could, developing a taste for Racine and Molière. "No matter how national, prejudiced, and so forth a people may be, there is a culture that stands out and above it all and to me the French is by far the greatest in all fields," he wrote to his parents after a month in Paris.

On one of his walks along the Boulevard des Italiens, in front of the Opéra, he encountered John McGraw, vacationing with Giants coach Hughie Jennings. McGraw remembered Berg, and the three Americans fell into one another's arms. McGraw had lost his way, so Berg directed him back to his hotel, the Continental. The Giants manager insisted that Berg join him for dinner that night, but Berg had a theater ticket, so they made a date for another evening. "John McGraw said a few things to me which I better tell after I eat with them," Berg wrote cryptically to his family. They did dine, and Berg came away triumphant. First he had a highball with Jennings, which tasted to him "like Berg's special mixture for constipation." The drink was on Jennings, who had a law degree from Cornell, but not much French. He ordered anyway and, in the Continental tradition, the bartender made him pay for his broken phrases, prompting Berg to gloat in a letter home,

"They charged him plenty—as they do all English-speaking peoples here but of course our boy doesn't come in there."

During the meal, McGraw asked Berg why he hadn't joined the Giants the previous summer, and after Berg replied with something modest, McGraw flattered him further, telling him that he was young and full of promise. "He is a most encouraging fellow—just as glad as could be to see me," Berg told his family. The visit also made an impression upon McGraw. Back in New York, he told an AP reporter all about it, exclaiming, "Who ever heard of a ballplayer spending his vacation studying Latin—and in Paris?"

That wasn't all Berg was studying. For the 32 francs, 50 centimes ($1.95) tuition fee, he received a card entitling him to attend as many courses as he wished. "I don't let a thing go by," he informed his family, and this was little exaggeration. His workload included five history courses, including a survey of seventeenth-century France—"which, if it becomes too one-sided, I'll tell the professor to stick the course up his !!!!"; eight classes in French and Romanic linguistics; five classes in French literature; one in the history of Italian literature; another in the history of Latin literature; comic drama; and a study of Latin during the Middle Ages. In all, he was taking twenty-two classes.

He liked to tinker with words, to know where they came from, how they'd evolved into the present spelling, pronunciation, and usage, and so philology interested him most of all. "Naturally the ideal language would be a combination of the Teutonic and Latinic elements and that's what English is," he informed his father, who, no doubt, agreed. Scrutinizing language lent him a forkful of humility, too. "No matter how well a foreigner speaks French, he remains a foreigner, that is, as far as the little nuances of speech are concerned," he reflected in mid-January.

Berg's professor of phonetics was the famous L'Abbé Jean-Pierre Rousselot, the founder of modern experimental phonetics. Not many students were interested in the subject, so

Berg received personal instruction. He also spent hours in the language laboratory, analyzing his own speech patterns, and he had a pleasant conversation with a doctoral student who was preparing a thesis on the American "r."

That was as close as Berg came to mentioning a friend. For all his enthusiasm for his surroundings, Berg was a loner in Paris, much as he'd been at Princeton. Diffident by nature, he could also sound intolerant—not a promising combination for striking up warm acquaintances. At various times he referred to the French as "nickel-squeezers" and claimed Frenchmen grew whiskers to "hide their dirty faces." Describing an evening out, he wrote, "A nigger is the same as a brother to a Frenchman—the other night a beautiful French woman sat next to me at the theater and on her left her husband, I guess, a dirty black nigger—if some of our Southern whites ever saw that, there'd be a riot." Libertine Paris likewise left him disgusted. "The women have the nerve to rule the streets here," he complained in one letter. "The French musical comedy stage is obscene, the women at times are absolutely naked," he huffed prudishly in another. As to the women he met, he struck a condescending tone. "I have been accosted many times; I always talk to them and send them away laughing." Clearly, there were a lot of experiments he wasn't ready for.

It went beyond a matter of maturity. That a man of such expansive academic curiosity was otherwise prone to the rigid, timid thinking of one of Sinclair Lewis's Gopher Prairie feed merchants was surprising. Berg's pleasures were not much different from those of the average tourist, while a fluttering feminine eyelash sent him stumbling into retreat, and the movable feast of painting, writing, and music that made Paris in 1923–24 the capital of the avant-garde he noticed not at all. True, he was young, only twenty-one, and since he was precocious in so many ways, perhaps it was to be expected that other things would come more slowly. Yet Berg in Paris as a recent college graduate really was not that different from the Berg who would return to the city twenty years later as a spy.

▼

If he was prepared for something, had been told what to look for, was carrying instructions, he was fine, even creative. Without guidance from a textbook, or a teacher, or a coach, or a parent, or a general, however, he grew confused and retreated.

The cumulative effect at the moment was that, even with the staggering number of courses he'd taken on, Berg had time on his hands. To fill it, he developed a habit he'd keep for the rest of his days: multiple newspapers. Paris was full of newspapers, and Berg read all he could get his hands on. Days began and ended in respectability with *L'Oeuvre* each morning and *Le Temps* in the evening. In between, he read *Journal des débats* and *Le Figaro*, whose political coverage he admired; *L'Action française* and *Le Gaulois* for the royalist perspective; *Echo de Paris* to get the Catholic side of things; *Le Libertaire* and *L'Humanité* to hear what the anarchists were foaming about. Hidden at the center of the bundle he hauled back to his apartment were the scandal sheets or, as he put it, "a flock of papers for the rabble." He was a careful reader, particularly when it came to international politics. Consistent with his burgeoning interest in linguistics, he kept a written list of the English words that appeared in French papers.

By January, he was missing baseball. "Well, pretty soon the bell will ring again to hit the old apple and believe me I'm anxious to show all the gents that I can do it and have enough confidence in myself to believe that I'll give 'em all a good battle," he wrote, slipping easily into the diamond jargon. Yet Berg didn't hurry back to New York to get himself into shape so that he could prove to Uncle Robby that he belonged in the major leagues. Instead, he toured Italy and Switzerland, and that indulgence quickly cost him.

CHAPTER 5

▼

Good Field, No Hit

J oe Cascarella was one of Moe Berg's teammates for the Boston Red Sox for portions of the 1935 and 1936 seasons. Cascarella was a pitcher who seldom pitched, and Berg was a reserve catcher who rarely caught, so they spent many afternoons together in the bull pen, watching their teammates do the playing. Whatever dash Cascarella's fastball was lacking, he wasn't missing personally. "Crooning Joe" liked stylish clothes, and had once been hired to sing on a Philadelphia radio show. Berg bewildered him. "It was very puzzling," he says. "Here was this man with a tremendous academic background in a game that didn't call for it. I asked this to myself numerous times: why would he select the ordinary game of baseball and devote so much time to it?"

Moe Berg wore a professional baseball uniform for nineteen years, more than a quarter of his life, and far longer than most men last in the game. He was many things ballplayers are not supposed to be: educated, intelligent, cosmopolitan, well spoken, Jewish, and slow-footed. He didn't hit many home runs either, only six as a major leaguer. His lifetime batting average was a feeble .243. It seemed odd that a man of such parts should have remained committed to something that freighted him with mediocrity.

Cascarella never asked Berg about his reasons for staying in baseball, but Diane Roberts did. In 1933, Roberts was a lithe young woman of twenty-two, living alone at the Wardman Park, a residential hotel in Washington. Huey Long, Henry Wallace, and Joseph Kennedy all kept apartments at the Wardman Park at the time, as did several members of the Washington Senators baseball team, including Moe Berg. Some of the Senators would spend their evenings together in rocking chairs on the hotel porch, ogling energetically when someone like Roberts passed. Berg didn't do this. As a consequence, alone among the Senators, he became Roberts's friend. "His manners were very good," she says. "He was very polite. He wasn't in the same class as those guys sitting in chairs as a gang, whistling at girls. He told me about going to Princeton and Columbia law school. He said he wanted to be an international lawyer. I said, 'Why do you play baseball?' He said, 'I love it. I could never stop.' "

He did love it then, as he always had. Yet, over nineteen seasons, it was an affection that evolved, the way some marriages do, from passion to comfort. Baseball served Moe Berg well. After a time it afforded him a lifestyle that he liked, and offered him a center that he needed. He, in turn, was a far more useful player than might be supposed. For a time, it even appeared that he would become one of the best of his day.

As BERG SAILED home from Europe in the late winter of 1924, the *Newark News* was busy keeping baseball in perspective for him. "He likes to succeed," the paper said, "but he will not make the mistake of many a collegian who has gone into professional sport and been mired in the life when he found he was only a second-class player. Berg seems too wise for that, his friends agree." Perhaps. Berg docked in New York, freshened his valise in Newark, and bought a seat on the Florida Flier, bound for the Robins training camp in Clearwater. Robinson watched Berg practice, saw that Paris had seasoned his French but had lent no brio to his hitting, and optioned him to the Minneapolis Millers of the American Association. Berg took the demotion poorly. He muttered something about becoming an instructor of foreign languages, announced that he was going home to Newark, and bought himself a railroad ticket. Long train rides can be wonderfully conducive to reconsidering. In Newark, Berg asked that his mail be forwarded to Minneapolis. It was spring. Nobody hired teachers in the spring. Besides, most ballplayers spent some time in the minors.

Berg joined the Millers in mid-April. His tardy appearance and the fact that the team was well larded with infielders kept him waiting until June before he was given a turn as the regular Minneapolis third baseman. He started well, batting close to .330 through the month, and found himself enjoying the ballplayer's life. On an off day during a series in Milwaukee, he and teammate Pat Malone—destined to become a fine pitcher for the Chicago Cubs—took a train south to Chicago, where they saw the Red Sox play the White Sox. Afterward, they went for a walk, looking over the city and listening to animated talk about Leopold and Loeb, young homosexual scions of wealthy Chicago families who were accused of murdering a fourteen-year-old boy and stuffing his corpse into a railway culvert. "Perverts," Berg called the defendants in a letter home, in which he went on to lump them with the "inactive college type" he'd seen at Princeton who read "perverted literature like Oscar Wilde and the Renaissance Italians and thereby take free license to copy them. The student in athletics," he advised, pointedly, "is also the healthier minded."

Through July Berg's batting average plummeted, and soon

he was back on the bench, where he remained mired, more or less, until August 19, when he was loaned to the Toledo Mud Hens for the remainder of the season.

Unfortunately for the baseball-mad citizens of Toledo, the 1924 Mud Hens were a lavishly bad team. The infielders were so ravaged by injuries that John Schulte, a catcher, had been pressed into duty at second base. At shortstop was Rabbit Helgeth, whose erratic fielding matched his random behavior. As Berg arrived on the scene, the team fined Helgeth $10 for poor play. He refused to pay, and was suspended, and Berg had a starting job.

Soon there was joy in Toledo. In an article headlined "Why the Mud Hens Are Playing Better Ball Now," the *News-Bee* writer explained that "Moe Berg is not a great shortstop, and he has his bad moments, but he is such a great improvement over Helgeth that he has restored confidence among the Toledo players and they are now able to go through a game without the fear that the hole in the shortfield would eventually prove their undoing."

Berg's worst moments continued to be as a hitter. After watching him play early in his career, the major league scout Mike Gonzalez filed a brief, remorseless dispatch that was such a true description of Berg, and a thousand ballplayers like him, that it made Gonzalez famous. "Good field, no hit" is what he wrote, and Berg's batting in Ohio—his average was a bruised .264 by season's end—was meek argument to the contrary.

Home for the winter, Berg took classes in French and Spanish at Columbia University's Graduate School of Arts and Sciences and reviewed Dr. John Gordon Andison's *The Affirmative Particles in French* for the spring issue of the *Romanic Review*. Berg evaluated the author's "detailed account of oui," on etymological, phonological, and morphological grounds, and concluded that while "the author advances no new theory . . . this thesis is a distinct contribution to the bibliography of Romance linguistics." By the time his essay was published in

April 1925, Berg was in Reading, Pennsylvania, making a distinct contribution of his own. They called him "the Great Moe" in Reading, where the word on whether this Berg fellow was a major league prospect was a resounding yes.

International League baseball had been in Reading since 1919, and the German farmers, cigar makers, beer brewers, and pretzel bakers of Berks County had yet to see a home team worth taking the afternoon off for. They got one with the 1925 Keystones, and in Berg local newspapermen had a player on whom they could spread praise thick as honey over butter. By early June he had been called everything from "a revelation" to "the whole show" to "the brilliant young shortstop." The difference was his hitting. Except for a mild slump in August, he bashed the ball around Lauer's Park with authority. On May 11, he had two home runs and a double against Syracuse. Eight days later his fifth hit of the game, a triple, defeated Jersey City. Soon the *Reading Eagle* reported that Berg "has been pickling the horsehide over the .300 mark all year and his sudden rise to batting power might chase the idea that he can't hit in the majors."

He played like a man of urgent appetites, with everything, both successes and failures, coming frequently and in profusion. On a sweltering June afternoon in Providence he made four errors, but slapped out as many hits, in an 8–5 victory. In June, the *Eagle* despaired over "a disastrous afternoon at shortstop," in which Berg errors cost his team eight runs. Come July, the *Baltimore News* baseball writer Roger Pippen was calling Berg and Keystones second baseman Heinie Scheer "the best double-play artists in the league."

The Keys reached second place on June 20 for the first time in franchise history, with Berg's batting average gliding close to .340 by late July. He hit three home runs in three days to close the month, before the slump cooled him off. The Keys stumbled with him, to fifth place, where they remained, for their highest finish ever. There was more verve left in Berg. On September 20 he had eight hits in eight at bats in a

▼

doubleheader against Providence. Nobody in the International League had ever done that. The Chicago Cubs offered Reading $25,000 for him. Chicago's South Side franchise, the White Sox, however, had earlier contracted with Reading for a $6,000 option on Berg, which they exercised. Berg finished the season with a .311 batting average, 124 runs batted in, and, more sobering, 72 errors. Then he hurried out of town. He was late for law school.

In 1920, THE outrage over the infamous 1919 Black Sox World Series gambling scandal had purged the White Sox of charismatic stars like "Shoeless" Joe Jackson and Bucky "Ginger Kid" Weaver, and without them the team's fortunes had sagged like worn bed ticking. By 1926, the roster was thin and management decisions seemed doomed to disaster—a prevailing discontent around Chicago which White Sox owner Charles Comiskey's latest elixir, his new shortstop, Moe Berg, would do nothing to appease. In early March, Berg announced that, instead of seizing this opportunity to rejoin the major leagues, he had decided to skip spring training and the first two months of the season to complete his first year of law school.

This was such an unusual choice that the White Sox had dismissed it when Berg advised them of his intentions during the previous August in Reading. They took him more seriously in late February, when each member of the throng of White Sox officials who visited New York in hopes of luring him out of the classroom was stoutly rebuffed. The White Sox star second baseman and manager, Eddie Collins, a former Columbia undergraduate himself, caused a stir when he visited his old campus to plead with Berg. Collins told him that to improve at baseball, he needed to play. "And what would I do if I broke my leg?" Berg retorted. Collins found that difficult to parry. He said he'd see Berg in June. "It was quite a disappointment to Manager Collins, who had counted upon Berg to handle the shortstop job when the season opens," said the *Chicago Tribune* article. Berg "was intent upon being an attorney and wants to finish his law education now so he can practice to some extent in the winter time while he is playing and then have an established profession when the time comes that he must quit the game."

Berg explained his motivations in a letter to Asa Bushnell, a Princeton alumni coordinator. "I have always considered the game only as a means to an end, because of its uncertainty, and the means are very important to me at this stage of life," he wrote. "It was a faster and more enjoyable way than any other to enable myself to finish my academic education and now a profession."

The demotion from Brooklyn to Minneapolis must have shaken Berg. Bernard Berg had long pressured him, the most talented of his three children, to attend law school and become a professional. It's entirely possible that before Berg left for Minneapolis, he brokered a compromise with his father. He'd continue to play baseball, but not at the expense of his education. Still, it was a curious time to undermine his chances in baseball. The fact was that, if he did break a leg, he could then study law. A job as a starting major league shortstop was an elusive prize, and for a man who liked the sport as much as Berg did, it was an odd decision.

Berg joined the White Sox on May 28. In his absence the team had signed Bill Hunnefield to play shortstop, and for much of the summer "Honey Boy" was a .300 hitter and Moe Berg a flannel-clad spectator. He was also a target for the japes of a Chicago press that had been annoyed by his law school decision. Mocking comments alluded to how rarely he played. When he was in the lineup, accounts of his spotty hitting and fielding tended to be gratuitously snide. In a game against Saint Louis, which the White Sox "lost because of the one error they made . . . our aspiring barrister Moe Berg was guilty of the mistake. He could never convince any jury of laymen that it wasn't his fault." In all, he earned the year's tuition money by playing in 41 games and hitting .221. His one moment of triumph came in the City Series, a best of seven post-season competition with the Cubs. In the seventh game, Berg's double off the left field wall at Wrigley Field drove in the series-winning run for the White Sox. "Moe Berg isn't much of a hitter, but this was a game where a decorum meant over $300 per individual, so Moe hit one," wrote Irving Vaughan in the *Chicago Tribune.*

Back at Columbia, in February 1927, Berg exchanged letters with Charles Comiskey, the president and owner of the White Sox. "The Old Roman" was imperious, notorious as a cheapskate, and prone to condescension with ballplayers. When Berg contacted him from New York in February, requesting permission to again report late for spring training, Comiskey began his reply unctuously. "My Dear Young Man," he wrote, "The time has come when you must decide as to the profession you intend following. If it is baseball, then it is most essential and important to the club and yourself that you report for spring training." He concluded by feigning detachment. "Whether or not you decide to play baseball, the Chicago Club must continue, so you may rest assured that whatever action you take will make no difference to us." Berg wrote him back, unconvinced, and Comiskey's next letter resorted to a less subtle means of persuasion: cold cash. "A player reporting after the season has opened naturally is way behind the other players—as was the example in your own case last year," Comiskey reasoned. This said, the owner added almost casually that "should you decide that you would report for spring training, I might tender you a contract, with an increase over the contract which you now have in your possession."

Berg didn't bite, and the White Sox went to Shreveport without him. That didn't mean that Berg was at peace with the situation. Up in New York, he was still struggling with the same indecision about professions that had been with him since his Princeton graduation. But now he felt he had come "to the cross roads," as he said to Taylor Spink in 1939. "It apparently would have to be baseball or law. Which? I loved the game and hated to quit." Berg hadn't told any faculty members at Columbia about his summer job, and few students knew about it either. One day in May, his quandary resolved itself unexpectedly. He called on Professor Noel Dowling to discuss a lecture. Arriving at the professor's office, Berg found Dowling reading the sports page and chuckling. "Great game, this baseball," he said, looking up at Berg. "You ought to get interested in it." Dowling told Berg that he'd played first base for Vanderbilt.

"Professor," said Berg, "I played shortstop for Princeton."

"Are you the Berg from Princeton?" asked Dowling. With that, out tumbled Berg's dilemma. Dowling was sympathetic. He told Berg to take extra courses in the fall, and promised to help arrange with the dean a leave of absence from law school the following year, in February 1928.

Berg spent his first three months of the 1927 season with the team in the same way he'd spent them in 1926, seated on the bench watching Bill Hunnefield play shortstop. In August came serendipity. Ray Schalk had been the White Sox catcher since 1912, and even now, at age thirty-five, he still liked to play when his body was willing. He chose July 21 for one of his rare appearances, and he chose badly. Julie Wera of the Yankees scored only eight runs in his major league career, but one of them came that day, when he ran over Schalk, injuring the little Chicago manager in his rush to the plate.

The team's regular catchers were Harry McCurdy and Buck Crouse. Crouse's locker was next to Berg's, and he liked to tease Berg about his weak hitting. "Moe," he said once, "I don't care how many of them damn degrees you got, they ain't never learned you to hit the curve." A few days after Schalk's mishap, Crouse split a finger in Philadelphia. The team moved on to Boston with only McCurdy left. In the third inning of a game on August 5, Red Sox outfielder Cleo Carlyle, running as though it was his only season in the majors—which it was —collided with McCurdy. Schalk was out of catchers. As he despaired in the dugout, Schalk heard a low, measured voice say, "You've got a big league catcher sitting right here."

It was Berg. He was referring to the husky backup first baseman Earl Sheely, who'd done some catching in the minor leagues, but Schalk didn't know that. "All right, Berg, get in there," he said. Dutifully, Berg began buckling on a chest protector and a pair of shin guards. Not only is it difficult to catch a baseball that is dipping and swerving at more than 90 miles an hour, for the unprepared it's also dangerous. "If the worst happens," Berg is supposed to have said, "kindly deliver the body to Newark."

It didn't. In his first game as a catcher since the Newark sandlots, Berg was terrific. The next day the team moved on to New York, where Schalk had a former Philadelphia Phillies catcher named Frank Bruggy on hand to meet the team. With Philadelphia, Bruggy had been known as "the Bruggy Boys," because he was so obese there seemed to be two of him. Bruggy hadn't caught in the majors since 1925 and the lack of exertion showed. He was fatter than ever. When Ted Lyons, scheduled to pitch against the Yankees, saw Bruggy, he told Schalk that he wasn't throwing to him. Schalk asked him whom he'd like as catcher. "Moe Berg," said Lyons.

Lyons was a future Hall of Famer, with an eclectic array of pitches. In his debut as a starting catcher, Berg would be contending with a brisk fastball, a darting curve, a knuckleball, and Babe Ruth. The 1927 Yankees were one of the strongest teams in baseball history. Led by Ruth, who would hit a record 60 home runs, they lost only 44 times. One of the losses came that day, as Lyons beat them 6–3, holding Ruth hitless. The defensive play of the game was made by, of all people, the novice catcher Moe Berg. With Chicago leading by one run in the fifth inning, Berg scooped up a poor throw from the outfield, spun, and tagged out New York third baseman Jumping Joe Dugan at the plate. Led by Lyons, the White Sox converged on their catching prodigy, shouting his name and clapping him on the back. "He went forward like a shortstop and picked up the half hop," said Lyons admiringly. "He caught a wonderful game and handled himself like an old-timer."

A few days later, *Tribune* columnist Westbrook Pegler re-counted the unfolding events with glee. "The distinguished Corean philologist confessed that he was secretly a catcher all the time instead of a shortstop, as everyone thought him. He has been catching very nicely and Mr. Schalk feels faint stir-rings of hope that some of his other players will confess to a secret accomplishment, preferably hitting. However, not to rely too strongly on a catcher who may only think he is a catcher, Mr. Schalk has engaged Mr. Frank Bruggy." Bruggy never played an inning for Chicago. Crouse's finger soon healed, and Berg caught eight more times in the last month and a half. He also amused himself by practicing his Spanish on long train rides with Carl Reynolds, a young outfielder from south Texas.

After the season, Berg returned to Columbia, while Schalk went off to Comiskey's retreat in Jerome, Wisconsin. Among the topics of their conversation was catching. "The catching department is something of a problem," reported Edward Burns in the *Tribune*. "At least one catcher who can flirt with .300 with his bat is needed." Berg's response was "Why not me?"

IF JOURNALISTS, CHARLES Comiskey, and perhaps some of his White Sox teammates, too, regarded Berg with a strand of enmity, it wasn't surprising. Berg's practice of skipping spring training and the first two months of the season left the impres-sion that he felt he had better things to do than play baseball. Everything might have been tolerated had he played well when he did show up, but thus far Berg's baseball career had been undistinguished. Comiskey was receiving very little for his investment.

Part of Berg's problem was that the game had never seen anything like him. Baseball at the time was full of country

▼

boys—rubes from mid-Atlantic mill towns, Great Plains farm-boys, and hayseeds from the deep South. Baseball had always had its share of college men, too. Christy Mathewson had gone to Bucknell, Lou Gehrig to Columbia; Frankie Frisch was "the Fordham Flash"; Eddie Plank went to Gettysburg College, and Chief Meyers was a Dartmouth man. But then, as now, nobody had ever tried to manipulate the baseball season to accommodate an academic schedule.

There had been one other exception, a right-handed pitcher named George Davis. "Champ" or "Iron," as Davis was called, was vice president of Williams College's Class of 1912, a speedballing pitcher for the baseball team, and a Phi Beta Kappa graduate. On July 16 of the same year, he began pitch-ing for the New York Highlanders. He was 1–4 for the team in ten games. Davis went to spring training in Cuba in 1913, but left to go home to get married. Fast and wild, he spent 1913 with Jersey City of the International League, striking out 199 batters in 208 innings and hitting 15 more. The Boston Braves brought him back to the majors for two games that summer. In 1914, he enrolled at Harvard Law School and missed spring training. He returned to the Braves with éclat, though, pitching a no-hitter against the Phillies on September 9 and helping the "Miracle Braves" to the pennant. It was a moment for any pitcher to savor, and especially so for Davis, who would win only five more professional baseball games. In 1915, law school again kept him in Cambridge through spring training, and after he received his LL.B. from Harvard in 1916, he became a full-time lawyer in Buffalo, where he learned to read seven foreign languages and became an accomplished amateur astronomer. His four-year major league record was 7–10.

Even Berg's most grudging critics had to admire the gump-tion he'd shown in offering himself to Schalk during the White Sox catching crisis. Berg came to regard that day as a splendid turn of chance. Catching, he decided, was his calling, some-thing worth postponing a law school diploma for. On February

15, 1928, Berg received a letter from John Grant, in the Columbia law school dean's office, securing him a leave of absence for the balance of the year. For the first time, Berg was allowing baseball's schedule to crowd his scholastic ambitions. Now he had a month and a half to learn the refinements of catching.

Three weeks before he was due at Shreveport for spring training, Berg traveled to a lumber camp in New York's Adirondack Mountains. Strenuous labor there tapered him into the best physical condition of his life. He awakened each morning at five and spent part of the day felling timber, sawing it into logs, and loading the logs onto sleds. Afterward, he took long runs through the sugar maple and yellow birch forests and sparred indoors. He reported to Shreveport on March 2, looking supple and fit to Edward Burns of the *Tribune*: "Moe Berg, who is allaying culture with his passion to become a catcher, arrived this morning as per schedule. . . . Moe being one of those lucky skinny devils who doesn't have to worry about his victuals, reported in good physical condition, except that the bottoms of his feet are tender as a result of sitting around in libraries all winter."

Shortstop Berg had always been too slow. Catchers, though, are notorious for trudging around the base paths, and Berg fit the essential criteria for the position: nimble reflexes, a strong arm, soft hands, and brains. In his crouch he looked the part too, balanced solid on his feet, angled slightly forward toward his pitcher, glove arm parallel to his thighs and thrust straight out beyond them—a firm, attractive target. The White Sox never did trade for a catcher. Crouse, McCurdy, and Berg were to share the position.

By May, the team had fallen to last place. On July 4, Schalk resigned, and Lena Blackburne became the new manager. To this point Berg hadn't caught much, but pitchers like Alphonse "Tommy" Thomas and especially Lyons liked the way he handled himself at the position and began to request him. He was becoming a pesky hitter, too, keeping his batting average above

▼

.300 into September, when it dipped to .246. By City Series time, the White Sox had rebounded to fifth in the eight-team league, and Berg had established himself as their starting catcher.

Previewing the City Series, Burns wrote a piece comparing Cubs catcher Gabby Hartnett, a future Hall of Famer, with Berg. Hartnett, he said, was the harder hitter, but both "are nifty dressers and single. They are deadly on high foul flies and throwing to second . . . the big difference between the two boys is that Hartnett drives one of the most costly of domestic cars, while Berg still clings to his boyish love for the bicycle. He can be seen riding every morning rain or shine in the vicinity of 53rd Street and Hyde Park Boulevard. Berg speaks from seven to twenty-one languages, while Gabby speaks but one—rock ribbed New England." The press was warming up to him, and why not? On a bad team, a witty man of broad interests made for a nice traveling companion and, more important, good rainy-day copy. The Cubs won the City Series 4–3, no thanks to Berg, who caught every game and batted .333.

Berg was by no means a famous player, but to Chicago's Jewish fans, his presence in the lineup was important. The largest Jewish diaspora from Eastern Europe to the U.S. had taken place around the turn of the century, meaning that American cities were now teeming with recent immigrants looking for a means of assimilation. For many, the National Pastime was perfect for the purpose. By absorbing the jargon, learning the rituals, adopting a team, and cheering along with a boisterous hometown crowd, men speaking heavily accented English began to feel a part of things. The paleontologist Stephen Jay Gould recalls, "My grandfather says he acclimated to this country through baseball," and Horace Bresler, a baseball enthusiast who grew up outside New York City, says his father had a similar experience. "My dad came from Russia to New York when he was seven and grew up in the Bronx. He had two passions in life. One was opera, one was baseball.

He was inclined to be refined, but when he could bring the conversation around to baseball, he was delighted. The assimilation is very important. I think baseball gives a lot of people who feel obscure a feeling of identity and belonging in a new place. The games always start with the national anthem. Baseball eased my father's entry into this country."

So enthusiastic were some Jewish White Sox fans about Berg that they tried to ply him with money. Earlier in the summer, pitcher Red Faber, playing his fifteenth season for the White Sox, had been honored with a "Day" by fans who presented him with $792. Clamoring for a "Berg Day," Chicago fans raised a staggering $25,000, only to have it turned down by Berg, who explained, "I've done nothing to merit it and besides, it would be an affront to a great player like Faber."

The same year in New York, where over a million Jews lived, McGraw finally found the Jewish player he'd long coveted for the Giants. Second baseman Andy Cohen was so popular with Jewish fans that the Giants hired a secretary to sort through his mail, poems were published in his name, the *Jewish Daily Forward* printed accounts of his play on the front page, and vendors at the Polo Grounds were instructed to bellow "Get your ice-cream Cohens here!" After the Yankees watched this go on for a summer, in October 1928 they were rumored to have proposed a trade with Chicago for Berg.

At law school in the fall there was trouble. Possibly it was the strain of concentrating a year's work into one semester, but whatever the explanation, Berg failed evidence and did not graduate with the Class of 1929, although he did pass the New York State bar exam later that spring. He was nonplussed in late February, when the White Sox traded outfielder Bibb Falk to Cleveland for catcher Chick Autrey. Autrey and Crouse shared the catching into early June. In seventh place on June 5, Chicago lost to last-place Boston 17–2, prompting Irving Vaughan to rage in the *Tribune*, "The White Sox are no longer comical, they are pathetic." Berg caught the next day, had two hits, and threw out two base runners. He had two more hits two days later, then three, and three more. Suddenly, he was a regular American League catcher again.

Good catchers have always been rare in baseball, but on a seventh-place team, a swallowtail jacket and a bad temper can be more interesting than a steady bat and a strong arm. Chicago's first baseman in 1929 was a twenty-one-year-old cotton-haired terror from Waxahachie, Texas, named Art Shires. That summer it was Shires, or the "Great Shires," as he insisted upon being addressed, and not Moe Berg who was the talk of Chicago. Shires was suspended following a gin-soaked spring training evening, which he brought to an unfortunate de-nouement when he whacked Manager Blackburne in the eye. There was, as John Kieran put it, "grave suspicion that [Shires] was a ballplayer," however, and with the paucity of such species in Chicago, Shires was portrayed as an ingenue, a victim of the demon gin, and all was forgiven.

When sober, Shires was a whimsical slugger, the only .300 hitter in the league who came to the ballpark turned out in spats, green and white striped pantaloons, a green jacket with pearl buttons, a walking stick in his hand, and a silk top hat nestled on his curls. In July, Shires began writing poetry, or "pomes," as he called them. The first announced, "They is a ballplayer / He is The Great Shires / Which he can paste the old apple / Whenever he tries." "It ain't such a hell of a pome anyhow," critiqued the author, "but it's a pipe I can clout better when I try than when I'm tired. Anyhow a writer told me poetry don't have to rhyme." Only when Shires read more in the newspapers about Babe Ruth and Lou Gehrig than about him-self did he resort to rhyme: "You may rave about Babe, / You may rave about Lou, / Why be so snooty? / The Great Shires is good too." He was endearing, and during a summer when *Tribune* articles began "Wanted: Some Hits," a hit he was.

Berg's finest season progressed without many superlatives, but on September 7 he made headlines for, of all things, stu-pidity. In the fifth inning of a game Tommy Thomas was pitch-ing against Washington, a runner was on third with the score tied at one when the batter hit a foul pop-up. Berg circled back, caught the ball, flicked it toward the mound, and began trotting toward the dugout. But that made only two outs, not three, and the delighted Washington runner scampered home to score what proved to be the winning run. After that, Thomas never tired of telling Berg, "You can speak a dozen languages but you can't count to three."

Eight days later, on the fourteenth floor of the Benjamin Franklin Hotel in Philadelphia, Manager Blackburne discovered Shires holed up in his room with a flask of gin. Shires reacted poorly to the intrusion and lowered his head. It took four men to subdue him. Blackburne got the worst of it. Shires bit the manager's finger, punched him in the eye again, and tore up his hat. He was suspended indefinitely. While across town the Cubs were winning the National League pennant, the White Sox were seventh in the American League and "a sick ball club" according to Comiskey. Three hundred people came to watch their final game against Detroit. Berg batted .288 for the season, and if that still wasn't quite on the rarefied level of Bill Dickey of the Yankees or of Mickey Cochrane of the Athletics, Berg was their peer defensively. Besides rarely making an error and putting a tremble in base stealers with his throwing arm, Berg was a clever caller of pitches and something of a psychologist. "He could make you believe you were the greatest pitcher in the world that day," said Tommy Thomas.

In New York, Berg repeated the evidence course, passed it this time, and received his LL.B. on February 26, 1930. At spring training in San Antonio, the White Sox starting catcher told Newark reporters, "I am in the pink." In his spare time he watched Mexican dancing girls and eluded American women. One day with a woman at his side, he approached the rookie shortstop Luke Appling and asked, "Luke, will you look after this lady for a few minutes?" An hour went by, and then another. Appling took the woman to lunch, put her in a taxi, and sent her home. The next day he saw Berg. "Hey, Moe,"

▼

he said, "what happened?" Berg smiled, turned, and walked away without saying anything.

Berg also managed to skirt the controversy that dominated March: the fate of Shires. After first spurning the White Sox contract offer, and thus winning himself a revised appellation, the "Peculiar Shires," at the end of March Shires agreed to a contract that stipulated he "follow baseball as a serious profession," and showed up for work in San Antonio wearing a garish diamond ring. Berg probably observed these antics with mild distaste. Both men were eccentrics, but Shires was a more typical baseball flake. He was uncouth, sophomoric, and hilarious. Berg, the elusive intellectual, always deflected attention and was careful never to flaunt his learning or to make an exception of himself.

If Shires was the extreme, many baseball players were unpolished, to say the least. Once, after a teammate subjected Berg to some particularly vile invective, Berg turned to the man and said, "That betrays a lack of vocabulary. You shouldn't curse. Don't you ever use a polysyllable?" To the press, however, he was a steadfast defender of all "the gentlemen I played with." The *Washingon Post*'s Shirley Povich says that "Moe was bemused and amused by ballplayers. Mostly he talked about them with benign amusement, never scorn or contempt." Privately he sometimes discarded the respectful air and could sound condescending, even caustic, while recounting tales of teammates who stumbled when reading comic books, but whatever disdain Berg felt for ballplayers, he kept to himself. And his affection for some of his teammates, Lyons and Thomas in particular, was genuine. Most teammates would have said that he was a fine man—that they didn't know much about him, but he was a very nice fellow. That was how Berg wanted it.

On April 6, the White Sox, working their way north to begin the season, stopped in Arkansas for an exhibition game against the Little Rock Travelers. It was a day with a tear to it. While he led off first base, Berg's spikes caught in the soil as he tried to change directions, and he felt a sharp pain in his knee. The next morning he was bound for Mercy Hospital in Chicago, where a serious injury was discovered. The White Sox would need a new catcher, and two months later Shires was traded to Washington for Bennie Tate. "Just call me Shires," he said, introducing himself to his new manager, Walter Johnson. Two years later, Shires was out of baseball for good.

And Berg? Berg didn't become a full-time lawyer. Instead, he made a life for himself as that consummate baseball mediocrity, the third-string catcher.

CHAPTER 6

You Never Knew
He Was
Around

On May 2, 1930, a puzzling notice appeared toward the end of Edward Burns's White Sox story in the *Chicago Tribune.* "If anybody in Chicago knows how Moe Berg, the first-string catcher now laid up in Chicago, is getting along," wrote Burns, "will they please communicate with the ballclub." Moe Berg had vanished.

The last people to have seen him were the nuns of Saint Catherine's convent. The nuns acted as Berg's nurses during his hospital stay, and were charmed by "Cousin Morris." He told such irresistible stories about baseball players, Notre-Dame Cathedral, and Masses he'd gone to as a child in New Jersey, and he spoke Latin as well as a priest. The nuns gathered at his bedside in virtual shifts, to giggle at banter that poured from him like lemonade. In return they indulged in some mild proselytizing, begged him to repeat a few Hail Marys every day—he was having none of it—and let it be known that they were praying for him anyway. Berg promised the sisters a New York City tour whenever they wished, and one winter a few of them took him up on it. The itinerary included a visit to Saint Patrick's Cathedral and a stop at Temple Emmanu-El. Perhaps the nuns knew that Berg had gone home to Newark, where his brother, Sam, now a doctor, applied heat treatments to the damaged knee, but probably they had no idea where he was. It was at about this time that Berg began compartmentalizing his life, moving quietly from destination to destination and scattering scant traces behind.

The years 1930 and 1931 were lost baseball seasons. Berg turned up in the White Sox clubhouse in mid-May, claimed he was sound in body, and was in the White Sox starting lineup on the twenty-third. With a sheared knee ligament still healing, this was foolish. The squatting alone must have been agony. Catching every day was out of the question, and Tate was soon acquired from Washington in the deal for Shires. Berg played in only 20 games all summer and hit a humiliating .115. He was a forgotten man in Chicago.

Only in October did Berg really go to work, beginning his legal career as a corporate lawyer in Manhattan. Satterlee and Canfield was a respected Wall Street firm that melded the pedigree of Herbert Satterlee, J. P. Morgan's son-in-law, with the academic prestige of George Canfield, a distinguished Columbia law school professor whose original partner was the future chief justice Harlan Fiske Stone. Satterlee and Canfield were gentlemen rainmakers whose discreet single-line annual bills for "services rendered" went to clients with names like Rockcfeller. When it came to hiring associates, the firm chose exclusively from the graduating classes at Harvard, Yale, and Columbia law schools, and their choices usually turned out to be Protestants. It was a plum job, and when Berg was offered a place, he took it. New York and New Jersey had plenty of Jewish firms, but by this time it was clear that Berg was drawn to patrician settings where he was the exception.

The firm—now Satterlee, Stephens, Burke & Burke—has

▼

long since disposed of its records from Berg's day and knows of nobody still living who worked with him, but Jim Dwyer, who started with Satterlee and Canfield in the early 1930s, says Berg had already departed by the time he began. So Berg's career as a downtown New York lawyer was brief, lasting three or four winters at the most. The work probably paid very well, but left him restless.

In April 1931, Chicago put Berg on waivers, and the Cleveland Indians claimed him. The Indians already had three catchers, Luke Sewell, Glenn Myatt, and Joe Sprinz. Berg was a speculation. If he could catch the way he had in 1929, fine. If his knee was too rickety or if he suddenly quit baseball to practice law, the outlay was only a few months' salary. Arriving in Cleveland, Berg was sure his knee was sturdy, and playing baseball, he said, "is what I want to do." Thereupon he came down with bronchial pneumonia. Berg had one hit for the entire season, and he may have done more for team owner Alva Bradley by taking his young son, Maury, to Cleveland's museums on rainy days than by anything he did at the ballpark. It was a thoroughly unobtrusive year. "He never caused anybody any trouble," says pitcher Willis Hudlin. "You never really knew he was around."

Moe Berg had always been a loner, and as he receded to the fringes of professional baseball, his eccentricities became more pronounced. Nobody had ever really known much about him. Now he became obviously unusual, and it began to occur to some people to wonder.

There were his clothes. Berg was a formal dresser for a ballplayer, and fussy about his wardrobe. He favored dark gray suits, white dress shirts, a black tie, black shoes, and, sometimes, a gray fedora. What made the sartorial Berg compelling was variety. There was none. He wore this same personal uniform every day of the year for the rest of his life. He had large, very flat feet, and when he could afford to, he bought shoes that were custom made to accommodate them. In more austere times, he settled for sturdy oxfords with rounded toes and thick soles, similar to those worn by metropolitan policemen. Some people were sure that he owned just one suit, one shirt, and one tie, but a group of his teammates learned otherwise. After luring Berg from the hotel where he lived, they went to his room, opened his closet, and found eight identical suits hanging neatly. Charlie Wagner, who would play with Berg on the Boston Red Sox, had a similar experience. Wagner, known as "Broadway Charlie" for his dapper appearance, was teasing Berg during a train ride. "Moe," Wagner told him, "we need to get you a light gray suit. We need to get you a new tie." Berg hauled down his suitcase from the luggage rack and flung it open to reveal ten identical ties. "See," he said. "I don't wear the same tie every day." Berg and the nuns must have made a striking portrait in black and white.

As to why he adopted the nearly monochromatic garb, Berg was always evasive. His sister's explanation was that he made a pact with his friend Enrique López-Herrarte when López-Herrarte's mother and Berg's father died in rapid succession. That couldn't be, however, because Berg began wearing black, white, and gray in the early 1930s, and Bernard Berg lived until 1942. The New York reporter Jimmy Breslin, a friend of Berg's in the 1950s, once asked Berg about his clothes. "He told me he was in mourning for the world," says Breslin.

Whatever the explanation, this form of dress was practical for a traveling man, flattering to Berg's olive complexion, and expedient for someone with a penchant for passing suddenly out of view.

There were also his newspapers. Berg craved newsprint the way some people yearn for coffee or tobacco. Walking along a city sidewalk, he cut a distinctive figure, with a stack of papers cradled under his arm and stuffed into his pockets, protruding like reeds from a marsh. Berg was as particular about his newspapers as his attire. Until Berg had finished reading a paper, it was "alive" and nobody else could touch it. When he'd finished, which he often signaled by throwing it on the floor, the paper was "dead" and no longer sacrosanct.

▼

The 1930s and 1940s were wonderful days for newspaper readers, since large cities usually had several competing papers. In Boston, for example, Berg could choose from the *Globe*, the *Evening Transcript*, the *Post*, the *Herald*, the *American*, the *Record*, and the *Traveler*. When a big story broke, Berg bought them all. At times he had newspapers arriving from every direction (in Chicago he ordered them shipped from New York)—French papers, the *Miami Herald*, the *Philadelphia Inquirer*, a West Coast paper from Los Angeles or San Francisco, the New York papers (he depended upon the *Times*), the *Washington Post*, the London papers a few days late, and the *Manchester Guardian*. When traveling, he carried a separate straw suitcase to hold them all, and he had contacts at train stops waiting to replenish his stock. The train would pull into the station, and there would be a boy, arms full of papers, looking for Mr. Berg.

Berg was obstinate about keeping papers until he had read them, and sometimes he acquired them at such a pace that he fell far behind in his reading. No matter; he set them in stacks on any available flat surface—chairs, tables, the floor. One of his friends, the baseball comedian and coach Al Schacht, surveyed Berg's room once and made a sarcastic reference to the piles of "dust collectors." "No, Al," Berg replied. "They're alive, and they'll stay alive until I've read them." He meant it. At the end of spring training every year, the clubhouse boys packed the team's equipment and shipped it north to Washington or Boston. In one trunk, neatly tied up to his specification in thick bundles, were Berg's newspapers. "If you read the *New York Times*, the *Washington Post*, and the *Boston Globe*, you don't need to go to college," Berg told a friend, the Chicago sportswriter Jerome Holtzman.

An eager conversationalist, even garrulous at times, Berg could be very funny. Yet for all the flow of talk, he kept himself to himself. He was as gray as the front page, and he behaved like a newspaper too; all the latest facts, but no reflection. "We knew a lot about [ballplayers'] private lives," says Shirley Povich, "but he was mysterious. You never saw him hanging around the hotel lobby like the other ballplayers. They just accepted Moe for what he was—a man apart." The game ended, and Berg showered, dressed, and disappeared. "He never told anybody what he did with his free time," says Eldon Auker, a Red Sox pitcher. "Nobody knew much about him," says former Boston infielder Billy Werber. "A great guy to be around," says pitcher Jack Wilson. "Always kidding, but he never told you anything. You never bummed around with him either. He'd get a cab and he was gone."

BERG WAS DAMAGED now, a weak-kneed catcher scrambling to stay in the majors. His physical decline came at a time when the national optimism he had known since youth had been stifled by economic collapse. The country's torpor paralleled his personal disarray, a fact that must have had resonance for an inveterate newspaper reader who had spent time working on Wall Street. Not that Berg had to sell apples or escort children to art exhibitions to hang on in the major leagues. He had two Ivy League degrees. He had studied at the Sorbonne. He was a lawyer. Even during the Great Depression there were jobs available to a man like this.

At heart, however, Berg was a sensualist, and he knew of no other job that would send him to so many places, install him in plush accommodations, present him a generous meal allowance, and offer him as much free time for reading, dining, and adventure as baseball did. The rhythms of the game complemented the lifestyle he preferred. The reason other ballplayers never saw him in his free time was that, as much as he enjoyed his hours at the ballpark, in his twilight years as a professional athlete life really began for him when he got into that cab and slipped away by himself.

Everything depended upon the association with baseball. Among ballplayers, he was something unique, a scholar in a roomful of muscle. And when he stepped out of the taxi, he achieved the inverse celebrity; to professors, actors, scientists, and politicians, he was the famous Moe Berg, the brainy baseball player. Baseball made him special in a way that drafting briefs never would have. So Berg would stay with the game as long as possible, lugubrious because he was no longer capable of playing it with distinction, yet elated still to be in uniform.

The Indians gave Berg his unconditional release in January 1932. With catchers scarce, however, on March 10 Shirley Povich reported that the Senators owner, Clark Griffith, had invited Berg to spring training in Biloxi, Mississippi. "Judging from Berg's record," wrote Povich, "the chances are that Griffith would be glad to get a better man." That said, Povich sidled up to Senators outfielder Dave "Sheriff" Harris and observed, "I see you've got a new catcher, Sheriff. What kind of a catcher is he?"

"We'll find out tomorrow," said Harris, an outfielder known for his hard line drives and hardhearted one-liners.

"I just want to tell you he speaks seven languages," said Povich.

"Yeah, I know," Harris retorted, "and he can't hit in any of them."

On March 13, Povich spoke to Berg, apparently for the first time, and discovered someone who would delight him, and so his readers, for the next three years. This time he wrote about Berg with all skepticism vanquished: "The average mental capacity of the Washington Ball Club was hiked several degrees with the acquisition of the eminent Mr. Moe Berg, late of the Chicago White Sox and Cleveland Indians, who has joined the Nats from the ranks of the free agents and is destined to do considerable catching in Washington regalia." Povich, an orthodox Jew, reported that Berg was "the most famous linguist in baseball with his command of languages variously put at from 7 to 27 . . . he laughs off the idea that he gives signs in Hindu, and declares that Yiddish will usually suffice."

Povich had found his man, and Berg, too, had found his. Berg was often petulant in response to articles like Povich's.

"I wish less attention were paid to my linguistic accomplishments," he huffed to the *American Mercury* in 1940. "Too much has been made of this by the newspapers," he said sternly to *Baseball* magazine editor F. C. Lane, when Lane asked him about Sanskrit. Actually, Berg was eager to accommodate journalists, and he cultivated them like so many marigolds. "I don't suppose there was ever a man in baseball who was more popular with the press than Moe," said Ted Lyons in a letter to Ethel Berg. Rick Ferrell, with whom Berg would play for the Red Sox, says, "Moe had connections with the top people— the owners, the writers, the manager. He associated with them more than he did with his teammates. I never saw him with other players."

Every day Berg sat in the dugout before the game and told stories to crowds of reporters. All his life, he made a point of befriending young sportswriters, from Povich and Kieran to Jerome Holtzman of the *Chicago Tribune* and Ira Berkow of the *New York Times*. It's no coincidence that Berg was in the sports pages without respite until he died. Not only was he unique, he was available.

More profiles of Berg were published than of any other journeyman ballplayer in history. He submitted to a surfeit of interviewers who later made outrageous claims for his linguistic, legal, and literary acumen, and elevated a well-educated ballplayer to a savant in shin guards. No matter how many languages reporters claimed that Berg spoke, there is no record of his ever taking real umbrage, much less demanding a correction. The exaggerations didn't bother him.

To the contrary, he accepted interview requests with alacrity and was at pains to give the writer what he wanted. Preparing a profile of Berg, Donald Stuart discovered, was no effort at all. "The minute he learned our reason for accosting him in the lobby of the Commodore Hotel, he ordered a taxi and, once inside, proceeded to interview himself," wrote Stuart. Make no mistake, Berg liked the company of reporters. It was pure pleasure for him to go walking to the Boston Public

Garden with John Kieran and translate the Latin inscriptions they found there, but he wasn't blind to the fact that Kieran's torrent of Professor Berg stories distinguished him from every other ballplayer in the business. "You kept me in the big leagues for years," he wrote Kieran shortly before his death in 1972, and both men knew there was some truth there. In 1929, he was a fine catcher. In the 1930s, when he was scarred and going to fat, his mystique helped him keep his job.

Yet it went deeper than clever pragmatism. Berg's voluble way with the media belied an essential elusiveness. "I was fascinated by him, respected him, admired him," says Povich. "He had a great attraction for writers. He brought up subjects that were always interesting. He was so cognizant of world affairs. He'd trace the names of certain writers. He'd tell John Keller, 'Keller's German for cellar.' He could charm or fascinate anybody. He just didn't talk about himself. He deflected always. You learned quickly not to ask him." There was the rub. All these stories Berg was distributing were incomplete. Professor Berg the linguist and lawyer was there, Moe Berg the person was not.

Why the camouflage? There was nothing sinister here. Berg was no villain. He was a baseball player speaking to men who wanted to write humor, to flatter rather than harm him. Besides, he was also an unusually talented and intelligent young man, not a charlatan of any sort. All true, but he was one more thing, a man with secrets.

THE 1932 SENATORS won 93 games and were the best team Berg had yet played for. Shortstop Joe Cronin, married to Griffith's daughter, Mildred, and outfielder Heinie Manush were powerful hitters; Alvin Crowder and Monte Weaver were two of baseball's better pitchers. Berg played in 75 games for the Senators, and though he hit only .236, he was potent when it mattered. After starting catcher Roy Spencer injured his knee, Berg caught regularly, and his defense made him an important member of a team that missed finishing in second place by a single game. He threw out 35 base runners and made no errors. "I would say that, barring Bill Dickey and Mickey Cochrane, Berg has caught as well as any man in the American league," said Washington manager Walter Johnson toward the end of the year. And now, best of all, Berg's solid defense was taking him abroad. In October he boarded a passenger ship bound for Japan. He was going to teach the Japanese baseball.

CHAPTER 7

Strange
Foreigner
with Camera

A few occasions in Moe Berg's life gratified him so much that he recalled them often in conversation or reverie, and over time they came to form who he was. Some people acquire a spouse, children, a home, furniture, an automobile, or an album full of vacation snapshots. Moe Berg never married, fathered children, took vacations, learned to drive, or owned much of anything besides the black, white, and gray clothes he wore on his back and the books he stacked in his brother's house. What he collected were experiences, signal moments gathered like pretty quartz stones along the shore and then fingered again and again until they were polished to a shimmer. As it happened, most of his experiences occurred abroad and included his few months at the Sorbonne, his wartime service in Europe, and his two trips to Japan, in 1932 and 1934.

An American missionary named Horace Wilson introduced baseball to Japan in 1872. Influential daimyo (feudal lords) decided that baseball was an American martial art and urged young Japanese boys to develop the American spirit by playing it. The spirit of kendo prevailed, though, with Japanese players attacking baseball like stoic gentleman warriors, practicing year-round through driving rain and bitter cold, prizing the man who fielded ground balls until his hands bled and treating umpires with exaggerated obeisance no matter how dreadful their decisions. The game quickly became very popular in Japan.

In 1913 and again in 1922, professional American players visited Japan. John McGraw and Tris Speaker, the Boston Red Sox brilliant center fielder, were part of the first entourage, and among those in the second were the famous umpire George Moriarty and a former National League utility infielder named Herb Hunter. Accustomed to the churlish ways of American players, Moriarty spent a few innings in a place where athletes lowered their eyes and bowed to umpires, and was certain he'd seen Erewhon. Hunter saw opportunity.

The Japanese knew nothing about the subtleties that make a superficially simple game yield endless complexities. They needed someone to teach them inside baseball: techniques, strategies, and psychology. Hunter reasoned that American major league players and managers would make excellent instructors. Acting as a conduit, Hunter traveled to Japan eight times between 1922 and 1932, and became known as "baseball's ambassador." In 1931, the newspaper *Yomiuri Shimbun* sought to cash in on the growing Japanese baseball craze by asking Hunter to assemble an American all-star team for an exhibition game tour against Japanese college teams. Collectively, the American team, which included Mickey Cochrane, Lou Gehrig, and Lefty O'Doul, hit .346 in 17 games. The next year Hunter brought not another all-star squad to pummel Japanese pitching, but three players to offer what amounted to baseball seminars at Japanese universities. Hunter hired O'Doul, the National League batting champion, to help with hitting, fielding, and base running; Ted Lyons to work with the pitchers; and Moe Berg to teach the catchers.

By the time the ship had reached Honolulu, Berg was already exulting to his family: "I am having a truly marvelous time—linguistically, sociologically, ethnologically, legally, and athletically." While in Hawaii, he looked at volcanoes, went for a seaplane ride, and watched the undulating hips of a hula dancer, to which he reacted as prudishly as he had to Parisian coquettes. "They tell me the hula is a sacred religious rite," he wrote, "but it looks like a vulgar 'come hither' dance to me."

Berg spent a good deal of his two and a half weeks aboard ship seated on deck or in his cabin, memorizing a small red Japanese grammar book, and when he got off the boat, he looked up at the signs along the teeming streets and knew what some of them said. *Yakyu-kai*, a Japanese newspaper, declaring that Berg was "a genius in language," said that he read through six elementary school textbooks during his less than two-month-long visit. He didn't, as the American sports press later liked to claim for him, become fluent in the space of a trans-Pacific voyage, but what is true is that in a short time he grasped more Japanese than most American expatriates or tourists could speak, and learned to write some characters in katakana, Japan's phonetic written alphabet. His effort alone delighted his hosts, who referred to him as "Scholar Berg, the Linguist."

On October 20, Berg, Lyons, O'Doul and his wife, and Hunter and his wife docked at Yokohama Harbor. Two days later the ballplayers began their circuit of Meiji, Waseda, Rikkyo, Teidai (Tokyo Imperial), Hosei, and Keio universities, the members of Tokyo's Six-University League. Towering over the Japanese ballplayers, the Americans spent five or six days at each school, teaching the finest baseball players in Japan to defend situations when runners are at first and third, to hit outside pitches behind a base runner so as to advance him into scoring position, and to confuse batters by varying pitch selection and location. Berg enjoyed coaching, but mostly he regarded it as an excuse to explore Japan, and what he saw of this most highly ritualized of societies left him feeling, of all things, insouciant.

Life in this new place where even the mundane—beds, clothing, food—was unlike anything he'd seen before, immediately fascinated him much in the way that Paris had. "I have never enjoyed a visit or anything more in my life than this one," he told his family on November 9. Japan was "a page out of a dream—streets, narrow, lined with shops, thousands of people going home from work on bicycles." He slept on a tatami mat, wore a kimono, read English-language newspapers, strolled past the fancy shops along the Ginza—he called it the Ginzberg—survived two mild earthquakes and a typhoon, stood in a crowd with thousands of Japanese for a glimpse of the emperor, and ate sushi with chopsticks and the attendant cacophony of appreciation good manners required. "You must inhale it with the noise of a steel-mill at full blast, sound your p's and q's, dot your i's and cross your t's and then when the food or drink has passed your gullet, you exhale a sound of satisfaction," he explained in a letter home.

He even made mild mischief. The three American ballplayers were dining in a restaurant one day when O'Doul became frustrated by the waitress's inability to understand his order. Berg scribbled something on a napkin and quietly handed it to her. "O'Doul ees ugliest mug I have ever seen," she read aloud from his katakana. "He ees also lousy baseball player. Someday he weel get heet with fly ball and get keeled."

He also attended a geisha party and afterward managed to maintain the acquaintance of three geisha girls, who served him dinner and accompanied him to plays. He liked one of

them best, was perhaps even infatuated, and definitely tried
to see her again when he returned two years later. She refused,
telling him she was married.

At Meiji, Berg had become fast friends with an English
teacher named Takizo Matsumoto. Matsumoto asked Berg to
call him Taki or Frank, and to teach his class. Berg did, and
so successfully that soon other professors and even the presi-
dents of Meiji and Imperial universities heard about him and
expressed interest in meeting with him to discuss Japanese
difficulties in learning foreign languages. Berg was intrigued
by the Japanese inability to pronounce the English letter "l,"
and he spent some time designing a means of using katakana
to combat what he later referred to as "the 'l' problem."

After completing his coaching assignment in late November,
Berg parted from the other Americans, heading off with Matsumoto to see some of the country. They traveled by train to
Nara, where Berg played with the tame local deer, Kyoto,
Osaka, and Kobe, and Beppu, where he and Matsumoto were
photographed together, wearing kimonos. Berg, curious about
everything and unaccustomed to being in a place where he
couldn't communicate, was studying Japanese continually.
Matsumoto helped him with it and, in exchange, Berg taught
him some French.

Vowing to stay in touch with Matsumoto, Berg pressed on
alone through Manchuria, which the Japanese had invaded,
setting up the puppet state of Manchukuo much to Chinese—
and American—displeasure. "Don't fear—safe," he told his
parents, and despite the Japanese soldiers he saw swarming
everywhere outside his train windows, it was. He toured Shanghai and Peking; stood at the Great Wall, which struck him as
more futile than magnificent; and then went on to Indochina,
where the snug skirts with long slits up the side worn by fash-
ionable women in Saigon caught his attention, as did the rick-
shaw drivers, who seemed to him "satisfied to be beasts of
burden." After a day of touring the ancient stupas and spires
of Angkor Wat, reclaimed from the Cambodian jungle—"the

▼

most thrilling sight I saw in the Orient"—he slept in a bed raised six feet off the ground to avoid snakes.

Berg saw as much as he did because he was an enthusiastic walker, undaunted by the sweltering Southeast Asia heat. In Siam, however, he was told it was mating season for "Mr. Tiger," as the Thais put it, so he did without his accustomed evening strolls and also declined an invitation to go tiger hunting. By New Year's Eve he was in Bangkok, a seasoned and carefree traveler. "I am always meeting people and leave them or have their company as I please," he told his parents. For Moe Berg, moving briskly across a fascinating landscape without obligation or connection was life at its best.

The trip continued through India and the Middle East. "I have decided to see it all . . . may never have the chance to see it again" was his reasoning when he petitioned his parents for some extra funds. He climbed a pyramid in Egypt, wearing his black necktie; crossed the Sea of Galilee; stood by the shores of the River Jordan, walked in the valley of Jehoshaphat; and made it to Berlin by January 30. The city was clogged with Nazis; Hitler had just become German chancellor. A few weeks later Berg passed through Newark, where he distributed kimonos, chopsticks, geta (formal wooden shoes), and, for his mother, a lamp. It was clear to his brother, Dr. Sam, who received a kimono, that "Moe was dying to go back to Japan." Instead, by February 26, he was in Biloxi, Mississippi, for spring training with the Senators. It had been the happiest few months of his life.

Still preoccupied with Asia as Berg must have been while riding an American train through the Delta crescent, he was no doubt gratified that he did not to have to think about scrapping for a catching job that year. Although the Senators had two other catchers, Luke Sewell, the starter, and Cliff Bolton, a raw, cigar-chomping rookie, Berg's value was proven. Of course in baseball, all jobs are ephemeral. In Biloxi, the *Post* described Berg hard at work, teaching Bolton the fundamentals of catching as "a rather poignant example of pure Christian

unselfishness and Christian charity being given down here by
a Jewish gentleman named Moe Berg. . . . Don't you see that
as soon as Bolton is good enough—Moe goes?" Implicit was
that Berg was no longer a young athlete but a codger whose
job depended upon his wiles. That he was only thirty suggested
as much about the ephemeral nature of a baseball career as it
did about the impression Berg left with baseball people. He
was ceded an avuncular role in the game in part because he
really was savvy and also because he always did seem a little
older than his years.

The year 1933 was a triumphant season for the pennant-
winning Senators and an unobtrusive one for Berg. He batted
65 times, hit a squalid .185, and played in only 40 games. Even
at the ballpark, his mind was drifting. Seated in the bull pen,
he enlivened the long summer afternoons by spinning tales of
the East for the relief pitchers. "Japan was the main subject;
he loved it," said Tommy Thomas, then also with Washington.
On trains, while his teammates played cards, Berg sat alone,
reading. Besides holding newspapers, the extra suitcase he
lugged with him was stuffed with scientific magazines, a chessboard, and plenty of books, including Lewis Carroll's *Through
the Looking Glass*. As a rule, Berg eschewed fiction, but for a
time he could be found poring over Carroll and a chessboard,
attempting to work out a more logical sequence of moves for
Alice's mad chess game.

A new member of the Senators that year was the talented
and temperamental left-handed pitcher Earl Whitehill, who
was married to Violet Linda Oliver, the California Raisin Girl.
During spring training, Cronin, now the team's "boy" manager, asked Berg if he would room with Whitehill on road
trips. "If we're going to win a pennant, we need harmony" was
Cronin's reasoning. Berg agreed, all the while thinking "that
Earl'd make fun of one suitcase filled with clothes and the
other with books. But it worked out satisfactorily. . . . Whitehill
wound up by winning us a pennant. Also by carrying my bags.
Both of them."

Earl Whitehill won a career-high 22 games, and on Ladies' Day, September 21, the Senators defeated the Browns to win the pennant. As the last out was recorded, the handsome Cronin sprinted for the clubhouse, a delirious crowd of women shrieking at his heels in what the *Post* called "the weirdest hare-and-hound fan-ballplayer chase ever witnessed." Berg didn't play that day, but on the Ladies' Days when he was in the lineup, Berg mugged for the crowd by circling under foul pop flies, tossing his mask in the air, and catching the ball with his glove and the mask with his bare hand.

The 1933 World Series against the Giants was decidedly less dramatic for the Senators than clinching the pennant had been. Whitehill's six-hit shutout in game three was Washington's lone victory in the five-game series. Berg didn't budge from the bench, as Sewell caught every inning.

CLIFF BOLTON HAD hit .410 as a pinch hitter for the Senators in 1933, and when Griffith sent him a contract that winter, offering an $800 raise, Bolton, who'd asked for more than twice that, chomped down on his cigar and refused to leave High Point, North Carolina. Holdouts were rare at the time, and thought to be dangerous for players, but Bolton was stubborn. So was Griffith, and when Sewell broke his finger in a spring training game, Washington was left to defend its pennant with Moe Berg as its starting catcher and Eddie Phillips and Elmer "Yahoo" Klumpp backing him up.

Berg was serene that spring. The Senators players were billeted right on the Gulf of Mexico in the posh Hotel Biloxi, and Mildred Cronin remembers walking into the sun parlor one evening to find Berg all alone with a large sheet of paper spread out before him on a table. When she asked him what he was doing, he replied that he was translating hieroglyphics.

On April 22, Berg went 3–4 as the Senators defeated the Athletics. He also made an error, his first fielding mistake since 1932. He had played 117 consecutive errorless games, breaking Ray Hayworth's American League record. Hardly anyone noticed. The team, meanwhile, had fallen into a pattern, winning a game or two, and then losing a pair. On May 5 came a scare when the talented rookie infielder Cecil Travis was struck on the skull by a pitch. But he would recover soon, return to the lineup, and hit .319. Phillips was doing most of the catching by then, and it was Travis's strong impression that this was fine with Berg. "He was studying all the time, more so than he was interested in baseball. He dressed up more than the rest of us." Travis didn't know quite what to make of Berg, and neither did anybody else in the ball club. "He was a private person, he didn't go out, he didn't converse," says Calvin Griffith. "We didn't know if he had dates with women."

Diane Roberts, Berg's pretty young neighbor at the Wardman Park hotel, says he did, although not with her. "I wasn't interested in Moe," she says. "I was just a playgirl. I had a different date every night. He was having an affair with the wife of a doctor in the hotel. He didn't seem to have many affairs with women. I asked him once why he didn't marry and he said he didn't have time. He was kind of a loner. You had to pry him open like an oyster." Berg was a loyal friend to Roberts in 1934. She had begun a romance with a young diplomat from Santo Domingo, who drowned. Berg heard about the accident at the ballpark. "Moe came to visit and said, 'You need a long walk.' We walked over the Connecticut Avenue bridge above Rock Creek Park. He began telling me about the stars. It was a good night to see a few."

Washington's embassies were always hosting fancy parties where the free food and drink and the well-dressed single women were all in plentiful supply. Charm and language skills are as useful as a silk evening jacket at such affairs, and Berg, who had both in spades, negotiated the diplomatic party circuit with considerable success. Yet sometimes what seemed suave to him struck others as rude. The American Bar Association was having its annual meeting that summer in Washington at the Mayflower Hotel. One day, instead of attending another meeting, J. Kemp Bartlett, an attorney from Baltimore, decided to take his teenage daughter Marjory to the Senators game. He hailed a taxi, and as the Bartletts settled into the rear seat, the front door on the passenger's side opened and a young man stuck his head in. "Mr. Griffith's Stadium, did you say you're going to Mr. Griffith's Stadium?" he asked, climbing in. "We were surprised, my father annoyed," Marjory remembers, but they permitted the man to stay. The stranger tried to make a little conversation. "He asked Daddy if he was in the Bar Association. Daddy said yes. The man said, 'I'm a lawyer too.' Daddy said, 'Hummph.' We rode in silence out to the ballpark. When we got there, the door opened, the man sprang out, said 'Thank you very much,' and disappeared into the crowd. This was the Depression. I said, 'Daddy, he left without paying his share.' Daddy gave me a withering look and said, 'That kind never does.' " The Bartletts' seats were near first base and close to the field. During the game, a pop fly was hit in their direction. The catcher threw off his mask and scrambled after it. "I gasped and said, 'Daddy, that's the man in the cab with us.' Daddy said, 'Hummm. I knew perfectly well he wasn't a lawyer.' " Of course, Moe Berg *was* a lawyer, as Marjory would come to know well over time.

Another person who met Berg that summer was Frank Slocum. Slocum's father was a roving reporter for the *New York American*. One day in Chicago, with Washington in town to play the White Sox, Slocum took young Frank up to Berg's room in the Del Prado Hotel for a moment. Slocum grew up to become a baseball reporter himself, and later assistant to the commissioner. That brief glimpse of Berg stayed with him, because in over five decades with the game, it was the only time he shook hands with a ballplayer wearing a white kimono and nothing else.

Luke Sewell returned to the Senators in mid-June. Ten days later St. Louis pitcher Bump Hadley hit him in the head, putting him on the bench again. The catching disorder mirrored the team's; the Senators dropped far behind Detroit, at one

▼

point losing 16 of 20 games. Something had to give, and it was Griffith. On July 25, with the *Post* reporting that "the Nats catching staff has been one of the chief drawbacks and contributors to the collapse of the club this season," Bolton was summoned to Washington, and his demands were met. To clear space for him on the team roster, Griffith decided to cut Berg loose. This was done without consulting his manager, and when Cronin heard about it, he—"chipper as a lark denuded of its vocal chords" all season, according to Povich—was furious. Cronin argued that one Moe Berg was worth ten Cliff Boltons, but Griffith didn't agree and gave Berg his unconditional release.

The retirement lasted four days. On August 1, Cleveland catcher Glenn Myatt broke his ankle sliding into a base, leaving the third-place Indians with only Frankie Pytlak to do the catching. The Cleveland manager was Berg's old friend from Washington, Walter Johnson. Johnson offered the reserve catching job to Berg, and the *Cleveland Jewish Independent* was soon reporting that "the most erudite player in professional baseball is a member of the Cleveland Indians."

Berg played sporadically through August. He made a spectacular one-handed catch of Hank Greenberg's foul pop on August 10, and tripled against Whitehill on the seventeenth, but there was ample time for other pursuits, like baby-sitting for Johnson's children. "Moe would take care of my sister and me, making sure we didn't trip and fall," says Caroline Johnson Thomas, ten that summer. "We had the run of the ballpark, and he made sure we didn't get into areas where we'd get hurt. I'd imagine Dad asked Moe to do so. Moe gave my sister an ashtray with his autograph embossed on it." In September, Pytlak injured himself, and Berg became the regular catcher. "He has performed in fine style, being largely responsible for the recent winning streak, which has practically clinched third place for the Tribe," boasted the *Jewish Independent*. Berg had played well enough, but hitting .258 in 29 games was nothing spectacular.

His performance on the "Football Special" to Princeton Junction, however, was highly impressive. Back in New York, he and John Kieran rode the train together out from Manhattan to see a Princeton football game. Kieran had with him a fat, dog-eared Latin dictionary, which he and Berg fell upon like starving men. They traced the roots of English words from Latin, through French and Italian, into their modern English forms, and they examined prized quotations from Cicero, Caesar, Horace, and Virgil. As the train arrived in Princeton, Berg pleased Kieran immensely by saying, "Imagine wasting time and money in a nightclub when you can have fun like this."

In October came Herb Hunter's greatest coup. For years, the Japanese had been imploring to see Babe Ruth. Ruth had always been unavailable, but now, after his last—and worst—season with the Yankees, the aging Bambino agreed to participate in a 17-game exhibition tour of Japan against a Japanese all-star team. Along with Ruth, Hunter had arranged for a gaudy roster that included Jimmie Foxx, Lou Gehrig, Earl Averill, Charlie Gehringer, and Lefty Gomez. Hunter took two catchers, Frankie Hayes of the Athletics and Moe Berg, a last-minute all-star selection. Rick Ferrell of the Red Sox had turned Hunter down, and when that happened, with departure looming, Hunter must have thought back to 1932, recalled how well received Berg had been, and extended the invitation. Berg, of course, was overjoyed.

By 1934, Japan was openly at odds with the United States, seething, in fact, with what Edwin O. Reischauer called a "general sense of discontent." Japan hadn't liked it at all when the U.S. sought to place restrictions on the size of Japan's naval fleet, and the frustration was exacerbated when American politicians condemned the Japanese incursions into China. The U.S. had grown powerful by extending its sphere of influence through Latin America; why could Japan not do the same in Asia? The notion that Washington, halfway across the world, wanted to be a player in the politics of the Pacific rim had led Tokyo to withdraw from the League of Nations and to double its military budget within four years. Avid reader of newspapers that he was, Berg must have been aware of Japan's growing disaffection with the West. Beyond the ecstatic crowds that gathered for a glimpse of Babe Ruth, hostility and paranoia were everywhere.

In particular, there was a manic fear of spies stoked by a fierce newspaper war between several Japanese newspapers. To Japanese eyes, every Brownie-toting foreigner was suspect. "They come ostensibly as tourists but in reality as military observers," warned one Japanese newspaper. "Despite the utmost vigilance of the police, the country is swarming with a particularly dangerous brand of spy," cautioned another. An American entomologist studying Japanese beetles suddenly found himself embroiled in controversy when he was accused of using the insect studies as a cover to scout an air base. When the National City Bank of New York, which had offices in Osaka and Kobe, commissioned scenic photographs from those cities for display in its Manhattan headquarters, a month-long flap ensued.

Memos from bewildered State Department officials testify to the fact that the U.S. was not dispatching flocks of spies to Tokyo any more than the hapless entomologist was training his beetles to observe dive-bomber flight patterns. Japan's fear of spies, however, accomplished at least two things. Among the Japanese, it created a sense of solidarity against invisible invaders. It also piqued at least one American visitor's sense of adventure.

In addition to taking his personal effects, Berg boarded the *Empress of Japan* with a leather case containing a 16-mm Bell and Howell automatic movie camera; a letter from MovietoneNews, a New York City newsreel production firm with which he had contracted to film sights from his trip and which seems to have given him the camera; books on the Japanese language; and some cards he'd made, with Japanese transliterations of American baseball terms, such as first base, right-handed batter, double, and triple. The thirty-two-year-old Berg worked hard at the language on the boat, but study didn't interfere with his social life. He liked to dance, and his tango and waltz partners included Ruth's stylish eighteen-year-old daughter, Julia, and a tall, long-legged eighteen-year-old blonde named Peggy Boulton.

Raised by cautious, protective parents, Peggy was now on her way to spend a year with the family of her uncle, Herbert Marler, Canada's minister to Japan. She had been accompanied to the boat, and her uncle would meet her in Yokohama, but across the ocean, she was on her own. High-spirited and very beautiful, she quickly became popular with the American ballplayers. Babe Ruth liked to toss silver dollars out over the ship's pool and watch Peggy dive for them. Berg preferred to flirt with her mind.

Traveling alone abroad by passenger ship for the first time and spending your evenings separated by a champagne flute from a tall, dark storyteller with a soft laugh and manners to match is the sort of moonlit, irresistibly romantic interlude that a mother tells her daughter about over and over for the rest of their lives. "She became a mascot for the team," says Peggy Boulton's daughter Jane Lyons. "With Moe it became something deeper. Mother said that it was how different he was from other players, how he stood apart. He was cultured. He was an intellectual. It was sparkling and fun as could be." It was also innocent, which is perhaps why, twenty years later, when Peggy Boulton Parsons ran into Berg at Union Station in Washington, they were unreservedly glad to see each other.

Berg's peers in baseball saw the sort of effect he had on people and envied him. "I wanted to be a person like Moe," says Joe Cascarella. "All the other members of the team felt Moe was special and different from them. On the ship the other players played games or got drunk at the bar. Moe studied Japanese. After two weeks of sailing Moe could speak some

Japanese, and Japanese people understood him. He spoke to regular citizens everywhere he went."

Although Berg wasn't completely fluent in Japanese, he was not above adding to his reputation as a quick study. In Vancouver, Ruth said to him, "You're such a linguist; do you speak Japanese?"

"No, I never had occasion to learn it," Berg answered. Two weeks later, on November 2, Berg greeted someone on the dock in Japanese.

"Wait a minute," said Ruth. "You told me you didn't speak Japanese."

"That was two weeks ago," came the reply. In later years, Berg would tell this story often, sometimes substituting Lefty Gomez for Ruth as his straight man.

Ruth had been in a malaise when he left the United States. Thirty-nine years old, with a body he'd lived in hard, the Bambino hoped to retire and manage a major league team, but none wanted him. Japan perked him up. Ruth arrived to find himself everywhere: on the cover of the program sold at ballparks; in newspaper headlines—"Babe Ruth, Sultan of Swat, Arrives," bannered the *Osaka Mainichi*; and in milk chocolate advertisements. Everybody wanted to see and fête him, and so the Americans were rushed from appointment to appointment—to welcoming ceremonies in which players and politicians exchanged messages of friendship, to garden parties, teas, luncheons with royalty, and dinner dances, and to private tours of department stores, castles, Buddhist temples, and, inevitably, a geisha house. At the last, the subtleties of young women attired in layers of silken costume, shuffling across a room to perform ancient ritual ceremonies, were lost on Ruth. He pawed at one increasingly flustered woman every time she passed. Watching nearby, Berg wrote down some characters in katakana and handed them to Ruth's victim. The next time she felt a large hand groping beneath her carefully tied obi, she paused, bowed, smiled sweetly, and said, "Fuck you, Babe Ruth." That, Ruth understood.

But Berg was having it both ways. He and Lyons, as two of the single men on the excursion, were treated to an evening at a brothel. Berg wasn't usually much of a tippler, but in filmed footage of this evening he looks plastered and engages in some public kissing and groping. Who knows what else transpired behind curtains?

At the ballpark, people waited in line for two days to become part of crowds of as many as 55,000. The Americans played 17 games in 12 Japanese cities against Japan's first-ever professional team, a collection of former high school and college stars who called themselves the Tokyo Giants. The U.S. won every game. Late in the series, the American team went so far as to lend some of its players to the opposition to even things out a bit.

The competition may have been lopsided, but nobody was bored. There were elaborate pregame ceremonies in which young women gave the players bouquets of flowers. One contest was played on a field in Shizuoka, set near the foot of Mount Fuji and surrounded by fragrant tea plants. Another took place in a driving rainstorm in a stadium at Kokura. The stadium had no bleachers, and with an enormous crowd on hand to see Ruth, 11,000 spectators knelt behind the outfielders in hip-deep water. One fan walked 80 miles to see that game. He carried a samurai sword with him, which he ceremoniously awarded to Earl Averill, who hit the first home run of the day. This was not so much baseball as opéra bouffe, and Ruth was the undisputed basso profundo. Responding to the shouts of "Banzai Ruth!" that accompanied him wherever he went, he led the American regulars with a .408 batting average and 13 home runs. Babe Ruth, said Ambassador Grew, was worth one hundred ambassadors.

The closest the all-Japan team came to scratching out a win came at Shizuoka, where a eighteen-year-old flamethrower named Eiji Sawamura lost 1–0 to Earl Whitehill. Sawamura struck out Ruth, Gehrig, Jimmie Foxx, and Charlie Gehringer, and the American players had abundant praise for him afterward. One U.S. team official even tried to lure him to the American majors. Sawamura demurred, however, and was killed in an airplane over Formosa during World War II.

Tragedy was close at hand, too. Five games were played at Shingu Stadium in Tokyo, which had been built as a shrine to honor emperor Meiji. With nascent fascism in Japan had come a large number of extreme nationalist societies. During the American tour, three members of the War God Society declared that Matsutoro Shoriki, the head of the *Yomiuri* newspaper and the producer of the trip, had defiled the Meiji shrine by permitting foreigners to play a foreign game on its sacred ground. In February, Shoriki was stabbed in the neck as he left his office.

And Moe Berg? He walked the penumbra. Berg appeared in six games and had two hits, fewer than anybody else on the team, including the pitchers. Berg didn't object and neither did the Japanese. "He's more a scholar than a baseball player," explained one reporter. The Mizuno corporation consulted him about the manufacture of baseball gloves, and afterward presented him with a specially designed black kimono filigreed with red baseball designs and Berg's name in Japanese. Meiji University asked him to deliver a speech, and Berg did, in English. "You have done us the honor of adopting our national game as yours," he said. "There is no greater leveler, no greater teacher of humility than competitive sports, and I sincerely hope that our innocent junket through Japan will serve to bring the countries whom we represent unofficially closer together." Speaking over Tokyo radio to the United States, he offered similar sentiments, concluding, "I hope an innocent adventure like ours will turn out to be a scoop of diplomacy without portfolio."

Berg was always happy to pose for photographs, but this was the one occasion in his life where he displayed an interest in taking them himself. He took the camera almost everywhere he went, shooting scenes on American trains and ballplayers boarding the *Empress* in Vancouver, storms at sea and parties in Hawaii, Ruth dancing with his wife aboard ship and crowds greeting the boat in Yokohama. The camera went with him to ballparks in Japan, where he recorded his teammates at play, and on trips to Nikko, Hikone, Kamakura, Nagoya, Osaka, and Kyoto. Through a train window he shot Mount Fuji in snow. Along the city streets he recorded women wearing traditional clothes, children playing juggling games, and the dense Tokyo traffic.

That Berg succeeded with this sort of behavior in a country obsessed about foreign spies is not as surprising as it might seem. Members of the expatriate community still traveled wherever they liked without incident. With politics what they were, things might have been different for American tourists, but tourists to Japan then were rare and, besides, Berg was no ordinary stranger but a celebrity guest whom nobody wanted to offend. Very few Japanese spoke any English, and for all the editorial bluster, Japanese policemen were leery of confronting foreigners with whom they could not communicate. Those who didn't recognize the large American were disposed to let him be.

There were limits to this deference. Taking pictures of the Tsugaru Strait, separating Honshu and Hokkaido, for example, was forbidden by the Japanese military, and Ruth himself was inspected by police during the team's crossing. Berg, however, had an uncanny ability to remain unobtrusive, to blend into the fabric of the moment. He was also fearless, and seemed to thrill at the idea of gathering sensitive material for his MovietoneNews travelogue during the crackdown on publicity. Berg may have heard Connie Mack say that he suspected that someone was listening in on his telephone conversations, but if he did, he wasn't intimidated. Dark eyes glowing, camera held high, he photographed the Tsugaru Strait, and got away with it. Toward the end of the trip, he dared himself even further.

On November 29, in a game played at Omiya, the all-America team pasted the all-Japan team 23–5. Frankie Hayes caught the entire game, and Moe Berg didn't play an inning. That was so much the ordinary that most of the American players failed to notice that Berg was missing. Those who did inquire about him were told that he was ill. In fact, his health was fine and Berg was twelve miles away, back in Tokyo. This man who genuinely loved Japan was preparing for the stunt of a lifetime—for a day, he was becoming Japanese.

Changing out of his oxford cloth suit and tie, Berg put on a kimono and a pair of *geta*, waved back his thick black hair, and parted it at the center. Under his arm he carried a bouquet of fresh flowers. So dressed, he headed for Saint Luke's Hospital. In the *Japan Advertiser* there had been a notice that Elsie Lyon, Ambassador Grew's twenty-two-year-old daughter, had just given birth to her first child, a daughter she named Alice. Berg had decided to pay Elsie and her new baby a visit.

Buildings in downtown Tokyo at the time were limited in height both because of earthquakes and because of a decree that no man should be able to look down upon the emperor's imperial palace. Saint Luke's was in Tsukiji, a residential neighborhood built on land reclaimed from Tokyo Bay. It was over a mile from the palace, so the seven stories with piazza and bell tower above made Saint Luke's among the tallest buildings in Tokyo. Saint Luke's rose like a single cornstalk amidst the brown field of low-slung wooden houses surrounding it. From the piazza, you could see for miles in all directions.

Entering the hospital, Berg asked in Japanese for directions to Mrs. Lyon's room. He was told to take the elevator to the fifth floor. How he got past the reception area was always a mystery to Elsie Lyon. Her mother was on hand and was behaving like a dragon, barring all visitors except those whose impending visits she'd registered with the desk. Perhaps the sight of a six-foot-one-inch burly man clad in a kimono and *geta* in a country where the men were generally lithe and half a foot shorter than Berg was sufficiently unnerving that he was waved on without a contest. At the fifth floor he alighted, dumped the flowers in a trash can, stepped back into the elevator, and pressed seven.

Off the seventh floor was the piazza, a nice place to have lunch. But Berg didn't stop there. Instead, he passed through a door and climbed a narrow spiral staircase to the bell tower, where, exactly as he'd been told, between the latticed windows on all sides was a stunning panoramic view of Tokyo. From beneath his kimono Berg drew out the movie camera. His hands appear to have been shaking in many of the four hours' worth of film he shot on his trip, but for the next twenty-three seconds they were firm as feldspar. The Bell and Howell was a powerful instrument, and as Berg panned the city, shipyards, industrial complexes, and military installations around Tokyo Bay, he also recorded Mount Fuji, sixty miles away. Finished, he secreted the camera, climbed down the staircase, and left. He had not so much as set eyes upon Elsie Lyon. On December 1, the American team played at Utsunomiya. Berg was there, and it was as though he'd never been gone. He didn't play an inning.

Following the Utsunomiya game, the Americans sailed to Shanghai on the *Empress of Canada*, where they played one game, and then completed their schedule in the Philippines with games at a Manila ballpark on December 9 and 10. In Manila, Berg was told that back in Cleveland the Indians had released all rights to his contract. He was now in every respect a free agent. So, camera in hand, he headed north.

On January 4, he turned up in Korea, where trouble finally found him. "Strange Foreigner Taking Photographs of Yalu Bridge," said the headlines in the next day's *Osaka Mainichi*. Berg had been riding in the observation car at the end of the Hikari Express, and as it passed over the bridge across the Yalu River dividing China and Korea a sentry saw him taking photographs. The sentry reported Berg to the Antung police, who arrested him, confiscated 25 feet of film, and set him free. Berg then set about making travel arrangements. He'd been wanting to take the Trans-Siberian Railroad.

In Manchouli he boarded the train for the six-day ride. Fabled a trip as it may be, taking the Trans-Siberian Railroad in winter is for long stretches bound to be a rather dull experience, especially when you don't speak Russian. Whenever the train halted, Berg walked outside and filmed the barren countryside. Once he got to Moscow, things picked up. Strolling about the city in the heavy, full-length overcoat he'd purchased, Berg was in the midst of filming Lenin's tomb when he was confronted by two plainclothes policemen who demanded his film. Berg gave it to them, and was sent on his way with a warning not to use his camera anymore.

Continuing his meandering, Berg came upon a board fence. He peered through a hole and discovered that the Moscow subway was being dug by a corps of women using picks. He couldn't resist. "I was young then, and what the heck" is how he later explained it. Out came the camera. Moments later someone was tapping his shoulder. It was a Red Army soldier, who took his passport and left him there. Berg told John Kieran that he stood on the corner for five hours in 20-below-zero weather before the soldier returned and handed him his passport without a word. Berg took this as a cue that his time in Russia was up. After he crossed into Poland, he was searched, and two rolls of film were taken from him. The overcoat had deep pockets, however, and when he arrived in New York in April, the souvenirs in his luggage included a ceremonial Japanese happi jacket, the Moe Berg kimono from Mizuno, a Russian fur hat, and two reels of film. Berg would never again visit Japan, but for the rest of his life he talked constantly about his time there.

CHAPTER 8

Mr. Berg, You've Been Brilliant

With no job in baseball waiting for him, Berg went home to Newark. That couldn't have been thoroughly pleasant. The Bergs had it in their minds that they were special, superior to other people, including their own. They often disdained gatherings of their by now sprawling extended family, and at the functions they did attend—Rose liked to go —they held themselves aloof, maintaining a discreet but emphatic distance. All three Berg children were professionals. Ethel had become a public school kindergarten teacher, Sam was an established young pathologist with a family practice on the side. For the most talented of the brood to breeze in from Asia and lounge about the house playing the prodigal son while everyone else contributed toward burnishing the Berg name wouldn't have done. Fortunately for Berg,

▼

another family, in Washington, was experiencing tensions of its own, and out of that strife came employment for him.

Clark Griffith had made his son-in-law the manager of the Senators in 1933, when Joe Cronin was as young as many rookies. All was well while the shortstop took them to the pennant, but at the end of the more dour 1934 season Cronin became expendable. In December, Griffith traded him with a flourish, sending him and Mildred to Boston for Lyn Lary and $225,000.

On April 11, 1935, the Red Sox played an exhibition game in Newark, on their way from spring training in Sarasota, Florida, to Boston. Berg appears to have gone to the ballpark and told his old chum Cronin that he was looking for work, because six days later, when the Red Sox opened the season on a chilly afternoon in the Bronx against the Yankees, Berg was with them. The usually hardboiled Boston press corps warmed to him immediately. "It was so cold at Yankee Stadium they say that Moe Berg, new member of the Red Sox, was talking Eskimo," cracked Harold Kaese in the *Evening Transcript.*

In the five years Berg played for Cronin in Boston, he appeared in an average of fewer than 30 games a season, which meant that he was doing very little catching and throwing. Some days he didn't even practice. The Red Sox were all out on the field warming up one afternoon, when Cronin glanced over toward the bench and saw Berg reading a newspaper. Cronin asked him just what he was doing, and Berg, looking up briefly, replied, "You lead your life and I'll lead mine and next year we'll beat the Yankees."

All this, obviously, Cronin could tolerate. His and Berg's was a symbiotic relationship. Cronin kept Berg in baseball, Berg gave Cronin advice. There was more. Cronin was a congenial man—"sweet-natured," Shirley Povich called him—but he was no intellectual, which may have pained him. "Joe Cronin liked to associate with the higher-echelon people," says Ted Williams, who began his lustrous career with the Red Sox in 1939. "He didn't waste his time with a lot of yokels." That people looked at Berg and thought of Cronin lent an aura of respectability to the manager, in much the same way that the brilliant members of a Parisian salon reflect well upon the wealthy woman who assembles them. Another personal quality of Cronin's was superstition. If you tried to hand him a two-dollar bill, for instance, he'd send you out to find a pair of singles. Moe Berg may have been his good luck charm.

Not that Berg was just an ornament. If that were the case, Cronin would have made him a coach. Berg could still catch, and do it well—a rare enough skill then, as now, as to make him valuable. Boston pitchers like Lefty Grove and especially Jack Wilson would request Berg, the way Tommy Thomas and Ted Lyons had with the White Sox. "A lot of guys thought that because he knew Joe Cronin was the only reason he was there," says Wilson. "But I'll tell you one thing, he was a great catcher."

Spectators groused about Berg's low batting averages, but not his teammates, who admired the way his mitt made peace with a scorching Grove fastball. What they questioned was his inclination. "He didn't care whether he played or not, he just wanted to be on the team," says Gene Desautels, who caught for the Red Sox from 1937 to 1940.

"He was a fine catcher; we all felt he was an intelligent catcher," says Boston infielder Billy Werber. "He had a good arm, he could hit occasionally, but he'd rather sit and talk baseball than play it. He liked to be around ballplayers, but he didn't always want to play. We all felt he was a little lazy."

Nobody was more aware of the games Berg wasn't catching than Rick Ferrell, who was catching them for him. At 150 pounds, "Little" Rick was one of baseball's smallest players, and one of its best catchers. The future Hall of Famer caught for Boston from 1934 until the team traded him during the 1937 season. He was resolute and, for his size, he was durable—two fortunate traits, considering his replacement. A reserve catcher generally catches the second game of a doubleheader, but not on the Red Sox when Moe Berg was the backup. "Joe Cronin's locker was two down from mine," says Ferrell. "We'd play a doubleheader in Boston and Moe'd come over to my locker after I caught the first game and say, 'Rick, you're the greatest catcher in the American League. Joe, let's not change the lineup.' So I'd catch two games. I didn't care. He didn't want to play unless he had to."

What to make of this lawyer who wasn't working on Wall Street, this linguist who wasn't teaching at Princeton, this ballplayer who didn't seem interested in playing ball? With Berg, potential was a red herring. Was he lazy? In conventional terms, perhaps. But Berg was not living a conventional life. His priorities were different from most people's. He was making use of baseball to plot a life of wandering curiosity. Nothing made him as happy or as comfortable as the routine of a ballplayer. "Isn't this wonderful," he said once. "Work three hours a day, travel around the country, live in the best hotels, meet the best people, and get paid for it." He had no new interests except those that developed casually within the confines of baseball's daily calendar. Many men could have been lawyers. It took an unusual person to resist convention, live by his wits, and form himself into the character that Moe Berg was becoming.

MOE BERG WAS an eccentric with a taste for conformity. He didn't at all wish to be one of the boys, but a level of acceptance among his teammates was important to him. He wanted them to like him, admire him, and—oh, perverse man—he wanted them to leave him alone.

On the baseball field Berg commanded respect by surpassing expectations. What teammates like Rick Ferrell regarded as simple indolence was also part of a subtle calculus designed to avoid failure. Most baseball players respond well to playing frequently. An aging Berg was the opposite. Unless there was nobody else to catch, he played only when he felt spry. In this way he preserved his reputation as a fine catcher, and elicited admiring comments from teammates like Red Nonnenkamp, a reserve himself, who found it "remarkable" that Berg could be "inactive for so long, and then Cronin would put him in and he'd really be something." As for all the games Berg didn't play, well, better to be seen as lazy than incompetent. Besides, the supposed indifference reminded his teammates that he had weighty interests outside baseball. For the Red Sox to believe that, as Nonnenkamp put it, "baseball wasn't his main concern" added to Berg's mystique. Baseball *was* his main concern. It made everything else possible. But why should he let them know that?

Berg was still a reticent man, but on certain subjects— namely, his travels—he could be downright loquacious. "In the bull pen he'd keep you spellbound," says Boston pitcher Jack Wilson. "For seven years we sat in the bull pen laughing and telling stories. He talked to you any time you wanted to talk. He'd talk about his travels. He'd tell you about something in Latvia and then in the next minute it was something in China or Japan." After one game Al Schacht remembered Wilson, full of excitement, blurting to him, "Al, you should have been in the bull pen this afternoon. Moe had us in Russia!" Some of the players couldn't quite follow Berg all the time, but the gestalt was enough. "Moe was really something in the bull pen," one of them said. "We'd sit around and listen to him discuss the Greeks, the Romans, the Japanese, anything. Hell, we didn't know what he was talking about, but it sure sounded good." Berg was proud of his storytelling, to the point where he collected stories about telling stories. "I was warming up a pitcher one day in the bull pen and we got to talking about that trip to Siberia," he told the Boston journalist Joe Fitzgerald in 1967. "It seemed everyone wanted me to talk about that. Well, the pitcher was called into the game, but we didn't realize it because we were still discussing Siberia in the bull pen. The umpires came running out to see what was wrong. They laughed when we told them. We could do things like that then."

Besides entertaining the relief pitchers, Berg's sagas of adventure naturally provided baseball writers with plenty of material. Berg even put in some time himself at a typewriter, taking the readers of the *Boston American* on the bull pen tour. Substituting for the "Mr. Boston" columnist, Berg composed an essay predicting that baseball would soon become an international game. He started off lamely with a mock comparison between the butterfingered French actors he'd seen in a Parisian production of *The Merchant of Venice* and sure-handed American outfielders, a device that had the unfortunate effect of appearing both strained and pretentious. After that, however, the tone shifted markedly, into a lively, thoughtful piece of writing. "It would be difficult to find even one major league club without at least one player in the first generation of people who emigrated to this country," wrote Berg. "Certainly the special attributes of the baseball player aren't confined to our people or those raised here. We have all seen Italians with supple shoulders, Russians with limber arms, Poles with prehensile fingers, and Greeks with speed of foot and endurance." Next he moved on to what he'd seen in Japan, the first country outside the U.S. to take a serious interest in baseball. "Here are people who less than 100 years ago had no intercourse at all with the outside world, and had their own distinctive Oriental manner of life, disporting themselves under the code of the Samurai with only swords. Yet in the morning paper you may read that Waseda University in Tokyo beat Yale at baseball. The Japanese are playing ball by the thousands." After describing the tea plants outside the ballpark at Shizuoka, and two store clerks he saw playing catch under a Tokyo street lamp at midnight, he concluded, "Perhaps the second generation of Japanese, born into baseball with mitts on their hands, will compete with us." Berg may not have been a writer, but there are professions that prize a man who sees what others don't.

The Red Sox traveled the country by Pullman car in the 1930s. Huge blocks of ice placed in special compartments above the car, and lower berths for all members of the team, made the train a cool and comfortable means of getting to Detroit or St. Louis. While most players divided into groups for poker or bridge games, Berg sat alone, reading. Beside him he kept a rice farmer's basket he'd picked up in Japan filled with enough books to last him the intervals between newspaper editions. He was a fairly rapid reader, but occasionally a single book was enough. "I remember one trip we went on," says Eldon Auker. "Moe got on the train. He was all excited. He had a book about four feet thick. The title was *The Holy Bible in 1000 Languages*. It must have weighed twenty pounds. He couldn't wait to sit down and open it up. He'd found it some-where in Boston. It made his day and, I guess, most of his year."

There was a benevolent quality to Berg's efforts at social-izing. When Jack Wilson confided that he was having tax trou-bles, Berg took him to an office in Washington and, just like that, Wilson's problems were behind him. Berg knew the New York ticket agent Sam Roth, and when the Red Sox were in town to play the Yankees, Berg arranged for passes to plays and musicals. He could provide the entertainment himself, too. In Boston, Berg once invited the whole team and their wives to a screening of his travel films. "Quite a few of us went," says Jack Wilson. "They didn't mean nothing to us."

Once in a while, Berg would spend an evening alone with a teammate or two. Bobby Doerr, a handsome young second baseman who joined the team in 1937, got a few brief whiffs of Berg's world. Berg would look at Doerr and say, "C'mon, take a walk with me," and off they'd go, usually on a tour of dime stores. In 1933, Berg had invested some money in Nov-elart, a stationery and film production company. He liked to visit the card departments to see what Novelart's competitors were up to. In Florida, he took Doerr through a private gam-bling casino. In New York, they paid a call on Jay C. Flippen, at the tomato-faced actor's apartment. Doerr was thrilled. It seemed to him that Moe knew everybody.

Berg also began spending time with the pitcher Charlie Wagner, who had joined the team that year. For all his color, Wagner was somewhat uncouth as a young man, "a raw-boned kid from Reading, Pennsylvania," he likes to say. Berg became his Pygmalion. "He helped me with English—a lesson every day in the bull pen," says Wagner. "We used to eat together. He taught me etiquette, eating, ordering at big hotels, how to treat waiters. He was a classy guy. We'd have nice long evenings of talk." Sometimes they went to Greek restaurants, where Berg ordered his meal in Greek. Wagner says that a waiter once told him that Berg "speaks better Greek than I do." In New York they would head for Leo Lindy's, then in its prime as a late-night roost for actors, musicians, horseplayers, and showgirls. Wagner thought it was wonderful. "You'd go to dinner with Moe," he says, "and before you knew it, there was a table of eight talking baseball."

Berg and Wagner also went out together at night in Boston. Backup infielder Boze Berger, Berg's roommate for a time, once joined them. "He was very fastidious when he ate," says Berger. "He ate everything on his plate in a certain order." That night the idiosyncrasy was taken to an extreme. First the three men ate spaghetti at an Italian restaurant. Then they moved to the Union Oyster House for oyster stew. Finally, it was on to a steakhouse for beef. Berg paid for everyone. "When he'd invite you out, he paid for dinner," says Berger. "He was generous."

These men were exceptions and they knew it. Although he didn't bluntly say as much, Berg's demeanor made it implicit that he discouraged invitations from his teammates. "None of us would ever think of saying to Berg, 'We're going to see Gary Cooper in a show, do you want to come?' " says Billy Werber. During the afternoon, Berg was a ballplayer. What happened after that wasn't anyone's business, something he made clear in the jocular, unflinching way that is appreciated in clubhouses. "Tom Daly and I ran into him on the street one night with some girl wrapped up in silver fox fur," says Jack Wilson.

"He said 'hello' and kept right on going. The next day in front of Berg's locker Tom said to me, 'How are you, Mr. Wilson?' I said, 'Just fine,' and walked right on by. Berg said, 'You sons of bitches. I have to put up with you until six. After that, I don't have to put up with you.' " Wilson took it in stride. He often joked with Berg about such behavior. "I used to kid him that he was a spy," he says.

Not that the Red Sox were scratching their heads in unison, wondering what Moe Berg was doing with his time. Most ballplayers were accustomed to Berg's ways and didn't think much about them. But Ted Williams noticed. "Secret," Williams called Berg, or "the Mystery Man." Neither nickname stuck. With Moe Berg, nothing did.

EVEN WITH A patron like Cronin, it was a tenuous time for Berg. He was a man nearing forty, trying to hold on in a boy's game. That old chestnut about needing to lose something to realize how much you liked it didn't apply. Berg knew, had known for years, that baseball was the life he wanted. Now in Boston he'd found the ideal place to live it. Boston was a refined city dense with bookstores, colleges, and newsstands. Compact in scale, with crooked streets, lancet windows, gas lamps, and lush public parks, Boston had a reserve, and, of course, so did Berg.

He was liable to turn up anywhere, but at least part of the time his days began at the Parker House, a stately Boston hotel. Berg liked to begin his morning in the bathtub. He perspired easily and, besides, believed in the therapeutic powers of hot water. Whenever possible, he took three baths a day. Finished with the first, he clothed himself in black, white, and gray and stepped out into the day. His first stop was usually the Old South News Stand, a venerable establishment in business since 1909, at the corner of Washington and Milk streets. Arthur Weisman, who worked at the stand, remembers Berg buying ten New York, Washington, and Boston papers a day. If there was a big local story, his take increased, and he carted away all six major Boston papers. Berg was friendly with Edward Bernstein and his partner, Larry Rosenthal, the owners of the Old South. While Weisman watched, Berg would sometimes walk a block away from the stand, where he would have whispered conversations with Bernstein or Rosenthal. It all looked very intriguing to Weisman, who, of course, wondered what was being said. The answer? Very little. "We were friends, but not close friends," says Rosenthal. "It wasn't necessarily deep. It was about movies, baseball. I wasn't anything particular to him. Just somebody who liked him." Bernstein had the same experience with Berg. "Nobody knew his business," he says.

For at least part of his life Berg fasted one day a week. It's impossible to say how many years he did this, because he didn't stay in touch with anyone on a consistent enough basis for them to recognize his eating habits. On non-fasting days, newspapers in hand, Berg repaired to a coffee shop, where he read through the morning. He liked coffee, and when he ate, he did so with relish.

If he wasn't going to the ballpark, Berg might turn up anywhere. He traveled Boston like a June bug, skimming from point to point, pausing long enough to lend it his imprimatur, and then on to the next. Wherever he went, people described him as a kind man, witty, gregarious, and . . . gone. He liked to take trips into Cambridge. At a newsstand in Harvard Square he could find the international newspapers that the Old South didn't stock. Cambridge was dappled with secondhand bookshops, and Berg was on good terms with the inventories—and the proprietors—of most of them. If his feet needed a rest or his mind wanted an infusion, he strolled into the rear of a Harvard lecture hall and sat in on a class. Berg helped Takizo Matsumoto gain admission to the Harvard Business School. They met occasionally, but not often enough for Matsumoto. He was lonely and in the winter wrote Berg plaintive notes, telling him he missed him.

Berg didn't miss anyone. He was too busy for that. He knew

the waiters at the Ritz and the secretaries of women's clubs. You might glimpse him at a demonstration on Boston Common or in the main reading room at the public library. Some of his old classmates from Princeton had settled in the Boston area. They all told Moe Berg stories and would have been eager to spend time with him, but Berg was hard to find. Marjory Bartlett of Baltimore, then a Wellesley undergraduate, wrote him once, care of the Red Sox, requesting baseball tickets. Back in the mail came an envelope containing four passes to a Sunday afternoon game. There was no note. At the ball game, when she waved, he tipped his hat solemnly, and thereafter avoided her eyes. She wrote again anyway, thanking him for the tickets and inviting him to dinner at Wellesley, and this time managed to pry a note out of him. "I was happy to repay an old favor" was all it said.

Margaret Ford had better luck. A young and attractive feature writer for the *Boston Sunday Herald* and a contributor to the *New Yorker*, Ford lived at her parents' home in Brookline, and that is where Moe Berg came to call. Most of the Fords were rabid baseball fans, so he talked first about the Red Sox, and then deftly turned the conversation elsewhere when it seemed to him that Margaret's mother might be bored by the subject. A week later, Berg returned to present Mrs. Ford with an old-fashioned bud-rose and violet nosegay. Margaret and her sister were each favored with a fleeting kiss on the wrist. Mr. Ford watched all this with a mildly puzzled expression on his face. Margaret thought her date was somewhat calculating, a player of social chess, "moving slowly, cautiously, making correct decisions, more meditative than coldly analytical."

Berg took her dancing on the roof of the Ritz. It was an elegant spot, with tiny yellow lights shining everywhere like forsythia, the splash of the fountains in the public garden audible below, and the houses on Beacon Hill glowing in the distance. They danced, and here Berg's movements were also slow, his decisions again were cautious, but this time, alas,

▼

they were decidedly not correct. "I, though no Ginger Rogers myself, had nevertheless a sense of rhythm, which bore not the slightest resemblance to Moe's," says Margaret. "What Moe was doing was indescribable. He wasn't running, he wasn't jumping, but he certainly was not dancing." Berg's lack of grace was not confined to the foxtrot. He indulged in some flattery (he'd read Margaret's work), some gossip (she thought him a conversational voyeur), and then, of course, at the end of the evening he was running, after all. None of this surprised the man Margaret eventually married. John Kieran was as baffled by Moe Berg as everyone else.

ASIDE FROM THE ties of his contract with the Red Sox, which bound him to Fenway Park for a few hours a day, Moe Berg lived as a peripatetic in Boston, a nonstop walker in the city. When the team took to the road, the names of the ballparks and the hotels changed; Berg's habits did not. With the Red Sox in Philadelphia to play the Athletics, Berg might hurry up to Princeton for a look at an exhibition of Islamic miniatures and calligraphy, to listen to Thomas Mann lecture on Goethe's *Faust*, or to visit one of his former professors' Greek classes. In New York, wending north toward the Bronx for a game against the Yankees, he sometimes stopped in at Columbia. St. Louis could mean Washington University in the morning and the Browns in the afternoon. In Washington, Cleveland, and Chicago, where he'd lived as a player, there were familiar haunts, from a newsstand in the lobby of a fancy hotel to a favorite side street café with a menu of red meats and red wines. He liked art museums, antiquarian bookshops, and public libraries with well-lit main reading rooms. And always he was game for an outing. He once went from Washington to Baltimore, where he recited Poe's "Raven," standing beside the poet's grave. Berg rarely drank much alcohol, and never smoked, but he liked people who did, and there were evenings when he set his elbow to oak, nursing a lone Bloody Mary amidst the fighters, molls, stars, and spenders. He listened for a while—he'd overcome some of his feelings of prudishness, so now bawdy stories pleased him—and then was out the door before anyone noticed he was gone. No "See you next time around" for this man.

Berg met people everywhere. They would say afterward that they knew him, but what did they know? Only what they saw. When Berg wasn't telling stories, he was asking questions. People liked to confide in him, were flattered that he was interested, and were too cowed to ask anything in return. Typical of the sort of person Berg liked was I. M. Levitt, director of the Fels Planetarium at the Franklin Institute in Philadelphia.

One day in the late 1930s, a tall dark man attended one of Levitt's shows and came up to talk with him afterward. Levitt thought the man's questions were intelligent. A few months later the man returned and introduced himself. Levitt liked baseball, and learning that Moe Berg of the Boston Red Sox was interested in the galaxies pleased him very much. After the show, they went out to dinner. Berg ordered a strip steak and ate every morsel, including, Levitt couldn't help but notice, the slivers of fat that marbled the edges of the meat. They had a grand time talking astronomy and linguistics. After that, whenever the Red Sox came to town, Berg left a pair of tickets at the "Will Call" window for Levitt and his wife. Before the game, they'd walk down to field level and talk with Berg while he warmed up the Red Sox starting pitcher. Berg looked at the pitcher and spoke to the Levitts out of the corner of his mouth. Never once did the Levitts see a game where Berg was in the lineup.

Levitt had been a semi-pro ballplayer in his youth and then had gone on to take four university degrees, including a doctorate from the University of Pennsylvania. Berg's marginal career in baseball made sense to him. "It left him time to do what he did best, and that is read," he says. In this respect, Berg reminded him of Benjamin Franklin. Franklin, Levitt felt, had provided himself with a superior education by reading, and Berg was doing the same. He'd taught himself astronomy, for instance, and to Levitt's mind, "he knew a hell of a lot about it." For years, Levitt tried to cajole Berg into giving a guest lecture on constellations. He never succeeded. Aside from the scheduled games with the Athletics, when Berg was certain to be at Shibe Park, Levitt couldn't be sure when his friend might turn up. One Saturday night, Berg walked into the planetarium with a tall, attractive, black-haired woman. They watched the performance and then left without a word or a wave to Levitt.

BERG PLAYED IN 38 games for Joe Cronin in 1935, hit .286, and smacked 2 home runs, a full third of the 6 he would hit in his career. One of his rare appearances came on September 22, when he emerged from the bull pen, not to catch, but to participate in a throwing contest against the Yankee catcher Bill Dickey. Promotions have always been popular in baseball, and match races were a prime publicity staple in Berg's time. Some of them were intriguing. In 1946, George Case, a speedy member of the Senators, barely lost a dash across the outfield to the Olympic gold medal sprinter Jesse Owens. Others were plain bizarre. Hans Lobert of the Giants once finished second—by a nose—in a race around the bases with a black pony ridden by a Mexican cowboy. On the twenty-second at Fenway, there were five events: a relay race, a 100-yard dash, a circling the bases race, a fungo hitting contest, and an accurate throwing competition. For the last, a barrel was placed on second base, and catchers rose from their crouch and tried to throw a ball into the barrel. It was always a delightful moment when a ball went shooting across the infield and then, *blup!* disappeared into the void. Berg lost to Dickey on this day, which was an upset. He was well known as the master of the barrel throw.

The season over, Berg moved his base of operations from a

Boston hotel to his brother's home in Newark. Back in his old neighborhood, he was the same elusive figure he was everywhere else. He could sometimes be seen handing out the grass-stained balls and splintered bats he'd cadged from the Red Sox to local children, fixing them a stern look while cautioning them to always keep their eye on the ball. In the morning he might go for a jog through Branch Brook Park or for a long walk. Wherever he went, he always went alone, sometimes carrying a briefcase. He boasted that nobody in Roseville knew him. One night he turned up unannounced in East Orange, at the home of his old friends from childhood, the Jenningses. He had with him the films from his trip to Japan and asked if anyone would like to see them. The Jenningses said yes, they would. When the footage shot from Saint Luke's appeared on the screen, Margaret Jennings Gahan says that Berg "intimated that this was an insight into the fortifications of Japan." Other than that somewhat cryptic comment, Berg didn't say anything. "He was a very shy man," says Gahan.

Roseville was still a bustling, fairly prosperous community, but for Berg, who had seen Tokyo and Bangkok, and who traveled first class during the season, it was dull in comparison. His family was many things—hardworking and bristling with opinions were two—but the Bergs were not relaxing to be around. Two years earlier Berg had invested with two partners in the formation of Novelart. Things seemed to be going well with the business. Even so, perhaps because he was still sometimes short of ready cash or maybe because he didn't want to make the effort, Berg didn't buy a house of his own. He was further constrained by his refusal to learn to drive. Berg relied on trains to get him out of Newark. His flat feet took him everywhere else. As for the law, if people he knew asked him for advice, he gave it. But his days of reporting to an office were behind him. He lived with his parents, spending as little time there as possible.

One of Berg's favorite winter pastimes was attending the six-day bicycle races at Madison Square Garden in New York.

He knew Willie Ratner, who covered the event for the *Newark News*, and Ratner could always fix him up with a press credential. According to Ratner, Berg liked to stroll among the foreign riders, chatting with them in their native languages, and sometimes gathering information for his host. Once, with the Belgian team ahead late in the race, Berg told Ratner that he'd heard one of the Belgian riders say in French that he was injured and would soon have to retire. Ratner filed a story to this effect, and came the afternoon, the newsboys outside the Garden were hawking a *Newark News* exclusive.

THE SUMMERS OF 1936 and 1937 were mournful periods for Red Sox aficionados. Although hundreds of thousands of dollars had been spent to buttress the lineup with expensive veterans like Cronin, Lefty Grove, Jimmie Foxx, Doc Cramer, and Eric McNair, the "Fenway Millionaires," as everyone now referred to the Sox, skulked to sixth and then fifth in the standings. Berg faded too, from .355 in June 1936 to .240, in the 39 games he had appeared in by season's end. After 9 games in June 1937, he was hitting .367. By the close of that season his mark was down to .255.

Between 1938 and 1940, the Red Sox began to rely on their own minor league system. What they found there—Bobby Doerr, Ted Williams, Dom DiMaggio, Jim Bagby, Jr., and Jim "Rawhide" Tabor—hoisted the team into annual contention with the Yankees. Amidst all this nubile talent, Berg, husky now with a nascent pair of jowls, suddenly became known as an exemplar. Down in Washington, Clark Griffith declared him the best handler of pitchers in the league, while Cronin, purring as usual when Berg was the subject, praised him as "an excellent example for young catchers." Well that he could hang his cap on that, because, as the third-string catcher behind Desautels and Johnny Peacock in 1938, Berg played in 10 games and batted only 12 times all season. He would have remained the best-known third-string catcher in baseball anyway, but that winter something happened that turned him into a national sensation, the epitome of brains meshed with strength, even for people who always turned past the sports pages. There are many means of establishing a broad reputation for genius, but few can match Berg's for economy. He simply entered a radio studio in New York, answered a few questions, and emerged thirty minutes later a certified quiz show king.

In contrast to some of the other, more popular prewar national radio programs, "Information, Please!" seemed banal. "Truth or Consequences"—the great rival of "Information, Please!" for a time—lured its audience less with its questions than with the outrageous slapstick situations, the "consequences" that followed an incorrect answer: a blindfolded couple had to keep up a conversation while feeding each other blueberry pie; an unfortunate soldier was forced to telephone his girl while an actress sat cooing on his lap. With "Information, Please!" the gimmick was intelligence. People sent in trivia designed to stump a highbrow panel of experts, and were given cash rewards if they succeeded.

Moderator and *New Yorker* book critic Clifton Fadiman— billed as the Toscanini of quiz—delivered the week's questions to three permanent experts: humor columnist and roundtable wit Franklin P. Adams, pianist and composer Oscar Levant, and John Kieran, who, Fadiman liked to say, "carries so much information around with him it's a wonder he isn't round-shouldered." Each week there was also a guest expert, the likes of whom included Alfred Hitchcock, Dorothy Parker, Orson Welles, Arthur Rubinstein, George S. Kaufman, Moss Hart, and Ogden Nash. "Information, Please!" was unrehearsed and spontaneous as the wind, so listeners came to rely upon Adams's and Levant's clever repartee, Fadiman's penchant for sly puns, and the always looming potential for embarrassment. Rex Stout, for example, got plot details from one of his own Nero Wolfe detective books wrong. Still, the real fun of it was hearing brilliant people reveal the breadth of their learning. Kieran, Adams, Levant, and Fadiman knew a great deal. For a guest to keep up with them was no mean feat.

It was undoubtedly by Kieran's agency both that Berg was invited to appear on the show and that Berg agreed to do it. Kieran knew how well read Berg was, and the sportswriter may also have heard about the game Berg's teammates invented to pass the time on the annual train trip north from spring training. As the train pulled into a new town, someone would sing out "Information, please!" and Berg would dutifully provide the essential characteristics of the place, its size, principal industries, famous natives, and more. In New York for the real thing, Berg made only one stipulation: no legal questions should be put to him. Why a lawyer wished to avoid the law, he didn't explain.

Edith Engel interviewed Berg before he appeared on the program, as she screened almost every prospective guest. In the brief time they spent together, Engel sensed that Berg was a complicated fellow. "You could tell how comfortable people were at digging into their own encyclopedia," she says. "He was very comfortable. He could call on difficult things without scratching his head. He put a finger on his intellectual file very easily. But there was a dichotomy because he didn't reveal anything about himself. I sensed there was a door closed and you shouldn't even peek through the keyhole. There was a charm about him but you worried about revealing Mr. Hyde if you went too far. He set his limitations and implied, 'Don't trespass.' " None of this speculation made Berg unsuitable for the show. Indeed, Engel thought Berg would do very well, and so she sent him onto the air.

On February 21, 1939, Fadiman introduced him. "Professor Berg catches for the Boston Red Sox," he said. "In addition, he's got a string of degrees long enough to hang yourself. A philological baseball player is something new on this program. Okay, Mr. Berg. I'll pitch 'em, you catch 'em." Then came the first question, and Berg didn't know that Tweedledum and Tweedledee quarreled over a rattle. This was surprising, given the time he'd spent studying the chess games in *Through the Looking Glass*. After that, however, he was dazzling. He identified the *bordereau*, a supposedly incriminating document from the Dreyfus affair, and the Willy/Nicky correspondence between Czar Nicholas II and Kaiser Wilhelm. "You do a lot of things besides catching for the Boston Red Sox, don't you, Mr. Berg?" asked Fadiman. There was no response, so the game continued. Berg knew that poi was a Hawaiian root eaten instead of bread, *loy* was the ancient French spelling of law, and soy, the word from which chop suey is derived. For an American-presidents-as-athletes question, he identified Teddy Roosevelt as a one-time boxer, Warren Harding as a former sportswriter, and threw in, free of charge, that Woodrow Wilson had played some baseball at Princeton. He said that Halley's was the most visible comet, and chose the sun as the brightest star in the sky. "Are you popular with your teammates, Mr. Berg?" asked Fadiman. A moment later the half hour was up, and Fadiman thanked him "for catching them so neatly. You've been brilliant."

Other people thought so too. Adams sent him a telegram in which he said, "Such a combination of wisdom and knowledge is so uncommon as to be conspicuous." Throughout the next summer, baseball writers recounted Berg's triumph. Several put him "on the stand" themselves for further question-and-answer sessions, which he endured gracefully. In a lengthy interview, Taylor Spink of *Sporting News* asked Berg what had led him to be on the show. Berg replied, "This may sound like hokum to you—because those folks really pay well. But I was induced to go on in order to do a missionary job for the game." He succeeded, at least according to baseball's commissioner. Kenesaw Mountain Landis called Berg over to his box one day in Chicago. "Berg," he said, "in just thirty minutes you did more for baseball than I've done the entire time I've been commissioner."

NBC received boxes of letters—24,000 of them, according to Berg—calling for more Berg, and so the following fall he

▼

was back twice, in mid-October and late November. His second show went fine. In a flat, somber, slightly nasal tone that had some Newark in it, he revealed how much he knew about Latin cognates, political history, and world geography. The third appearance was another matter. Here the first question was a lark—a change-up, in baseball argot. Each man was asked to give the date of his wedding anniversary and of his wife's birthday. "Mr. Berg, are you married?" asked Fadiman. "I am not," said Berg. He sounded tense. Kieran consistently knew the most answers, but he didn't know this one and restored the atmosphere of levity by botching Margaret's birthday. After the laughter subsided, Fadiman, moving on, addressed Berg again. "Mr. Berg," he said, "you were once a lawyer among your spare extra vocations, weren't you?" "I refuse to answer," replied Berg. The question dealt with the distinction between "immaterial" and "irrelevant," and as Kieran fumbled with it, Fadiman appealed to Berg. "What would you say to that, Mr. Berg?" Berg had meant it when he said no law questions. "Who am I to judge?" he said. "To a legal mind I'm sure these two words have nothing in common whatsoever," snapped Fadiman before asking a new question. A sensitive man might well have construed Fadiman's final remark as an insult. After it, Berg attempted to answer almost nothing in what was easily his worst performance, and he never again appeared on the show. "He was not very forthcoming," Fadiman remembers. "We didn't get to know him at all." Fadiman and others on the show had suspicions about Berg. They thought he was a spy.

BY 1939, ONLY a handful of players—Lefty Grove, Ted Lyons, Charlie Gehringer—had been in the American League for as many years as Berg. His longevity, his press clippings, and his success on the radio made him a celebrity, or, more properly, a celebrated curiosity. Famous as he was by now, very few people actually paid attention to Berg's baseball career. They followed men who excelled, like Jimmie Foxx, the Red Sox brawny first baseman. With Foxx, the game was everything. With Berg, baseball was a prism that revealed a singular personality. Foxx meant home runs. Berg meant intelligence, mystery, and the hint of adventure. One man made you cheer, the other made you wonder.

To Jewish fans, Berg meant something more. American Jews were looking for heroes. They had one in Hank Greenberg, the Detroit Tigers handsome, slugging first baseman. A second-generation American Jew from the Bronx, Greenberg had become one of the best players in baseball. This success was an inspiration to vast numbers of Jewish Americans, particularly those of Greenberg's generation. Many immigrant Jewish parents pushed their children to transcend cultural inferiority "by virtue," says Philip Roth, "of that cultural elixir known as a good education." Greenberg helped people believe there was another way. Bert Gordon, a retired Detroit real estate broker, told Roger Angell, "I don't think anybody can imagine the terrific importance of Hank Greenberg to the Jewish community. He was a God, a true folk hero. That made baseball acceptable to our parents, so for once they didn't mind if we took a little time off from the big process of getting into college."

Moe Berg was a foil to Greenberg. Greenberg punctured the stereotype that Jews were unathletic. Berg suggested that you could get a top education and be a ballplayer, too. "Hank Greenberg, by being a star, was the shining knight," says Don Shapiro, who grew up in Detroit. "Moe Berg, by being an intellectual, confirmed our ideals. He was a legend in the sense that we all knew about him, knew how smart he was. He was important to Jews because he confirmed that you could be an intellectual and an athlete and an American, too. He was to wider society first a ballplayer and a towering intellect. He was Einstein in knickers."

Greenberg was a source of ethnic solidarity. Toward the end of his 1938 pursuit of Babe Ruth's home run record, each turn

at bat sent swells of anticipation through Jewish neighborhoods, where Tiger broadcasts murmured from radios on every
porch. Greenberg assumed the burden of being a hero to Jews,
while Berg distanced himself from religion. Yet even if Judaism
was of limited spiritual importance to him, opposing players
would have reminded him at every opportunity that his blood
was different. Harry Danning, a Jewish catcher for the New
York Giants in the 1930s, says, "They called you lots of names.
Everybody did. You were supposed to ride the other team."

Berg didn't like to discuss his brushes with anti-Semitism,
and when he did, his stock response was "If you do your job
and stay out of trouble, you won't experience such things on
a broad level." Publicly, Greenberg also minimized what he'd
experienced. Yet to close friends who pressed him on the matter, he admitted that at times the ethnic slurs he absorbed were
painful, and made him want to fight. Berg, a proud man who
never responded well to teasing of any sort, undoubtedly felt
the same way when opponents called him "a dirty kike," which
they did. It may have been a day when ethnic slurs were just
part of the game, but it was also a period in history when reports
of Jewish genocide were beginning to emerge from Europe.
However it is dressed, hostility rarely feels pleasant, and it
couldn't have pleased Moe Berg. This was especially true when
it came from his teammates.

Most of the Red Sox members treated him fine. "What the
hell, he was Jewish, I was German, Cronin was Irish," says
Eldon Auker. "Moe Berg was well respected. I never heard
any slurs." Pitcher Joe Dobson says that he "never thought
about him being Jewish at all."

Others, however, weren't so oblivious. Sometimes it was just
a matter of the relief pitchers engaging in friendly bull-pen
banter. Jack Wilson, who was fond of Berg, would take a minor
Berg transgression as an opportunity to ask him "what the
rabbi would think of that." It was all in jest and Berg knew it.
"He'd say, 'The hell with the rabbi,' " says Wilson. "He didn't
seem interested in religion." Yet, when he is discussing the

loquacious and sometimes abrasive Al Schacht, a Red Sox coach who was Jewish, Wilson no longer sounds so puckish. "There's one son-of-a-bitch Jew who wasn't liked," says Wilson.

Players could be just as crass about Berg. "The people on the ball club didn't like him," says Billy Werber. "He wasn't of their stripe. He was Jewish and people were less tolerant of that then." Pitcher Herb Hash says he had little to do with Berg, explaining, "The Jewboys didn't associate with us as much as with their own kind." At six foot one and 200 pounds, Berg was a large man, and not one to trifle with. If Red Sox members were casting anti-Semitic aspersions his way, they were probably doing so out of his hearing. Still, he would have known that when some people looked at him they thought "Jew," even if they said nothing. This must have pained a man who went to lengths never to appear the social exception.

TED WILLIAMS JOINED the Red Sox in 1939, a headstrong, jubilant bundle of sinewy talent. Cronin asked Berg to watch over him a little, help break him in. At first Williams had trouble getting along with some of Boston's veteran players, but he and Berg grew fond of each other in a distant sort of way. "He liked me as a player and a kid," says Williams. "I think he liked my young, enthusiastic approach to it all." This self-portrait contrasted vividly with Williams's impression of Berg. "Moe was only sixteen years older than I was, but he was much more subdued than the average guy even of that age. Not a lot of pep or vinegar." Not a lot of playing, either. Berg batted 33 times in the 14 games. "Gentlemen," he would say when Cronin sent him in, "does everyone still get three strikes out there?"

Berg had been serving mostly as a bull pen catcher and aide-de-camp to Cronin for two years, turning in reports on young pitchers and working with the catchers. Now with a strapping backstop named George Lacy on hand, Cronin decided to make coaching Berg's official position. On February 2, 1940, the Associated Press reported, "The linguistic Moe Berg, who has mastered all the finer arts except hitting, will be missing from the baseball box scores this coming season for the first time in seventeen years."

As a coach, one of Berg's first tasks was to do for the rookie outfielder Dominic DiMaggio what he'd done for Williams. At spring training, Cronin asked Berg to room with DiMaggio. On March 10, soon after they moved in together, DiMaggio injured an ankle tumbling into Johnny Peacock at the plate during an intersquad game. The next day Cronin and the Boston owner Tom Yawkey came to see how he was. Berg was out, but he'd left a signature; the only chair in the room was covered with a neat pile of newspapers. Yawkey and Cronin were tempted into a little fun. They scattered the papers all over the room and then, giggling, escorted DiMaggio out. When DiMaggio returned to the room, he found the papers gone and Berg's closet empty as well. There was a note: "Dominic, you have too many friends—my newspapers are too important to me."

DiMaggio found Berg intelligent and unobtrusive, though he wondered about him. "I thought, here's a bright guy, what's he doing playing baseball? He couldn't have been making much money. If he had many pairs of clothes I didn't see them." Although he claimed on a government application to be earning as much as $15,000 a year from the Red Sox, Berg's actual salary was $7,500 in 1941. Together with his earnings from Novelart, he was probably earning between $10,000 and $12,000, a good middle-class income for someone with no dependents. Yet for a man with expensive tastes, even one who was unburdened by a mortgage and didn't accumulate possessions, high living could consume it all quickly.

DiMaggio wasn't the only young player who had questions about Berg. Many of the Red Sox members wondered what exactly his baseball job was. The *Boston Globe* wrote of "the effervescent Moe Berg, who will work with baby pitchers," but

Cronin had hired a new pitching coach, Frank Shellenback, to work with the prize young prospects Herb Hash and Bill Butland. "I don't really know what Berg was doing," says Butland. Hash didn't either. He remembers that Berg "was real quiet, stayed mostly to himself and had an armful of newspapers morning, night, and noon."

In late March 1941, after training in Sarasota, the Red Sox sailed to Cuba for some exhibition games on the baseball-crazed island. Berg had a grand time. He brushed up on his Spanish and, according to Wagner, "spoke it better than the guys who sold orange juice." (He didn't write it quite as well, however. In a Cuban restaurant in Tampa, Berg and John Kieran saluted the chef by carving into the wall "comer nemos comides"—this is one of the best meals we have ever eaten. The sentiment was nice, but the grammar was lacking. The past participle of *comer* is *comido*.) On the boat from Florida, Berg told Doerr about Cuba and told a lot of things to a married American woman who fell for him completely and allowed herself to be seduced.

Except to give the very clear impression that, as Cronin put it, "he was a charmer with ladies," Berg kept his romantic life as secret as anything else. Certainly he could be a devastating flirt, able to come at a conversation from so many angles. People saw him with attractive women now and then, but never the same one twice. He could be slightly lubricious; on the back of a photograph of a woman named Kelly he wrote in a memo to himself, "Kelly has a beautiful leg and what a fanny."

In 1941, Berg spent a second summer amusing himself as the bull pen coach. The Red Sox had a teenage midget batboy named Donald Davidson, and sometimes Berg would hoist Davidson onto his knee and help him with his French and Latin lessons. Davidson's parents were amazed when he brought home A's in Latin and French. Berg did some composing of his own, too. In May, he received a letter from Edward Weeks, the editor of the *Atlantic Monthly*. Weeks said that he wondered a lot about pitchers—"how they learn to be cooney," as he put it—and wanted Berg to write him a "paper" explaining what it takes "to be better than the average." Berg mulled over the proposal and accepted. In September, Weeks published a lissome, erudite, and thoroughly winning piece of prose, in which Berg held forth on pitching, as he'd been asked to do, and catching, as seemed only reasonable.

"Pitchers and Catchers" remains the most concise adult primer on the essential art of baseball. Still regularly anthologized, it runs ten book pages in length, and between the stout first sentence ("Baseball men agree with the philosopher that perfection—which means a pennant to them—is attainable only through a proper combination of opposites.") and the terse, cryptic finale ("The game's the thing."), Berg concerns himself with the nuances of the sport that separate players of comparable physical abilities. At first glance, some of Berg's conclusions read like bromides, but one doesn't object, both because the writing is so smooth and also because there is always the understanding that Berg was among the first to approach baseball with such literary seriousness.

His essay is full of pleasures. "Good fielding and pitching, without hitting, or vice versa, is like Ben Franklin's half a pair of scissors—ineffectual" is typical of the bright, pithy tone. There are phrases in Latin and French, explanations of phenomena like the two o'clock hitter—a man who is a slugger in batting practice and futile during the game—and why catchers give the signals—since they crouch, they can hide them more easily than the pitcher can. The dead-ball era came to an end after World War I, says Berg, because of changes in the availability of foreign ingredients and adjustments in yarn-winding technology. He tells his reader how to throw a forkball and a knuckleball and discusses the many ways pitchers seek to get an edge on hitters, or, as he puts it, "to fool the hitter—there's the rub." Wily Ted Lyons, for example, constantly varied the pace of his windup and the style of his delivery. Fastball specialist Lefty Grove waited a year to throw his forkball, and then in a moment of crisis, flabbergasted an opposing batter by sending him one of the slower pitches.

"Pitchers and Catchers" is dense with such detail, sharp testament to Berg's enthusiasm for baseball and the amount of time he spent thinking about it. After all, who else would discuss probability and pitch sequences, compare testy pitchers to recalcitrant judges, and then add the cheerful disclaimer "Judges, if you are reading, please consider this *obiter.*"

Of course catching was a real and very specific interest, and the catching portion of the essay is perhaps the best. Berg's model catcher does not just possess, as he says, a good pair of hands, grace, rhythm, bent knees, and a straight back. He also "has to be able to cock his arm from any position, throw fast and accurately to the bases, field bunts like an infielder, and catch foul flies like an outfielder. He must be adept at catching a ball from any angle, and almost simultaneously tagging a runner at home plate. The catcher," says Berg, "is the Cerberus of baseball." The physical requirements set forth, Berg discusses the mental side of the job—calling the game, disguising signs, remaining alert to anything that will lend an advantage, for "the catcher is an on-the-spot witness," the only defensive player with a view of all that happens on the ball field. Finally, displaying grace that would have been a credit to any catcher, Berg explains that "pitchers help catchers as much as catchers do pitchers," and thanks his old White Sox teammates Red Faber, Ted Lyons, and Tommy Thomas for teaching him to catch. For a largely unsentimental man, such an essay, ending with such an acknowledgment, takes on the qualities of a professional summing up, with a few notes borrowed from a dirge.

For Berg seemed to be aimless, drifting through the seasons. It was now four years since he'd really done much of anything. The *Boston Globe* sports columnist Arthur Siegel asked him about it. "Arthur," said Berg, "I seek no other man's shoes. If I've misdirected my priorities, and I'm confident that this is

▼

not so, I've had a pretty fair time in lost country." Berg meant exactly that. As a man with choices, he had decided to spend the first part of his life in pursuit of a good time, and he knew of nothing that pleased him more than the rituals of a ball-player's summer. Sam Berg, who despaired over his talented brother, knew him well enough to shrug and say that "he was happy in that he lived the life he loved." Another time Sam said, "All it ever did was make him happy." But Williams, who spent three summers with Berg and was famous for possessing the sharpest eyes in baseball, noticed something else. "I don't ever remember seeing him laughing," he says.

CHAPTER 9

Southern Junket

M oe Berg was an intensely proud man and privately found it dismaying to be perceived as a curiosity. As a coach, Berg didn't have to worry any longer about wearing the embarrassing mantle of the catcher who never caught. Yet from catcher to coach, the job description hadn't changed, and much as Berg liked baseball, watching 154 ball games a summer from his perch in the bull pen must at times have made him restless. Coaching also carried with it less cachet, for no matter how sparely a man plays, "baseball player" is a far more impressive title than "baseball coach." Not that he was complaining. This was the existence he'd chosen, among many possibilities. But now a bit of the polish was rubbed from the Berg mystique.

With the war came something better. Much better. Berg was leaving baseball behind for a career so well suited to his personality that it would make him a star: espionage.

When he was a baseball player, Berg's strong throwing arm, quick instincts, and savvy understanding of a complicated game made him a competent professional, nothing more. Only because of personal traits ancillary to baseball did he become famous. But that intelligent, eccentric personality was exactly what made him an unusually successful intelligence operator. Because he was a man who found it easy to make other people talk about themselves while keeping himself a secret, and because he was a loner with a penchant for disappearing, Berg was the perfect spy. It was one of the ironies of his life that he won considerable fame during a largely inconsequential career as a ballplayer, while the truly valuable intelligence work he did for his country he was forced to keep as classified as he kept himself.

As EARLY AS 1934, when he carried a movie camera to the top of Saint Luke's Hospital in Tokyo, and perhaps long before that, Berg had known the pleasure of pilfering secrets under risky conditions. At the time, the United States had no central institution dispatching agents to gather intelligence in foreign countries. That changed with World War II.

Months before the American entry into the war, it became clear to President Roosevelt that the U.S. needed to know more about what was happening abroad than military and naval intelligence, the FBI, and the State Department were providing. Roosevelt appointed a New York lawyer and World War I hero, William "Wild Bill" Donovan, as coordinator of information, authorizing him to create an American version of England's famous intelligence corps, MI-6, which had been sending the world's secrets back to London since the sixteenth century. A year later, Donovan's organization became the Office of Strategic Services (OSS), the first American intelligence agency.

Donovan wasn't the only prominent New York Republican to extract an intelligence franchise from a Democratic president. Among the most vital U.S. national security concerns during the world war were its borders to the south. Oppressive poverty, mercurial politics, and the local perception that Americans were plundering imperialists made many South and Central American countries seem vulnerable to fascists bearing sacks of money and ill will toward Washington. With that in mind, shortly after the fall of France in the summer of 1940, Nelson Rockefeller, the youthful scion of the billionaire Manhattan petroleum family, proposed an organization that would fan U.S. representatives throughout South and Central America to further the national defense by encouraging close bonds of friendship between neighbors. This idea appealed to President Roosevelt, and by July 1941 the organization had developed into the Office of Inter-American Affairs (OIAA). During the war, Rockefeller would cede some of his turf to the grasping FBI director J. Edgar Hoover. As things turned out, the FBI was responsible for all secret intelligence in Latin America; the OIAA handled political and economic intelligence and propaganda in the region; and the OSS contented itself with as much of the rest of the world as the British and Douglas MacArthur would permit.

IN A SPEECH he delivered at the 1940 Boston Book Fair, Moe Berg concluded, "Montaigne said a few hundred years ago, about Paris, what I feel strongly about our way of life, our country—'I love her so tenderly that even her spots, her blemishes, are dear unto to me.' " The reference was a touch maudlin, but the characterization was true enough. There was never any doubting Berg's loyalty. He learned it from his parents, who, like so many other grateful immigrants, bred a patriotism in their children that was unwavering and absolute.

In Boston during that summer, the newspapers were full of ominous stories from foreign places where Berg had once been very happy. What he read left him uneasy, disquieted with the world and with himself. It was probably then that he told Arthur

▼

Daley, "Europe is in flames, withering in a fire set by Hitler. All over that continent men and women and children are dying. Soon we too will be involved. And what am I doing? I'm sitting in the bull pen, telling jokes to the relief pitchers."

In November Berg arranged an interview with officials from Rockefeller's office through an old friend, the Guatemalan diplomat Enrique López-Herrarte. Nothing much came of it for a while, but in June 1941 Berg was invited to a discussion on the role of sports in the hemisphere defense program, and by autumn, one of Rockefeller's assistants was telling him that they were "anxious" to hire him as a cultural ambassador to teach sports throughout South and Central America. By Berg's account, the lobbying was so intense that one Rockefeller aide even came to the ballpark and went out to the bull pen where Berg was warming up Lefty Grove; Berg had to field job pitches between tosses from Grove.

Berg's angst increased as the U.S. entered the war. Hearing over the radio that Japanese Zeros had bombed Pearl Harbor, he sat down with a pen, paper, and a sense of righteous indignation to sketch out his thoughts. At 4:30 PM, writing in not very cogent English, he notes that most Japanese people are "kindly, hospitable, cheerful, and kindly disposed towards Americans," and that the hope of the world is "a charitable regard for others, live and let live—an aristocracy of the intellect, i.e. of people who think and not live by the sword— there is room for all—there must be a league of nations—an international police force." At 5:00, this time in perfectly legible katakana characters he writes, "I don't like to appear to be a soothsayer but I predicted in the year 1922 that there would be a war between two philosophies, fascist and democratic." Fifteen minutes later, back in English, he snaps, "It is now here and all the pseudo-patriots will have to shut up." Then his tone softens. "I feel sorry for the Japanese, as well as Italians and Germans who see as we do; Matsumoto, Takizo must be having a bad time today." That was as close to fond sentiment as Moe Berg got. Japan had meant a lot to him, and so had Matsumoto.

Grim as he said the war made him feel, Berg had yet to leave baseball and make a commitment to Rockefeller. Initially the idea of sponsoring sports programs in Latin America pleased him. He wrote enthusiastic letters to Washington and prepared a three-page memo in which he extolled the democratic virtues of sports. But Rockefeller's interest in him had set Berg to thinking that he might have better options. Doing some lobbying of his own, he managed to get an interview with the FBI, which he hoped would give him work. They would not. Rockefeller, however, seemed willing to permit Berg plenty of flexibility, so on January 5, 1942, he finally accepted a revised OIAA assignment, agreeing to travel in the South and Central American republics to monitor health and fitness, at a salary of $22.22 per day. Technically he was taking a position as a propaganda official, a virtual flack for the U.S. government. But as Berg had discovered in Japan, a nervy man out on his own can improvise.

Ten days later, on January 15, newspapers around the country reported that Berg was retiring from baseball to go to work for Rockefeller as a special consultant. For sportswriters, this was yet another chance to reheat some old Moe Berg stories while joining the jingoistic clamor that had seized a country still reeling from the Japanese sneak attack. Jerry Nason, describing Berg's assignment in the *Boston Evening Globe*, said, "The Brain, so styled, won't be on the business end of an anti-aircraft gun or nipping a Jap warship off first base with a torpedo, but the kind of work he will be doing will be just as vital, maybe more so, right at this moment." Nason also mentioned, among many, many other things, that Berg could "ask directions of a Greek shepherd . . . or even lecture in Sanskrit." These were signal accomplishments, no doubt—especially the lecturing, since Sanskrit is not a spoken language—but what use they would be in Panama or Brazil was more dubious.

Berg himself was at pains to emphasize the importance of his assignment with Rockefeller, telling the *Newark News*, "I have no intention of making a so-called goodwill tour in the hemisphere countries to the south. This program goes much deeper. It may take in, for instance, health and athletics, nutrition and diet, and a study of the best means of promoting goodwill between the hemisphere countries. It is a long-range program that must go on for centuries." This was pretty heady stuff for a ballplayer, and editorial interest went beyond the press box; *Time* and *Newsweek* carried Berg stories too.

Amidst all the hoopla, Berg's excitement at beginning a new career was tempered by an unsettling family development. Bernard Berg had been in poor health for some time, and on January 14 he died. He had slipped away before anyone could tell him that Berg was off to war.

BERG TOOK HIS oath of office on January 21, and then went to see John Clark at the OIAA headquarters in the Commerce Building. Tall, with gray-blue eyes and a long, narrow face, Clark had gone to Dartmouth with Rockefeller, worked as an editorial writer for the *Washington Post*, and studied Latin American affairs on a Nieman Fellowship at Harvard. Now he was chief of the Division of Basic Economy, and Berg's superior. Clark may have suggested Berg's name to Rockefeller and, in any case, knew all about him, right down to what he carved on the walls of Florida restaurants, as he demonstrated with his first question. As soon as Berg sat down, Clark asked, "What's the past participle of *comer?*" Berg was horrified. He and Clark would become friendly—they went to a Senators game together, where Berg cupped a hand over his mouth, lowering his voice an octave so that the players on the field could hear him below the noise of the crowd—but around this boss, Berg was always wary.

Berg joined the OIAA at a hectic time. With long-range radio broadcasts to Latin Americans from Berlin, describing

Hitler's triumphs and promising them that expelling the Yankees would lead to a better life in the barrio, and with Abwehr agents busily promoting the cause in person, many U.S. observers of Latin America, right up to President Roosevelt, feared that Nazi-backed putsches or even German invasions were imminent. The OIAA fought back with its checkbook, strewing money and favors across the region.

Brazil was of particular concern, primarily because its squat, cigar-puffing dictator/president, Getúlio Vargas, was a shameless opportunist. "I never had a friend who couldn't become an enemy or an enemy who couldn't become a friend" was Vargas's mantra, and he abided by it with impunity. In the late 1930s, while proclaiming his loyalty to the pan-American friendship cause and permitting Washington to finance, among other things, a new Brazilian steel industry, Vargas was conducting a brisk trade with Germany, exchanging coffee, rubber, and cotton for weapons. The U.S. wanted to make Jeep tires of the Brazilian rubber crop, and with a large German expatriate population in Brazil, and rumors of beachheads that were supposedly being scouted by Nazi submarines, it needed Vargas's cooperation to other ends. Perhaps the most crucial interest was the so-called Trampoline to Victory. As the U.S. contemplated entering the war in Europe, an ideal alternative to the Newfoundland-Iceland-Scotland transatlantic air route was a southern cross, bouncing from the hump of northeastern Brazil over to Africa.

While the proximity of the U.S. military was the most certain means of keeping Vargas in line, petting a reluctant neighbor was preferable to pulverizing him, and so the OIAA sought to ingratiate itself with Brazil by coddling the golfer Mario Gonzales on his U.S. visit, mounting an exhibition of the painter Cándido Portinari's pictures at the Museum of Modern Art in New York, and hiring him to paint murals at the Library of Congress in Washington. Versions of Hollywood films bound for Latin America were edited so that lovers were now always traipsing off to Rio instead of, say, Paris. A less flashy but more

▼

meaningful OIAA Brazilian venture was sponsoring a nation-wide sanitation project.

The OIAA made gestures of this sort all across the region. To protect the Panama Canal, and the many American battle and supply ships that went through it, from possible Japanese attack, the U.S. wanted to mount defenses on the Galápagos Islands. The Galápagos belonged to Ecuador, which, at the time, was quarreling with Peru, so the OIAA cleared out the Peruvians and, in exchange, the U.S. was granted use of the Galápagos. The Peruvian refugees were then supplied with rice, beans, machetes, and cooking oil to help them get started at home. In Honduras, when United Fruit sent its ships to the Pacific to carry troops, Honduran banana workers were thrown out of work. The OIAA appeased the situation by hiring the banana workers to build new Honduran roads. Free food was sent to Venezuela, where the U.S. coveted iron ore; Bolivia received tin-mining technology; and the Chilean ski team was invited to Joe Louis's training camp.

Moe Berg, meanwhile, was in Washington, waiting. His original travel orders were to depart on a six-month trip, beginning on January 7, but that hadn't happened, and for months nobody could quite seem to find anything for him to do. So he amused himself. By February, he'd met with officials at the OSS, who either asked him to make a lengthy radio address to Japan or accepted Berg's proposal to do so. In any case, Berg did speak to Japan, over short-wave radio, on February 24. Almost certainly Berg did not write his lines in Japanese, but the text was his, and once it was translated for him, he delivered it in Japanese. Mixing history and personal anecdote, Berg portrayed Japan's longstanding friendship with the U.S. "I ask you," he said at one point, "what sound basis is there for enmity between two peoples who enjoy the same national sport?" Later he remonstrated, "I know your glorious history, about your Samurai, the Cult of Bushido, your love of Confucian classics. I was impressed by your hospitality and customs—all these things I still admire. But you betrayed your friends—you made a sneak attack on Pearl Harbor while your Ambassadors Nomura and Kurusu were carrying out diplomatic conversations with us; you have lost face and are committing national seppuku." The speech, of course, had no effect upon the war, but for Berg's purposes, pleasing Donovan was something to put in his pocket for later.

One more export the U.S. had sent to Latin America was troops, installing many thousands of them in bases from the Caribbean to the Pacific coast in what was, in effect, a vast protective shield. By April, it had been decided that Berg would serve as a roving civilian inspector, charged with looking for ways to improve the life and living conditions of the U.S. soldiers stationed in the bases. If the terms of the assignment sounded vague, that was fine with Berg. He was to leave in midsummer, and before that he moved about Washington, consulting with agencies of every stripe, from the Army to the Red Cross to the OSS to the FBI. He described this activity in a memo to Rockefeller as necessary preparation for his mission, and maybe he saw it that way, but it's also true that Berg was quietly making his services available to agencies other than the one that employed him—agencies that conducted real espionage.

In a meeting with an FBI Foreign Funds official, Berg asked if he could be of any assistance to the Bureau while in Latin America, and the coy response was that "the Bureau would always appreciate receiving information which would be of interest to the Bureau." Berg concluded the meeting by saying he'd be back in touch before leaving the country, to make arrangements for transmitting information. During at least two of his conversations with officials from other offices, Berg described the films of Japan he had made back in 1934 and offered to screen them, much as he had in the past for friends and teammates. On July 11, Medical Corps Captain Robert Rutherford sent Berg a note that said, "We were able to get more good from your movies than would have been accumulated over several months of looking through texts and travel magazines." Two days later, Berg was writing to John McClintock at the OIAA to explain that the Pictorial Records Section of the OSS was "interested" in his films, which Berg would screen as soon as copies could be made of the portions "that were considered essential to the generals and admirals and interested persons in the intelligence service." Berg was due to leave on his mission the following week, and he promised that he would be ready.

He wasn't. On July 17, Seymour Houghton of the OSS thanked Berg for "making it possible to view your film and for your untiring efforts during the screening of it. Mr. John F. Langan, a member of our staff, reports your film to be of strategic importance." A week after that, Berg dispatched a memorandum to Rockefeller, inviting his boss "as my guest" to a July 28 screening of the films. "All the interested personnel of the intelligence services are attending." Berg sent copies of the memo also to Clark, McClintock, and seven other OIAA officials. The interest in his films had Berg ecstatic. Writing to his mother, he said, "I'm going to show my moving pictures to all the intelligence officers of all our armed forces—that means the officers of Army, Navy, Marines etc. who put together all information and give it to the fliers who bomb Tokyo or Berlin, or the army that attacks—I'll tell you what they say—I think I have pictures nobody else in the world has."

On the thirtieth, in a letter to his sister, Berg reported the reaction to the screening. "The movies were received triumphantly," he said. "They wondered how I got them—now they can make pinpoint recognition of warehouses, gas tanks, docks, factories, etc." Berg had seen Rockefeller that day, who by this time had enough experience with him to know how well he responded to flattery. "He told me some nice things," Berg reported. "That I was the only one in the office who could handle police chiefs, newspaper editors, local people [Spanish speaking] etc. in the other Americas to see how our troops were being received etc." Rockefeller invited Berg to dinner on August 11, which meant Berg's mission was again delayed. Berg didn't care. He was in the thick of things, providing his government with crucial information.

Or was he? Just how important to intelligence people were the seconds of footage Berg had recorded from the roof of Saint Luke's Hospital and elsewhere around Japan? Berg had last been in Tokyo in 1934. When U.S. intelligence needed information about Tokyo, rather than rely on an eight-year-old film made by an amateur, they were much more likely to go to intelligence experts who had been in Japan more recently, which, in fact, they did. For the surprise B-25 raids on Tokyo, Yokohama, Osaka, and Nagoya, led by Lieutenant Colonel Jimmy Doolittle from the aircraft carrier Hornet on April 18, 1942, Doolittle says, all bombing targets were plotted by Captain Steve Jurika, a former assistant U.S. Navy attaché in Tokyo who spoke fluent Japanese and had been in Japan for seven years, as recently as 1941. Beginning in 1939, Jurika spent two years preparing meticulous bombing maps for every neighborhood in Tokyo, highlighting gun batteries, political buildings, factories, barracks, highways, and railroad tracks. In 1944, when the Japanese learned what Jurika had done, they murdered his mother, who lived in the Philippines. There were plenty of published sources readily available as well, because Tokyo's topography had not changed significantly since the American Charles Austin Beard had helped to rebuild the city after the great earthquake and fire of 1923. Similarly, photographs were on hand. Jurika himself had taken a great many. He also had a movie camera. Except for a persistent but almost certainly apocryphal story that has Berg's film being used to plan the Doolittle raids, no archival or trustworthy published evidence has emerged to suggest that Berg's films were put to any use during World War II.

So why did Berg attract so much interest in July 1942? For several reasons. In a time of war, no intelligence officer turns down a prominent man who claims he has valuable footage of the enemy capital. Japan was a distant, mysterious place, and just because there was abundant information about the

country didn't mean that more was unnecessary. Berg, no
doubt, made his film sound intriguing. He was a terrific storyteller, a vivid embellisher, who took himself very seriously.
When he recounted the lengths he'd gone to, in order to get
to the top of a building that was undeniably a terrific vantage
point, he made people curious. But the generals and admirals
who, according to Berg, described the film as "essential" did
so on the basis of what Berg told them about it. They had yet
to see it for themselves. When they did, they would have taken
the films for what they were: brief, amateurish panoramas
made by an adventurous person using a movie camera for the
first time.

The enthusiastic notes Berg received following the screening
must be ascribed to decorum. How else to respond to an eager,
well-known man who had gone to so much trouble? Berg
worked for the OIAA, and was extending himself by arranging
screenings for other agencies. He deserved the thanks and
appreciation. Afterward, his films were probably filed away
with the burgeoning monograph on Japan and forgotten.

But just because the screenings were not of military importance does not mean that they weren't useful to Berg. The
early months of the war were a frenetic time in Washington.
Military people were besieged by businessmen from New York,
bankers from Cincinnati, insurance salesmen from Omaha, all
eager to join the war effort and certain of their own utility.
Amidst the thirsty mob of prospective dollar-a-year men, Berg
had been noticed. Less than a year before, he'd been a bull
pen catcher. Now he had commanded a powerful audience in
Washington.

Rubbing shoulders with so many people whose business was
secrecy made Berg, in Washington, more secretive in public
than ever. In the months following the publicity blitz that accompanied his joining the OIAA, Berg was conspicuously reserved or, as John Kieran put it, "Always a mysterious bird,
Professor Berg has become even more mysterious since he
joined up with the forces of Nelson A. Rockefeller, the coor-

dinator of Inter-American Affairs." Berg was rarely seen at Griffith Stadium, even when the Red Sox were in town, and when he ran into anyone on the sidewalk who knew him, Kieran said that "he would put up a warning finger across his closed lips, nod solemnly, and move off mysteriously without saying a word." One day he did stop for a long chat with the gossip columnist Walter Winchell, but Winchell was the exception. On August 22, Berg boarded a plane in Miami, flew to Panama, and began his assignment.

BERG'S ENTHUSIASM FOR improving the lives of American soldiers was so evident, his desire to please so sincere, his pedigree (ex-ballplayer) so attractive, and his funding from Rockefeller so generous, that any skepticism from military base commanders and embassy diplomats evaporated in the tropical sun. Berg would arrive at a base, look up the commanding officer, and explain that he was "just trying to help the boys in their dislocation." Dressed in a white shirt and khakis—a sartorial concession to the climate, and one he would never make again—and setting his own itinerary, Berg went everywhere that airplanes, Jeeps, and his feet could take him; he had a high time and managed to carry off his work with aplomb.

He stayed a week in Panama, consulting with the American ambassador as well as various generals and admirals, touring gun batteries and other fortifications designed to protect the canal, and concluding, in the journal he later submitted to Rockefeller, that beyond "a natural bit of griping," morale was high. Then he was off, flying first to Costa Rica. To get to an isolated aircraft warning station, he rode a Jeep through jungle bristling "with bushmasters and coral snakes, baboons, jaguars and wild cats." Two days later Berg was on the arid, coastal plain of Talara, Peru, in far western South America, where a dusty runway faced Japan. He pronounced the soldiers' drinking water "excellent," and described a beach covered with wooden crosses put up in memory of natives killed by sharks.

▼

There were plenty of other fish in the Pacific, and Berg recommended that the barracks be supplied with six sets of deepsea fishing tackle. Other diversions he thought the men could use included a movie theater, athletic equipment, radios, a Victrola, and a series of books on Peruvian archeology, geology, history, and folklore (Berg felt that American soldiers and sailors should take an interest in local culture). He bought all of the requested recreational equipment that he could, and promised to order the rest from the U.S. He also commented on the shortage of condoms and widespread venereal disease in the town of Piura.

Berg's journal for Rockefeller is as much a literary travellog as a morale evaluation. In his Galápagos entries, he takes time to explain that the islands arc named for large turtles, describes the soldiers singing and drinking beer beside the ocean at dusk, tells Rockefeller how pleased the soldiers were with the Victrola records he'd brought them, urges the purchase of fishing equipment here, too, and since there were no women on the island he visited, relates that he told the commanding surgeon that he had a "great opportunity to write a definitive report on man without woman."

September brought him to Salinas, Ecuador, "the venereal Utopia," where Berg discouraged a colonel who wanted to ban his men from the syphilis-infested town of Salinas, since that might "reflect on the hospitality of the Ecuadorian people, as well as the lack of restraint on the part of our boys." Nazis, meanwhile, were warning the local people to "keep their 'nice' girls away from our 'bad' boys," which, said Berg, "Ecuadorians take in stride." By mid-September he'd been to Guatemala and Honduras. Back in Panama, he wrote to his mother and sister: "Never felt better—working all the time, but it is a great pleasure to me—I like it—the Embassy here thinks I'm doing a great job. Nobody has been accepted by the military like me. I talk their language and they know I am for them." Then it was off to Trinidad, with stops at bases in Colombia,

Aruba, Curaçao, and Venezuela en route. Besides sampling tomato omelettes and seeing tarantulas and centipedes, he presented gold baseballs to the winners of the Trinidad softball championship.

For Berg, the work was tantamount to a wonderful holiday adventure. Life was dull for American troops in this mostly peaceful part of the world. When the exotic former catcher appeared out of the mists, it was a rare break in the monotony. Wherever Berg went, people were delighted to show him the sights. So it was that, between post inspections, he lay face down with a pair of binoculars in the glass nose of a British B-18 bomber during an unsuccessful hunt for some of the German submarines that were taking a heavy toll on Allied shipping. He was also treated to dinner at the best Chinese restaurant in Aruba, and he began October with "a fascinating journey through the heart of the Dutch Guiana jungles—tigers, jaguars, wild cats, snakes, alligators, dense bush, Indian villages and unique, au naturel, 'bush nigger' Djuka villages, and seeing the 'bush niggers' come out to shore in their homemade pointed canoes, both men and women, mostly naked." There were fully clothed American soldiers in Guiana too, and sitting with them, Berg learned that the Yankees had won the first game of the World Series.

Thousands of miles from Broadway, Berg was still bumping into people who'd met him, or had wanted to. Just before he left Belém, Brazil, for the port of Natal, Berg was asked to delay his departure and greet Navy Secretary Knox, which he did. The next day, Berg cheerfully awakened hours before dawn to see Knox off. In Natal, Berg encountered Don Griffin, his former Princeton classmate, serving in the air transport command. Griffin he ignored, giving him the hush sign as he passed. Elsewhere about town, Berg visited dance halls, where enlisted men "of good family" hired out prostitutes. "Perhaps if these service men had an alternative they might curb their indulgence" was his thinking. Berg did his best. By the time he left them, the soldiers at Natal had ice-cream freezers, a boxing ring, and new furniture and lamps for their recreation center.

He got to Rio on October 19, and there he encouraged the wives of naval officers to think of ways to keep the servicemen out of the bars. Bounding about town, he met Mrs. Vargas, who was "very pleased and showed great interest" in his work. Three days later she dispatched a messenger to ask Berg if he would set up similar programs for Brazilian soldiers. Berg couldn't do that, but he happily shared "my ideas on the subject." He also attended a luncheon of the American Society of Rio de Janeiro, where he encouraged sending Christmas presents to the servicemen and stressed the pleasure the men got when personal notes were enclosed.

In Washington, nobody had any idea of what Berg was doing with himself, as Ethel Berg discovered when she wrote to John Clark asking for information about her brother. "There isn't much that we here in Washington know of Mr. Berg's trip," he responded. "We feel that Mr. Berg himself does not know very much in advance his own plans." A letter Ethel had sent care of Clark had not gone out because, it was explained, "we did not know where to send it."

Through December, Berg stayed in Rio, where, after receiving word from Rockefeller that the last installment of equipment for the troops stationed in Brazil was on its way, his business changed. Now he was nosing around, taking meals with Brazilian coffee and newspaper barons in places like the Jockey Club and the Lobby Grill at the Copacabana Hotel, trying to get a sense of how the quicksilver Vargas and other Brazilian political leaders were feeling about the Nazis. He was a little late. By this time most of the German spy rings in Brazil had been smashed, and Argentina had become the Latin American center for German espionage. Still, it was important to keep abreast of Vargas. A year earlier, when he had finally renounced Brazilian neutrality and signed on with the Allies,

Vargas had simultaneously sent word to the German ambassador that he wanted to be on good terms with Hitler.

In January, Berg went down to São Paulo, where local lawyers and professors told him that "the naziphile element still exists high up in Brazilian military circles." Back in Rio on January 17, an ex-consul from the Brazilian embassy in Italy passed along word that Mussolini was in poor health. Three days later, Arturo da Silva Bernardes, a former president of Brazil, told Berg that Brazil was no longer a democracy. Although this hardly constituted a revelation, Berg urged him to write about Vargas for the *Atlantic Monthly*. February took him to Recife, where he heard about assassination plots within the Brazilian military ranks. Describing his various meetings to Rockefeller, Berg noted, "In all my visits and talks with the above Brazilians I made clear that although I was making an official trip my status with them was unofficial and off the record." By poking around in this way, Berg had turned his soft propaganda assignment into a secret operation and delicately imposed himself on a new profession. He was acting, more or less, as a spy.

Berg filed this Brazil portion of his journal under separate, "confidential and secret" cover from the rest of his reports, which resumed on February 9. It seems unlikely at this or any other time on his trip that he also sent a report to the FBI, but if he did, it remains classified.

Berg returned to Natal on February 11, for President Roosevelt's visit, as well as for consultations with doctors about prostitution. At 3:30 A.M. on Valentine's Day he was awake to watch the A-20 bombers load up and take off for sorties in Asia and the Middle East. Gazing at the pilots and bombardiers, Berg noticed "among these boys some anxiety, even fear, but on the whole, magnificent courage." On February 17, he was back in the U.S.

At the Commerce Building, Berg prepared his reports for Rockefeller. He had finished the Brazil section by February

27, and the rest was complete a month later. In all, it totaled close to sixty single-spaced typed pages. "At times," admitted Berg in the cover letter accompanying the report, "I felt obliged to enter into details that may seem excessive." That was putting it delicately, but Rockefeller didn't chastise him. Instead, four days after he received Berg's materials, the coordinator wrote him a letter of praise, thanking him "for all you've done. . . . Only someone with your experience and knowledge of international as well as human problems could have handled this situation with such tact and effectiveness." Clark, however, was responsible for Berg's official evaluation, and he was a more rigorous critic. On a scale of one to nine, he gave Berg a five. In almost every performance category Berg received "good" marks, although Clark said that Berg's "effectiveness in meeting and dealing with others," his "initiative," and his "physical fitness for the work" were all "outstanding." This was fair. If Latin America had proved anything about Berg, it was that he was willing to go anywhere, that it was as easy for him to befriend people in foreign places as it had been in Boston or Washington, and that when it came time to leave, he was gone without warning or remorse.

Now, however, he was in Washington with no job. Certainly, he didn't want to work for Rockefeller anymore. Not many ambitious people did. Clark, writing to his brother-in-law, explained, "We are all uncomfortable, perversely, over the growing realization that Latin America becomes more and more of a back eddy as the war moves east and north . . . there is a glaring headline that papas are to be drafted and I think I shall not accept a deferment unless someone can think up something a little more significant for me to do." The logical alternative was to move from the Commerce Building to Q Building, where the OSS offices were, and that is what Clark, and an OIAA employee named Charles O'Neill and Berg all did. "Berg left for the same reason Clark and I did," says O'Neill. "There wasn't the fear there had been in the first year or two. There was no more alarm in Peru that the Japanese were coming.

We thought there was more necessary work elsewhere. The OSS was looking for people like us. They knew something of what we were doing and they contacted us."

In June, Berg resigned from the OIAA. He had spoken with an OSS colonel named Ellery Huntington, who thought Berg was excellent OSS material. Huntington was a lawyer who had known of Berg since his days as a Princeton shortstop, and had worked with him at Satterlee and Canfield. These were just the sort of clubby, rep-tie connections that the OSS thrived upon. The hiring process would take a while, but Berg could wait. He had something else on his mind. Her name was Estella Huni, and he was in love with her.

OR MAYBE HE wasn't. What was clear, she was beautiful. Tall and slender with delicate bones, wavy brown hair, a pale complexion, and large brown eyes, at times she resembled Paulette Goddard's gamine in Chaplin's *Modern Times.* Only in appearance, however, because Estella was no waif, but a sophisticated and challenging woman.

Estella's father owned the New Haven School of Music and was an opera baritone, her mother played the violin, and Estella also became a musician, a pianist. In 1926, at sixteen, she left New Haven for England, where she had won a scholarship to attend the elite Matthay School of Pianoforte in London. In 1934, she was alone in New York. Her parents had both died, and Estella had sold the music school. When Berg met her, probably in the mid-1930s, she was supporting herself by giving recitals and teaching piano.

He must have seen quickly that this was a woman who could keep up with him. Years later, Estella would be selected as a contestant for the television quiz show "21," but feeling too shy to compete against Charles Van Doren, she withdrew her name. She read as much as Berg did, everything from Greek mythology to the *New Yorker,* and spoke Italian, German, and excellent French. French was Berg's best foreign language too, and presumably they spoke it together, since she signed her love letters to him "Etoile." Even better, one of her hobbies was etymology. Berg's heart must have leapt the first time he visited her apartment and saw her huge, well-thumbed dictionary resting on its brass stand.

Estella was witty, enthusiastic about everything from opera to haute cuisine to puns to tennis to President Roosevelt to riding to newsreels, and full of fun when around people who could keep up with her. Dull company, on the other hand, made her impatient and sulky. Her ambition was to be an actress, and though she never attempted to be one, she was suitably vain, she lied about her age, and she had social pretensions. Like Berg, she was photogenic and enjoyed being photographed. Although she wasn't wealthy, she lived on East Sixty-sixth Street, on the posh Upper East Side of Manhattan. A snug apartment at the best possible address was more important to her than spacious quarters in a more modest neighborhood. And one more thing, she was Christian.

London had made an Anglophile of Estella Huni, and back in New York she moved in a patrician circle where many of her friends were English aristocrats. But Moe Berg was better company. They were two vivacious, intelligent people, absorbed in the world around them, and they had a lot of fun together. Berg loved to be out on the town in New York, and so did Estella. They went to nightclubs—to Toots Shor's, and Billy Rose's Diamond Horseshoe for the glittering floor shows. During the baseball season she visited him at the Parker House in Boston, and when the Red Sox had a day off, they were off to Plymouth Rock and then to Cape Cod where, on the beach, Berg wore black bathing trunks with a white undershirt.

Berg wasn't much interested in music and heard Estella perform only once, but she succeeded in introducing him to opera, urging him to read the librettos, and he grew to like Puccini's *Madama Butterfly*. She also taught him to play the piano a little. While she knew Berg, Estella followed baseball and became a lifelong Red Sox fan. Berg could be harsh about anything from overpacking to using poor grammar, and sometimes his impatience spilled over and he yelled at her. This was something. Moe Berg, who never lost control of his emotions, yelling. Another time he wrote her a poem, "To the Girl of East 66th Street."

Berg didn't introduce Estella to a great many people. One evening, when they unexpectedly encountered a group of ballplayers at Lüchow's Restaurant, Berg told them that she was a friend visiting from Romania, a countess who couldn't speak a word of English. So for the next hour, Estella didn't say anything to Berg in English. She thought it a wonderful lark. This sort of behavior was to be expected from Berg anyway, but there was a practical explanation for his reserve about Estella and hers about him. They were living together out of wedlock, which wasn't something respectable people flaunted in 1940. The situation appalled Bernard, who refused to meet her, but Rose, Sam, and Ethel all did. Ethel was jealous that Moe bought Estella gifts, something he rarely did for his family. Sam fell for her completely. He referred to his brother's lover as "the most beautiful and cultivated and intelligent girl I have ever known."

In early May 1944, Berg left her for the war in Europe. She started off game, declaring that although he was "difficult to get along without," she wanted him "over there as I know how much it means to you." Three weeks after that, she wrote, "There is absolutely no need for you to worry or be concerned about me." In mid-June she was thrilled when a package from London arrived, filled with "such a fascinating mélange of papers, rags, cuttings and programmes," as well as two grammar books. His communications soon grew sparse, and her resolve wavered. She hinted that she was lonely, and then, perhaps trying to stir up a bit of proprietary jealousy, told him, "I look best I have in two years." When he did write, she was "a different girl." But more often, when the postman came, there was a letter from Sam, stationed in the Pacific, and silence from Berg. Berg used the distance to create distance.

Many couples survived the war, but Moe Berg and Estella Huni did not. Eventually, she sensed what was up and married an engineer, a navy officer she met in New York. Years later she said she was relieved, that Berg had been a physical addiction and ultimately would have been impossible to live with.

Estella Huni came closer than anyone to putting an ear to Moe Berg's soul. After her marriage, she settled in New Jersey, where she raised a family. She died in 1992. Aside from one brief, awkward afternoon when Berg called on Estella and her husband, it can't be said whether Estella ever saw Berg again or even how much she thought about him. She never spoke about him, even to her children, who describe their mother as an extremely secretive woman who was a mystery to them. "In many ways," says Christine Curtis, Estella's daughter, "my mother was as elusive as Mr. Berg."

CHAPTER 10

Remus Heads
for Rome

It is uncertain whether William Donovan had a direct hand in making an OSS man of Moe Berg, but without question Donovan liked unusual, talented people. He was one himself. At the Argonne forest, during his World War I days as an infantry colonel leading New York's "Fighting Irish" 69th Regiment, his response to an order to retreat under brutal enemy fire was to command a charge. "What's the matter with you?" he hectored his terrified troops. "Do you want to live forever?" They charged. "You wouldn't believe the appeal he had," says Ned Putzell, who was an OSS executive director. "Donovan's the only guy I've ever met who had physical and intellectual daring."

Donovan was a lawyer, and in peacetime his professional integrity was the stuff of pulp allegory. During prohibition in 1923, as the U.S. district attorney for western New York, he sent his burly enforcers through the front door of the oak-

▼

paneled Saturn Club in Buffalo, where some of his law partners and in-laws, not to mention Donovan himself, were prominent members. But it was at war, where the rules grew vague and the result was what mattered, that Donovan flourished.

Donovan didn't simply create the OSS, he set the tone for the organization and infused it with his personality. He wanted the OSS to be a place, as he wrote President Roosevelt, for "calculatingly reckless" young men of "disciplined daring." Donovan admired gusto and whimsy. "He was a rather small, rumpled man with pale yet piercing blue eyes," remembers Julia Child, who, before she became a famous chef, subsisted on boiled water buffalo as an OSS file clerk in China. "He could read an entire document by looking at it. He was intensely personal, so everybody just loved him." The OSS was created with the country headed for war, leaving no time for Donovan to assemble it meticulously. "He didn't really try to organize it, he just authorized it," wrote Stanley Lovell, a chemist whom Donovan hired as his director of research and development. Lovell's experience was fairly representative. "For my activities [Donovan] laid out the objectives in the broadest possible terms and left me wholly free to develop unorthodox weapons and stratagems." Donovan gave Lovell a well-guarded building and a generous budget and left him on his own to make devices. Soon enough Lovell was designing bombs that looked like crustaceans, sacks of Chinese pancake mix filled with explosive batter, buttons and shoes with secret compartments, and a false documents plant staffed by some of the nation's most notorious forgers, who churned out ersatz Swiss passports and counterfeit Japanese yen.

In a sense, Donovan's OSS was a bohemian organization filled with dazzling people who were handed assignments and told to make of them what they could. He hired "Circus King" Henry Ringling North; *Grapes of Wrath* director John Ford; assorted Vanderbilts, Du Ponts, Mellons, and Morgans, as well as members of Murder, Inc.; the bartender at the New York City Yale Club; professional wrestlers and leading ornithologists; John Birch; Tolstoy's grandson and Toscanini's daughter; sexy journalists; and professors of religion from small Midwestern colleges. "We had," says Geoffrey Jones, president of the Retired Veterans of the OSS, "all kinds of egomaniacs and crazies."

There were risks to constructing an organization in this headlong fashion. Washington panjandrums clung to their turf and could be waspish on the subject of the new adventure in town. "Oh so silly," they scoffed. "Oh so secret and oh so social." Some of the OSS gaffes *were* horrendous and, as it happens in war, men died because of them. But behind the lines, in places like Burma, France, Italy, and neutral Switzerland, OSS operatives and contacts also made important contributions to the Allied victory. Among the most effective of them was a man whose personal qualities came to represent all that was promising and doomed about the organization, the old Red Sox catcher Moe Berg.

"Donovan would have liked Moe Berg personally," says OSS veteran Monroe Karasik, "because he took delight in having people around him who were first class. He wanted the best." As the architect of an organization that thrived upon spontaneity, the OSS director embraced Berg's unpredictable ways. He could also empathize with Berg. Donovan was born poor, Irish, and Catholic, in the shadow of the grain elevators down by the docks in Buffalo's hardscrabble first ward. He first attended Niagara University and then moved on to Columbia, where he was the second-string quarterback behind Berg's future White Sox teammate and manager Eddie Collins. Donovan remained at Columbia for law school. He was too talented, too ambitious, and too charismatic for anyone to hold him back for long, but in 1929, political triage briefly succeeded. President Hoover had promised to make him his attorney general, and then, when it seemed to him that the nation couldn't bear a Catholic, he went back on his word. So Donovan and Berg had similar backgrounds and some of the same scars, too. There were plenty of differences; Donovan became the consummate insider, while Berg was the opposite. But they also shared one more important quality. Both men were fascinated by secrecy.

IN EARLY JUNE, the OSS deputy director of operations, Ellery Huntington, wrote a memo introducing Berg to the chief of the Special Operations Branch, Lieutenant Commander R. Davis Halliwell. "I can vouch for his capabilities," said Huntington. "He would make a good operations officer either here or in the field." Berg paid a visit to the OSS offices at Twenty-fifth and E streets and then, suddenly one day, he left Washington. His brother, Dr. Sam, was stationed with the Army Medical Corps in Stockton, California, and Berg telephoned him there to say he was coming out for a visit. Long-distance wartime travel was almost impossible for civilians, so when Moe arrived in Stockton, Dr. Sam asked him how he got there. Berg said that he'd come in an army plane. "What the hell are you doing in an army plane?" asked Dr. Sam. Berg put his finger to his lips. It was a baffling visit for Dr. Sam. Berg brought Chico Marx along for dinner one evening. Sam hadn't known that his brother socialized with the Marx brothers, but Berg wasn't explaining that, either.

When he returned to Washington in July, Berg checked into the Mayflower Hotel and filled out his OSS application. Such requests for information were generally fruitless with Berg. During his Red Sox years, when the publishers of *Who's Who in Sarasota* sent him a form, what Berg mailed back was either puckishly evasive, puerile, or in poor taste, depending upon how you felt about it. It most definitely was not informative. Beside "Full Name" Berg wrote "Mohammed Montaigne"; his "Profession" was "narcotics"; for "Birth Place" he wrote "Bed"; his "Wife's Name" was "Venus de Milo"; as "Names of Children" he included "Abortia and Miss Karridge"; and his "Winter and Summer Addresses" were simply the "Out of Town News Stand" (in Harvard Square). When it came time

Bernard Berg
at work in the
pharmacy.
(*Charles Owen
Collection*)

Rose Berg was beautiful and good-humored, and her children were
devoted to her. (*Charles Owen Collection*)

Before she became a respected Newark teacher, Ethel Berg was an aspiring actress. (*Courtesy of Elizabeth Shames*)

Little Moe.
"Send me to school like Sam and Eth."
(*Charles Owen Collection*)

Counselor at Camp Wah-Kee-Nah. "There isn't a boy who doesn't jump with glee to play ball with me." (*Courtesy of New York Public Library*)

At the Princeton sundial on graduation day, June 19, 1923. (*Charles Owen Collection*)

The best baseball player in Princeton history.
(*Courtesy of Princeton University*)

A semester at the Sorbonne. "I am the happiest one in the universe." (*Courtesy of New York Public Library*)

Chicago White Sox catcher. "I don't care how many of them damn degrees you got, they ain't never learned you to hit the curve." (*Charles Owen Collection*)

Rookie shortstop with the Brooklyn Dodgers.
(*Charles Owen Collection*)

A patient at Mercy Hospital. "And what would I do if I broke my leg?" (*Columbia University Law Library*)

A young lawyer with a white-shoe firm. "I have always considered the game only a means to an end." (*Associated Press/Wide World*)

中野五吉

Berg visited Japan twice. In 1932, he tutored young Japanese catchers and visited a geisha house with Ted Lyons. (*Charles Owen Collection*)

In 1934, he made clandestine films (*Charles Owen Collection*) and then traveled across Asia by train. (*Columbia University Law Library*)

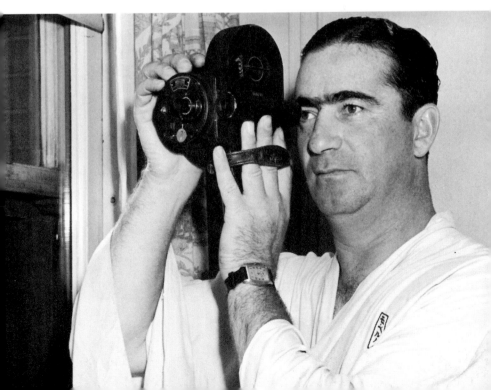

At spring training in Florida with "Black" Jack Wilson (*UPI/Bettmann*) and visiting the Franklin Institute's observatory in Philadelphia. "Isn't this wonderful. Work three hours a day, travel around the country, and get paid for it." (*Columbia University Law Library*)

The aging Red Sox catcher. "I've had a pretty fair time in lost country." (*UPI/Bettmann*)

"*He's saving it for his newsboy...*"

• The question of what ball players do in the winter falls into the same general classification as "What happens to your lap when you stand up?" But our John Kieran has given us a good tip.

For at least part of every day, winter and summer— says Mr. Kieran—Coach Moe Berg of the Red Sox reads The New York Times.

One day when the Red Sox were playing in Detroit, Berg's Times arrived late. And Manager Cronin was astonished during a hot third inning to find, ensconced in the team dugout, the boy who brought Moe's paper!

Moe Berg — ball player, lawyer, alumnus of three universities — is typical of Times readers in his feeling that nothing else can take the place of The Times . . . an attitude that advertisers wisely capitalize. For 22 years, The Times has published the largest share of newspaper advertising in New York City.

The New York Times, April 23, 1941.

Berg and Estella Huni.
"The most beautiful
and cultivated and
intelligent girl I have
ever known," said Sam
Berg. (*Paul Kahn*)

Visiting his brother Sam in California in 1943. "What the hell are you doing in an army plane?" (*Charles Owen Collection*)

Moe visits me a few days before departure for overseas.

On Heisenberg's trail. En route to Florence, Aldo Icardi dressed Berg in fatigues. (*Charles Owen Collection*)

Berg bicycling and skiing with Paul Scherrer.
(*Charles Owen Collection*)

Watching a baseball game in the Polo Grounds press box with Jerome Holtzman (at Berg's left) and (*Columbia University Law Library*) chatting in the Yankee Stadium press room with Casey Stengel (left) and General Groves. "You'd be at a game and he'd be behind you, you'd look up again and he'd be gone." (*Charles Owen Collection*)

The perfect spy. "There were a lot of strange people in OSS. He was certainly sui generis." (*Charles Owen Collection*)

Still portrait with newspapers. "I don't know where I'll be tomorrow." (*Charles Owen Collection*)

to list "Additional Data," he scribbled "Smyrna figs, disa &
data & nuts to you."

Joining the OSS was something he badly wanted to do,
however, and so here he was forthcoming, making it one of
the rare occasions where Moe Berg willingly divulged personal
information. As his home address, he listed the house Dr. Sam
had purchased at 156 Roseville Avenue, Newark, instead of
the apartment he'd grown up in on South Thirteenth Street,
where Ethel still lived with their mother. Most of the time, of
course, Moe stayed at Estella's when he was in the New York
area. His character references included an old Princeton professor, Christian Gauss, and Eddie Collins, then the Red Sox
vice-president. Berg was much closer to Boston owner Tom
Yawkey and to Joe Cronin, still the manager, but Collins had
played football with Donovan. Rockefeller was also a character
reference, while Enrique López-Herrarte, Ted Lyons, and Milton Kahn, Berg's partner in the Novelart stationery business,
were named as friends. In the otherwise accurate educational
history he supplied, Berg failed to list the time he'd spent at
New York University in 1919–20, before transferring to Princeton, and he claimed to have graduated from Columbia in 1928,
when the truth was it was two years later.

The language section of the OSS application clears some of
the ambiguity surrounding the number of languages Berg
could speak, and how well. Berg delighted in the conspicuous
possession of foreign newspapers, and likewise took every opportunity to break off conversations with English-speaking
friends for brief, animated chats with foreign-born taxi drivers,
toll collectors, busboys, and tourists. Yet, when in the company
of his friend Sam Goudsmit's wife, Irene, a native German
speaker, or OSS major Max Corvo, who spoke fluent Italian,
Berg was more reticent. If they proposed speaking in German
or Italian, he always demurred. With French he was more
agreeable. "He had a nice accent," says Ned Putzell, who spoke
it with Berg.

On the OSS form, Berg lists his French, Spanish, and Por-

▼

tuguese as "fair," and his Italian, German, and Japanese as "slight." When he was speaking it regularly, Berg's French was good or excellent, but he had not had much occasion to use it since 1923, so "fair" was the best available substitute for "rusty." During the six months he was in Latin America, his Spanish and Portuguese undoubtedly improved, and spending the summer of 1944 in Italy would be a boon to his Italian. Berg knew varying amounts of Hebrew, Yiddish, Latin, Greek, and Sanskrit, but he left them off his OSS application. This was probably because he thought they were irrelevant to OSS work and, with Yiddish and Hebrew, he may have thought that being Jewish might make him a less desirable candidate to the OSS. There should be no question that Berg was a gifted student of languages. During his life he also took a passing interest in, among other languages, Russian, Polish, Mandarin Chinese, Arabic, Old High German, and Bulgarian. Real fluency in a foreign language, however, is something else, and although Berg didn't object to sportswriters ascribing it to him, he would not do so himself. Sam Goudsmit, a native of Holland, who spoke fluent English, Dutch, and German, good French, and some Italian, met Berg just after the war and knew him for many years. Goudsmit says Berg was "a linguist, certainly, but his command of the spoken foreign languages was not as fluent as reported. He listened and understood, but said little in any language. When he spoke it was important to pay attention."

Berg submitted the application to Halliwell on July 16, showed him the letter of congratulations Rockefeller had written him back in April, and was vague and apologetic about his trip to California. It was a special mission for the White House, he explained. He was sorry, he couldn't elaborate. The next day Halliwell requested an expedited security check on Berg, appending to it a note that explained his "belief that we should get our hands on him as fast as possible." He also wrote to Huntington: "It is evident from Berg's conversation with me that his mission for the White House indicated that considerable responsibility had been placed upon him and that he was entrusted with a most confidential mission since he was last in this office." There is still no explanation for this mission, but in one respect, at least, its effectiveness is undeniable. It impressed Halliwell, which is exactly what Berg intended. The OSS snapped him up.

By August 2, Berg had agreed to a meager annual salary of $3,800 and had taken the oath of office, swearing that he'd keep all information he obtained undisclosed unless authorized. After pushing him through the hiring process with such celerity, nobody could think of what to do with him. Finally, it was "believed best . . . to keep Berg's assignment somewhat amorphous."

The first OSS agents were trained by the British in England, but by the time Berg joined on, Donovan had established his own camps in Maryland's Catoctin Mountains, not far from President Roosevelt's retreat, Shangri-La, and at other locations outside Washington. Apprentice spies were tutored in silent killing, safecracking, bridge blowing, and lock picking. They learned codes, ciphers, and how to install listening devices; they were taught hand-to-hand combat by Major Don Fairbairn, the former chief of the Shanghai police. Fairbairn was grey-haired and well into middle age at this point, but he was still spry as a terrier as he passed along the particulars of gouging out a man's eyes with a knife, shooting to kill, and using judo to disarm knife-wielding attackers. Recruits were sometimes dumped miles from camp, handed a compass, and told to return without talking to anyone. There were stress interviews, construction problems—moving a range finder across a swollen river was one—and also a terrifying OSS fun house replete with dank, narrow passageways, sudden drops, and a surprise meeting with a papier-mâché Hitler, whom the OSS men were supposed to shoot in the head on sight. This capture-the-flag approach to espionage training largely left it

▼

to the recruits to study what they thought might be helpful, and some men responded by spending their time in Maryland preparing for war by reading mystery novels.

It's not certain how much instruction Berg received, but he did take the final training test, which was to slip inside a heavily guarded American defense plant and come away with classified information. One OSS man forged a letter of introduction as an engineer, with FDR's confidant Harry Hopkins's signature on it, filled out a job application at a factory that made bomb sights, was given a tour, and walked out at the end of the day with a bomb sight in his pocket. Berg wasn't so fortunate. A forged piece of White House stationery got him into the Glenn Martin aircraft factory, where he aroused suspicions and was confronted. When Berg revealed who he was and what he was doing, the incident caused a mild scandal in Washington, where there was much concern that the OSS would be used for surveillance of American citizens. The situation also didn't help refute the notion that the OSS was a bunch of bunglers. Perhaps because this supreme OSS test was more of a stunt than anything else, or possibly because Berg was, as Putzell says, "so valuable in other ways," Glenn Martin was treated as a peccadillo, and in September Berg was assigned to the Secret Intelligence (SI) branch of the OSS and given a place at the OSS Balkans desk.

In Washington, Berg followed the movements of Peter, the exiled teenage king of Yugoslavia, who had fled the country for England in 1941, and was now a student at Cambridge; he monitored intelligence reports from the Balkans, and reviewed mission proposals, such as an October plan to sabotage shipping on the Danube by arming Romanian agents with speedboats, bazookas, and Stanley Lovell's explosive shellfish. He was also responsible for looking out for the second-generation Slavic Americans and Slavic-born aspiring U.S. citizens whom the OSS had recruited and trained for missions to rival factions of the Slav resistance, led by the Serbian Chetnik nationalist General Draža Mihajlović and the Communist Croat Josip Broz, known as Tito. The fatality rates on these parachute drops were extremely high, and when one mission was repeatedly delayed, Berg found himself saddled with a group of terrified Slavs. He resorted to playing bursar, handing out beer money every night so the men could go off and distract themselves.

Finding himself tied to a desk, proctoring other people who were bound for hazardous missions, could not have satisfied Berg. He thrived upon motion. OSS travel orders were usually as easy to come by as war bonds, but through summer and into fall they eluded him.

Instead, he traveled the corridors of Q Building, feeling out his peers. During these tête-à-têtes, Berg was his usual self, ferreting as much as he could from the person he was talking with, while veiling himself in yards of gossamer wit and erudition. Berg treated Q Building like a Borgian villa, fixing everyone he met with quiet suspicion. "Be careful," he warned an OSS man he met later in Europe. "Many of our own people are not to be trusted."

Ballplayers might not have been aware of what Berg was doing, but here he was dealing with spies whose job was to notice, and some did. Not that they held it against him. The people Berg met in the OSS, like William Horrigan, were as enchanted by him as everyone else was. Berg had lunch or dinner a few times with Horrigan, but meals were all. "We weren't poker players," says Horrigan. "We didn't date, and the reason we didn't date was that Moe never had a date. He did for chrissakes, but he didn't with you or me. He did by himself. I don't know where the hell Moe was living."

Toward the end of the year there were plans to send Berg to Turkey, but before that could happen, Horrigan intervened. Horrigan was a New York lawyer who had become friends with Donovan when Donovan argued a case for him before the Supreme Court. Horrigan had been training agents in Algiers, but had recently been called back to Washington for a pressing assignment, a delicate job that would require a partner. "I didn't need a muscle-boy, a guy who could jump out of parachutes or take submarines," he says. "I needed a bright, competent fellow. They wanted me to see a bunch of people around the world. That's why I got Moe. I brought Moe in, and they were very happy with him. At that time, what they were talking about was the greatest mystery of life." It was also the greatest secret in the world. Who better to help guard it than a man who didn't trust his own brother?

JUST BEFORE CHRISTMAS in 1938, Otto Hahn, a German radiochemist, was experimenting with uranium by bombarding it with neutrons and getting results that were, as he wrote his collaborator, the Austrian physicist Lise Meitner, "fantastic." Delicate and soft-spoken, Meitner was also of Jewish descent, and she was in Sweden because of it. Earlier in the year she had slipped out of Germany by train, one step ahead of the Gestapo. Meitner could keep her emotions clasped as tight as the bun into which she wrapped her hair, but not now. She wrote Hahn back immediately to tell him that his "results are very amazing," and indeed they were. Hahn had discovered that the strange transformation of uranium atoms under neutron bombardment was fission. Meitner then explained that, as the nucleus of an atom fissions, it releases tremendous amounts of energy. Atomic physics at the time was an intimate community of scientists to whom the implications of Hahn's discovery were immediately apparent. Gazing out his Columbia University office window at the bustle of a New York City afternoon, the Italian physicist Enrico Fermi made a small cup of his hands. "A little bomb like that," he said, "and it would all disappear."

Hahn had not simply split the atom, he had divided physics. At least that is how the Hungarian physicist Leo Szilard saw it. Between 1933 and 1941, more than one hundred prominent scientists, including Szilard, Fermi, Emilio Segrè, Eugene Wigner, Edward Teller, and Hans Bethe, fled countries all over Europe for the United States. But others, including Hahn, Carl Friedrich von Weizsäcker, Fritz Houtermans, Paul Harteck, Max von Laue, and Werner Heisenberg, were still in Germany. Heisenberg, a short man of freckled, boyish mien, who played the piano beautifully, doted on his children, and kept photographs of scientific friends on his desk, was the greatest theoretical physicist in the world. Heisenberg had been offered several jobs in the U.S. during the 1930s, but always refused, saying "Germany needs me." Under Hitler, the Germany he knew had been contorted into something he hardly recognized. Yet, painful as that was for him, the ground was still German, and for Heisenberg that meant you were loyal to it.

To Szilard, Fermi, and the rest, Heisenberg's patriotism was troubling. Late in the summer of 1939 at a party at the University of Michigan, the Italian physicists Ugo Fano and Edoardo Amaldi watched Fermi and Heisenberg talking together off in a corner. "See Fermi, see Heisenberg, sitting in that corner," whispered Amaldi. "Everyone in this room expects a big war and the two of them to lead fission work on opposite sides, but nobody says!" German science had supplied Adolf Hitler with some of the most lethal and expensive military technology in world history, from tanks to submarines, which he had always thrust at Europe with enthusiasm. And as the Dutch-born physicist Sam Goudsmit put it, "In science, as everyone knew, the Germans were way ahead of everyone else." Heisenberg was the man physicists in the U.S. counted most likely to husband a successful atomic bomb project. Worse, they were sure he was well along in the process. Once he got wind of what an atomic bomb could do, Hitler would have left him no choice.

The refugee and American scientists did not, of course, share these concerns with their neighbors or discuss them with journalists. Instead, Szilard badgered Albert Einstein into addressing a confidential letter to President Roosevelt, informing him that the Kaiser Wilhelm Gesellschaft (Institute for Physics) in Berlin-Dahlem had been taken over by the military, and urging him to pour more funds into the incipient American atomic bomb program. Fritz Reiche, who left Germany in 1941 for a job at New York's New School for Social Research, carried a message from Houtermans, playing Cassandra, that said, "Heisenberg will not be able to withstand longer the pressure from the government to go very earnestly and seriously into the making of the bomb . . . they should accelerate if they have already begun the thing." Eugene Wigner heard about this and, says Arthur Wightman, the Princeton physicist, "he was scared silly."

Wigner wasn't alone. The Germans had conquered Czechoslovakia, the site of Europe's only uranium mines. They had Norway, too, and thus the heavy-water plant at Rjukan, where, in 1941, production was said to be increasing. (Heavy water slows down neutrons, encouraging fission in uranium 235, the pure form of uranium necessary for a chain reaction.) Physicists in the U.S. placed macabre bets upon when the Germans would finish. Certain the U.S. program was lagging, scientists in Chicago moved their families to the suburbs, since the city seemed a likely German target. A miasma of rueful calculation accompanied every advance by the atomic scientists working in universities scattered across the U.S. If we are here now, and Heisenberg had three years' head start, he must be . . . It was the stuff of thwarted sleep and tormented dreams. "I had many sleepless nights," the British physicist James Chadwick remembered in 1969. "But I did realize how very, very serious it could be. And I had [in 1941] to start taking sleeping pills. It was the only remedy." It was into this rarefied world of brilliant, sleepless men that William Horrigan ushered Moe Berg in late 1943.

In June 1942, the American bomb project became a military program, and in September it was taken over by Colonel Leslie

Groves. Groves was a tendentious man with a penchant for stuffing his pockets with chocolate turtles, and had dunes of flab at his waist to show for them. He didn't look like an agile organizer, but he was. Trained as an engineer, Groves had overseen the construction of the Pentagon. Now forty-six years old, he wanted to lead troops, not scientists building a fantasy weapon. When he accepted the assignment, Groves extracted a promotion to general out of the military, and during the next few months made even less effort than usual to curb his bilious humors. Still, the physicists came grudgingly to appreciate him. "I detested General Groves, but I admired him," says Philip Morrison, then a consultant at the Metallurgical Laboratory in Chicago. "A narrow, bigoted, stubborn, vain, tireless, resolute person."

It took Groves a while to come around on the physicists, too. For many of them, the impetus to engage in morbid work behind barbed wire fences in remote Los Alamos, New Mexico, was the fear of a German bomb. Groves seemed unconcerned. He and his scientific director, J. Robert Oppenheimer, concentrated on building their own bomb instead of worrying much about someone else's. It wasn't until the fall of 1943 that the Danish physicist Niels Bohr told British intelligence officers that Heisenberg had asked him whether it was moral for a physicist to build an atomic bomb. Bohr's inference from this was that Heisenberg's progress was already significant. Groves finally took note.

Secrecy was a fetish with Leslie Groves. When he invited twenty-eight-year-old Army Corps of Engineers Major Robert Furman to his office to discuss atomic intelligence, he removed from his safe a physics textbook and referred Furman to a section on atomic energy. "I told him, 'I already got this in college,' " says Furman. "That upset him. He thought it was a secret." Groves needn't have worried. In Furman, Groves, who habitually browbeat everyone from Szilard to *New York Times* editors to keep everything about the American atomic bomb mum, had hired a Manhattan Project intelligence aide for whom secrecy became such a consuming habit that, forty-five years after joining the Manhattan Project, when all of the atomic secrets were out, Furman still could not bring himself to talk about some of it. Furman was a civil engineer, who had worked for Groves during the construction of the Pentagon. He had no special knowledge of atomic science, but then, who did? "A very unusual time we were living through," he says. "The nuclear age was just breaking upon us. It was as if you were Wilbur Wright and hadn't yet flown."

IN JULY 1943, John Lansdale, a Texas-born lawyer working as Groves's army counterintelligence aide, felt he could not ignore information from British intelligence that the Germans were working on an atomic weapon in southern Germany. He devised a plan to send a military force to Europe, equipped with scientific expertise, to see what the Germans were doing. The ten-man Alsos Mission—made up of soldiers and of MIT, Cornell, and Bell Labs scientists—was designed as a multi-tiered scientific intelligence operation so that nobody, not even most of the men who were part of it, would know that its real objective was to learn about atomic weapons. Groves approved the Alsos Mission, although when he heard the name Lansdale had given it, he reacted with an irritation that went beyond even Groves's routinely truculent standards. "Alsos" is the Hellenic name for groves, and in his zeal for secrecy, the general could not abide the allusion. Still, to change the name would call attention to it, and so Alsos it was. Colonel Boris Pash, a White Russian by birth and a swaggering martinet by nature, was given command. In early 1944, Groves made his relationship with Lansdale permanent, hiring him away from the army as his security and intelligence chief. One day when the general idly asked Lansdale what he thought about kid-napping Werner Heisenberg, Lansdale was shocked. "I regarded that as an absurd thing to do," he says, "and I would have no part of it.

Trying to learn about Hitler's atomic bomb program without letting slip anything about theirs was a subtle task for Groves and Furman. Groves's intelligence policy was similar to that of a hunter who looses a pack of sturdy hounds on the same vague scent and waits to see which dog will scare up the fox. With one exception: the dogs all know about one another. A number of people helped Groves determine the extent of the German bomb program, but such was the general's passion for secrecy that he didn't always tell them about one another. Groves's reasoning was that he had a pressing need to know what Heisenberg was doing, he couldn't divulge much about what he *thought* Heisenberg was doing, and he certainly wasn't telling anyone what *he* was doing. Better, then, to supply a number of people with sketchy information and see what they came up with. After creating the Alsos Mission to track down Heisenberg, Groves approached Donovan, at the OSS, with the same task.

In late 1943, Horrigan and Berg were assigned to Project Larson, an OSS operation designed by OSS Chief of Special Projects John Shaheen, in which the stated purpose was to spirit Italian rocket and missile experts out of Italy by boat and bring them to the U.S. What most people at the OSS didn't know was that Larson was a subterfuge which had quietly been altered to accommodate Groves and Furman. Groves and Furman didn't care about missiles or rockets. They wanted the OSS to go to Italy and interview Italian physicists to see what they knew about Werner Heisenberg and Carl Friedrich von Weizsäcker. Larson, then, was largely a smokescreen, another of Groves's careful strokes to obscure his real objective, a project within the Larson project, filed under the name AZUSA.

Soon thereafter, on an early November evening, at 5:00 PM, Moe Berg was called into the office of Colonel Howard Dix.

▼

Major Furman—no affiliation announced to Berg—was there as well, watching silently while Dix handled the meeting. A New York patent lawyer and an engineer in peacetime, Dix ran the OSS Technical Section for Donovan, and all AZUSA files went directly to him. His large, somewhat oblong head was balding, and he wore spectacles. The combination gave him an owlish appearance, which was nicely complemented by his sober, businesslike demeanor. Nobody joined the OSS without some taste for intrigue, however, and Dix was no exception. In conversation he liked to speak in a personal patois, in which, for example, Moe Berg was known as "the Black-Haired Boy" and the Soviet Union was "the North Country." Here, with the Mysterious Major and the Black-Haired Boy on hand, Dix mustered a dramatic flourish appropriate to a most dramatic occasion. "They can take us at a second to midnight if they get this thing first," Dix told Berg. "Find out what they're doing, and we've got it won." With that, Dix ushered Berg into the company of those who were privy to the deepest secret of the war. Under Furman's gaze, Dix didn't explicitly say what that "thing" was, but Berg got the idea. "Most of the talk was cryptic," he wrote later in notes to himself. "But enough was said to reveal to Moe Berg his newest mission without spelling it out." Berg's job, as he understood it, was to go to Italy, talk with a series of scientists, most of them at the University of Rome, and try to learn from them where the German physicists were and what they were doing. Furman says that Berg was told "damn little" about the Manhattan Project, but he concedes, "You've got a good spy like Berg, a big organization like the OSS, they probably figured it out. We told people generally what to look for without telling them why. A guy like Berg could learn more than you wanted him to. He was their hot rod, one of their best."

He also still read the newspapers, which were filled that December with lurid speculation about the wonder weapons that Nazi propaganda was always touting. On December 22, the *Washington Post*'s Earnest K. Lindley mused that "the Berlin radio's reference to blowing up half the globe would seem, to a layman, to hint at progress in the release of atomic energy." Three New York papers, the *Daily News*, the *Herald-Tribune*, and the *World Telegram*, carried a United Press report out of Lisbon on December 31, which reported that the "latest travelers to arrive here from the Reich said today that Germany's long-vaunted 'secret weapon' is based upon the principle of energy released from split atoms." And in an article headlined "Can the Nazis Blow Up Half the Globe?" *Newsweek* magazine imagined a scene where a single, high-flying airplane dropped bombs that made an explosion "so tremendous and all-inclusive that in a fraction of a second the entire community had been wiped from the face of the earth." It was an exciting, frightening time, and Berg had real, urgent, and highly confidential responsibility. In his grave, furtive way, he was ecstatic.

And then everything paused. The Alsos Mission had departed for Italy in December. (Before Pash left, Groves told him that if the new German secret weapon were possessed even by a country like Uruguay, Uruguay could then dictate terms to the rest of the world.) Berg and Horrigan, assigned to do the same job as Pash, were scheduled to leave Washington that month as well, but their travel orders became hopelessly delayed. The American Fifth Army, under General Mark Clark, commanded the Italian theater, and was recalcitrant on the subject of permitting them entry. Weeks would turn into months as the OSS tried unsuccessfully to prod the approval out of the stonewalling Fifth Army.

At first, Berg used the impasse to good advantage, shuttling up to New York, where Estella lived, and to various libraries and offices where he was learning science as quickly as he could stuff it into his head. He read Max Born's *Experiment and Theory in Physics* and accounts of Chadwick's work with neutrons. He studied quantum theory and matrix mechanics, which led him to Heisenberg and his uncertainty principle.

▼

William Fowler, a Cal Tech, Nobel Prize–winning physicist who met Berg shortly after the war, says that Berg taught himself a great deal of physics. "I think Moe understood Heisenberg's uncertainty principle as well as I did," he says.

Among the people Berg consulted were several scientists at the U.S. Office of Scientific Research and Development, including its chief, Dr. Vannevar Bush, and an electronics expert named Eugene Fubini, who'd come to the U.S. from Italy in 1938. Bush gave him a glowing letter of introduction, a sign of how seriously the OSS mission was being taken. Fubini on the other hand gave him nothing. "He asked about atomic weapons," says Fubini. "He sure did. But I could not help him. I felt he was not a technically competent guy, but a person who tried hard to find the truth." Berg was briefed by rocket and guided missile specialists, and on Italy's Guidonia supersonic wind tunnel and its director, a young, gruff, and brilliant aerodynamics specialist named Antonio Ferri.

Toward the end of December, Berg took a train to Schenectady, N.Y., where he met with a General Electric physicist named Guy Suits. When he began a discussion, Berg liked to first take a man's measure during an exchange of what amounted to little more than innocuous banter. If after a while he felt he could trust the man, he laid out his mission and asked for advice. Suits seemed discreet, so Berg told him that he had decided that Switzerland was the best locus for personally investigating the German scientists. Switzerland was a neutral country, and the only place outside their own country where German scientists could attend scientific meetings, which they liked to do, not least because the schnapps, cheeses, and chocolates that were no longer available in Germany were still in ample supply in Zurich and Bern. Suits had received his doctorate in physics under Paul Scherrer, the head of the physics department at the Eidgenössische Technische Hochschule (ETH), the Federal Technical College in Zurich. Scherrer had been providing useful AZUSA information to Allen Dulles, the OSS Bern bureau chief, and it was Scherrer whom Berg had really come to talk about. Berg knew that Scherrer had friends in the German scientific community. Could he trust him with highly sensitive information? Suits said he thought he could. Berg asked Suits for a letter of introduction to Scherrer, and Suits obliged him.

Back in Washington, Berg and Horrigan, now known by their OSS code names of Romulus (Horrigan) and Remus (Berg), were filling their satchels as well as their heads. They requested two Kodak cameras, a movie camera, and a dozen pairs of women's nylon stockings. On their request form they said that these would be given to high-ranking Italian officials, but the situation smacks of intentions of another sort. Stockings were nearly impossible for European women to get during the war, something which would not have escaped a sometime gallant like Moe Berg.

The New Year arrived with matters very much unchanged. Pash and the Alsos scientists were gnawing their fingernails in a fancy Naples hotel, waiting for the Fifth Army to liberate Rome; Berg and Horrigan were stranded in Washington, waiting for the Fifth Army to liberate them; and Groves was pacing back and forth in his offices in Los Alamos, Oak Ridge, Hanford, and Washington. British intelligence had by this time concluded that there was no German bomb project and had sent Groves a lengthy report saying so, but Groves and Furman weren't buying it. "In this conclusion it is felt the British are skating rather thin" was the acid American comment scrawled on the bottom of the report. At a meeting in Chicago with Morrison, Luis Alvarez, and other scientists on the morning of January 2, Furman sat listening and worrying about the succession of ominous possibilities that came flying across the conference table. The Germans were increasing heavy-water production; Niels Bohr had been told that Heisenberg had built a chain-reacting pile in 1941; it might be possible to build a bomb without a huge industrial effort, using teams of skilled artisans instead. The meeting went on like this until deep into the afternoon.

Four days later, Hitler's propaganda minister, Joseph Goebbels, announced that teams of German chemists and physicists were working at a feverish pace in underground laboratories to complete "the uranium torpedo." Furman's feeling was that it was a 10 percent chance that the Germans were doing something. Maybe the British could take such a chance, but he was not ready to. He had several hundred nervous scientists working at a feverish pace in New Mexico who weren't convinced. How could he be? Besides, the last anybody had heard from Heisenberg was that he was reported to have said that he was at work on a bomb.

IN LATE JANUARY, William Horrigan was transferred to Burma to set up an invasion for Lord Mountbatten, leaving Berg to work in the way he felt most comfortable—alone. Not that he was going anywhere. The month passed with more failed appeals to the Fifth Army and the news that the Anzio Beach landing had been botched. It would take months now to get to Rome.

Boris Pash knew all about such delays. By early March his Alsos Mission was back in Washington. He had spent weeks waiting for the OSS to whisk them at night by submarine from a desolate shoal near Rome for delivery to the Alsos scientific specialists in Naples. It never happened, and the beachcomber's sack full of explanations and requests for patience from the OSS in Italy left Pash emptyhanded and caterwauling with irritation.

Elsewhere, there was at least some good news. Swarms of American B-17 Flying Fortress bombers disabled the Norwegian heavy-water plant at Rjukan. Then, when the Germans attempted to salvage the stock of partially purified heavy water by smuggling it out of Rjukan in the bottom of a ferryboat, Norwegian saboteurs blew out the boat's hull with plastic explosive, plunging the heavy water—thirty-nine drums—to the bottom of an icy lake. This was not all. From Switzerland came word that Heisenberg would be speaking in Zurich at some point that year.

Months of waiting in Washington were getting to Berg. Now he really did possess government secrets, and he began to take extraordinary measures to protect them. For some reason, he had developed a powerful dislike for the head of the Larson project, John Shaheen. Shaheen's and Howard Dix's offices at Q Building were situated in such a way that you could look from one into the other. Berg visited Dix frequently, and when he did, he'd crouch down low so Shaheen couldn't see him, sometimes even hiding under the desk. He was adamant; Shaheen must know nothing about him. In March, Shaheen filled out an efficiency report on Berg, giving him the highest possible rating in all twenty-seven categories, but Berg knew better. Shaheen was not to be trusted. By now there were several people at the OSS whom Berg regarded as enemies, but he wanted even his friends, like Margaret Feldman, to keep their distance from him. Feldman, who worked as an OSS liaison to the State Department, learned to walk right past Berg in public without showing any recognition. "Moe was a guy with all sorts of turmoil going on inside him" was Earl Brodie's impression. One more concern with Berg was his finances. He'd never been particularly careful about money, and now the combination of the repeated delays in obtaining his overseas travel permission and his expensive tastes meant he was piling up quite a tab at the Mayflower Hotel in Washington.

And then, when all seemed vexing and fruitless, the travel orders were finally approved. Before Berg left, Furman wanted to see him. This time, it was Berg's turn to listen. Furman was blunt and efficient, and Berg found it easy to organize a running account of the meeting into six sections, which he set down on a pad in his cramped, spidery script and labeled "FUR-MAN/SECRET." Furman wanted to know which German and Italian scientists were alive, where they were located, and what their travel plans were. Berg was to learn what he could about German secret weapons, but he was never to breathe the words "radioactive" or "atomic bomb." Dutifully, Berg wrote "TA-BOO" beside each word. He was always to be on the lookout for recently constructed industrial complexes, and if he found one, he should be ready to provide diagrams of its antiaircraft defenses. In February, the Allies had bombed the Kaiser Wilhelm Gesellschaft in Berlin-Dahlem, because Heisenberg's laboratory was there, and Furman wanted an account of the damage and he wanted especially to know if there were any casualties beyond test tubes. (Furman was hoping to kill people.) Last, he requested a status report on the supply of rare metals in countries throughout Europe. Berg's notes don't say so, but it's likely that at this meeting Furman supplied him with the list he carried with him to Europe of German and Italian scientists, a spy's dossier, which had been annotated with comments ranging from age and home address to political affiliation. Heisenberg, for example, was described as a forty-two-year-old Protestant who was "pro-German but anti-Nazi." Among the notations Berg made on his copy were numbers ranking the various scientists in order of importance. Among the Italian scientists, he placed a large "1" beside Edoardo Amaldi, a thirty-five-year-old anti-Fascist who "May be in touch with Germans."

On May 4, dressed in black, white, and gray, with $2,000 in OSS travel funds in one pocket and a .45 pistol in the other, Berg reported to a military airplane hangar outside Washington and boarded a plane for Europe. The travel orders permitted him passage to London, Portugal, Algiers, and Italy, and were signed by Donovan himself. The general couldn't usually be bothered to sign travel orders, but this was no usual mission.

▼

CHAPTER 11

A Perfect Spy

War meant upheaval for many people, but not for Moe Berg. Right down to his black necktie, he did not alter himself. The chaos around him did not change the rhythms of his life. He remained a quiet traveler, whose days were still packed full of mysterious interludes with people who saw him just once and never forgot him.

Boarding the airplane on May 4, 1944, for the long flight from Washington to Newfoundland to Scotland to London, he settled into a seat beside one occupied by George Shine, a major assigned to join Army General Omar Bradley's staff. As Shine told Thomas Powers many years later, he was soon curious. Not only was Berg wearing his accustomed black, gray, and white mufti in a plane filled with military men dressed in olive drab, but not long after takeoff a pistol slipped out of his pocket and fell into Shine's lap. Berg looked at his neighbor sheepishly. "I'm inept at carrying a gun," he said. Shine recommended that Berg stash the pistol inside the belt at his waist. No luck; soon enough the gun was loose again. And again. Finally, Shine offered to stow Berg's gun in his bag, and Berg, who apparently had been supplied with a gun but not with a bag or holster, accepted. Berg then shortened the long day of flying for Shine by regaling him with stories of his travels in Japan and Russia. When they got to London, Shine gave Berg back the gun and told him where he'd be staying.

Berg checked into Claridge's Hotel and ate a meal of sallow vegetables accompanied by one small morsel of beef. This wouldn't do. The next day found him beside Shine again, dining as Shine's guest in hearty style at the American officer's mess. Berg returned the favor by taking Shine to a restaurant—Estella had suggested several from her days at the Matthay School—and choosing their wine by château and year. Berg was in fine storytelling form during these dinners, and the two men talked for hours. They made a date to have lunch on May 9, but Berg asked that it be tentative and, in fact, he never appeared, so Shine ate alone. Berg had admitted that he was in the OSS, and had mumbled something about going to see Mark Clark by submarine, but Shine really had no idea of what Berg was doing, nor would he ever meet him again to ask.

Malcolm Muggeridge described the OSS men he saw in London as arriving "among us, these aspiring American spymasters, like innocent girls from a finishing school, anxious to learn the seasoned demi-mondaine ways of old practitioners," but if guns bewildered Berg, MI-6 and London did not. London was the headquarters of the European Theater of Operations for the U.S. Army, and Berg found no shortage of people to see there. On May 11, for instance, he met with a navy colonel named William Moore, with whom he discussed Toledo, the Allied intelligence code name for biological warfare. Moore told Berg that the British were so skittish on the subject of, say, being bombarded by disease-bearing rats that they "take the view that Toledo is never to be discussed." Berg shared some documents with Moore, who copied them, thanked Berg for his trouble, and sent them in to his superiors, claiming he'd found them himself.

More useful was H. P. "Bob" Robertson, professor of mathematical physics at Princeton, whom Guy Suits had encouraged Berg to look up when he got to England. In the U.S., Robertson had interviewed scientists for work on the Manhattan Project, and had been fully briefed. Now he was working outside London as Vannevar Bush's liaison with British scientific intelligence. As a young physicist in 1925, Robertson had gone to Germany for two years to work as a research fellow in Göttingen and Munich, where he met many of the scientists who now concerned Berg. Robertson dearly loved a party, and at Princeton in the mid-1930s he had hosted a lively one every Tuesday night for people at the Institute of Advanced Studies, which were attended by the likes of Niels Bohr, I. I. Rabi, Eugene Wigner, and Werner Heisenberg.

He and Berg hit it off immediately. Robertson was a jolly, irreverent soul who liked Ivy League football, difficult crossword puzzles—he raced through them—chess, Greek literature, Scotch—he drank and consumed it the way a ten-year-old boy does strawberry pop—ribald jokes, and outrageous clothing ensembles, such as black shirts with road-stripe yellow ties. Berg found his company infectious, and they had begun a promising friendship when Berg disappeared. Even the people at the OSS office at 70 Grosvenor Square had no idea where he was.

He resurfaced in late May, wearing a trench coat on an airplane bound from Casablanca to Algiers. Berg was seated on the aisle, and across from him was a tall young man wearing an 11th Airborne Division uniform. Geoffrey M. T. Jones, not an 11th Airborne man at all but an OSS major, thought Berg was a war correspondent. Then he saw Berg's OSS-issue wristwatch, identical to the one he himself was wearing. Jones made sure Berg got a look at his watch too, and as they walked off the plane, Berg said to him, "I'm Moe Berg. I'm supposed to go to the Aleti Hotel." That was the best hotel in Algiers, on the level of the Ritz in Paris. All the generals stayed at the Aleti. Jones, on the other hand, had a room at a fleabag hotel. He told this to Berg. "Why don't I come stay with you," said Berg, and to Jones's amazement, he did. The hotel had no restaurant, so the two men went across the street to a dingy café and drank muddy Algerian coffee. Berg told Jones he was on his way to Yugoslavia by submarine. "Would you like to come with me?" he asked. Jones's mission had been scrubbed, leaving him with no posting, so he said, "Sure."

On his own, Berg visited the OSS Algiers bureau, where he met the head of the French intelligence desk there, yet another patrician New York lawyer, named Henry Hyde. Berg didn't volunteer anything about where he was going, but Hyde had a pretty good idea. There were only two places U.S. military transport planes went from Algiers in June 1944, Cairo and southern Italy.

New orders, meanwhile, came through for Geoffrey Jones, sending him to the south of France to smuggle in equipment before the Normandy invasion. Jones was on his way, and he didn't see Berg again until after the war.

Back in Washington, the last Howard Dix had heard was that Berg was bound for Turkey. Istanbul was a valuable OSS listening post, but it is nowhere near Italy, and why Moe Berg was headed that way when he was preparing for important business in Rome, the meager OSS paper trail leaves unclear. A Sergeant E. G. Pothblum was convinced that Berg was in Istanbul, though, because he forwarded some books and dictionaries Berg had left in Washington to him there on May 12. On May 29, he fired off a cable for Berg in Istanbul, reminding him to send in his reports as quickly as possible.

The Germans had been falling back from Rome, and the city was at last liberated at the end of the afternoon of June 4. The OSS, screened out of so much of the war, was finally in on something crucial, and the whereabouts of the agent in charge were unknown. Dix was frantic. On June 5 an urgent cable from him arrived at the OSS offices in London, Cairo, and Algiers: "In the event that Berg has not taken action in Italy . . . he should leave immediately . . . he will be too late if he does not do so."

Berg may not, as Earl Brodie says, have felt he was "in anybody's control—he was in business for himself," but his assignment was always his guide. On June 1, he was not in Turkey at all, but at the OSS base in an old Caserta, Italy, castle, near Naples. Three days later he had crossed Italy by Jeep to Bari, on the Adriatic Sea, where, on the fifth, he was having dinner with Air Force General Nathan Twining and another general when word arrived from Rome that the city had been liberated. After Berg showed Twining his letter from Vannevar Bush and explained how important it was that he get to Rome, Twining gave him a plane back to Caserta. Then a command car sped Berg on a four-hour ride from Caserta to Rome. After the rubble-strewn cities he'd seen out the command car window en route, Rome seemed to him "a ray of sunshine, no sign of war."

On June 6, Berg checked into the Hotel Excelsior, a sumptuous accommodation not far from the Villa Borghese, and met with an OSS operative who knew his way around the city. That afternoon, Berg was led through streets crowded with euphoric Romans to 50 Via Parioli, a handsome home not far from the University of Rome physics institute on Via Panisperna. This was where the occupant of the chair in experimental physics, the man with a "1" marked beside his name on Berg's list of scientific contacts, Edoardo Amaldi, lived with his wife, Ginestra, and their children.

Berg was at least the second American to visit Amaldi that day. Boris Pash had already paid a call to Via Parioli. Pash's Alsos scientists had gone their separate ways back in the U.S., but with Mark Clark on the fringes of Rome, Pash had scurried back across the Atlantic on his own. For all that trouble, it was a brief conversation, and one that filled the colonel with rage. After accepting some food that Pash had brought for his children, Amaldi told him that he had never once heard from the OSS while Pash was in Naples that winter, which meant that all the OSS tales of woe and submarines were so much rotten fish. Pash did his best to keep his anger in check, instructed Amaldi that he was not to leave Rome, and departed.

Pash need not have worried that Amaldi was going anywhere. Amaldi was the only member of the famous Gruppo di Roma, University of Rome, physicists not to flee Fascist Italy during the war. Though he detested Mussolini, Amaldi had refused teaching offers in the U.S., remaining behind, he said, "to help Italy." The son of a University of Padua mathematics professor, Amaldi was a first-class experimental physicist who had worked closely with Fermi, studying the effects of bombarding the atomic nucleus with neutrons. Their collaboration had lasted until 1938, when Fermi left for the U.S. because Fascist racial laws threatened his Jewish wife, Laura. Once he was gone, so was the group, for the others had been dispersing as well. Emilio Segrè went to California, Bruno Pontecorvo to Paris, and Franco Rasetti to New York. As for Amaldi, he was drafted into the Italian army in 1939, for a year of African service. Then, after the university managed to coax his discharge, in 1941, Amaldi censored himself. At a clandestine meeting he attended with several other physicists, it was decided that they would do no more work with fission, because they saw only one way that it could lead, and they did not want to become involved with the construction of weapons. From September 1943 to February 1944, Amaldi was forced to abandon his family and go into hiding from the Germans. Eventually he would become known as the man who saved Italian physics. Now, early in June, with the city at long last liberated, weary as he was, he felt elated.

When a second unexpected knock came at her door that day, Ginestra Amaldi opened it to find another American standing outside, asking for her husband. Whereas the first had worn a military uniform, this one had on a white nylon shirt and a black tie. She invited him in and went to get

Edoardo. Amaldi usually rode a bicycle to work, but he had hidden it in a wardrobe during the German occupation. At the moment, he was in the process of removing and reassembling the bicycle, so Berg's first glimpse of this scientist he had waited so long to see found him covered with grease. Berg was brief. After presenting the Amaldis with chocolate, coffee, and greetings from Fermi, he got down to business. Amaldi had to go immediately to the United States. The physicist demurred, saying that he would be glad to talk with Berg in Rome.

That evening, Boris Pash says, he was drinking chianti at the Albergo Flora when a shaken Amaldi arrived at his table. Amaldi told Pash that he was sorry but, in spite of Pash's wishes, he was leaving Rome for Naples with an American army captain under orders directly from President Roosevelt. The captain, said Amaldi, was awaiting him in the lounge downstairs. Pash got up from his table, descended to the lounge, and there found a large man sprawled in an easy chair. Pash says he introduced himself to the "sloppy, smug" captain, who remained seated and said, "Colonel, looks like you and I are going to have to reach an understanding." Pash says he thought this "attitude was unfriendly and domineering," and felt compelled "to call him down."

"Attention!" barked Pash, by this point feeling not a little unfriendly and domineering himself. This was an understandable reaction for a man who felt he had been gulled by the OSS all winter and now sensed another "bluffer." This "big hulk" of a captain, according to Pash, was Moe Berg, who now clambered to his feet, protesting that he had to escort Amaldi to Naples. It was important. The Alsos Mission was waiting for him there. Pash, of course, *was* the Alsos Mission, which he made clear to Berg with a fine spray of invective that concluded, "You have no business in Rome. If I run across you again, I'll bring charges, and I can think of plenty. Now get out."

Strange things occur between spies, especially spies who, unknown to each other, have been given the same job. Yet elements of this skirmish strain belief. Berg might not have known about Pash, but Furman did, and while briefing Berg in Washington before he left for Europe, Furman would not have told Berg to take a precious source like Amaldi to Alsos in Naples when Alsos had cleared out long ago. At one point, there had been plans for the OSS to transport Amaldi to the U.S. from Caserta, so that might have been it, except that the OSS could have done that without Alsos. Then there is the matter of the captain's bars. To date, Berg had refused to wear a uniform, and had dressed in his usual clothes that afternoon when he visited the Amaldis. Even if he did intend to take Amaldi south for interrogation at the Naples OSS station, located outside the city in Caserta, he wouldn't have needed a captain's uniform to do so.

Something happened that night, however, because the next morning Berg was back at the Amaldi house, nonplussed. Amaldi wasn't home. He had gone to the university and, slave to schedules that Amaldi was, Berg was assured that he would not be back for lunch until 1:15. Berg could wait if he liked. Roman summer is sweltering, especially if you are in a white nylon shirt. Berg agreed to wait. With one of Amaldi's young sons, Ugo, watching, Ginestra ushered Berg into her husband's study and left him there. Berg sat at Amaldi's desk for two hours, staring out a small window at the family garden and trying his hand at smoking cigarettes. Berg's method of smoking was to take three or four puffs, stub the cigarette out, and light up a new one.

He had done this ten times when, promptly at 1:15, Edoardo Amaldi walked through the door. Amaldi delayed his lunch for no man, so his conversation with Berg was brief. Berg asked again if Amaldi would not get onto a plane and go to the U.S. to help the Allied war effort, and again Amaldi refused. Berg tried to insist, and Amaldi was firm. He would be glad to help, but in Rome. If Amaldi was perturbed about the imbroglio with Pash, he and Berg smoothed it out, and Berg left, relieved. Ginestra then went into the office, emptied Berg's ashtray, and presented the barely smoked cigarettes to Marco, the family porter. Tobacco was scarce in wartime Rome, and Marco was delighted. He unwound the cigarettes and put the tobacco in his pipe. It was those cigarettes that forever endeared Moe Berg to the Amaldi family.

A hearty meal helped too. Amaldi, like almost everyone else in Rome, had been eating very little, and was glad to accept Berg's offer of a large dinner. They went to eat at the Arturo Restaurant, on Via di Ripetta, where pasta and meat were eaten with gold forks. Berg spoke in English, probably, or French, but not in Italian, for he spoke no Italian with any of the Amaldis. His patient questioning during this dinner and in subsequent meetings gradually disclosed what Amaldi knew about the German bomb program, which was very little, but in its own way revealing.

Amaldi told Berg that he had not worked on atomic physics since 1941, because the University of Rome was not properly equipped for such experimentation. His opinion—he stressed it was only that—was that the Germans were working on an atomic bomb, but he thought that it would take them ten years to complete it. Amaldi's only contact during the war with the German scientific community had come in 1941, when Otto Hahn visited Rome for three days at the behest of the German Cultural Institute. Amaldi rated Hahn the most likely German to lead an atomic bomb construction project, and said he was also concerned about the chemist Walther Bothe. Although Heisenberg was a first-class theoretical physicist, he was not an experimental physicist, and hence seemed to Amaldi less capable of managing a large industrial project. Amaldi, Berg reported in his cable to Dix, "was somewhat surprised and delighted in our interest in him . . . he would be willing to go to the United States for a reasonable length of time on AZUSA." Evidently, gold forks and Marco's tobacco had helped change the professor's mind.

During these early days in June, Berg was also spending time with Gian Carlo Wick. Wick was a fine theoretical physicist. He got his probity from his mother, Barbara Allason, a Piedmontese journalist and translator of Goethe's *Faust*, who had been jailed in the late 1920s after a letter of support she wrote to the Neapolitan anti-Fascist intellectual Benedetto Croce fell into the wrong hands. As a teenager, when asked by a friend to ski across the French border and help carry anti-Fascist leaflets into Italy, Gian Carlo Wick had readily agreed. Later, while he was teaching at the University of California during the fever of red-baiting Senator Joe McCarthy's popularity in the 1950s, the university ordered its faculty to take a loyalty oath. Wick was no Communist, but such rituals reminded him of Mussolini, and he chose to resign rather than comply.

In 1931, Wick had gone to Germany to study physics. One of the professors he got to know there was Heisenberg. Heisenberg liked the young Italian theoretician—they shared a common interest in classical music—and treated him with an affection that Wick never forgot. Once a week, Heisenberg had invited Wick and other students to his home for spirited evenings of talk and Ping-Pong. Back in Italy, Wick had served as Fermi's personal assistant for five years. Still, it was Heisenberg who had first encouraged the young physicist's ideas about the magnetic moment of the neutron, by referring to them in one of his articles. Fermi was less demonstrative initially, but he thought highly of Wick too. When he left for Columbia in 1938, Fermi recommended Wick for his chair at the University of Rome.

Berg took Wick to a trattoria, perhaps the same at which he hosted Amaldi, and made an effort to get acquainted. At one point, Berg informed Wick that he was a Renaissance man, explaining that, among other things, he knew Latin well. Berg did know some Latin, but it was soon apparent to Wick that Wick knew much more. This was nobody for Berg to be engaging in a duel of scholarly one-upmanship, for Wick was a highly cultivated European intellectual. His first language was French, as a boy he had spoken in German with his Austrian grandmother, he read Greek and Latin, and he knew some Russian and Danish besides. For pleasure, he listened to Brahms or Verdi, read Huxley in English and Flaubert in French. Berg seemed superficial to Wick. He thought Berg postured to give the impression that he knew more than he did. But Berg was lucky. Wick was, says the physicist Jack Steinberger, "a very dear guy and kind, much more than most of us are." Wick wished to offend no one, especially a host, and so, while any number of physicists would have dispensed with a man who put on such airs, Wick answered Berg's questions in excellent English, giving no hint of annoyance.

Wick made it clear that he had done no atomic research, but that the subject, of course, interested him as a physicist. Wick had last seen Heisenberg in the summer of 1942, when he traveled to Munich and Berlin-Dahlem to deliver a series of lectures on cosmic rays. They had spent time together in Berlin and Munich. Wick had not broached the subject of politics—he didn't want to snoop—but his feeling then was that Heisenberg was anti-Nazi. At one point Heisenberg had said to him, "Must we wish for a victory of the Allies?" Wick felt that Heisenberg had said this rather pointedly. Still, Wick believed that Heisenberg's feelings for his country were too strong for him not to serve it. Wick told Berg that during his visit, the Germans had been extremely secretive on the subject of atomic energy, but Heisenberg's teacher, the German physicist Arnold Sommerfeld, had assured Wick that Heisenberg did not think it possible to build a reactor in the near future. Could anyone else? Wick mentioned Bothe, as Amaldi had, and Klaus Clusius.

Wick said he missed Heisenberg, but at least they had managed to keep in touch by letter. He said that a postcard from Heisenberg had come dated January 15, and he allowed Berg to see it. Berg's pulse must have quickened. A piece of mail from Heisenberg! He decided to neglect to return it, and when he and Wick parted that day, the postcard went with Berg.

Berg arranged, through the U.S. Naval Intelligence unit in

Rome, for a photostat of the filched postcard to be made and sent to Washington. He also translated it himself, and included excerpts in his June 17 cable to Howard Dix. The complete postcard is only one subdued paragraph. Heisenberg tells Wick that his Leipzig institute has been destroyed, but that the Kaiser Wilhelm Gesellschaft is "still standing." Heisenberg's Leipzig home and his father-in-law's home in Berlin-Dahlem are damaged, so he has moved his family to the Bavarian Alps, while he sleeps at the Harnack Haus in Berlin-Dahlem. "The time in which one could think calmly on physics is so far away," he writes at one point, "that it seems as if ages had passed in between."

And Wick knew more. He told Berg that Heisenberg had since left his temporary quarters in Berlin and was now living in the southern part of Germany. Could Wick be more specific? The scientist seemed flustered. Probably he was grappling with several things. He felt personal loyalty to Heisenberg and he was ashamed to be leaking information about him to people who were indifferent to Heisenberg's fate. There was also Wick's reluctance to believe that Heisenberg could be doing something as hideous as giving the bomb to the Fascists, an instinctive aversion to Berg, and his strong sympathy for the American's cause. Instead of sorting all this through, Wick compromised. He explained that Heisenberg had gone to "a woody region" of southern Germany, but he would say no more. In his cable, Berg supposed that Wick's reticence was because he was afraid of bringing "harm to Heisenberg."

By this time, the Fifth Army had taken over the Excelsior, and Berg had relocated to another plush hostelry, the Savoia, nearby on Via Ludovisi. He was in the heat of his first assignment, and if he was wondering how good a job he was doing, the answer came from Donovan himself, who passed through Rome with his entourage on the twenty-seventh. The general was in town for only twenty-four hours, but he made a point of seeing Berg and soaking him in a profusion of praise of the sort that was calculated to keep a man with Berg's weakness for hyperbole going all summer. Now Berg could report to his mother, "I am in the best of health, having a great time and very happy." Berg couldn't yet say exactly where Heisenberg was or what he was doing, but he had already provided Groves with the most useful atomic intelligence of the war thus far, and he had only just begun to look.

THE OLD RELIGIOUS city of Rome was sultry with summer and boisterous with gratitude in June 1944, and Moe Berg took full advantage. The OSS supplied him with a handsome black and white Alfa-Romeo sedan and Aldo Icardi, a twenty-three-year-old OSS major and former University of Pittsburgh cheerleader, to drive it for him. Five or six days a week they swept around the city together, from address to address. Leaving Icardi parked behind the wheel, Berg would get out of the car by himself, ring at the door, and disappear inside. Berg never told Icardi what he was doing, and Icardi, under orders not to pry, never asked.

Berg visited more than a dozen scientists during June and July, but none seemed to know about the Germans. He kept in touch with Amaldi, who permitted Berg to look through his files. It was probably there, between June 11 and 15, that Berg turned up an issue of the German physics journal *Zeitschrift Physiks* that contained an article on neutron diffusion. Somehow Berg got it into his head that Philip Morrison, back at the Met Lab in Chicago, needed to have a look at it, and instead of pouching the periodical off to Morrison, Berg chose to deliver it personally. Traveling to the U.S. from Italy was no puddle jump under the best circumstances, and now it required Berg, at minimum, to change planes in Casablanca or Algiers and again in Washington. Yet Morrison swears that one day in mid-June, direct from Rome, Berg appeared at his office, sweaty, fetid, and very tired, clutching the journal. Morrison recognized Berg's name. For years he'd been hearing about this "linguist and man of daring." Morrison took the magazine

▼

from Berg and saw immediately that he'd read it. *Zeitschrift Physiks* came to the Met Lab library every month through a Swiss distributor. Privately he thought the situation ludicrous, Berg not a little naive, and the deficiencies in his briefing appalling. But Morrison didn't inform Berg that his trip was pointless. Something in Berg's eyes told him not to do that. Instead, Morrison courteously thanked Berg for his trouble and sent him back to Icardi.

In Rome, it was more knocking on doors. Berg enthusiastically reported everything by triple-priority cable, and on June 20, a cable for him from Washington arrived, via Algiers, telling him to "radically condense" his reports if he wanted to keep such priority. Berg didn't listen. Throughout the war, his reports are consistently longer and more detailed than those sent in by most OSS operatives. Berg was curious and it showed. He was also fascinated with the human side of things, the tiny plots and subplots, the nuances and details that turn the quotidian into something revealing. When he could, he went back to his sources time and again, asking further questions, sorting, and embellishing until complicated matters seemed to him complete.

These sources were not only physicists. Throughout World War II the OSS was also soliciting word on an array of German and Italian weapons, rumored and real. In addition to his AZUSA files, from late June through July and into August Berg pouched lengthy reports on new German radar technology and radar jamming equipment, infra-red radar detectors, countermeasures against U.S. radar, the Luftwaffe's radio-directed missiles, and collaborations between German and Italian factories. He supplemented his reports by sending in logbooks, microfilm, blueprints, and diagrams that he'd sifted from Italian military files. If documents required translating, he did it himself. When he needed something explained, he consulted Italian scientists and engineers until he understood.

Berg's pouches went first to Stanley Lovell, the OSS Research and Development chief, and then were distributed by

Lovell to military development committees, including the National Defense Research Committee and the National Advisory Committee on Aeronautics. Soon notes of appreciation began arriving at the OSS, expressing enthusiastic thanks for the documents from Italy. Lovell and Donovan, in turn, both wrote to Berg in July, saluting him for "an outstanding job" of pouncing upon Rome. They meant it. By sending home the details of new Italian military technology, Berg was performing the primary task of an intelligence organization, which is to eliminate surprises. Lovell and Donovan were pleased because Berg was making the OSS look good.

Rome wasn't all work for Berg. Even war couldn't change some things, and so his mornings began with a walk to the Excelsior, where he read the newspapers, six Italian one-sheet dailies, French papers when they were available, *Stars and Stripes*, and the British military publication, *Union Jack*. Then he had breakfast at the Excelsior or back at the Savoia, and walked to the office he was using on Via Sicilia. At noon he might return to his hotel room for one of the two or three showers he took every day. After work, he explored.

If the days were warm, the evenings were cool that summer, and Berg took advantage, visiting the Forum and the Colosseum in the purplish Roman twilight. One night he took a boat ride on the Tiber. On another, he and Captain Max Corvo, the OSS Secret Intelligence chief for Italy, went to hear a symphony orchestra. Probably it was by himself that Berg visited what he referred to as "the old ghetto," the Jewish section of Rome. He met a group of Italian Jews there who told him stories of Catholics sheltering Jews behind fake walls in their homes during the German occupation. Berg refrained from commenting on the atrocities in his conversations, letters, and notebooks. His tone sounds as matter-of-fact describing the Jewish ghetto to his mother as it does when he tells her about his appointment to meet the Pope. If Berg had a strong emotional reaction to the Jewish genocide, he was true to form and kept it to himself.

   Sometimes during the day in Rome, instead of giving Icardi
an address, Berg would take the young major sightseeing. They
went to the Baths of Caracalla, to the Colosseum, and for a
leisurely stroll through the Vatican, with Berg pausing frequently to tilt back his head and read aloud the Latin inscriptions. Berg also liked to visit Roman cemeteries, where he
pointed out to Icardi the graves of famous poets, writers, and
soldiers. Robert Furman came to Rome on June 19, and Berg
treated his boss to the Vatican tour as well, guiding him
through the religious, artistic, and social history of Saint Peter's
in his distinctive grave, low-pitched nasal voice, which Furman
always found "a very sincere way of talking." With both Icardi
and Furman, Berg laughed as he noted the irony of a Jew
explaining the Catholics to a Christian. Furman left Rome for
Naples on the twenty-fifth, and after Donovan had come and
gone two days later, Berg had been through a rite of passage.
Not only had he submitted excellent reports; his superiors
had met his eyes, measured his reserve, and found that they
trusted him.

   In one of their conversations, Furman told Berg that, as
soon as possible, he was to investigate the Galileo Company,
an optical laboratory in Florence. The principles of lens as-
sembly depend on a system that is much like the one used to
compress fissionable material in the building of plutonium
bombs, and there was much concern that the Galileo Company
was in close contact with Germany. Furman also made sure
that Florence would be spared any further unseemly conflicts
between Berg and Pash by sending the Alsos Mission to
France.

   Florence was still German-held territory, but Corvo was
headed that way to inspect the front lines, and when Berg told
him how anxious he was to get to Galileo, Corvo gave him a
seat in his Jeep. As they drove north on July 3, an old Latium
road took them through Viterbo and Bolsena and into Acqua-
pendente, in time for lunch at the Hotel Milano. Some of the
hotel's rooms had been wrecked by bombs, and the restaurant

menu had suffered too. It read in full: barley soup and fried
eggs. After eating, they followed brightly clad Algerian troops
astride mules into Siena, just as the city was liberated. Corvo
photographed Berg at Siena's medieval central square, the Piazza del Palio, standing erect and uncomfortable in the mid-
afternoon heat, his suit jacket buttoned, his shoes covered with
dust. Beyond Siena, the German retreat had slowed, and the
Americans could advance no farther. Berg went back to Rome.

There he began the business of recruiting the serious young
Italian aeronautical engineer he'd been told about in Washington, Antonio Ferri. Until the German occupation, Ferri had
worked at the Italian aeronautical research center at Guidonia,
not far from Rome, where he had been in charge of the supersonic wind tunnel, which simulated high-speed flight conditions. Ferri's specialty was supersonic flow (air flowing at
speeds higher than Mach 1), which made him of great interest
to the National Advisory Committee on Aeronautics, where the
secret testing of high-speed aircraft was going poorly. NACA
wanted someone like Ferri to help usher in the jet age by
improving its wind tunnel in Langley, Virginia.

The problem was finding Ferri. Three days after the Germans occupied Rome on September 10, 1943, Ferri had gone
to Guidonia, bluffed his way inside, destroyed what equipment
he could, and departed with a trunk full of documents. Then,
one step ahead of the Germans, he fled 150 miles north, to a
tiny Apennine Mountain grain-farming village where his family owned land. After installing his wife, Renata, and their three
young children in his grandfather's farmhouse, Ferri disappeared into the mountains and, along with his brother, a history
professor, organized a group of local people, refugees, and
soldiers into an anti-Fascist partisan guerrilla band. They spent
the better part of the next year blowing up bridges and preying
upon German patrols. Rumors of the bandit scientist reached
the Germans, who came looking for Ferri in March. They
burned the farmhouse to the ground, but the Ferris had been
warned. Renata escaped with the children to an Adriatic fishing

▼

village, where she was told that her husband had been seen lying dead on a bridge. In July, word came from Antonio. He was not dead, but in liberated Rome, and eager to see his family.

In June, Berg had gone to the Ferri house in Rome, and found nobody there. He asked around, and was sent on to the home of Ferri's mother-in-law, with whom he left his name and address. When Ferri got back to Rome in July, he was glum about the state of the world and what science was doing to it. He told friends he was considering becoming a fireman. Ferri contacted Berg, though, and began to work with him, translating some of the documents he'd removed from Guidonia the year before.

On July 25, a cable arrived from Furman, urging Berg to get to Florence and investigate Galileo. But the British and the Russians were courting Ferri, and Berg was reluctant to let him out of his sight. He was also now dispatching information, culled from Italian military files, on radio-guided bombs, German radar, bomb sights, and aerial torpedoes. This was just the sort of intelligence that had won him approbation earlier in the month. Berg decided that it was more important that he stay where he was.

Ferri and Berg seem to have liked each other from the start. Berg further ingratiated himself by befriending the Ferri children, whom he taught to play baseball. "My children loved him," says Renata Ferri. "We hadn't heard of baseball. It was something those crazy GI's would do." On August 4, Berg sent a twelve-page report to Washington that included blueprints of the Guidonia wind tunnel, Ferri's experimental records, and flight test data. There were also accounts of what Ferri had seen during his visits to inspect German wind tunnels in 1938, 1940, and 1942. Berg concluded by reporting Ferri's willingness to work in the U.S.

During the next week, Berg received a flurry of technical questions from London and Washington, which he distributed among his Italian scientific and military contacts. On August

10, he sent word to Furman that he intended to fulfill his Florence mission, but seven days later he was still immersed in enemy tank communications. Then, at last, he headed north toward Florence.

It turned out he hadn't been wasting time after all. Florence still belonged to the Germans, which Berg learned when he got to the Allied camp in Poggibonsi, a small town near the city. There he was reunited with Icardi, who had left Rome toward the end of June, and was now in charge of small groups of Italian agents who conducted nighttime infiltrations behind the German lines, looking for fuel and ammunition dumps. While he waited for the city to fall, Berg stayed in a GI tent, played boccie with the soldiers—he was no better than anyone else—and indulged his near mania for cleanliness by rigging up a shower. He hung a five-gallon tin can from a trellis and punched small holes in the bottom. Then, two or three times a day, he filled the can with water and stood beneath it and scrubbed himself as though he were crawling with vermin.

The soldier's life briefly intrigued Berg. He asked Icardi about the evening infiltrations, and Icardi told him that the scouts traveled by dead reckoning, plotting their route by using the stars. Berg knew how to do that. One night he asked if he might go along, and Icardi said he could. He found Berg a uniform and some boots and off they went, through fields and over stone walls and fences. The evening was uneventful, but traveling across unbroken ground raised terrible blisters on Berg's flat, tender feet, and he never went again.

Berg seems to have liked wearing the uniform, though, and did so as long as he was in camp. The days of waiting grew tedious, and so Berg and Icardi went sightseeing. By August 20, the Allies were in Florence, which became the setting for one of the more fantastic of the many apocryphal Berg stories. Wearing a German officer's uniform, he is supposed to have entered a still-occupied Florence and slowly toured the Galileo factory, wielding a swagger stick and an arrogant sneer. This never happened. Groves would not have permitted such a risky

▼

stunt, and Berg knew it. Besides, with the city about to be liberated, there was no point in taking such chances. When Berg entered the sand-colored stone headquarters of the Galileo Company, a business suit was on his back and Icardi was at his side.

Shell and sniper fire was still audible from some sections of Florence as Berg, Corvo, and Icardi crossed the Ponte Vecchio and drove into the lovely old city of the Medicis. Florence was nearly without food and water, and as they checked into the Excelsior Hotel, the OSS men were troubled by the incongruity of a string quartet doggedly playing Boccherini and Bach at teatime in the hotel's main salon while most of the city scavenged for crusts.

Berg went straight to work. He spoke with the owner of the Galileo Company, Dr. Paolo Martinez, who told him that the company produced range finders, periscopes, searchlights, and telescopes, but nothing Groves would have found threatening. Furman's gaze meanwhile had shifted west. After Eisenhower's successful invasion of France and the subsequent drive toward the Seine, France and Switzerland were now accessible. Berg's long but meatless Galileo report arrived in Washington on the desks of men who were preoccupied by these new opportunities and impatient for Berg to attend to them.

On August 21, the same day Berg was transferred from the OSS Special Operations to the Technical Section, Howard Dix instructed him to hurry to Paris and find the French physicist Frédéric Joliot-Curie. Berg was also asked to interview a French pathologist said to have information on German bacteriological warfare. There were other plans brewing, to send him on to Stockholm, where Lise Meitner lived, and to Zurich. But there was a problem with getting Berg to do any of this. The OSS had lost track of him again. As far as Howard Dix knew, Berg might be anywhere between Rome and Algiers. He sent him urgent cables to both cities. But in fact, Berg was still in Florence.

By the time he got back to Rome, Stanley Lovell had received a formal request from a delighted National Advisory Committee on Aeronautics, requesting that Antonio Ferri be brought to the U.S. at once. Berg would not receive instructions to this effect until September 2. By this time, Boris Pash and the new Alsos scientific chief, Samuel Goudsmit, were in France, tracking Joliot-Curie; another OSS agent, Martin Chittick, was looking for the French pathologist; and Moe Berg, who loved Paris, had vexed his superiors by fiddling in Rome.

On September 6, Antonio Ferri signed a ninety-day contract for $2,500 and travel expenses to go to the U.S. Sixteen days later, an OSS agent named Peter Tompkins brought Ferri into the U.S. The scientist had no passport and very little English, but both came to him, as did his family, for he never left.

As for Moe Berg, on September 14 he reported to the OSS headquarters in London. It was the beginning of a rather calm three months.

A FEW DAYS after returning to London, Berg sat down to write his mother and sister a letter. Berg's feelings for his family were always the most affectionate when there was an ocean between them, and now he was solicitous, asking after everyone, including the neighbors, promising to write to Dr. Sam in the Pacific, begging them to pardon his "seeming negligence," and enclosing photographs of himself in Italy. "Have a wonderful job and enjoy doing it," he told them. "Rome," he said, "was beautiful. I worked hard, but enjoyed it." He closed by telling them where he was—"at Claridge's Hotel, London, living in luxury at the moment."

This was true. With nothing pressing him, he gamboled around London, sightseeing, foraging in old bookshops, and dropping in on people like Michael Burke, Robert Thompson, and Henry Ringling North at an OSS flat on Sloane Street. As life in cities being pelted by buzz bombs goes, theirs was tranquil. North liked to tease Berg about his clothes and noticed that Berg liked women, especially a young Finn named Helvi, whom Burke had introduced him to. Not that Burke or North ever felt particularly close to Berg. He seemed to them charming but remote. Burke thought Berg an ideal undercover agent, because he "possessed an unusual capacity to live alone contentedly for long periods of time."

In London, Berg was not so much solitary as hither and thither. During a dinner party outside London at Soames House, a mansion with sunken bathtubs and gold faucets made famous in John Galsworthy's *Forsyte Saga*, he met a blue-eyed captain named Clare Hall. Hall was working as an advisory liaison between scientists and the military. Berg had a car and driver that night, and he gave Hall a ride home to her apartment near Marble Arch. After that they began dating, going out to dinner or to an occasional play. Contrary to the testy British descriptions of Americans in London during the war —"overpaid, oversexed and over here"—between Berg and Hall matters remained chaste. At the end of each evening, Berg would peck her on the cheek and leave.

With H. P. Robertson, the talk, at least, was bawdy. Berg had resumed his informal physics seminar with the Princeton scientist, conversations that were inevitably spiced with Robertson's boisterous accounts of, say, an English butler who instructed overnight male guests to push a button on the wall if a mistress was wanted during the night. Hall, who also knew Robertson, says that "Moe was having the time of his life during the war."

The OSS European Headquarters was moved to Paris in September, and Berg went there at least once in early fall, but mostly he was in London. He saw Robert Furman in London when he passed through, as well as Groves's man in the United Kingdom, Major Horace "Tony" Calvert. Calvert valued the company of someone with whom he could speak freely about his work, and he and Berg strolled for hours, going into bookstores and talking. Berg was wearing a gray fedora to ward off the damp, musty chill of autumn in London, and Calvert thought he looked "the picture of what you'd think a spy would be."

Estella was also on Moe Berg's mind. He mailed her newspaper clippings and theater programs, and asked Howard Dix to forward his regards. Dix sent word back to Berg that he had told her that Berg was "behaving himself and having a good time, and that above all . . . doing an excellent job for us." Dix sensed Berg's need for flattery and encouragement, and played a version of the doting grand-uncle, stroking his black-haired boy, off in the thick of things, by providing him with modest services—passing along the baseball standings, the latest gossip from Q Building, and word from the National Advisory Committee on Aeronautics that Ferri was doing well at his work.

In 1942, MEMBERS of the Manhattan Project began floating the idea of abducting Werner Heisenberg from Germany. By the time the OSS became involved, these impolite suggestions became two kidnapping missions, where the unspoken option was murder. The first involved a burly former Mexican border patrolman named Carl Eifler. The second designated kidnapper was a man who had once caught for a living—Moe Berg. We know about these plans because old records suggest them, and old men talked about them. Carl Eifler did, and so did Moe Berg.

The first Heisenberg kidnapping proposal came from a pair of refugee scientists. Heisenberg had plans to give a lecture in Zurich in December 1942. "I have to confess that Victor Weiss-kopf and I thought of kidnapping Heisenberg at the latest in 1942," says Hans Bethe. At that early stage in the war, the scientists that Groves and Furman consulted for counterintelligence purposes were virtual looms spinning out fresh ideas, most of which were dispensed with like so many pillings and nubbins. Kidnapping and murder present problems of turpitude beyond the difficulties of execution, and so Bethe and Weisskopf were flatly rejected.

Yet, smart men were racked with fears of what Heisenberg might be doing, and relieving such concerns with one brief, violent gesture was more appealing than most people liked to admit. Behind closed doors, in hushed tones, proposals like Bethe's and Weisskopf's were made repeatedly. It was probably in the last days of 1943 that Groves sat in Robert Oppenheimer's office and listened as the Manhattan Project scientific director quietly suggested that "if [he] was fearful of German progress in the atomic field [he] could upset it by arranging to have some of their leading scientists killed." Groves sent the idea along to Army Chief of Staff General George C. Marshall, who responded sourly. "Tell Groves to take care of his own dirty work," he said. In January 1944, Philip Morrison weighed in, suggesting to Furman that "it would be wise to kidnap such a man as Von Weizsäcker." That was soon dismissed, but by Valentine's Day, Groves had passed his Heisenberg dirty work along to General Donovan, who found nothing vulgar about any opportunity to increase the OSS role in the war. The job called for someone unbothered by fear or scruple, and Donovan knew a man like that.

Carl Eifler never liked to be far from trouble. Just over six feet tall, broad as a brown bear, at 280 solid pounds, Eifler was a graduate of the elite Los Angeles Police Academy and had worked for a time as an undercover U.S. customs inspector, tracking smugglers through the Mexican mountains. After several Scotch whiskys, he once shot a three-inch-square cigarette box off a man's head. Another time, standing in a barn lit only by a dim lantern, he blasted a glass off the head of a loudmouth who dared him to try it. Eifler was more than a crack shot. He considered himself "well qualified in the art of boxing," and his threshold for pain was such that when flying scraps of metal were imbedded deep in his leg, he found a scalpel, and "I operated on myself."

Eifler became friendly with General Joseph Stilwell in California in the 1930s, during his days in the army reserve, and it was "Vinegar Joe" who urged Donovan to hire him for the OSS. Stilwell commanded the American troops in Burma, India, and China, and in May 1942, he had approved Detachment 101, an OSS guerrilla mission based in India and extending deep behind Japanese lines in the northern Burmese jungle. He recommended Eifler as the leader of the mission.

The plan was for the American agents to train Kachin tribesmen and then work alongside them, disrupting Japanese supply lines by sabotaging airstrips, bridges, and railroad tracks, and by sniping at troop columns. When Donovan paid Eifler a visit to see how things were going, most of what he saw in Burma impressed him. Nonetheless, Eifler, who had suffered an injury when he lost his balance in a pounding surf and was thrown head first against some rocks, was soon back in Washington. In February 1944, Donovan sent Eifler in to see Robert Furman. Furman had talked over an upcoming assignment with a few other men and rejected them. Now he sketched it for Eifler. A German scientist was making a dangerous new weapon, and Furman wanted him stopped. Eifler doesn't like to discuss killing—"it's nobody's business how many men I killed," he says—and Furman didn't ask him to. In somewhat ghoulish terms, he made it clear that Heisenberg should be kidnapped. Eifler was told "to deny Germany his brain." Would that be possible? Furman asked.

"I said yes," says Eifler. "This was the first time someone had just said yes to him."

"My God," said Furman. He had his man.

Over the next few months, Eifler was allowed to design a mission that nobody would have mistaken for either a likely success or just a kidnapping. Eifler would capture Heisenberg, presumably in Berlin, lead him out of the country on foot, and put him on an airplane in Switzerland. They would fly over the Mediterranean, ditch the plane, and parachute into the water, where both men would be picked up by a waiting submarine. Stanley Lovell supplied Eifler with guns for silent killing, and in late June, ever game, Eifler was in Algiers, on his way to Germany, when Donovan met him on a balcony above a busy street and called it off. Eifler was told "We got the secret," meaning that the atom had been split, but that was just politesse. The real reason was common sense.

That cautious men like Furman and Groves should have temporarily gone along with such a wild scheme suggests how badly they wanted to be rid of Heisenberg. What now changed was the kind of man they chose to pursue him. Moe Berg was not the ruthless field soldier Carl Eifler was, but he was a very intelligent man—not a bad quality when you are in the business of denying brains.

This time, things would be more subdued, developing at a measured pace over the course of several months, until a sudden turn of events hurried years of concern into sudden climax.

By the autumn of 1944, Berg's translation of Werner Heisenberg's postcard to Gian Carlo Wick had been supplemented by enough other intelligence from the Alsos Mission in France and from the OSS Bern bureau for General Leslie Groves to feel certain that Heisenberg was living in Hechingen, a village on the edge of the Black Forest in southern Germany. In his autobiography, Groves writes that Tony Calvert intended to send Berg to the Black Forest via Switzerland, until Groves interceded: "When I heard of Calvert's plan for Berg to go into the Hechingen-Bissingen area, I immediately stopped it, realizing that if he were captured, the Nazis might be able to extract far more information about our project than we could ever hope to obtain if he were successful." Groves's account is somewhat misleading. Groves and Furman kept firm control of the AZUSA Mission, and no plans of this importance got beyond the suggestion stage without their participation. Further, the mission to Germany that was plotted toward the end of 1944 was by no means intended to send Moe Berg into

Germany on his own. Several other men were to join him, and in October they began trickling into London, with no idea what they were there to do.

One of them was Jack Marsching, a graying World War I veteran with heavy jowls who was dispatched to the OSS London offices at the end of September to serve as the head of technical reports. Berg and Marsching sniffed the air and detected the same thing: bad chemistry. They hated each other instantly. Berg soon complained that Marsching was withholding AZUSA information from him, and Marsching responded with an aggrieved memo to Dix: "If Mr. Berg did not receive information promptly, he was to blame because he only paid the office infrequent visits and after finally obtaining his address, it was necessary to phone him when information or instructions for him were received. His attitude was inclined to be impatient, critical and extremely independent." If Marsching seems a bit like an old prune, Berg was hardly gracious. Sounding not a little self-important, he told another London OSS man that he would rather quit than work with Marsching. It is a measure of how much Dix, Donovan, and Groves had come to value Berg that Dix's solution to the cat-fight was to pull Marsching out of England.

With Marsching gone, the AZUSA roster at the beginning of November included two OSS agents, Earl Brodie and Edmond Mroz, and one scientist, Martin Chittick, the chemist who had gone to Paris for Berg in June when Berg had been unable to extricate himself from Italy. It would have been only natural for Berg to want to meet them all, but Moe Berg didn't meet people, he investigated them, looking them over the way a shopper examines a supermarket tomato. Marsching he rejected. Brodie he'd already spent time with in Washington and liked fine. He reminded himself of this during their one brief encounter in London. Brodie was on his way back to his room one night when a large man emerged in his path from the dimly lit doorway of an Italian restaurant, scaring the wits out of him. It was Berg. "Can you get anything back to the States?"

he whispered to Brodie. Brodie said he could. Berg handed him an envelope and melted away into the evening. Brodie got the envelope back. "He knew all about me, had me totally figured out," says Brodie.

Chittick hadn't yet arrived in London, so only Mroz remained to be examined. Mroz was a chemical engineer who had spent the first part of the war as an air force navigator. In January 1944, the OSS asked for him, rushed him through training school, and put him on the *Aquitania*, bound for London in September. Nobody told him why, and Mroz didn't ask. Mroz was working at the OSS office in Grosvenor Square, under Marsching, when one day he received a telephone call from Berg, inviting him to lunch at Claridge's Hotel. They met in Berg's suite, where a succulent mixed grill was delivered to them. As they ate, they talked. Mroz recognized Berg from newspaper photographs, but he didn't really follow baseball. When Berg brought up the game, Mroz said that baseball was too slow for his taste. Berg raised his thick eyebrows. He told Mroz some of his Trans-Siberian Railroad stories, which Mroz enjoyed, and then, gradually, the direction of the conversation turned to fission. Mroz said he'd used a mass spectograph to separate isotopes, but other than that, he didn't know much about it. He knew chemistry, not nuclear physics. After two hours, the lunch was over. "I didn't ask him why he wanted to talk with me," says Mroz. "We were both fighting the same war. That was it. We were all compartmentalized. We didn't know what the other guys were doing." Berg might have liked working with a man who thought like that, but he never got the chance.

WHILE BERG WAS dining on grilled sausage and lamb chops with Ed Mroz, Boris Pash, Samuel Goudsmit, and the Alsos Mission were visiting the liberated northeastern French city of Strasbourg, where Carl Friedrich von Weizsäcker taught physics at the university. The professor's files contained a large sheaf of correspondence, diaries, notes, and computations, and Goudsmit began reading through it all at once. On one letterhead was printed Werner Heisenberg's secret address and telephone number in Hechingen. After all the effort expended in looking for Heisenberg, now you could just ring him up! Goudsmit kept reading in silence until, suddenly, he startled Pash by blurting, "We've got it!"

"I know we have it," said Pash, who preferred to do the yelling. "But do they?"

"No, no," he was told. "That's it. They don't."

When he calmed down, Goudsmit could put it more cogently. "Germany had no atom bomb and was not likely to have one in any reasonable time" is the jubilant summary of the situation in his memoirs.

Washington was informed immediately, and soon, inevitable as sunset, came the doubts. Was Goudsmit absolutely certain? Well, he was virtually certain. Could he prove the documents weren't decoys, plants? No, he couldn't do that. And so forth. Meanwhile, General Groves had seen a photograph of a new industrial complex in the Hechingen area. Immediately he was sure that it was the German uranium separation factory. A bit of digging by the British revealed that this was no Oak Ridge, but rather an act of desperation. German geological engineers were trying to squeeze fuel from a seam of shale. That a country this strapped for oil could be supplying the necessary resources for an atomic weapon did not seem impossible to Groves, and as long as there was possibility, AZUSA and Moe Berg were still in business.

In late November, Berg's position at the heart of the American atomic intelligence mission was strengthened even further as he was fully briefed by the OSS and Furman on Flute, the code name for Paul Scherrer, the director of the Physics Institute at the Eidgenössische Technische Hochschule (ETH) in Zurich. Berg had discussed Scherrer with Guy Suits during

▼

his visit to General Electric, before leaving the United States, so he knew something about him. As a young man, Scherrer had done exciting atomic investigation, but at the moment, in middle age, he had a reputation as a man grown indifferent to research who was now preoccupied with organizing physics lectures that were famous throughout Switzerland.

Scherrer was well placed for espionage within the intimate community of the world's great physicists. With its shops, museums, concert halls, and restaurants, Zurich had always been a popular spot for scientists' lectures and conferences. During the war, Switzerland's neutrality made the country the single permissible destination outside Germany for the German physicists, meaning that Scherrer had access that nobody else did to Gentner, Von Weizsäcker, and his trusted friend Werner Heisenberg. With this in mind, the OSS Bern bureau chief, Allen Dulles, and one of his favorite agents, an oil company lawyer named Frederick Reed Loofbourow, cultivated Scherrer's friendship. Over time, Scherrer became a prized OSS source. This was brave of him. Nazi spies were ubiquitous in Swiss cities, and the Swiss government dealt harshly with citizens who compromised the country's neutrality. Scherrer told nobody that he cooperated with American agents, but he did, making Flute an OSS asset of incredible value.

At times, however, Scherrer seemed uneasy. After Dulles warned Donovan that the scientist was "heavily overworked" and would respond well only to those who approached him with "the greatest care and tact," Furman decided that Scherrer might be more comfortable if one man from the OSS or Alsos was assigned to work with him. The choice for the job was Berg. At the same time, on Dix's recommendation that "his work since assignment to this section has been of high caliber and exceptional importance," Berg's annual salary was raised $800, to $4,600. Much as he always liked signs of approval, what Berg really wanted was something to do. He had been beached in London for a long time, and after the excitement of Italy he was impatient for more.

On December 8, word out of Bern announced that Werner Heisenberg was planning to give a lecture in Zurich on or about December 15. Two days later Berg was in Paris, where a GI named Bud Leavitt, in peacetime a sportswriter from Maine, spotted Lefty Groves's old catcher ambling down the Champs-Elysées, with five newspapers under his arm. "Don't ask me what I'm doing here" was Berg's greeting. "What are you doing here?"

For most of the four or five days he spent in Paris, the truth was that Berg couldn't have answered his own question. The plan had been for him to go to Germany to search for an industrial complex, in the company of Mroz, Brodie, and Chittick. Now, suddenly, he was on his own. Only on his last day in Paris, during a meeting at the Ritz Hotel with Sam Goudsmit, were Donovan's and Groves's instructions forwarded to him.

Berg and Goudsmit probably met for the first time in Paris, and they would stay loosely in touch for the next three decades, mostly at Goudsmit's behest. Goudsmit was fascinated by a man who liked to probe other people's souls even more than he did. The scientific head of the Alsos Mission was a Dutch Jew from the Hague. He and another Dutchman, George Uhlenbeck, discovered in 1925 that electrons are not static but are always spinning. Two years later, Goudsmit became a professor at the University of Michigan. "That fellow Goudsmit," another physicist once said, "he talks physics, but he talks a lot of other things, too." Goudsmit was particularly curious about secrets. While in Holland he had studied detective techniques, and there is reason to believe that Alsos began a sideline career for him in espionage that lasted all his life.

Goudsmit was a good-natured man, but the war made him bitter. In March 1943, his mother and father sent him a farewell letter from a Nazi concentration camp. Loyal Germans were not people for whom Goudsmit had any sympathy. Detestation is more like it. As for his old friend Werner Heisenberg, Goudsmit was irritated by his refusal to leave Nazi

Germany, and privately faulted Heisenberg for not trying to use his influence to save his parents. That may explain why Goudsmit, after reviewing documents in Strasbourg that, he says, made him certain that Germans were not building an atomic bomb, did not now hesitate to tell Berg that he might have to kill Heisenberg.

Late in his life, in one of his several brief attempts at writing an autobiography, Berg jotted down bits of what Goudsmit told him in Paris. He also discussed his orders—sometimes in oblique terms—with several people, so the situation can be pieced together. Goudsmit told Berg that Heisenberg would soon be in Zurich to give a lecture. "Gun in my pocket," wrote Berg in his notes. Goudsmit was European and Berg, he would have known by now, was interested in foreign languages. So Goudsmit dramatically switched to spoken French while presenting Berg with the option of using that gun to murder Heisenberg. "Nothing spelled out," noted Berg, "but—Heisenberg must be rendered hors de combat."

Berg didn't like to talk about himself in any language, but even he eventually found the facts of his Zurich assignment impossible to keep a secret. Toward the end of his life, Berg became friends with George Gloss, the owner of a book shop in Boston. Berg roamed the store, piling up tall stacks of books, which he would ask Gloss to hold for him behind the counter so that he could buy them at a later date. That date, Gloss knew, would never come, but he didn't mind. Gloss liked Berg. When Berg had finished his browsing, Gloss would always bounce off his stool, propose a meal, and off they would go. For one of those meals, Gloss's fifteen-year-old son, Ken, accompanied the two men to Patten's Restaurant in Boston, where he ate and listened, wide-eyed, as Berg told his father what Goudsmit had told him. "He said he definitely was there to assassinate Germans if they were inventing the bomb," says Ken Gloss.

Except for the evening when he stopped him on the sidewalk and asked him to mail a letter, Berg avoided Earl Brodie when they were both in London in 1944. But five years later, quite unexpectedly, Brodie learned what had pulled Moe Berg out of England so suddenly. Brodie was visiting Washington from his home in California, attending a convention at the Mayflower Hotel. It was nearing ten o'clock one night when he felt like smoking a cigar. He went into the Mayflower's tobacco shop and was selecting a Cuban panatella when he sensed a presence. He turned and saw Moe Berg. Something about Berg's manner told Brodie not to recognize him, so he paid for the cigar, walked outside, and, as he was lighting it, Berg appeared at his side again. "Have you time to take a walk with me?" he asked.

Berg was obviously feeling low, and so Brodie kept him company, walking beside him mile after mile, hour after hour. Berg was in better shape than Brodie, who had to strain to match his pace. Brodie began to feel worn out, and nervous as well about an early-morning meeting, but he could tell that Berg was down and had not the heart to abandon him. It was good that he didn't, because the conversation began to grow very interesting. Berg was doing most of the talking, and Brodie noticed that "while not many people knew much about him, Moe seemed to have made it his business to learn a great deal about everyone. He was his own FBI." But eventually on this night, Berg did have something about himself to reveal. He told Brodie that Werner Heisenberg had been lured out of Germany to give a lecture in Zurich in late 1944. The lecture would be open to the public, and Berg was told to attend. "He'd been drilled in physics, he'd had a lot of one-on-one training and had been told to listen for certain things," Brodie says Berg told him. "If anything Heisenberg said convinced him the Germans were close to a bomb, then his job was to shoot him—right there in the auditorium."

The last person to see Berg in Paris was Tony Calvert, who was staying with him at the Ritz. Calvert handed Berg a cannister of heavy water, to present to Scherrer as a token of American appreciation. Calvert and Berg had dinner together

▼

and then talked late into the night. Groves, who wanted his intelligence staff to know as little as possible about what he was doing, hadn't bothered to mention to Calvert that Berg had been authorized to shoot Heisenberg. Berg didn't tell him either. That was characteristic too. Berg kept a secret as well as Groves did, one of the reasons that the general grew to trust him.

As BERG HURRIED toward Switzerland, strange things had been happening elsewhere. In Rome, liberation sent the university into a happy delirium of gratitude, which took form in a liberal bestowal of honorary degrees upon several "Allied officers," who were recognized for "services rendered to the university." Berg was not an officer, and what a spy who arrived after the liberation and spent most of his time interviewing people and even trying to convince some of them to leave the University of Rome for new work in the United States did to merit the titles "Grand Benefactor" and "Honorary Doctor of Laws" is unclear. The doctorate's Greek and Latin inscriptions are no help. They say that Berg was "eminently deserving of this honor" and laud the "intelligent and affectionate work he performed toward the reconstruction and rebirth of the maximum cultural institute of Rome." Part of the explanation may be the familiar one with Moe Berg: people just liked him.

WHEN MOE BERG arrived at the ETH small lecture hall in Zurich on December 18, he had not come as Moe Berg. Berg believed that one of his most useful personal qualities for spy work was a dark, saturnine complexion, which allowed him, as he once put it, "to fit in," with equal success in Tokyo, Berlin, or Morocco. To support this impression of himself, he liked to tell the story of something that had happened to him in Rome. He was walking down the street one day, when two American officers pulled up alongside him in a Jeep. "Let's ask this guinea where the hotel is," one of them said. Before they could say anything more, Berg said, "You can't miss it, it's three blocks up with a green awning."

"Where'd that guinea learn to speak such good English?" one of the officers said to the other.

"Princeton, Class of 1923," said Berg, and walked away.

At Werner Heisenberg's lecture in Zurich he was equally convincing. By various accounts, Berg identified himself as a Swiss physics student, an Arab businessman, and a French merchant from Dijon. Berg was forty-two years old that day, so the student's would seem to have been the least plausible mask, but that is the one he chose, and Heisenberg did not question it.

It was an interesting choice of identity for Berg, and a revealing one. With the exception of his three years at war, from the time he injured his knee as a member of the Chicago White Sox most of Moe Berg's adult life was spent reading, observing, and asking questions. For his most stressful assignment, he would pose in a role that was for him no role at all. He was comfortable as a student and this was no time to be flustered.

Berg arrived for Heisenberg's presentation in the company of another OSS agent, Leo Martinuzzi. They left their winter coats and hats in an anteroom, walked into the lecture hall, and joined the modest audience of twenty professors and graduate students who had come to hear the world's greatest physicist discuss his recent thoughts on S-matrix theory. Berg's German was passable at best and no better than his knowledge of physics. He would have had difficulty following such an advanced scientific colloquium in English, never mind in a foreign language he hadn't studied since Princeton, and so he didn't really try. Instead, he looked around and, as usual, he saw more than most people would have.

After struggling to set up a blackboard, Heisenberg began speaking at 4:15 P.M. from typewritten sheets of paper and, like any good student, Berg took copious notes. Initially, he was entranced by the sight of this man he had been hearing about for so long. To Berg, Heisenberg appeared frail, about five foot six and no more than 110 pounds. Berg knew the physicist to be forty-three, but he decided he looked a few years past that. Heisenberg wore a dark, three-button suit, a ring next to the pinkie on his right hand, and a quizzical smile; he kept his left hand in his pocket and paced as he talked. For a while, Berg played Holbein, embellishing and perfecting a vivid description. He gazed at Heisenberg's "artistic" hands; his heavy eyebrows, which seemed to him to "emphasize movement of that part of bony structure over the eyes"; and then at Heisenberg's reddish bristle of hair gone bald at the crown. Berg made a quick sketch of the last. "Looks like Furman," he wrote, but that wasn't it. He tried again. "Like Irish author Gogarty." The recondite allusion was to the poet Oliver St. John Gogarty, Joyce's model for Buck Mulligan in *Ulysses*.

Berg's scrutiny did not go unnoticed by Heisenberg. "H. likes my interest in his lecture," Berg jotted. Heisenberg, of course, had no idea of what Berg was really up to, an irony that was not lost on Berg. "As I listen, I am uncertain—see: Heisenberg's uncertainty principle—what to do to H.," he wrote to himself. "Discussing math while Rome burns—if they knew what I'm thinking."

It must have been frustrating not to understand what was being said, so Berg looked around the room and took solace from Scherrer, seated in the front row and, it seemed to Berg, "despairing because he doesn't understand the mathematical formulas on the board." Scanning the audience, Berg noticed a man with deepset eyes who was shivering in the drafty room. It wasn't until after Heisenberg had finished speaking that Berg realized this was Carl Friedrich von Weizsäcker. In his notes, Berg drew up a seating chart, and beside Von Weizsäcker's name he wrote "Nazi."

Berg's assignment had been to look Heisenberg over. He was to fire only if he heard indisputable evidence that a German bomb was nearing completion. Berg wasn't exactly sure what he had heard, but it didn't seem terribly threatening, and nobody else seemed to find anything amiss either. Heisenberg was no Scherrer, but he was a good speaker, and most of the Swiss professors and students in attendance agreed with young Herman Waftler, who listened intently and found Heisenberg's presentation "very interesting because it was quite new for us." You didn't murder a man for that. The pistol stayed in Berg's pocket, so did the "L"—lethal cyanide—tablet Berg was carrying in case he needed to dispose of himself. The lecture ended, and he and Martinuzzi went to get their wraps.

After collecting the coat and hat, Berg returned to the seminar room to greet Scherrer. "Dr. Suits sends his best regards from Schenectady and I have a little bundle for you," he said. It was 6:40. Scherrer told Berg to meet him in his office in fifteen minutes.

Reassured by the presence of Martinuzzi, whom he knew, and the letter from Suits, which Berg would now have presented, and pleased by the cannister of heavy water, Scherrer was frank and animated. Scherrer said that he had spent the past few days with Heisenberg, who had confided in him.

There was plenty of interesting news from Heisenberg, and Scherrer passed it on to Berg at a brisk clip. A friend of Heisenberg's had seen Hitler recently and described him as "well and working." Scherrer was convinced, he said, that Heisenberg was an "anti-Nazi." Heisenberg's family was living in a small Bavarian town outside Munich, and Heisenberg saw them only once every five months. That was one of the reasons he was so glad to be in Switzerland. He could buy them chocolate and other treats for Christmas in the Zurich shops. Heisenberg himself was working in Hechingen, "on cosmic rays, not AZUSA." Berg underlined the latter phrase for emphasis. It amused Berg to learn that Heisenberg had spotted an American reconnaissance plane flying above Hechingen, taking photographs.

Berg was convinced by Scherrer's portrait of Heisenberg as an "anti-Nazi." So, instead of now scheming a denial of his mind, Berg proposed to "transplant" Heisenberg and his family to the U.S. He didn't mention the original plan, which, almost certainly, he always kept from Scherrer. This was a wise choice. Heisenberg and Scherrer disagreed politically, but the war was only a caesura in their lifelong friendship.

Scherrer seemed to think transplanting Heisenberg to the U.S. a fine idea, and told Berg he would pass the invitation along to Heisenberg. He also asked Berg to come to a dinner he was hosting for Heisenberg at his large Zurich home later that week. Berg said he would be there.

HEISENBERG HAD ACCEPTED Scherrer's dinner invitation with the provision that he would not have to talk politics. But at the party he found himself confronted by a number of angry men and women who had agreed to no such restraints and immediately put Heisenberg on the defensive. Werner Zünti asked Heisenberg what he was doing. "I am working on theoretical problems of ballistics" was the reply. "We assumed that wasn't true," says Zünti. Another inquisitor wanted to know how Heisenberg could remain in a country led by Adolf Hitler. "I am not a Nazi but a German," came the familiar justification. Something else Heisenberg was not was a diplomat, and eventually it showed. When Gregor Wentzel all but sneered, "Now you have to admit that the war is lost," Heisenberg replied, "Yes, but it would have been so good if we had won." This was one of those piquant remarks that makes tasty gossip for years to come, and few heard about it sooner than Howard Dix, courtesy of a Moe Berg file a few days later.

At the end of the evening, Berg timed his departure to match Heisenberg's, and when the scientist left the house, Berg joined him on the sidewalk. Together they set out, walking through the cold and quiet of a Zurich winter night. Artificial lighting was used sparingly in Zurich during the war, so the few lamps that were on at that hour shone like stars against a sky of pitch. It was an ideal moment for murder, but again Berg resisted. He had just heard Heisenberg say that the war was lost for

Germany. Were Heisenberg poised to unfurl an atomic bomb, he would probably have spoken differently or not at all. Berg asked more questions, "pestered" Heisenberg with them, in the scientist's words, and mixed in a few bromides as well. Apparently, Berg's Swiss-accented German aroused no suspicions in Heisenberg. In fact, if it is possible to ignore someone while maintaining a conversation with him, Heisenberg managed it. He didn't know who Berg was and did not bother to ask. Eventually, he and Berg parted company, never to see each other again. It had been a marvelous exercise in anticlimax.

Anything else would have been absurd, for the whole situation was charged with improbability. If Heisenberg was supervising a bomb project, it seems unlikely that Hitler would have permitted him a long public visit to Switzerland. Besides, only a large dose of OSS wishful thinking finds Heisenberg, with his bomb nearly built, telling a lecture hall full of foreigners about it. Then there is the matter of timing. It might have made sense to steal and shoot Heisenberg in 1942 when Bethe and Weisskopf first suggested it, but by December 1944, it was too late. "I have no doubt that those were [Berg's] orders and that he would have done it, but it would have made no difference," says Philip Morrison. "With our project you could shoot Fermi in 1944 and it would have made no difference. A year before the [American] bomb, 100,000 people were working on it. By 1944, Heisenberg was no longer very valuable."

HOWARD DIX WROTE a letter to Berg on December 22 that sounds more like a note from father to son than spymaster to spy. "It is our hope that you will have an interesting time at your present location," he said at one point. Referring to Berg's $800 raise, he instructed, "You should now feel like a millionaire." And then in closing came, "May you have lots of fun doing the work." Mixing lighthearted sentiment with secret business was a specialty in the devotedly collegial OSS, but in

▼

fact, Berg did live it up for the rest of the war, and his nearly constant companion in play was Paul Scherrer.

There were several reasons for this friendship, and chief among them was Scherrer's boundless enthusiasm for the United States. Scherrer had returned from his first visit there, in the late 1920s, brimming with praise for everything American, from the physics to the theater to the chewing gum. After that, he began encouraging former students to go to the U.S. "Everything from America is good" was Scherrer's assistant Georg Busch's dry assessment of his boss. Scherrer's daughter, Ines Jucker, agrees. "That Moe Berg was an American and was a way for [my father] to help America was what interested him about Berg," she says. "He was interested in the progress of physics."

If affection for America prompted Scherrer to supply information to the U.S., it was Moe Berg who put him at ease while doing so. Scherrer had been assisting Allen Dulles and Frederick Reed Loufbourow before meeting Berg, but Scherrer was not always comfortable with them. He and Berg were more compatible. Scherrer was not Jewish, but he was more than tolerant of Jews. There were several German Jewish refugees working illegally in the ETH physics department, and Scherrer protected them from the Swiss police and from pro-Nazi colleagues. Personally, Berg and Scherrer shared the near-contradictory qualities of being both secretive and ebullient. "When my father and Berg were together, they were always alike, they were fun," says Ines Jucker. "Both liked bicycling, swimming, and a good late dinner. Berg would always say, 'We will have good food!' " And they were simpatico in at least one more respect. Both were fiends for newspapers, happily beginning their day with as many as could be supplied.

Berg took a room in a hotel not far from Scherrer's house, and apparently came to know him during frequent meetings at three places in Zurich: Scherrer's home, his office at the ETH, and the Kronenhalle, Scherrer's favorite Zurich restaurant. Hulda Zunnsteg operated the Kronenhalle for sixty-four

years, during which it became, in equal parts, literary café, art
gallery, and purveyor of exquisite European cooking. Zunnsteg
had a fondness—and an eye—for good painters, and they liked
her, too. Among the regulars who ate the Kronenhalle's rich
chocolate mousse and supplied the no-less-renowned wall dec-
orations were Marc Chagall, Joan Miró, Georges Braque, and
Henri Matisse. In the bar are two Picasso paintings and a series
of lamps designed by Giacometti. Between 1915 and 1919, a
table was reserved for a visiting writer from Ireland, and every
day James Joyce would come in, sit down, and scribble away
at *Ulysses*. Between 1912 and 1916, Albert Einstein held col-
loquiums with his students in the billiard room upstairs. Berg's
pocket full of OSS-issue Swiss francs made it easy to repair
there often.

Scherrer's interests spread well beyond physics. He read
history, literature, and philosophy for hours at home every
evening, favoring Herodotus and English novels. So he and
Berg had a lot to talk about. They mixed conversations about
the whereabouts of German scientists with more whimsical
discussions. Scherrer was a teacher, and one of his gifts was
the ability to simplify complicated scientific ideas so that
nonspecialists could understand them. For Berg, who had to
write reports full of science of which he sometimes had only
vague comprehension, Scherrer was very helpful. On the day
after Christmas, the two men met at the ETH, and after Scherrer taught Berg something about uranium chain reactions, he
put down his black pen, and Berg picked up a red one and
sketched a diamond. "My explanation to Professor Scherrer
of game of baseball," he wrote beside it afterwards. On other
days, Scherrer mused about how long it might take Germany
to build its bomb—he guessed two years—and supplied news
of Walther Gerlach's nervous breakdown and rumors of a powerful new German flamethrower.

The OSS had left Berg free to roam, Dix asking only that
Berg supply him with an address "so that we can get in touch
with you when necessary." Zurich may not have had much

light at night, but the war brought a luster of a different sort. Taking refuge in Zurich were artists from all over Europe and, for a brief time, they transformed the ancient city of bankers and clockmakers into a flourishing artistic center. During this slightly bizarre Renaissance, Scherrer saw the likes of Richard Strauss performing his own operas and Kate Gold acting as Nora in Ibsen's *A Doll's House*. For some of these events, seated beside Scherrer was his family and "Bushie," as the Scherrers had taken to calling their new American friend, Moe Berg.

Until the end of the war, Groves and Furman were never completely convinced of what their intelligence operators had been telling them for years—that there was no German atomic bomb. And who could fault their doubts? In Belgium, German-controlled radio broadcasts were urging citizens to flee because "atomic power is about to be unleashed . . . wherever it is dropped all animals and plants cease to exist, huge areas of land are scorched, woods are consumed, and any human being caught in this hurricane is shattered to smithereens." Groves's wad of newspaper clippings on the subject grew ever thicker as well. Under the circumstances, it was good to have Moe Berg at Paul Scherrer's elbow.

Mostly, that is where he remained. In Zurich, he would drop by Risling Strasse for a long talk about books. When the Scherrers went skiing in the eastern Alps, Berg went too. Once the weather warmed, the Scherrers went to a house they rented for weekends and holidays on Lago Maggiore, a beautiful Swiss lake five minutes from the Italian border, and again Berg accompanied them. To the Scherrers, Berg was "lustig" (full of fun). He and Scherrer took moonlight swims in the lake, and liked to go for long bicycle rides. Across the lake was the Italian village of Pino, and Berg invented a song about Scherrer and himself called "We Are the Boys of Pino." The Scherrers thought he sang abysmally, but they didn't mind. He was so "lustig." "He was really in the family," says Ines. "A little bit like a cousin."

Such strange things were going on in the world that the

Scherrers readily accepted Berg and didn't think to wonder much about why he dressed in the same style of clothes every day, much less what he was doing in Switzerland. The Scherrers had plenty of American visitors, and they assumed Bushie was a bodyguard whose job was to protect Paul and to evacuate him if the Germans arrived to take over the Institute. Paul Scherrer never enlightened his family. During his life he seems to have confided in nobody, including his closest colleagues, what he and Berg were really doing, and before his death in 1969, he burned his personal papers. It was only in 1992 that Ines Jucker learned, as this book was being prepared, that her father had been passing secrets to the OSS through Moe Berg.

Berg did not visit the Scherrers again after the war, though for years he faithfully sent a card at Christmas. He would always remember his few months with them warmly, even wistfully, and they felt the same way. "Life in Zurich during the war was a happy time for me," says Ines. "It's because of that happy time that I like to think about Bushie. It could be that it was a happy time for him in our family because he had no wife or children." Ted Williams never saw Berg laugh during his last three seasons with the Red Sox, but in Switzerland the Scherrers knew a different man. "We never saw him sad," says Ines.

THERE WAS SOMETHING surreal about tranquil Zurich, when elsewhere in Europe there was so much turmoil. Elsewhere for Moe Berg, in 1945, was two hours away in the Swiss capital city of Bern, where the OSS Swiss station chief Allen Welsh Dulles had his offices in an elegant four-story apartment building. Dulles had slipped into Switzerland from France hours before the Swiss borders hissed shut in November 1942, and there he remained, sealed off from the rest of the world, until the end of summer 1944. Dulles was a determined, inventive man, and his isolation did not stop him from accumulating some of the best intelligence Donovan received during the war.

▼

Dulles learned about the existence of the German weapons research plant at Peenemünde, and he established ties with resistance leaders from several countries, including the group of Germans who would plot, unsuccessfully, to assassinate Hitler in 1944. He turned American businessmen stranded in Switzerland into valuable intelligence analysts, and cultivated a German foreign office official named Fritz Kolbe, who kept him supplied with documents from Berlin. Long before the German capital was divided, Dulles was sending files out of Bern, arguing that the U.S. should be as wary of Soviet Communism as it had been of European Fascism.

Bern was even quieter than Zurich. But just because he couldn't hear the screams or smell the blood didn't mean Dulles could put the war out of his mind. He was fighting a vile enemy that specialized in pogroms and torture, and he never forgot it. Everything he asked other people to do was focused on defeating Germany, to the extent that he forbade his staff from skiing—he didn't want any broken legs—and when a member of the American legation in Bern announced his engagement, Dulles worried that marriage would interfere with the man's work. Dulles liked calm, level-headed operatives. He had been hearing about Berg's imminent arrival since August, and now, when the long-awaited agent finally made his appearance, Dulles found he did not like Moe Berg, did not like him at all.

Berg would pay periodic visits to Bern to pick up communications from Dix, and send off his own. The OSS Bern station was located at 24 Dufourstrasse, a few minutes' walk from the Aare River, in a wealthy, tree-lined section of Bern. On the first three floors of the building were offices, and the top floor held radio and cable equipment. Twenty-four Dufourstrasse's front door was always opened by an elderly Englishman who had fought with Lawrence in Arabia and knew where to find Scotch whisky in Bern when shop owners said there was no more. Beyond him was a close-knit, relatively conservative group of analysts, secretaries, and cipher clerks who looked up at Berg with curiosity. "I remember I was in the office and this guy came through," says one of them, Bill Hood. "Somebody said, 'Do you know who that is?' and I said, 'No.' They said, 'It's Moe Berg, the baseball player.' He was conspicuous in Bern. He didn't have an Ivy League suit. He looked, if anything, like a cop. He wore a six-button suit, with all the buttons fastened, which brought the suit up quite high. You didn't really see things like that around the office. I thought he had funny ties. I concocted that he was wearing an old umpire's uniform, replete with steel-toed shoes. He had no bonhomie. He was very forbidding. There were a lot of strange people in OSS. He was certainly sui generis."

Bern was full of refugees, travelers, bankers positioning themselves for postwar business with the Americans, and spies—spies of every stripe and nation, who staked out bars and restaurants as their own. The Germans, for example, favored the Hotel Schweizerhof, the Poles liked the Café du Théâtre, and the Americans generally went to the Bellevue. Berg ate alone in cafés, where he read the newspapers and looked around, embellishing, for postwar recitation, accounts of Bern as a den of iniquity where spies of every country sat having dinner in the same room, faintly acknowledging each other as they worked their knives and forks.

At night, Berg would sleep in a guest room in Dulles's plush home in Bern. If Berg was following his usual policy of running a personal background check on everyone he worked with, he would have seen that, for all his clucking about discipline, Dulles was a devoted womanizer, who liked to tell exciting stories starring a mildly reluctant and endlessly successful undercover hero—Allen Dulles. The presence of a competing raconteur could not have pleased Berg.

Like all station chiefs, Dulles liked to know what was going on in his backyard, and Berg was saying nothing about what he was doing. From Berg's point of view, he had been assigned to a top secret project and was accountable only to Dix, Donovan, Furman, and Groves. What he did, and how he did it,

▼

was nobody's business but theirs. Switzerland, however, was
a very delicate base of operations. For it to be revealed that
Allen Dulles was not really a special representative of President
Roosevelt, but an American spymaster, would have outraged
the Swiss. Dulles felt responsible for what went on in his baili-
wick, and he had no patience with an independent operator
who could compromise work that had been careful years in
the planning. "Moe was secretive with what he told [Dulles],"
says Ned Putzell. "One time I was talking with Dulles and he
was furious because Moe hadn't come clean about something.
His face would get red, his mustache would twitch; he foamed
to beat hell. If Moe had been able to get into his good graces
it would have been different, but they agreed to disagree."

Nor did it help that Berg treated everyone at 24 Dufourstrasse like his office boy. The staff was irked by this character
who came strolling into Bern, insisting upon priority for his
work. "There were a lot of other people who thought what
they were doing was just as important, so you had inevitable
problems," says Cordelia Dodson, who worked as an intelligence analyst for Dulles and later married Bill Hood. "The
main thing about Berg was that he demanded service and
everything dropped to take care of him. Everyone thought that
Berg was something of a prima donna."

Dulles certainly did. In a memorandum he sent to Donovan
toward the end of March, shortly before Berg was scheduled
to make a brief trip to Sweden, Dulles wrote, "Confidentially,
he [Berg] is as easy to handle as an opera singer and [it is]
difficult for me to find time these days to coddle him along.
His work is at times brilliant, but also temperamental. When
he leaves here this time, I think it preferable that his contacts
be developed by Cabana [Martin Chittick] and [Max] Kliefoth
and that he not return here for the time being." Donovan's
approach in such matters was to pat each man on the back
and tell him he was doing a wonderful job. It was common
knowledge in Bern that Donovan was personally fond of Berg.
Dulles was also a big enough man to recognize the value of

Berg's relationship with Scherrer. He swallowed hard and did not press the issue.

THE INFORMATION BERG was sending to Washington from the top floor of 24 Dufourstrasse wasn't as dramatic as his cables describing the meeting with Heisenberg, but intelligence work rarely manages such excitement. Berg did spend an afternoon scrutinizing the Swiss scientist and Nazi sympathizer Walther Dallenbach, while concealed behind a curtain in the private Zurich library where Dallenbach was working, but that was an unusually charged moment. The work of espionage has much in common with the dogged days of digging and sifting that archaeologists put in while searching for the remains of a mosaic.

Through the month Berg continued to spend most of his time with Scherrer. Scherrer wanted badly to visit the United States, to take up a temporary assignment either with the Aerojet Corporation or at the California Institute of Technology, and Berg said he would see what he could do.

"This is very urgent," came Berg's March 19 dispatch to Washington. "He expects an affirmative answer." That was understandable and so was Groves's reply. "Nothing doing," said the general. As long as there was a war in Europe, Groves wanted Scherrer in Switzerland, where he could provide him with information. At the moment, all Groves would approve for Scherrer was a cache of physics magazines and four Goodyear atom-smasher belts that the scientist had asked for. Berg grew anxious. A trip had been planned for him to Sweden, where he was to interview Lise Meitner. But Scherrer had been very important to him. "Please trust my judgment," he wired back, "that I should not leave without definite word from you that invitation will be forthcoming when time suitable." The sense he got from Washington was that Scherrer would be taken care of.

Berg spent Easter Sunday bicycling, swimming, and drinking wine at a Swiss lake with Scherrer. Slim and fit, wearing sunglasses with his dark suit and fedora, Berg cut a sleek figure that contrasted with the skinny-legged, shaggy-maned Scherrer. A few days later Berg was off. With the war obviously ending, another OSS agent, German-born Max Kliefoth, who was a World War I flying ace under the "Red" Baron von Richthofen, was put in touch with Scherrer, and Berg left for Paris by command car.

Everything was now concluding at a breathtaking pace that must have dizzied men accustomed to the sluggish tempo of intelligence work. General Patton and the Third Army were steaming toward Berlin with Pash, Goudsmit, and Alsos right behind them. On April 12, Berg met with Donovan for breakfast in Paris. President Roosevelt had died earlier that day, and, like most Americans, Donovan and Berg were stunned. Many Americans would remember where they were when FDR died the way they would again in 1963, after John F. Kennedy was killed. Berg, a loyal Democrat who loved Roosevelt, was certainly among them. To be sitting across from the commander of the OSS made the occasion all the more memorable for Berg, especially when Donovan, who excelled in sentimental moments, comforted him. "FDR knew what you were doing," he said. It was as though God himself had smiled on Berg. Twenty years later, Berg was still braced by Donovan's words. He copied them down in a notebook and added, "And what I was doing was known to few."

Donovan wanted Berg to visit the physics institute in Göttingen as soon as it was in Allied hands. Then he was to go to the U.S. In Paris, Berg secured travel orders from Washington, and then he left for Germany. An airplane took him from Wiesbaden through Weimar and on to Göttingen by April 18. At the famous laboratories where Scherrer and so many other prominent physicists had been trained, Berg met Furman and Goudsmit and gave them the long version of his rendezvous with Heisenberg in Switzerland. The exciting story contrasted rather markedly with what Furman, Goudsmit, and Berg saw in Göttingen, and indeed with what Alsos would find in Munich, Heidelberg, Hechingen, and every other place they visited—nothing. There had been no German bomb. In fact, the Germans had not even come close. In Hechingen, Alsos dug up two tons of uranium, two tons of heavy water, and ten tons of carbon that the Germans had hastily buried in a field. Hidden in a cesspool were reeking documents that confirmed what Groves's intelligence had been reporting since he began asking. As Goudsmit would put it in his memoirs, "It was so obvious that the whole German uranium setup was on a ludicrously small scale."

While Alsos completed its job of destroying or carting off scientific equipment and rounding up Heisenberg and the rest of the German physicists, interviewing them, and sending them off to England, where they would be held at the Farm Hall estate, Berg headed west. He passed back through Paris, was in London on April 23, left the next day, and was home for dinner at his mother's in Newark on April 25.

CHAPTER 12

Always Good Company

During the waning days of the war in Europe, a fresh conflict, a cold war, was beginning. The United States, the only country that was building and would soon successfully test an atomic weapon, began to take measures to prevent its French, British, and Soviet allies from making one for themselves. Once the American investigation of the small Swabian Alpine towns of Hechingen and Bissingen revealed that German physicists had failed badly in their efforts to build a bomb, the task of American atomic intelligence shifted. The next four months were, in effect, a secret war within a war, as the U.S. attempted to hoard the human and material components of atomic bomb building. Physicists and rare earths were conscripted in the way soldiers once plundered pretty women and gold florins. What that pioneering cold warrior Allen Dulles had been saying for a year or more was now implicit; Soviet Communism was the new enemy.

On May 2, while briefly resuming his residence at the May-flower Hotel in Washington, Berg received orders from the OSS to go to New York, San Francisco, Los Angeles, and back to Washington. Berg's itinerary was revised two days later. He was redirected to London, Paris, Naples, Stockholm, and then back through Switzerland and Germany. One of the reasons for the sudden change of plans and the quick departure was that another restless traveler wanted Berg's company. Bill Donovan didn't just like to hire interesting characters, he liked to surround himself with them, even in the sky. Donovan was off to Western Europe and Berg went along for the ride, sharing Donovan's handsomely appointed transport plane with the assortment of bird colonels, navy captains, civilian VIP's, and OSS officials who made up the general's entourage. Berg took the front port-side seat, two seats back of the cockpit. Seated directly behind him was his old Camp Wah-Kee-Nah charge, Monroe Karasik, now working for the OSS. Toward the rear of the plane weighty conferences were in session, Donovan presiding. Karasik began to notice that "every now and then, an important person, head bent, would walk up the aisle engaged in serious contemplation. A lot of contemplation was taking place, and every single contemplator would pause at the end of the aisle to take counsel with Moe. I would hear snatches. 'Moe, what do you think of that young southpaw—can he last more than three innings?' and 'Moe, when you saw Tyrus Raymond Cobb on the coast, did he . . . ?'" Berg never left his seat, but he had company across the Atlantic.

In London, the OSS brass stayed at Claridge's Hotel, where Berg received word from Dix that his pleas on behalf of Scherrer had come to something. Scherrer would be officially invited to spend July through October in the U.S., dividing his time between the West Coast and the Schenectady home of his old student, Guy Suits. After a few days in London, it was on to Paris, where Donovan, Berg, and the rest checked into the Ritz. John Kieran turned out to be staying there too. He was thrilled to see the long-lost Professor Berg, and attempted to prise out of him what he was doing in Paris. Kieran got no further than anyone else, leaving him to grumble that Berg's security was three grades higher than top secret.

Yet, at least once on the trip, Berg did betray himself. From Paris, Donovan and company continued east. At a field hospital in eastern France, Donovan paid a visit to a friend who was recuperating from the loss of an arm. Wounds made Berg squeamish, and so he stepped outside the tent. Nearby, some young GI's were playing catch with a baseball. Berg watched for a while and then couldn't resist. "Let's see the ball," he said. He threw once, and one of the soldiers said, "You're a pro." He snapped off a second toss and the voice responded, "You're a catcher." He caught and flicked the ball back a third time and the game was up. "And your name is Moe Berg!"

On May 30, Berg sent in a request to Groves. There was to be a Jubilee Celebration at the Russian Academy of Sciences in Moscow and in Leningrad from June 15 to 28. A number of American scientists would be attending. Berg proposed to join them, and suggested calling himself a secretary or an aide as a cover, but Groves placed the gala off limits to anybody who knew anything about Los Alamos or AZUSA, and he pointedly suggested that Berg get himself to Sweden as fast as he could.

Back in London, Berg obediently went about securing the necessary travel orders and a cash advance in Swedish kronas. June 24 was spent in Oslo, drinking beer in a pub with a group of American soldiers. On the twenty-sixth, he sat waiting while Lise Meitner read a letter from Paul Scherrer introducing her to "Dr. Moe Berg" and inviting the exiled Austrian physicist to take up residence at the ETH in Zurich. With her solemn face, hair wound tight into a bun, and formal way of speaking, Meitner had always seemed a prim, somber woman. She was, in fact, terribly high-strung, and never more so than when she met Berg. For seven years she had lived in exile from Austria, her work compromised, her money and property stripped away from her because she was of Jewish descent. Now the radio had begun to tell her what had been happening at places like Belsen and Buchenwald to the millions of Jews she had left behind. The tossing sleep Meitner had managed after learning of the concentration camp atrocities was plagued by nightmares. She had fits of uncontrollable weeping. And now an American stranger had arrived on her doorstep. Meitner was in a mood to pour out her feelings, and her ensuing conversation with Berg was probably a long one.

Berg doesn't seem to have asked anything of her that first day. Instead, he played the kind messenger, delivering Scherrer's letter and listening sympathetically while she talked. That night Meitner sat down and wrote a lengthy letter to Scherrer, in which she described her recent work, expressed her hostility to the likes of Von Weizsäcker and Heisenberg, and responded to Scherrer's offer of a job. She said she would consider going to ETH, and modestly detailed the number of graduate students and the sort of laboratory conditions she would require to do her work properly. It was after midnight when she closed the letter by saying, "Dr. Berg was extremely friendly; this does one so much good after the long years of isolation."

The next day Berg was invited to tea. Meitner mentioned Hahn, and now that they were friends, Berg had a suggestion. Why didn't she write to her old friend and partner? Berg would see that the letter got to Hahn in the United States. When he left that day, Berg carried the letter for Scherrer, a copy of one of Meitner's articles, which she'd inscribed to Berg "With many thanks and kindest regards," and a letter to Hahn.

Typed single space in English translation, Lise Meitner's letter to Otto Hahn covers a full page and a half. Meitner revealed nothing about her future plans or how she felt about the Russians. Still, as pleasant letters to old friends go, this was pure poison. "I feel that I have so much that I want so desperately to say," she begins. And then after she gives "full assurance of my unwavering friendship," sheets of outrage come pouring across the page. "How could a man who had never raised a finger against the Criminal of the last years ever be of any possible aid to Germany?" she demands. "That is the great tragedy of Germany, that you all have lost every kind of standard of righteousness and fair play. . . . You consciously worked for Nazi Germany, without, as far as is known, ever making a single attempt even at passive resistance. I must write this," she explains, "because there is so much at stake for Germany." And then she leans into him even harder. "Undoubtedly to salve your conscience, you have now and then helped some miserable human being, but millions of innocent people were murdered and 'nary' a protest was heard." She tells him of the disturbing things she has been hearing on the radio and faults Hahn for his reluctance to "see things clearly," because "it was too uncomfortable." She closes by asking Hahn, "Please let me know how you are," and asks him to forgive her because "the American is waiting, hence the haste." These concluding soupçons of endearment sound as strange as a back-alley thug bending over the man he has just jumped, asking how he is feeling, and apologizing for kicking in his ribs so untidily.

Otto Hahn was not in the U.S., but imprisoned in Belgium and bound for Farm Hall with Heisenberg and the other German scientists. He was soon to contemplate killing himself, after hearing of Hiroshima, and so it is perhaps merciful that the scathing letter Lise Meitner thought she was sending to him was actually written for Moe Berg. Hahn would never read it. Berg had no desire to do favors for Lise Meitner, and asking her to write to Hahn had been a ploy. Berg only wanted to know what she would say to Hahn, her professional confidant. Eventually the letter landed in Groves's hands, but first Berg read it, probably as soon as he was a few blocks from her home. He must have thought it remarkable. At the least, it reminded a man of what he'd been fighting for.

ON JUNE 30, Berg was back in Paris. Or, the OSS thought he was. Arrangements were being made for Scherrer to leave for the U.S. on or about July 19. It was hoped that Berg would accompany him. Berg left behind traces in the form of a hefty bill at Claridge's Hotel in London and back in Sweden, where he took some leave time, but by July 26, he was more than accounted for; he and Scherrer were in Howard Dix's office in Washington, discussing how to keep Meitner from the Russians. Berg suggested that the Rockefeller Foundation might support her work under Scherrer.

After Washington, Berg escorted Scherrer on his visits to Cal Tech and Aerojet in California. They traveled using aliases—Scherrer was Peter Sherman, and Berg, Morrell Bush—and had a good time. In San Francisco, red ink sketches came to life as Berg took Scherrer to a San Francisco Seals, Pacific Coast League, baseball game. Berg's old friend Lefty O'Doul was managing the Seals, and the well-traveled O'Doul knew how to present a tourist with a memorable occasion. He invited Scherrer to watch his first professional baseball game from the Seals dugout.

Returning home to the East Coast seemed to have an awkward effect upon Berg. He didn't want to be recognized, but then he did. At Washington's Griffith Stadium one afternoon, his old teammate Rick Ferrell was catching for the Senators, and Berg called out a greeting from the stands. "I'd turn to say hello," says Ferrell, "and he'd shush me like everything was secretive. I just wanted to say 'hello.' I guess all he wanted was a wave." The same sort of thing happened on a side trip to New York with Scherrer. They met up with Berg's OSS friend from London, Michael Burke, and Scherrer announced that he was eager to visit Manhattan's venerable celebrity haunt, the Stork Club. Berg was reluctant to go, "for fear of being recognized," said Burke, so it was agreed that Burke would take Scherrer inside for a drink while Berg waited outside in the shadows of a doorway across the street.

It was only around OSS people that Berg seemed comfortable. He passed one afternoon in Howard Dix's office with Dix and Margaret Feldman, telling them war stories. Feldman had always thought Berg "the perfect operator for OSS," an opinion that grew firmer now as she listened to him talk about the aborted submarine trip to see Amaldi in Italy, and his meeting with Meitner. Berg also described playing catch with the soldiers, although, as was often his habit when it came to storytelling, he changed the details some. He placed himself amidst a group of GI's in Germany who lacked only a second catcher to complete two sides of nine for a game. Berg volunteered to give it a try, although, he said, he'd never played any baseball before. With his first throw down to second base he was discovered. A voice straight out of Brooklyn exclaimed, "Jesus Christ! Moe Boig! And here you are in Goimany!"

The true version stood up fine without the embroidery, but Berg could be excused for his tinkering and, indeed, for feeling out of sorts that August. He had always been reluctant to give up secrets, and now one he had been guarding for close to two years was out in the instant it took to turn part of the Japanese city of Hiroshima into a pot of boiling black oil where tongues of fire scorched the bodies of men. Aside from whatever distress he may have felt at such vast destruction—he never talked about that—divulging the existence of the bomb meant, in a sense, that it was no longer his. He was not a scientist who could boast the tangible accomplishment of having helped to build the uranium bomb. The spy's currency is that he knows what others don't, and now everybody knew about the atomic weapon. And besides obviating his wartime activities, Hiroshima and Nagasaki somehow diminished them. Little Boy was the news of the century. Heisenberg's bomb never existed. A callous man might have dismissed Berg's work as a wild goose chase. Berg could have been excused for privately wishing that he had uncovered a German bomb and stopped it. If he'd shot the evil Heisenberg and thus scuttled Hitler's atomic bomb, that would have been something *heroic*. What he had done, of course, was also something heroic, but it required much complicated explanation, and explanations weren't permitted.

One person who grasped the fading resonance of Berg's work right away was Whitney Shepardson, the head of the OSS Secret Intelligence division. Shepardson wasn't so much out to celebrate Berg as he was eager to keep his job. There had been plenty of talk that Harry Truman was not well disposed to the OSS, that the new president intended to disband the organization. It was with that foremost in his mind that three days after Hiroshima, and even as a plutonium bomb was exploding over Nagasaki, Shepardson wrote formally to Berg, requesting that he set down a narrative of his AZUSA work before he returned to Europe. "We are entitled to claim credit, at the appropriate time, for our contribution and that contribution has been very largely through you," he wrote. "I don't think there is anyone in the organization who can make this record correctly and in detail except yourself." He closed by saying "how much it has meant to the organization that you have been working on this revolutionary subject." Berg didn't do it. He spent the rest of his life trying to write that narrative, but he never could.

WITH THE MANHATTAN bomb project, AZUSA, and the entire war over with, Berg and Paul Scherrer left for Zurich on September 14, Scherrer carrying one of the coveted copies of the just-published Smyth report titled *Atomic Energy for Military Purposes*. Six days later, President Truman signed an executive order terminating the OSS as of October 1. It would wind up its business as the Strategic Services Unit (SSU). Personnel reductions would begin immediately. Berg, meanwhile, had been instructed to read an OSS report on Soviet interest in German scientists and then pay another visit to Lise Meitner's home in Sweden. He must have found it all confusing. At the same time that the SSU was continuing to give him important secret work to do, it was sending him terse messages demanding that he make immediate account of the $13,058.49 in cash advances he had withdrawn during the war.

▼

A letter Howard Dix wrote him on October 1 added to a sense of unraveling. At first, Dix was all business. He instructed Berg to go to Rome to make sure that Amaldi, Wick, and their peers resisted the Russians, and also suggested that Otto Hahn should be asked to write to Meitner. Then Dix became desultory. Groves could not finance Meitner's proposed appointment in Zurich with Scherrer, he said, because Congress had "almost shut off the money spigot." Donovan would be no more help to Berg either. He was going back to practicing law. Dix described the "very grand" farewell speech the director had given on the twenty-eighth. As for Berg, Dix suggested that he be back in Washington by November. Berg had been hoping to go to Japan, in the wake of the atomic bombs. Dix wrote again on October 4, to say that the SSU could not send him there, and that it could probably do nothing more for Meitner. In a third letter, dated October 9, Dix told Berg that he would be leaving SSU at the end of the month to become a lawyer in New York.

Berg pressed on without Donovan and Dix. In the months before Hiroshima, the U.S. had placed the best German physicists in protective custody, but now the Russians were mining Eastern Europe for second- and third-level scientists. Groves wanted to know who the Russians were interested in and what they were offering them, so Berg climbed into a command car with Tony Calvert, two other agents, Pete Oates and William Warner, and a large supply of Spam and Hershey bars and drove to Vienna. After completing their business in Austria, Calvert went to see the Russian commanding general about cutting back to Germany through Soviet-occupied Czechoslovakia and couldn't get a straight answer out of him. This went on for three days until, finally, Calvert, Berg, and the rest piled into their car, drove across the Danube, yelling "Amerikanish" as they passed the Russian guard station, and drove on back roads to Prague. While passing through the countryside, they were stopped by half a dozen roving Russian soldiers. Berg reached into his pocket, pulled out a letter with a large red

star on it, and held it up. The soldiers saw this, saluted, and
backed off. If they'd been able to read English, they would
have known that they were being intimidated by a piece of
Texaco oil company stationery. Warner thought this brilliant.
Berg intrigued him. Berg's suit was threadbare, and his shoes
had holes in the sides. It turned out that Berg had cut the shoes
open to relieve pressure on a pair of painfully swollen bunions.

The ride continued through bombed-out Dresden to the
Russian sector of Berlin, which they entered "without a hitch,"
according to Calvert, on the late side of a rainy night. The
German science publisher and Allied spy Paul Rosbaud had
supplied them with a list of people to look up in East Berlin,
and they did. By this time it was clear to Calvert and Berg that
the Russian policy was to start by making a scientist a generous
offer. For someone they truly coveted, this might mean a dacha
on the Black Sea. Bachelors were tempted with the prospects
of a beautiful Russian mistress. If the offer was refused, the
scientist was then bundled off to the USSR against his will.

All this took about a week, and when it was done, Calvert
and Berg melted back into West Berlin. "Berg was always good
company wherever you went," says Calvert, who still keeps a
photograph of Berg in Prague on a wall in his office. "He was
quiet on the trip. He stayed in the background most of the
time."

CAME NOVEMBER, BERG was attending a lecture titled "La
Désintégration Atomique" by the French physicist and suspected Communist Frédéric Joliot-Curie at the Grand Am-
pithéâtre de la Sorbonne, in Paris, and paying a two-week visit
to Rome. In December, while SSU accounting officials fretted
about his expense records, Berg moved about on the Continent,
blithely continuing to withdraw money from special funds
when he ran short.

In early January, he requested 147 Swedish kronas. He was
visiting Lise Meitner again. Meitner had been given a tem-

porary position as a visiting professor at Catholic University in Washington, but one of the world's greatest scientists might reasonably expect to attract better work than that, and Berg went to see her to make sure that no tempting offers were coming from Moscow. The sight of Berg enraged Meitner. Some time after Berg's first visit to Stockholm, in June, a member of the British diplomatic legation had mailed a second letter from her to Hahn. In that letter she referred to the letter Berg had promised to deliver to him. In Hahn's reply, he said that he had never received it. "It was very personal," she said petulantly to Berg. Thinking quickly, Berg assured her that nobody had read it, and comforted her with the news that Hahn was in England and well taken care of. All the while curses tumbled through his brain. "It's fun to be double-crossed like this," he wrote sarcastically in notes he made after leaving her. "Why didn't the London people censor Meitner's latter letter to Hahn if they saw fit to deliver it?"

After Berg managed to calm her down, Meitner told him that she would not accept any Russian offer, and that Gustav Hertz, a friend of hers from Berlin, had probably gone to Moscow against his wishes. As for herself, a physics institute in Sweden wanted her to teach nuclear physics there after her term at Catholic University, and she was considering it. Meitner said that Hiroshima had come as a surprise to her, and that she was "sorry that the bomb had to be invented." A measure of how successful Berg had been at appeasing Meitner is that when he left, he was carrying a short note and a package of groceries Meitner had asked him to deliver to the aged German physicist Max Planck. Meitner worried that Planck wasn't getting proper things to eat.

Usually after Berg met someone, it was the other person who was left wondering about him, but with Meitner, the reverse was true. Berg never saw her again, but he talked about her for the rest of his life, sometimes in such a way that people came away from the conversation convinced that Berg had been her lover. But it wasn't Meitner that he loved. He loved the work. It was time for him to go home now, but he wasn't ready, and for the time being, nobody forced him.

Rather, they sent him on two more important errands. On January 23, he was in Zurich for Joliot-Curie's lecture at the Zurich Physical Society on atomic disintegration. Joliot-Curie had been fulminating against the U.S. and its atomic secrecy everywhere he went, and nothing in the Zurich version of the diatribe came as much of a surprise to Berg, who had heard it all before in Paris. As he had been doing for months, Joliot-Curie proposed that European countries form an atomic bomb bloc against the United States. Before the lecture, Joliot-Curie bragged to Scherrer that the French government provided him complete autonomy in his work, and in a conversation with Gregor Wentzel afterward, the French physicist made no effort to conceal his pro-Communist feelings. Berg sent in a report to Washington, recording all this and warning that Joliot-Curie could be expected to "continue his demagogic tactics all over Europe." Yet Berg wasn't worried, and neither was Washington. The feeling was that Joliot-Curie was more of a nuisance than a threat and that his talk of a European bloc wasn't worth the candle. Scherrer, for one, had promptly told Joliot-Curie that Switzerland wasn't interested. And neither, it seemed, was the Soviet Union. Berg learned that when Joliot-Curie attended the jubilee meeting of scientists in June, he was not permitted to visit the Moscow Physics Institute.

January ended, and February began for Berg with eight days in Copenhagen, where he paid a hasty call on Niels Bohr. An emissary of Peter Kapitza, a leading Russian physicist, had been seen leaving Bohr's house, and this concerned Groves, who knew that Bohr was a dreamer who believed that the best way to keep the world safe was to keep it free of atomic secrets. Two days after Nagasaki, Bohr had published an article in the *Times* of London, calling for "free access to full scientific information" and the "abolition of barriers hitherto considered necessary to safeguard national interests but now standing in the way of common security against unprecedented dangers."

▼

Groves also knew that in 1944 Kapitza had sent a letter through the Soviet embassy in London inviting Bohr to the Soviet Union in 1944. He suspected that Kapitza's emissary was a Russian agent. This led the ever-paranoid general to imagine that Bohr was taking it upon himself to encourage the sort of nuclear openness he was advocating by sharing his considerable fund of atomic knowledge with the Russians. But the only things Bohr had given to the Russians were some American physics journals. Berg got something better. Bohr's younger brother, Harald, inscribed a copy of one of his own books to him. Then Berg checked out of the Hôtel d'Angleterre, leaving behind his usual magnificent bill.

Berg's work with Meitner and Bohr pleased Dix's military replacement, Lieutenant Colonel S. M. Skinner. Skinner recommended that Berg be given a raise in salary, on the grounds that his work "has been of the highest caliber and exceptional importance. It has involved the necessity for unusual discretion, tact and fidelity to purpose. It has also required an exceptional degree of technical competence as well as personal courage." All this netted Berg an increase in salary, to the still nowhere near princely sum of $5,600 a year. It was a gesture of approval more than anything else, and Berg took it in hand and disappeared.

Throughout the war, Berg could be counted on to show up unannounced in London every few months. Since the German surrender and the foreclosure of the London OSS office, Berg had taken to using the army's Manhattan Project liaison office at 31 Davies Street behind the U.S. Embassy as his temporary base of operations. Generally this meant that he would ride up the erratic elevator to the liaison office when he was looking for someone to join him for supper at the Savoy Hotel. "He always liked the best places and had special tastes," says Lyall Johnson, who was executive officer of the liaison office. "He made himself very comfortable and made the people who served him tell him their life history, standing up there stiffly, telling him about themselves." Now, however, when an inquiry came into London from Washington asking for Berg's whereabouts, nobody at the liaison office had any idea. Through the rest of February, March, and April, yet another series of increasingly distraught cables wondered what had become of Moe Berg.

He reappeared in May. It turned out that he had gone skiing in Switzerland, where he had injured his leg.

One reason that the SSU was looking for Berg was they wanted to know how he'd been spending their money for the past two years. "Mr. Berg has returned several times to the United States, but has rendered no accountings . . . these facts indicate procrastination and avoidance of financial responsibility," came one indignant memo from the chief of SSU special funds to General John Magruder. Lieutenant Colonel Skinner argued in reply, "Berg's mission is of such value that it should not be endangered by a lapse of morale in him through demanding a specific accounting," and Magruder agreed. "I have no concern about the systematic and appropriate use of funds on the part of Mr. Berg," he wrote on March 20. By May, however, Lieutenant Colonel William Quinn, the head of the SSU, had become puzzled on two counts: why Berg was not yet back in the U.S., and what he had done with $19,012.99 in unvouchered special funds.

Berg was in Frankfurt, making notes to himself on Joliot-Curie. He had been told that the scientist had 200 tons of uranium and that there were three functioning atomic piles in France. Although he felt he had followed European atomic science very closely since October, Berg still had very little specific information about whom the Russians were interested in, whom they had already approached, and what countries were attempting to build piles on their own. The Dutch, for example, were rumored to have begun one, but Scherrer said not, and Berg believed him. All this was important to know, but as he moved about Europe, from France to Germany to Switzerland and to England, Berg was raising more questions than he was answering. At Nuremberg, the Chief U.S. Council

wondered what Berg was doing there, and General Edwin
Sibert of Army Intelligence let it be known to Edward Green,
commander of the U.S. Naval Reserve in Europe, that he "did
not like the idea of various individuals 'freewheeling' through
the [European] Theater."

You couldn't cross generals like that, and the SSU moved
to correct the situation. As usual, it took a while to locate Berg,
but in late July, Lieutenant Colonel Quinn met him in France
and asked him to go back to Washington. Berg protested that
he was onto some useful information, but Quinn was adamant.
"You are ordered back," he said, and so Berg boarded a plane.

In Washington he met with procedure, and it didn't agree
with him. He didn't like being told what to do, he resented
being questioned about money, and he didn't want to be home.
Disquieted and morose, in August he turned in two boxes of
.32 Colt automatic shells, kept his pistol, and resigned from
the SSU. In September he was told that his outstanding funds
now totaled $21,439.14. The SSU ordered him to explain it
all in writing by October.

Since early December 1945, meanwhile, the ever-loyal
Howard Dix had been writing and rewriting a letter outlining
Berg's exploits, in a prolonged effort to nominate Berg for the
Medal of Freedom. In one draft, Dix described Berg's entering
Italy by submarine in April 1944, when entering in June and
by command car was the truth. In another draft, Dix wrote,
"It must be borne in mind that Miss Meitner was under German surveillance all the time in Sweden, and frankly, the question in my mind is how Mr. Berg ever accomplished the ends
without being incarcerated; I do not know." Again this was
misleading. Berg had seen Meitner after the war had ended,
when it was perfectly safe to visit her. Yet Dix knew only what
Berg had told him, and besides, people expected medal rec-
ommendations to burst with tales of daring more than they
looked to them for scrupulous accuracy. Filled with mistakes,
exaggerations, and several quarts of hyperbole as Dix's letters

were, they met their purpose. On October 10, Berg was awarded the Medal of Freedom.

Citations usually describe what the honoree has done to be worthy of a medal, but Berg's activities in Europe were classified, a problem that his citation skirted by omitting the details of his work. The heart of it reads: "In a position of responsibility in the European Theater, he exhibited analytical abilities and a keen planning mind. He inspired both respect and constant high level of endeavor on the part of his subordinates, which enabled his section to produce studies and analyses vital to the mounting of American operations."

Berg was simultaneously being celebrated for his work and hounded out of the SSU. This wasn't unusual. Medals, in fact, were sometimes awarded to soften reluctant departures from service. But Berg was having none of it. On December 2, he rejected the award "with due respect for the spirit with which it is offered," acknowledged his debts in full, and asked that his Siberia and Japan films be returned to him. In January, Larry Houston, the former counsel to the OSS, went to New York to see him. Because Berg's work was so secret, very few people had known much about it, and records were kept to a minimum. Despite these obstacles, Houston had been looking into things and had calculated that, in all probability, the government owed Berg money. They met at the Pennsylvania Hotel, where what Berg had to say was as black and white as his shirt and tie. Houston remembers that Berg "was nice, very pleasant and said flatly, 'I don't want any of your money.' He was that angry." Houston got back to Washington and wrote to Berg, explaining, "There is no desire on the part of anyone to collect or to permit you to proffer any sum of money" and going on from there to praise "your accomplishments and your exceptional abilities." Silence. In April, Houston decided simply to close Berg's accounts, reasoning, as he wrote in an SSU memo, that "Berg's services were of great value, inestimable in dollars and cents, but in all probability far exceeding the cost to the government for Mr. Berg's two and a half years of service." Houston, who went on to work as legal counsel to the CIA, says, "Everyone I knew thought highly of [Berg], but he was not an easy man to deal with."

MONEY AND ORDERS weren't the source of Berg's snit so much as symptoms of a more complicated agitation. Simply put, he didn't want the war to end. The OSS had tolerated his eccentricity, rewarded his spontaneity, prized his work in a way that nobody ever had, and had also treated him like a pasha. The work had been perfectly suited to him. He had lived in the company of brilliant Europeans, probing at them while keeping himself a dark secret. Berg didn't want to give up this life. He was confused and angry that the OSS was gone.

And it wasn't as if the work had dried up. If anything, the situation seemed more dire than ever. Whereas in 1944 the U.S. had to concern itself only with a possible German bomb, scientists now were telling the government that one might come from Russia, France, Argentina, or any number of other places. The atomic recipe had worked. Anybody might now be trying to mix one up, and American scientists sounded even more frantic than they had when they were fretting about Heisenberg. Harold Urey, who had worried so loudly about the German atomic bomb while working on uranium separation at Columbia during the war, was now referring to "the most dangerous situation that humanity has ever faced in all history." A few years earlier, Chicago scientists were removing their families from the city for safekeeping. Now the hysteria was such that average people all over America were fleeing to remote places to dodge the impending nuclear apocalypse. All this, and Moe Berg, who had been the first American intelligence man trained to attend to such problems, was in from the cold.

In notes he scrawled on the back of an envelope but then left out of the letter he sent to Colonel Quinn declining the

Medal of Freedom, Berg says that when he saw Quinn in France, he knew he would be unable to accept the award, because "the whole story of my humble contribution [cannot be] known or divulged." These notes closed with a strange remark. "The medal embarrasses me," he said. Berg meant that if he couldn't tell people what he'd done to earn the medal, he didn't want it. For the twenty-five years that remained in his life, Berg would yearn to violate his promise of secrecy and talk freely about his war experiences in Europe. But, except for dropping his guard a few times, he refrained. It was hard for Berg to talk about himself on any subject, let alone one that was classified. And there was another, more practical reason not to say anything. He wanted to remain in the intelligence business.

CHAPTER 13

▼

A Life Without
Calendar

Though the war was over, Moe Berg was back in the
United States, living much as he had in Rome, London,
and Zurich. He was telling nobody where he was going
or what he was doing, appearing and vanishing without wave
or warning. The deception had changed. Whereas previously
he had been hiding the fact that he did espionage work for the
government, now he encouraged people to think he was a spy,
when the truth was that he was doing nothing. Save a few
lacunas, which included a bungled assignment from the CIA,
Berg's last twenty-five years were without regular employment
of any sort. Baseball and intelligence work had kept him in
nearly constant motion, permitting him much discretion in the
use of his time while providing a skeletal structure to his existence. Now the structure was gone, and Berg's became a life
without calendar. Unleashed from his moorings, he wandered

aimlessly, unburdened by appointment, salary, or obligation. This talented man who could have supported himself in so many ways chose instead to become a vagabond, living on wit and charm and the kindness of friends.

Always elusive, Berg now began to defy chronology. Whereas previously his movements could be marked along the immutable points of a baseball schedule and traced through the trail of documents recording his wartime activities, in the ocean of time that was the last third of his life there were very few buoys to chart his passage. The signal events of his life had all occurred, and so Berg gyred through an amorphous span of years. He watched baseball games, he traveled, he paid visits, he fled and traveled some more, and all the while he hoped for one of the government's infrequent calls.

For many World War II veterans, the war had been a disruption, and after the German and Japanese surrenders, they returned home to resume their lives. For Moe Berg, however, war had provided him with a life he loved, and returning home was the disruption. There was nothing there to anchor his attention. Until he left her to go off to Europe, Estella Huni had come close. She had brought him companionship, intimacy, and diversions, both social and intellectual. But she was now married, which inconvenienced Berg more than it buffeted him. Instead of sharing an Upper East Side Manhattan apartment, he was forced to move into the house of his brother, Dr. Sam, on Roseville Avenue in Newark. He had no better place to go. What he did have were big financial problems.

Shortly after his return to Newark, Berg received a telephone call from the Internal Revenue Service, requesting that he come in to their office and explain several years of expense deductions on his income tax return. An appointment was made for the following day. Berg arrived wearing his fedora and a fur-collared topcoat. The agent assigned to the matter knew who Berg was and he was nervous. Berg was not. He handed the IRS man a slip of paper with a Washington tele-

▼

phone number written on it and asked him to call. The agent went into his supervisor's office. The supervisor listened, took the slip of paper, and dialed the number himself. When Washington picked up, the supervisor explained who he was and that he was auditing Morris Berg's tax returns, and then the person in Washington began talking. A moment later the supervisor hung up and told the agent not to trouble Mr. Berg anymore.

The problems of the Novelart Manufacturing Company were not so easily solved. In 1933, Berg had been a founding investor in the stationery and film company with his friend Milton Kahn, who served as the managing director. For a while, with orders received from well-known department stores like S. S. Kresge, W. T. Grant, and F. W. Woolworth, and theaters from Virginia to Texas, the partnership did well. When Berg left for the war, he had reason to believe that his original investment of $4,000 had earned him a considerable profit. On December 11, 1944, Kahn contracted to provide the government with $117,000 worth of writing portfolios. A year later, he entered into a repricing agreement, assuming a debt to the government of $16,341. When Berg returned to the U.S., $7,500 remained unpaid and the company was on the verge of ruin. In the fall of 1950, Kahn incorporated, disconnected the telephone at the company's new Long Island City headquarters, and filed for bankruptcy. He was granted a discharge of his debts in early 1951. The government proceeded against Berg for the $7,500, plus 6 percent annual interest.

Berg had made none of Novelart's financial decisions, and might have been more than justified in filing for bankruptcy himself, but he resisted. At the time, bankruptcy was still publicly regarded as something approaching chicanery, and Berg would not consider it. Perhaps he was confident that the crisis would dissolve. But this time there was no appreciative OSS or mysterious voice on the telephone in Washington to hoist him from the financial morass. By stoically maintaining his honor in the Novelart affair, Berg put himself in for years of misery.

Accounts of how the demise of Novelart affected him vary. Berg may have focused his resentment on a government that pursued him for money when he felt it should have been welcoming him home as a hero. In any case, Berg's initial response to the situation was to ignore it.

The simplest way to have satisfied the government was for Berg to have taken a job and begun to make payments on the debt. He didn't do that. Ted Lyons, the new manager of the White Sox, offered him a coaching position. Berg declined. Red Sox owner Thomas Yawkey would always have found something for one of his favorite players to do in Boston, but Berg never asked him to, and when Yawkey tried, he was politely rebuffed. Berg did not apply for a teaching position, join a law firm, advertise his legal services, or even list himself in the Newark or Manhattan telephone books.

For years, he ignored all the government entreaties to resolve his debts. "He loved the United States, he was incredibly patriotic, but he didn't consider that the IRS had anything to do with the United States," says Berg's friend Sayre Ross. It wasn't until 1953 that the government moved in. Berg returned to Newark from a CIA assignment in Europe, and was contacted by FBI agents, who knew that he had been earning money and wanted to know how he intended to make good on his Novelart debts. Berg paid $500 and offered $200 more, to complete a compromise settlement. When the agents talked the matter over with him, Berg told them that he would earn $9,000 for the year, but he would reveal nothing about the nature of his government work except to say that he had no tenure and his employment might cease at any time. The government division charged with evaluating the situation recommended against accepting the compromise, noting that Berg's "past history indicates that he might be able to earn much more than his present salary if he should leave govern-

▼

ment service and go back into business. He appears to be a man of middle age, in good health and of sound mind."

Berg was not able to earn more than his salary at that time. In fact, he earned far less. For 1954, his total income was nothing. His bank account held $200, and he had not another asset in the world, except for his battered old catcher's mitts and some worn gray suits. By May 1955, after borrowing money to pay his 1953 income taxes, he was more than $12,000 in debt. In January 1956, he made another compromise offer, of $1,500, on the Novelart claim against him, and this time the offer was accepted. Berg told the FBI that he would borrow the remainder of what he owed from a friend in Washington, and apparently he did, ending the protracted affair for everyone but the friend, who probably never got his or her money back. According to Ethel Berg, the situation "depressed him deeply—yet he did not speak of it."

The failure of Novelart did not stop Berg from working. He stopped himself. Berg owed his tatterdemalion days to more than a hatred of offices and a loathing for routine. He didn't work because his chosen employer, the CIA, did not want him, and for another most convenient reason: he didn't have to.

OF THE 13,000 people employed by the OSS in 1945, the CIA kept only 1,300 on the payroll. To his endless disappointment, Moe Berg was not one of them. Technically, he had resigned from the SSU, but the truth is that he had been cast aside, and he still pined for the work. Secret work fascinated Berg, even obsessed him. He spent hours filling notebooks with cryptic thoughts on the craft of intelligence work. "You can't get intelligence by sitting & saying nothing," he wrote one day. "Must learn to observe everything—where placed . . . my experiences in Moscow (1935)—Berlin (1933–35)—hotel rooms—things moved," he scribbled on another. He holed up in Washington hotel rooms and sketched out lengthy CIA mission proposals that sometimes covered sixty or seventy sheets of hotel stationery. In 1951, for example, he begged the CIA to send him to Israel. "A Jew must do this," he wrote in his notebook. For years, when he arrived home in the evening at his brother's house, Berg would ask Dr. Sam, "Did any mail come for me from Washington?" With one exception, the response from Dr. Sam and the CIA was always no.

The CIA was not spoiling to disappoint Berg. It did not ask him to do things for it at first because he had made such trouble for his SSU administrators at the end of the war. Then, when he was given some work, he did poorly enough that there was no reason to trust him with anything more. As with so much about Berg, this failure was a function of personality. The same qualities that made Berg the quintessential OSS agent led to problems at the CIA.

The OSS overlooked Berg's unpredictable movements, dilatory response to some orders, overlong reports, and shoddy accounting for large sums of money, and it soothed his quarrels with Jack Marsching and Allen Dulles. In General Donovan, he had a sympathetic boss whose sensibilities meshed happily with his own. The CIA would reject Donovan and his adventurous style of intelligence, bringing a more disciplined approach to the business of fighting Communists. Or, as Richard Helms, director of Central Intelligence (DCI) between 1966 and 1973 and an OSS veteran, puts it, "The difference between the two organizations, basically, was that the CIA, since it was operating in peacetime, had to set up far more regulations on what people and agents were doing." Station chiefs, for example, would now always be told which agents were coming into their territory, and what their purpose was. The Agency would brook no more scraps like the one between Berg and Dulles. General Donovan, says Helms, "was not particularly interested in organization or administration," and neither was Berg. Still, for all this, the CIA gave Moe Berg some work to do in 1952. Urgent voices in the U.S. were asking what kind of new atomic weapons the Soviet Union might be building, and Berg knew something about gathering intelligence on enemy bomb programs.

In 1952, the American zeitgeist was fear—cold, damp, corrosive fear. After 1950, when Klaus Fuchs, tall and slim behind tortoise shell glasses, was arrested in England for the crime of using his over-soft voice to turn over atomic secrets to the Russians, American intelligence began to wonder not just how much the Russians knew but who was telling them. Worried into a frenzy of suspicion by the likes of Harry Gold, Kim Philby, Ethel and Julius Rosenberg, and Allan Nunn May, and goaded by the long, paranoid lash of Joseph McCarthy, some Americans saw traitors everywhere. In Washington, in 1952, CIA director Bedell Smith confessed that he was "morally certain" that "there are Communists in my own organization."

On February 5, 1950, in Oak Park, Illinois, a frightened man was moved to write the FBI director J. Edgar Hoover a letter in which he stated, "In connection with the current A-bomb spy developments, I may be able to present you with a possible lead. The subject is Moe Berg." The man—he begged the FBI not to "mention my name in any way"—had met Berg at Claridge's Hotel in London during the war, where he learned that Berg, the son of Ukrainian parents, was "quite favorably disposed to Soviet Russia. In view of his extensive travels to Switzerland and Sweden, it is possible that he might have passed important information to Soviet agents." He felt that the FBI "would do well to investigate [Berg] thoroughly." Hoover, always glad to oblige, dispatched an agent to meet with Berg's accuser at a bar, where the man backed off a little. He "stated that although he was not particularly suspicious of Berg, he felt that Berg did have an immense amount of valuable information pertaining to the atomic bomb in his possession." All this was neatly taken down and filed away without any public disclosure. It is probable that Berg, a vigorous American patriot to the end, was never told that his government had investigated allegations that he was turning over secrets to the Russians.

Another man with an immense amount of valuable information about the atomic bomb was Enrico Fermi's prize student, the dashing Italian scientist Bruno Pontecorvo. Nearly as brilliant a tennis player as he was a scientist, Pontecorvo had been an employee at Harwell, the British atomic research establishment, when on September 2, 1950, during a vacation, he and his family disappeared from Helsinki, Finland. It was eventually revealed that Pontecorvo was now playing his tennis in Moscow, but what remained a mystery were his reasons for defecting and what he was telling the Soviets.

American intelligence was still puzzling about this ten months later, when Berg proposed going to Europe and tracking down some of his old scientific contacts to see what they knew about Soviet atomic science, about Pontecorvo, and about postwar German nuclear research. "We said, 'great idea,' " recalls an official in CIA Eastern European and German operations at the time. Berg filled out an information questionnaire, on which he claimed "good" facility in only three languages, and listed the Riggs Bank in Washington and a Washington hotel as credit references. To the CIA that said "I don't live anywhere." Berg was given a fat $10,000 contract, an airplane ticket, and an expense account, and off he went.

Berg landed in Europe on July 11, and spent several months there. It was like old times. He visited Scherrer in Zurich and Amaldi in Rome, and spent plenty of time in London. He later told friends that he went to the Black Forest in Germany to interview Anna Anderson, allegedly Anastasia, the daughter of the last czar, and considered her "a complete fake." Slipping effortlessly into his OSS routine, in each city Berg slept in posh hotels, dined on magnificent meals in the finest restaurants, and kept no receipts for the several thousand dollars it cost him. Very quickly he lost touch with his superiors at the CIA.

His operations file began to fill up with pieces of paper that asked "Where is he?" "What's he doing?" and worried that "the operation is going down the toilet."

Eventually Berg found his way to the old spa town of Bad Homburg, not far from Frankfurt, where he paid an unannounced visit to Michael Burke and his wife, Timmy. Burke was in charge of American covert activity for the area, and lived in a large house near the park that ran through the center of town. Berg moved into the guest house behind the Burkes' house. After breakfast on his first morning there, Berg went with Burke into Frankfurt. While Berg was gone, a maid tidied up the guest house, making the bed and arranging the newspapers that had been scattered around the room into a neat pile on the desk. Berg returned later in the day, took one look at the room, and became very upset. "No one is to disturb my newspapers," he told Burke with some vehemence. For the maid, he left notes beside the newspapers that said, "Don't disturb—they're alive." The maid did not set foot in the guest house again until Berg had left. She couldn't. Berg had confiscated her key.

The Burkes were fond of Berg, and enjoyed a pleasant fortnight with him. He always wore a kimono to breakfast. At dinner parties he was shy—Timmy had the feeling he was always "sizing people up"—but when the three were alone, Berg told wonderful stories about his days in Japan. One Sunday, he joined Timmy and her French poodle for a walk in the Bad Homburg park. All was amicable until they rounded a corner and Timmy recognized an acquaintance. "Oh, there's Bobby Van Roijen," she said. Berg shot away from her and hid behind some bushes. It was late fall and the bushes had no leaves, so Berg in his dark overcoat was plainly visible. "Who's that man?" Van Roijen asked Timmy. "A friend," she replied smoothly. "He had to go to the loo." Timmy and Van Roijen waited for a few minutes, and eventually Berg emerged from the bushes and walked back to the house with Van Roijen, Timmy, and her poodle. Nobody said a word. Timmy told her husband about what had happened, and Michael Burke was delighted. "Oh, that's Moe," he said. "I once was with him at Rockefeller Center and suddenly Moe just left me and hid behind a column. After a while he came out. We carried on and he never explained anything."

When he got back to the U.S., the CIA was perplexed by Berg. He wouldn't reveal anything. "We said to him, 'Who did you see, what did they have to say?' " says a CIA officer who spoke with Berg at the time. "It was not very solid. It was, well, flaky. He was tantalizing. He'd talk about schemes and people with great enthusiasm and you'd say, 'Moe, tell me about this,' and it disappeared in a cloud of fluff. I sometimes felt that when Moe told things, some of it might have been embroidering." The comments that began appearing in the operations file now said that Berg had failed to find out anything in Europe but wouldn't admit it.

Berg seems to have learned nothing from his OSS accounting experiences after the war, for now he could provide the CIA with no expense record at all, and when pressed for one, he lost his patience. "Oh, for Christ's sake, quit being bureaucrats," he complained. Had he produced something of value, the Agency might have been willing to do that—the CIA abounded with brilliant profligates—but all Berg could offer was obfuscation. The CIA had been patient. When his contract expired in 1953, after a brief lapse it was renewed. Nobody was asking Berg to do very much, however, and desperate for work, he tried to latch onto a CIA project he'd heard about. He pitched himself as a bargain, arguing that since he was already being paid, he would be doing valuable work for nothing. "Thank you, no" was the answer. When his contract expired in 1954, this time the CIA chose not to renew it.

In 1966, Berg tried again. His work proposal was received optimistically, he was given CIA security clearance, and he was invited to Washington to discuss a possible assignment. He did not impress. The Berg CIA file now bulged with comments that said that he was more unpredictable and more irascible than ever, a man who insisted upon operating as a loner, not as part of a team, who couldn't conform to accounting requirements, and who delivered an unsatisfactory product. No assignment was extended to him, and the security clearance was terminated.

Berg, of course, didn't tell people any of this. He once explained to Sam Goudsmit that he broke with the CIA in 1960 because it was anti-Semitic and because he couldn't get along with Allen Dulles. Dulles was the deputy director of the CIA from 1951 to 1953, and then the DCI, until November 1961. Berg had never forgiven him for their wartime spat in Bern. Donovan died in 1959, and Dulles was an honorary pallbearer at the funeral. Berg told Ted Sanger that if Donovan had known Dulles had a hand on his coffin, "He'd have jumped out and run away."

While there is plenty of evidence that Berg blamed his troubles on Dulles, there is none that Dulles aggressively impeded Berg at CIA. People who worked with Dulles describe him as a practical man, willing enough to overlook personal differences with a subordinate if he thought he could get good work out of him. "Dulles was a big fella," says Bill Hood. "If he saw a use for a guy like Berg, he'd have said, 'Well, maybe he's matured.' He wouldn't have held a grudge. He just wanted to get on with the job." As a rule, the CIA takes care of its own, and it might have looked after Berg had he played by their rules. But he did not because he could not. Allen Dulles wasn't the source of Berg's problems, Berg was.

With no Donovan or Groves to protect him, Berg withered into obsolescence as the profession that had made him a hero shook him loose. "He was a real romantic, I guess," says a man to whom Berg reported at the CIA. "He had a wonderful notion of being a buccaneer, an independent operator. Intelligence doesn't work that way. I would have thought that—particularly in those days [the 1950s]—if he had produced anything of value, people would have overlooked the idiosyncrasies, overlooked his freewheeling methods of operation."

But the results were not good, and the style was out of favor. "A Berg who is wandering around the world doing all sorts of jobs is just the sort of fellow we didn't want—they attract too much attention," says Richard Helms. "Risk taking within structure" was what the CIA preached to its operators. Controlled risk takers are rare, and Berg, like most people, was unsuited to these living games of chess. An intelligence man should never advertise that his business is secrets, and Berg did so constantly. "The goal of the craft is natural appearance," says Charles McCarry, a retired CIA deep cover agent. "A man who says 'Shsh' makes people who are inside either very nervous or very contemptuous."

Monroe Karasik, one of Berg's colleagues at the OSS, managed to follow Berg's career and concluded, "Moe was an amateur and quite a good amateur, but in the end an amateur. The people you won't ever hear about are the real professionals. Moe had all of the qualifications, but I don't think he ever became a pro. It starts with the ability, but you must always attend to it. Moe did not take the time to become a pro. People who succeed in this métier thought he was useful but limited. In a certain sense he resembled a beagle. They have marvelously sensitive noses. They smell something utterly delicious and then they smell something else utterly delicious. That's why beagles run away a lot and get lost." Berg was a determinedly non-introspective man, and may never have known why exactly he failed at the CIA. And when he did poorly at the assignment he was given in 1952, and came home to find government agents pressing him for the Novelart money, he did not stop to analyze his plight. Instead, he turned tail, ran away, and got lost.

Broke, disappointed, and disinclined, Berg did have one asset that no government could strip from him—his personality. People were drawn to him, they always had been. "Every success he had came from his personality," says Harry Broley.

▼

"He was a hard man to walk away from. He was loaded with charm." Even at the CIA, it wasn't that anyone had disliked Berg. The CIA man who supervised Berg's 1952 assignment says that Berg "engendered great affection. He was a delightful personality, fun to be with, a real extrovert with a high level of energy." Berg's personality had become an impediment to his intelligence career, but it would be an advantage elsewhere. When he couldn't make a living at the CIA, Berg began traveling from place to place, visiting.

An unplanned, itinerant existence is unthinkable for most people, but Berg was comfortable with it. He acknowledged as much in 1954, writing in a notebook, "As always, fluid. If I'm in the vicinity, I'll be there." And when Russell Gray invited him to speak to his Princeton class in 1959, Berg was again candid about his circumstances. He refused to make a speech—"It wouldn't become me to address guys who knew me at seventeen"—and made no promises to attend the gathering. "You know I'm a vagabond," he told Gray. "I don't know where I'll be tomorrow, as a matter of fact." Like George Orwell, down and out in Paris, Berg found that poverty "annihilates the future." After the war, Berg discovered that friends would happily supply him with lodging, meals, clean underwear, suits, and even pocket money just because they liked to be around him. For most of his last twenty-five years, Berg permitted all sorts of people that pleasure and came to believe that he was doing them the favor.

Berg dressed in wash-and-wear suits, nylon or rayon shirts that could be wrung out in a sink each night and required no pressing, and thick black policemen's shoes, ideal for a man prone to bunions and who often walked great distances. His luggage consisted of a small ditty bag that held only a razor and a toothbrush. He rarely bought train tickets. Instead, Berg made friends with train conductors, who considered it a privilege to be his host. Then, leaning back in his free seat, Berg would open his newspaper and read while the train hurried him on to a city that he'd just decided to visit. Today's destination was tomorrow's point of departure. Instead of a locus, he had only datelines.

Since Berg himself rarely had any idea where he'd be from one day to the next, other people could hardly be expected to keep up with him. After Berg returned home from Europe in 1946, Howard Dix tried, but almost immediately found that it was a hopeless pursuit, as he told Earl Brodie. "I do not know where your black-haired boy friend is . . . I do not know whether he may be on a trip or not." One good place to check was Princeton. Berg passed through frequently, and never more so than during home football Saturdays in the autumn of 1946.

Each time he went to Princeton that year, Berg liked to stay over for a night or two at H. P. Robertson's house. His pattern of arrival never varied, and eventually took on the ritual qualities of a ceremony—a faintly absurd ceremony. Berg would telephone the Robertsons on a Friday from somewhere in town—Firestone Library, perhaps, where he liked to read the newspapers—and announce, "I just came in for the game." This was a cue that the entire Robertson family learned to heed. "But you must stay the night with us" was the practiced rejoinder. Berg would refuse. He just couldn't. The Robertson family member would insist. An instant later Berg had capitulated. Someone hurried over to the library to pick him up, swung by the train station so he could collect his ditty bag, which was conveniently, yet not presumptuously, stowed in a public locker, and then brought him to the house, honor intact, ready for a rousing weekend.

On Saturday, Berg and Robertson would go to the football game at Princeton's Palmer Stadium and cheer for Robertson's son, Duncan, a right tackle on the team. Afterward, back at the house, Berg and Robertson, born talkers, told stories. Neither would discuss the war, Robertson refusing to broach the subject even with his family. Berg, however, liked to drop small hints about what he'd done in Europe. "He was evasive," Duncan Robertson remembers. "You pieced together little things." When it came to baseball, Berg was more forthcoming. As with everyone, he liked to tell the Robertsons stories of his trips to Japan. He told the family that when he was in Japan, nobody could tell him apart from the Japanese. The Robertsons were skeptical. "I don't know, he didn't look Japanese," says Robertson's daughter, Mariette. "He was twice as tall as they were." A man from *Life* magazine was once in the family living room, discussing with Robertson whether the curve ball curves. Berg became infuriated that someone was trying to dupe his friend. "Professor," he cried, "I don't want you to be taken in by this. I know a curve ball curves." And then to the room, "I'm not gonna let them them make a fool out of the professor."

On Saturday evenings, Berg tagged along with the Robertsons to cocktail parties hosted by the Institute of Advanced Study scholars. These were hard-drinking affairs, where the physicists gulped down martinis and wondered what would happen to the bomb they'd just made, now that the politicians had their hands on it. Berg met all sorts of people—anyone from Johnny von Neumann to Niels Bohr to Robert Oppenheimer might show up—and many of them were delighted to talk with "the smart baseball player." They were even more pleased when they found he could discuss their work with them. For many years after Robertson left to teach at Cal Tech in 1947, Berg would be asked to Princeton parties on his own.

Berg was also invited to spend two afternoons at the Princeton home of Albert Einstein. In December 1946, Pocket Books published an anthology of articles culled from the pages of the *Atlantic Monthly*. Included were Berg's piece on pitchers and catchers and an essay by Einstein on the atomic bomb. Sometime after this, Berg and John Kieran paid a call on Einstein. Einstein asked the two men to explain the "theory of baseball" to him, and with the help of a pencil and paper, they tried.

Einstein quickly lost his patience and vowed that he could not understand baseball now, and would never try again. That was Kieran's version. Berg described the afternoon differently. According to Berg, "the Professor" made him a glass of tea, played his violin for him, and then announced, "Mr. Berg, you teach me baseball and I will teach you the theory of relativity." Then, after a pause, he said, "No, we must not. You will learn relativity faster than I will learn baseball."

After the Robertsons moved to California, Berg stayed at the Trenton Inn, which was partially owned by his Princeton friend and classmate S. Lang Makrauer. Makrauer never charged him, and sometimes Berg installed himself there for weeks. In the spring, Berg liked to go to Princeton baseball games and even to practices. While he was sitting in the stands in 1957, his eye fastened upon Dick Edie. "For some reason he showed up at a lot of baseball games I played in," says Edie. "You'd look in the stands and there'd be a guy in a black suit with a *New York Times* and an umbrella under his arm. Then he'd disappear." Eventually Berg introduced himself, and after that, sometimes he would be invited to Edie's eating club for dinner. Edie wrote his undergraduate thesis on the history of Princeton baseball, and while he was aware that Berg had been a star player in his day, what Edie didn't know was that Berg would sometimes sit in Firestone Library, copying out page after page of the thesis verbatim into his notebooks. One day, he transcribed twenty-seven pages.

Through the 1950s and 1960s, Berg returned again and again to Princeton, though changes at the University troubled him. Princeton decided to begin admitting women in 1968, which Berg thought was a mistake. "My God, Sam," he once exclaimed to his brother. "This is not the college I once knew." He always remained a habitué of Princeton football games. At one of them he met a Lawrenceville School mathematics teacher named Robert Wallace. When Berg came to Princeton on a weekday, he might spend the morning at the library, join

Wallace for lunch, and then Wallace would give him a ride to the train station. Once Wallace's mother ate lunch with them at the Nassau Inn. Berg made a fuss over her, and Wallace never forgot it. Berg told Wallace just enough about his role in the war so that, without knowing any of the details, Wallace came away convinced that Berg was a hero who had risked his life many times. Wallace had one more impression of Berg. He sensed that he was lonely.

On Saturdays, Berg liked to pass the time with sportswriters like Harvey Yavener of the *Trenton Times*, who were assigned to cover the football games at Palmer Stadium. Yavener and another Trenton newspaper writer, Bus Saidt, got to doing things with Berg outside Princeton. They'd pick him up from his brother's house in Newark and take him places. At toll booths on the New Jersey Turnpike, Berg would read the toll taker's name plate and work his trick of identifying what country the person's ancestors came from and where in that country they'd lived. Yavener and Saidt, who paid for the tolls as they paid for all expenses when Berg was along, were amazed. When Saidt celebrated his fiftieth birthday, Berg insisted they go out to dinner to celebrate. Berg brought a date, and Saidt paid the check. Saidt didn't mind. He enjoyed Berg's company, and so did Yavener, who thought Berg was the "most charming person I've ever known. He was warm and made people feel good about themselves. You were flattered that he spent time with you." Berg paid his way with stories. He'd tell the sportswriters about his war exploits and about exotic women, but if they ever asked what he was doing at the moment, he held his finger to his lips. Yavener and Saidt assumed he was working for "the government." Berg's form of departure encouraged that impression. "He was like a ghost," says Yavener. "He'd appear and disappear." They weren't the only ones in the Princeton press box wondering about Berg. Sooner or later, everyone did. Morrie Siegel of the *Washington Post* once asked Bill Wallace of the *New York Times*, "What does he do?"

"Nobody knows," said Wallace.

In the late 1940s, Ted Berg was a young boy growing up in Elyria, an Ohio town twenty-five miles west of Cleveland, when his first cousin once removed Moe Berg came for a visit. Berg stayed for a few days and then, on a snowy night, he asked to be driven to the airport. Ted and his father took the front seat, Berg sat in back, and off they went. They neared the airport, and were traveling on an access road separated by a chain-link fence from the end of a runway, when Berg said he wanted to get out. The terminal was not yet in view, and all Ted could see was snow-blanketed fields. It was a dark night, cold and still. Fresh snow was falling. Ted had noticed that Berg wore leather shoes, and no galoshes. Berg asked the man and the boy in the front seat to drive away without looking back. Ted peeked anyway, but Berg had already disappeared.

When Berg telephoned to say he was in Philadelphia, his friend I. M. Levitt from the Franklin Institute was always glad to host him. Berg would arrive at the house, the pockets of his overcoat stuffed with newspapers. After the catching up was done, the two men liked to play a game, using Levitt's giant, two-volume unabridged dictionary. Levitt would open the book and pick out a word at random, and it would be up to Berg to give its derivation, root, and meaning. Levitt says Berg was never stumped. They stayed up half the night talking, playing, and nibbling cookies, until Levitt's wife, Alice, finally dragged her husband off to bed. Berg would wave good night, saying he intended to do a little reading before he went to sleep. That wasn't all he did. One night Levitt awakened in the middle of the night and went into the bathroom, where he discovered Berg's freshly washed underwear and socks drying over the bathtub, as they always were when he traveled. When the

▼

Levitts got up at seven, Berg, as always, was dressed and waiting for them. The clothes were gone from the bathroom. But if you brushed Berg's arm in the first part of the day, you'd notice that it was damp.

Berg never looked exactly shabby to Levitt, but he sensed that Berg was enduring hard times, and it baffled him. "I can't understand, with his abilities, why he could possibly be impoverished," he says. Levitt surmised that Berg's life "was spent keeping current, reading every paper he could get his hands on." Berg never asked Levitt for money, but Levitt occasionally gave him some, and Berg never refused it.

OKLAHOMA CITY, OKLAHOMA

Berg was Tony Calvert's surprise guest in early 1954. He seemed to Calvert "to be at loose ends. He put up a good front but you could see from his dress and his conversation that things weren't the best." Calvert was in the oil business, and Berg had oil on his mind. He'd just been to Alberta, Manitoba, and Saskatchewan, looking over Canadian oil fields, visiting the Icelandic collection at the University of Manitoba library, and sending out postcards on which he scrawled "X marks my room" and neglected to sign his name. On December 31, in the University of Alberta campus bookstore, he copied down into a notebook the complete titles of twenty-four books that interested him, from *Man the Tool Maker* and *Ukrainian Grammar* to *Latin for Pharmacy Students* and *Introduction to English Law*. What he was doing in Canada his notebooks make less clear, but during this period in his life, it appears that Berg attempted to form several different investment consortiums. In 1953 it was to be an oil deal. Two years later it was stainless steel.

People who knew him were always hearing rumors that Berg had his money in a Minnesota mining company or in Louisiana natural gas. But what money? As he had confessed to the government collectors, and which they verified, there was none. He made copious lists of potential investors and customers, but there is no evidence that he made any money for himself, and according to his brother, Berg squandered plenty from other people. Calvert was not one of them. Berg called him another time, to propose that Calvert back him in a deal that involved Israeli drilling rights. Calvert told Berg that Calvert Oil was too small an outfit to handle something like that.

CALIFORNIA

A few months after leaving Calvert, in the spring of 1954, Berg turned up in Oakland, California. Early one evening, Earl Brodie came home after work, opened the front door, and there was Berg seated in his living room, one leg crossed over the other, giving Brodie's two-year-old daughter, Andrea, endless up-and-down rides on his shoe. Berg had arrived by foot, he stayed for dinner, charming everyone with his thoughts on ballet, opera, and literature, and then late in the evening he announced that he was leaving. Brodie offered to give him a lift to the airport or to call a cab, but Berg declined and walked out into the night. "I think there was a flying saucer out there waiting for him," says Brodie.

H. P. Robertson was now teaching at Cal Tech, and Berg headed south to see him. Robertson would go to his office during the day, leaving Berg to amuse himself. One morning he rode into Los Angeles with Robertson's daughter, Mariette, a UCLA junior. When Mariette picked him up after classes to bring him home, Berg asked her to stop by Los Angeles City Hall for a few minutes. He said he had to meet someone in the men's room. She agreed, waited outside for him, and then drove him home. She knew Berg pretty well, knew that he was "entertaining" and "told lots of lies," but what happened in the men's room she never found out.

▼

The Robertsons were plotting to fix Berg up with another house guest, Johnny von Neumann's sister-in-law, Bushka, who was visiting from her home in England. One afternoon it was arranged that the two were left alone at the house, where very quickly the proposed match became a perfect mess. Bushka had two sons at home in England, and Berg asked her what sort of gift she was going to take them from her American visit. She said she didn't know. Berg had a suggestion. "Why don't you take them a nylon shirt?" he said. And then, "You can wash mine now, so you know how to wash them." That was about as romantic as it got.

Robertson introduced Berg also to William Fowler, the Cal Tech physics professor and future Nobel laureate. Fowler, like I. M. Levitt and so many of the men who admired Berg, was a baseball fan. Robertson had told Fowler that Berg was "a very smart man," and Fowler, a lifelong Pittsburgh Pirates supporter, was easily persuaded. "He was magical," says Fowler. "I was always surprised at the depth of his knowledge. No subject could come up on which Moe didn't have comments that were quite intelligent and apropos." They talked mainly about baseball, but in this and subsequent meetings, Berg was always eager to know about new developments in physics, and Fowler was soon telling Berg what he was doing in the lab. "A lot of that stuff was classified," he says. "I knew with Moe it would stay classified."

Fowler never knew how to contact Berg, but he didn't need to. Berg found him. At Physical Society meetings in Washington and New York, Fowler would be standing with a clutch of physicists between sessions, discussing the presentation they had just heard, when there would be Berg, listening right along, taking it all in. He and Fowler always exchanged a big hug and made plans to have supper together. "I kind of felt that Moe didn't have much money," says Fowler. "I always put his dinner on my hotel bill. I'd invite him to dinner, and afterward, he'd just vanish."

It was through Antonio Ferri that Berg met Theodore Von Karman. Berg stayed in loose touch with Ferri, now a professor at the Brooklyn Polytechnic Institute, and his wife, occasionally meeting them for dinner. Ferri liked to include scientific friends and colleagues in these outings, and once, when Von Karman was in New York, he came along.

The Budapest-born Von Karman had revolutionized the American aviation industry with his ideas on supersonics, rockets, and airborne weaponry. Despite his mother's warnings that the U.S. was full of gangsters, Von Karman had come to Cal Tech in 1930, and by the time Berg met him in the mid-1950s, he had founded or had a part in founding some of the United States' most powerful military research and development organizations, among them the Aerojet Corporation, the Rand Corporation, the Jet Propulsion Laboratory, and the NATO Advisory Group for Aeronautic Research and Development (AGARD). He was a fun-loving Jewish bachelor with an earthy sense of humor and great personal warmth, and he and Berg liked each other from the start.

Von Karman moved from place to place almost as much as Berg did, and so they met up in New York, Washington, and a few times in Ithaca, during Von Karman's terms as a visiting professor at Cornell. One year, a Japanese scientist, Yasujiro Kobashi, was also at Cornell. Von Karman was not a baseball fan, but Kobashi was, and with that in mind, Berg wrote a name in Japanese characters on a blackboard. With a wink at Professor W. R. Sears, who was also in the room, he asked Kobashi who that was. "Cone-ee Mock—great manager of Philadelphia Athletics" was the response. Berg picked up the chalk and wrote out another name. Kobashi was baffled. "Connie Mack," he read aloud. "Who is that?" That was, of course, the correct pronunciation of Mack's name, proving Berg's point that many Japanese mispronunciations of English words are

▼

due to faulty transliteration. There was more to Berg's friendship with Von Karman than displays of erudition. In 1956, when Berg flew out to Pasadena to see Von Karman, it was to discuss the legal issues involved in helping Von Karman's brother to leave Hungary, in the wake of the Soviet crackdown.

Ferri owed his job in the U.S. to Berg, and through Von Karman, in 1958, he did Berg a favor in return. It was obvious to Ferri that Berg was having financial difficulties, and he suggested to Von Karman that he help him out. It was no easy business getting Moe Berg to take a job. No matter how strapped he was, the work had to satisfy his pride, appeal to his curiosity, and accommodate his distaste for regular working hours. Von Karman had something in mind that would cover all that. He asked Berg to accompany him to the 1958 AGARD meeting in Paris, and Berg accepted.

On Berg's government employment form, Von Karman noted, somewhat generously, that "Mr. Berg is an expert in the field of foreign diplomacy and public relations." Berg was paid $50 a day and called a consultant. AGARD's aim was to encourage European countries to develop weapons technology of their own instead of relying on the U.S. defense industry to do it for them. This was not a subject upon which Berg could offer much consulting expertise. In one of his notebooks, Berg described his job more accurately, writing, "My new career to see scientific friends—bolster." He was, in fact, a lobbyist and a personal representative for Von Karman. If Berg didn't know much about aeronautical science, he did know some scientists, and Von Karman wanted him to talk with them.

The assignment went from mid-May to late July, 1958, and Berg managed to squeeze plenty of activity—and plenty of visiting—into the two months. Von Karman appears to have asked Berg merely to listen to what people were saying about AGARD. It was the ideal assignment, since the lines between business and what Berg would have done anyway for pleasure were vague. Berg worked most effectively when he had a broad mandate and was left alone to carry it out. He nosed around Europe, talking with people who covered him with banalities —AGARD was "doing things," one general told Berg in hushed tones over lunch—and reporting them, somewhat breathlessly, to his boss. In late June, Berg went to Copenhagen for three days to present a letter to Niels Bohr from Von Karman, inviting Bohr to speak for twenty to thirty minutes on "How physics became the key science on planning of the defense sciences."

The AGARD job gave Berg a chance to revel in his past. In Zurich, he had fondue with Paul Scherrer; he lunched in London with Bob Robertson, and walked around the city with the publisher/spy Paul Rosbaud. Excited, Berg filled his diaries with cryptic notations. "Can't go with this bastard—black marketeer," decided one. "Goldfinger," said another. He sent postcards from Paris that said only "X marks my spot," and signed one to Goudsmit as "Meaux Beurregue." He met ambassadors in elevators, and in Paris he attended a party hosted by the American deputy chief of mission, who just happened to be Cecil Lyon.

Twenty-five years earlier, it had been the birth of Lyon's daughter, Alice, at Saint Luke's hospital in Tokyo, which Berg used as a ruse to enter the hospital and pan the city with a movie camera from the top of the building. Alice was at her father's party in Paris, and Berg was thrilled to tell her the story of how he'd taken advantage of her birth. Not content with that, he used a full page of his report to relate the story to Von Karman. According to Berg, his films "may have been interesting later to our air force." After implying that he'd provided the source material for the Doolittle raids, Berg also suggested to Von Karman that only a squall had come between his films and Trinity. "Incidentally, on that same Japanese tour, I was able to photograph the fortified harbor of Shimonoseki, which I believe was the target of our first atomic bomb, but shifted to Hiroshima on the account of weather." Storytelling was not without preparation. In his notebooks Berg copied Elsie Lyon's maiden name, Grew, over and over again, without further comment, like a prayer.

As he became older, Berg became a creature of lists, at times recording names to no apparent purpose. Just after he returned from Paris, he sat down and wrote out sixty-three of them. Sometimes he named people he knew well. Just as often, however, there were names of people he'd scarcely met, like Eugene Fubini, the electronics specialist whom Berg had consulted with briefly in Washington during the war. In addition to appearing in some of Berg's American lists, Fubini received postcards from Berg when Berg was abroad. "I don't know why he did it," says Fubini. "I have no idea."

Whenever Berg was out of the country, he conducted mass mailings of postcards to friends and acquaintances. Before writing out the cards, he made lengthy lists of possible recipients, sometimes copying out more than one hundred names in his notebook before writing out several revised versions of the list. What was odd was that the people he wrote to were often accessible to him for visits, which Berg avoided. As soon as he left their town, however, he got in touch. The messages could be very witty and a little bizarre as well. Sam Goudsmit received a postcard from Cuba that read, "Fidel Neroes—Mo Burns—Cuba Libre?"

BOSTON, MASSACHUSETTS

Boston was Berg's favorite American city. He liked New York for its glamour and moxie, Washington meant intelligence work, but Berg loved Europe, and Boston was as close to Europe as the United States got, with its rows of elegant, corniced town houses, the Public Garden's duck pond full of children astride swan boats, the dimly lit old shops and narrow thoroughfares with names like Milk Street and Louisburg Square, the gentle timbre of streetcar bells, and educated people who remembered—certainly they did!—the brilliant old Red Sox catcher. In the 1950s and 1960s Boston had the feel of a town. Wherever Berg went, people were stopping him on the sidewalk to talk. When he was in the pink financially, Berg liked to stay at the Parker House, hard by the Boston Common. As his bank account wasted to nothing, he moved over to the Vendome, a once grand hostelry on Commonwealth Avenue that had slipped considerably and now let some of its rooms by the month. There were rumors that Berg stayed there for nothing.

Berg's life in Boston in the 1950s and 1960s resembled his days there as a member of the Red Sox, except, of course, that there was no baseball to fill his afternoons. On a typical Boston morning Berg would go to the Old South newsstand to buy as many newspapers as he could carry. He lugged them to a café on Washington Street, where he drank coffee and tore out articles he wished to save. Nearby was the Goodspeed Bookstore, and when the papers were dead, Berg might walk in, greet the owner, Arnold Silverman, and spend a few hours poking through the shop's dusty aisles. Once he'd filled up a carton with books, Berg would pay for them and, invariably, arrange to pick them up some other time. His reading tastes were eclectic. He liked books on linguistics, he read romantic poetry, he was interested in Heine, Napoleon, etymologists, and humorists. Novels he seems to have resisted. Silverman never knew what Berg was doing in Boston. "Every time he came up to town he was always on a confidential mission of some sort," he says. "We suspected he was probably working on a divorce case." Silverman noticed two other things about Berg. He had huge, spread fingers, and as the years went by, his appearance was increasingly seedy and his suits were never pressed.

A few blocks from the Goodspeed was the Brattle, the oldest antiquarian book shop in the country. Plenty of book collectors visited the Brattle, but to the Brattle's owner, George Gloss, Berg was something different. Berg was in the habit of setting aside Tyrolean piles of books and then, finally, after hours of

consideration, opting to buy perhaps two of them. Gloss might
have been vexed by this shopping practice, but he wasn't. Berg
fascinated him.

One of the attractions of the trade for Gloss was the inevitable stream of characters who populate used-book stores.
Berg was his favorite. Who else claimed, as Berg did, that he
bought dictionaries to see if they were complete? Whenever
Berg came to the store, Gloss would take him out to lunch or
invite him to the family house. Berg would repay the hospitality
with stories. He told Gloss about Heisenberg, he told him about
Einstein, he said that during the war he had memorized full
pages of German telephone books, he explained that he'd been
called home from the war because he knew too much about
the Manhattan Project, and he told Gloss about Japan, hinting
that the government had encouraged his filming stunt from
the hospital roof. "He talked about himself all the time, going
to France, Germany, Japan," says Gloss's widow, Dorrit. "He
wasn't interested in other people. He was more interested in
talking about himself." In front of Gloss, Berg played his
games with foreign customers or foreign waitresses, listening
to their voices and telling anyone who was around where the
person came from. At a French restaurant, he spoke in French
to a waitress who asked him, "What part of France are you
from?"

In 1965, in a fit of temper, Berg stopped talking to Gloss.
Gloss was at pains to understand what he'd done to cause a
fissure in the friendship, and to fill it, he wrote Berg a note at
the Vendome, saying that he'd like to take him to lunch and
was giving him the four cartons Berg had filled with books but
then left behind the counter unpaid for, "as a small token of
my regard for you and the great pleasure you have given my
family and customers." The friendship resumed, as always, on
Berg's terms. Gloss, for instance, always wondered what Berg
did for a living, but he knew he wasn't supposed to ask him,
and so he never did.

When Berg did haul away his books from the Goodspeed

or the Brattle, they often went no farther than the Old South newsstand. "He used my stand as a repository," says Larry Rosenthal, who accepted letters and packages addressed to Berg and routinely held them for six months, until Berg appeared to collect them. In exchange, Berg went for lunchtime strolls with Rosenthal on the Boston Common and told him stories about baseball, about Japan, about women, and about the war. He tended to embellish. Rosenthal learned that Berg had posed as a Swiss professor during Heisenberg's talk, that he gave lectures in German to the Germans, and that he worked with a partner until one day the partner disappeared and Berg found him floating face down in a ditch full of water. "The conversation wasn't particularly deep," says Rosenthal. "I wasn't anybody particular to him. Just somebody who liked him. George Gloss was the same. George had the books he needed. [Berg] didn't have any close friends. He never spoke about anybody, never mentioned anybody else. I guess he was a loner." Rosenthal noticed something else. Berg always had plenty of time.

He killed it in a number of ways. People would encounter him loping across the Common, a book about thirteenth-century French grammar in his hands. He spent hours telling stories to spellbound off-duty waiters at the Ritz, and hours chatting with Joe Cronin in his office. Cronin was the American League president from 1959 to 1973 and kept his offices in Boston, in the IBM building. Having Berg drop by was especially nice for Cronin, because his old teammate seemed to know everyone and, always fancying the role of the conduit, was delighted to put Cronin in touch with people.

At a coffee shop on Newbury Street, Berg met young Richard Gurner, who worked for a classical music station. During Gurner's break time, he would come in and talk with Berg, who told him stories about baseball and Japan. "He seemed to have all the time in the world," says Gurner. Jean Makrauer, the wife of his Princeton classmate S. Lang Makrauer, would be on errands and spot Berg in a telephone booth, look again, and he'd be gone. Once she was buying a paper at a newsstand and somebody said, "I'll do that." Berg paid for the paper and disappeared.

Sometimes he eschewed hotels and stayed with the Makrauers in Wellesley, arriving with, at the most, a toothbrush, a canvas bag full of used books, and the dirty suit he wore on his back. When Jean went into the bathroom during the night, she found the suit, freshly washed and hanging from the shower nozzle to dry. The Makrauers' twelve-year-old daughter, Susie, had an upsetting experience with Berg. One day he put his arms around her and hugged her in a way she didn't like. She ran away from him, up the stairs, and, with Berg in pursuit, hid under her parents' bed. Berg knelt beside the bed on his hands and knees, and began asking her questions about herself. Finally he got up and went away. After that, whenever she heard that Berg was coming to visit, she made herself scarce. If he frightened Susie, he seemed to have special fondness for the Makrauer's young son, Fred. When the Makrauers were heading north to Maine for a visit with Fred at his summer camp, Berg came along. "I would see him walking through Boston," says Fred, "and he'd appear out of an alley, say 'Hello, Freddy,' and he'd give me $100. He would do it on my birthday, ten years in a row. I think it's because he loved Dad." Possibly. Yet, when he talked with other people about S. Lang Makrauer, Berg referred to him cuttingly as "Slang" and derided him for hiding the fact that he was part Jewish.

It was at the Parker House, just after the war, that Berg again came upon Marjory Bartlett and her father, Kemp Bartlett, the Baltimore Orioles lawyer. Marjory had worked for Vannevar Bush at the Office of Scientific Research and Development during the war. Now she was running a natural history camp for children, editing a wildlife magazine, and writing books. She had married a Princeton man, Ted Sanger, and was living with him in Boston. Up for a visit from Baltimore, Kemp Bartlett had taken his daughter to the Parker House dining room for breakfast. Now, gazing across the room,

Mr. Bartlett told his daughter that a man at another table had been looking at them through the entire meal. Just then, the man came walking by and passed their table with no sign of recognition. Marjory exclaimed, "Mr. Berg!"

"Miss Bartlett," he said, without skipping a beat. "Mr. Bartlett." He bowed gravely over an armful of newspapers. There were two empty chairs at the table, and at Marjory's urging, Berg settled his newspapers into one and took the other for himself. He stayed for a few minutes before making his excuses. Marjory told Berg that she was living in Boston. She hoped she would see him again. Berg nodded, smiled, and left. Marjory admired Berg, but from the start he unsettled her, in the same way that he had Ted Williams. "His smile was a bare uplift of the mouth," she says. "I never saw him laugh."

This was not for lack of opportunity. Three years later Tommy Thomas, the manager of the Orioles, and his wife, Alice, were in Boston, and asked Marjory Sanger to join them for lunch in the French Room of the Vendome. The restaurant was one of Boston's finest, with a skilled chef, an imposing maître d', and a huge salad bowl set on a pedestal at the center of the dining room. A light scent of fresh garlic drifted through the room. Besides Mrs. Sanger, Thomas had invited Red Sox owner Tom Yawkey and his wife, Jean; Joe and Mildred Cronin; Ted Lyons; and Moe Berg. At one point, Thomas said to Marjory, "I hear you met Moe in Washington." Marjory thought to respond by telling the story of the taxi ride to Griffith Stadium, but she caught an icy glance from Berg and said "Yes, I did" instead. As she got to know Berg better, Marjory came to believe that he was as conscious of appearances as anyone she had ever met. She had the feeling that everything he said had been carefully measured first, as if to see how it would look in print. There was something unnatural about that, she thought, for such self-consciousness made him seem perpetually on edge.

After an extravagant meal of pressed duck, the waiter presented the bill to Thomas. Thomas pointed to Berg and said,

▼

"Give it to *him*." Marjory gasped, but everybody else was laughing. Berg said, "That's a very old joke, Tommy." Thomas pulled out his billfold and paid. "In the beginning of our friendship, that's the sort of thing that would make Moe turn pale," he told Marjory. "Now no one ever expects him to pick up the tab." Marjory didn't know what Berg did for money. He once told her that he had his shoes made in Europe, but "that is my only extravagance." You needed good shoes to walk as far as Berg did on bad feet. In the French Room, Marjory noticed that the cuffs of Berg's white shirt were filthy.

The Sangers spent the warm months living in a seventeenth-century house in the Massachusetts countryside, some twenty miles outside Boston, and it was while they were living there that they heard from Berg again. Ted owned a music shop, The Listening Post, and he would go into Boston by train to work there while Marjory wrote at home. One day the telephone rang. It was Ted, asking Marjory to meet him in Boston for dinner at the Athens Olympia restaurant. He had a surprise for her. The surprise turned out to be Berg. Berg had some newspaper clippings with him, which he presented to Marjory. They were reviews of her books. He asked her if she'd seen them. "Yes," she replied. "If I'd known him better, I'd have said no," she remembers, for Berg seemed hurt. "He was very disappointed and sulky all evening," says Marjory. "He wanted to be the one who showed them to me. He regarded most people as living in a kind of vacuum until he enlightened them." Ted was enthralled by Berg, and while Berg indulged him with warm conversation, Marjory had the feeling that she had offended Berg and was now being shut out. The Sangers paid for Berg at the end of the meal, as they did the many times they dined with him after that.

The Sangers moved into Boston when the weather cooled, and saw Berg from time to time. He would turn up without warning, and they would take him out to dinner at the Union Oyster House or another restaurant that he selected. Berg never seemed embarrassed about his status as the perpetual guest.

"I think he felt he earned it," says Marjory. When the Sangers proposed inviting some of their other friends, Berg would never allow it.

All this time, the Sangers had no clear idea what Berg was doing with himself, although he led Marjory to believe he was working for the CIA. In Boston, he always said he was staying at the Parker House, which was expensive. But about personal details Berg was vague, always deflecting. Ted Sanger didn't mind. Berg fascinated him. "We just clicked right off," he says. Marjory liked Berg's Old-World courtesy, admired his brains, and appreciated the clever postcards he sent now and then. But she was growing weary of his stories about the photographs he took from the top of a hospital in Japan, and tired of hearing about Paul Scherrer and Lise Meitner and Werner Heisenberg. He talked endlessly about Meitner, whom, he said, he'd assisted in her escape from Nazi Germany to Sweden. This wasn't true, but Marjory didn't know that. All she knew was that Berg seemed infatuated with Meitner. "He saw himself as a knight in shining armor come to rescue her."

Berg told very few people about his life in the OSS, but Marjory Sanger he told too much. His sluices had no controls. "He talked about his missions until it got to the point where he said so much you stopped listening. You couldn't eat. He demanded full attention. I saw a whole filet mignon grow cold on his plate. He was exhausting. His stories were awfully involved. Full of foreign places and people with foreign names. There was a lot of physics and chemistry that I couldn't follow. In his stories he was always cunning and brilliant, and nobody ever got the better of him. My part of the war was over. I wanted to move on. I thought he was living in the past. He never talked about the present." Her husband's business was music, but Marjory never heard Berg talk about music. Hers was writing, but her books and articles were never discussed either. Berg's stories dominated all conversations, and Marjory began to feel suffocated by them. "It was an event to know him," she says. "You can't say that of many people. He was brilliant and memorable, but he was like a sponge. Little by little he absorbed you. You began to feel diminished. I admired Moe, but I found him fatiguing. There were times when I almost feared I was going to be quizzed."

In the fall of 1958, the Sangers were in Stow, and Ted brought Berg out to visit for a long weekend. In the mornings Marjory would first take her husband to the train station, and then go up to Concord with Berg to buy him the *Boston Herald*, the *New York Times*, the *Christian Science Monitor*, and the *New York Herald-Tribune*, all of which she was permitted to pay for but not to touch. After she cooked breakfast for Berg, he would insist that Marjory accompany him for a long walk across the pine-needle-strewn paths in the woods. Later there was shopping to do, dinner to cook, and Ted's commuter train from Boston to meet. Marjory found that Berg was "constantly seeking attention," and felt relieved that he punctuated "his monologues" with "a lot of bathing." The old house had one bathroom, and Berg's fetish about baths meant that Marjory made a few trips to the woods. After his baths, Berg liked to make complimentary jokes about Marjory's thick, soft towels. They were monogrammed with her maiden initials, M.B., which were, of course, his initials too.

On a Monday morning, Ted and Berg walked into the kitchen to announce that Berg was having such a good time that he was staying on for a while. Marjory's face fell. Berg caught on immediately. "All right, Marnie," he said, voice gone cold. Ted drove him to Boston. For the next few days Ted was furious, but the rift seemed to heal with time.

That winter, the Sangers moved into a house in Cambridge, and in February, Teddy went off to Maryland to visit his mother, promising to be back on a Monday evening in time for dinner at Henri IV, a Cambridge restaurant. On that Monday, just before seven in the evening, the doorbell rang, and when Marjory opened it, Moe Berg was standing in front of her. "Come," he said, "I've come to take you out to dinner."

"Moe," she said, "that's awfully kind of you, but Ted's not

here yet. When he comes home, we're going to Henri IV, and I hope you'll come with us."

"Ted's not coming back," said Berg.

"Yes, he is. He's visiting his mother."

"No, he's in England." Ted, it turned out, was leaving his wife. "I pulled out somewhat dramatically," Ted says.

From then on, Berg was Marjory's constant companion. They ate lunch and dinner at out-of-the-way restaurants, with Berg always paying the check, took long walks around Harvard Square, and went on day trips to Walden Pond and to Wellesley. They went to bookstores, where Berg would make tall stacks of books and then leave without buying any of them. Marjory heard nothing from her husband.

After several weeks of this, Marjory says that "Moe seemed to change the tempo, and instead of trying to divert my attention from my shocked sense of loss, humiliation, and rejection, he started talking of divorce and finding me a lawyer and taking me to Baltimore to face my father. I never needed to *face* my father, and he'd hardly have wanted to see me with Moe." Marjory noticed another change. Whereas previously Berg had taken her to drugstore soda fountains and small cafés for meals, now they dined in posh restaurants and in plush hotel dining rooms at the Ritz, the Somerset, and the Copley Plaza. Berg still paid for everything, and was attentive and considerate, especially to the Red Sox fans who were always stopping by the table to say hello to the old Boston catcher and his slender blond companion.

One day, Berg invited her for breakfast at the Parker House, where he was staying. There was no sign of him in the lobby, so Marjory called up to his room. "Marnie," he said, "I'm here. Come on up." When Berg opened the door, he was still in his pajamas, with a Japanese kimono over them. "Come in," he said. "Breakfast is just about ready." Marjory told him that it had been her understanding that they were eating in the dining room. "I thought it would be cozier up here," said Berg. Berg had never made the slightest sexual advance toward her, and Marjory didn't think romance was quite his intention here either. She suspected something darker. "All of a sudden I thought there might be a photographer," says Marjory. "My father had warned me about doing anything incriminating." She told Berg she'd rather not. "What do you mean?" he demanded. "We've known each other for a long time." She left anyway.

After two months with Berg, Marjory knew there would be no reconciliation with her husband. Berg seemed annoyed that she was still upset. "He's not worth grieving over, you know," he said. At about this time, Berg told her how he'd come to be involved in the breakup of her marriage. He said that Ted had gone to Maryland to see his mother, and then met Berg in Newark to discuss the situation. (Ted Sanger says that Berg met him in New York and saw him off at the pier when he left for England.) Berg told Marjory that his response to Ted's request that he be the one to tell Marjory that he was leaving her was "I can't do this." But Berg had done it.

"I asked him if he'd be the one to tell her," says Ted Sanger. "How he expressed this to her and how he interpreted it was out of my hands." Marjory always suspected that her husband had been bankrolling Berg, but Sanger says that's not so. "I didn't ask him to stay in a hotel and take care of her," he says. "I just asked him to break the news to her. I asked him to make things as easy as he could for her. I knew it would be hard on her. He was my missionary, not my agent. It was the role the fates dealt him and he accepted it." How Berg, who had no money, was able to escort a woman to restaurants every day for two months while staying at a fancy hotel remains a mystery.

Marjory agreed to a divorce. Ted Sanger says he asked Berg to handle it for him, but Berg refused and recommended a Boston attorney instead. After that, Marjory never saw Ted or Berg again, although Berg did send her a postcard from Cuba. Following the divorce, the country house in Stow was put up for sale, and that summer, Marjory drove up from Baltimore to clean it out. The house was full of old newspapers, and it seemed obvious that Berg had been living there in a squalor of newsprint. Upstairs she found similar chaos, but what she did not find were her towels with the embroidered M.B. In the end, they had proved irresistible.

BERG HAD BEEN staying in Stow, and with Ted Sanger. When he got back from England, Sanger found that Berg was, as he put it, "living a bit pillar to post," and took him in. With Marjory Sanger, Berg had gone to restaurants. With Ted, he went to church. Sanger thinks that church for Berg was a lark. "He was a very undoctrinaire person," he says. "He didn't care about religion. He cared about honesty and morality. I don't think he ever set foot in a synagogue." In the morning, they got up, bought the newspapers, and found a place to have coffee. They talked a lot of politics and had a true bachelor's time together. Sanger found it liberating. "We were not responsible to anybody else," he says. "We were two people who thought we knew a lot. In a sense I was sitting at his feet." At night they went out to diners where Berg met sports fans. Sanger always paid for dinner, and if they stepped into a book shop and Berg wanted something, Sanger slipped him the money for that, too. Once they went up to Hanover, to see a Dartmouth College football game. Nelson Rockefeller was there, and he and Berg shouted hearty greetings to each other. The association lasted a matter of months. Then Sanger remarried, and he didn't see much of Berg after that. Sanger speculates about Berg that "maybe he was an unhappy man" and says, "I think the times with me could have been an escape."

DURING THE "TED and Marnie affair," as Berg referred to the divorce in his notes, he went to a cocktail party in Cambridge, where he met a young, whipcord-handsome bachelor named Harry Broley. Broley was a consultant for the Arthur D. Little Company. He had once worked in naval intelligence, loved baseball, and liked old bookstores, and he and Berg hit it off immediately. They began going to Red Sox games at Fenway Park and to Cambridge bookstores together. Broley says that the Sangers' divorce had depressed Berg. "Moe had a kind of romantic streak," he says. "He was against marriage to begin with, but if you do get married, Moe felt you should stick it out." Broley gave him something new to think about.

At the moment, Broley was working on a baseball project for Arthur D. Little. The city of Buffalo was contemplating building a downtown ballpark for a possible franchise in the Continental League, a new professional baseball league. It was Brolcy's job to assess for the Buffalo Redevelopment Foundation the likelihood of professional baseball coming to Buffalo and the facilities a professional team would require, and to evaluate proposed bond issues involved with raising the money to build a stadium. Broley invited Berg to go to Buffalo and assist him, and Berg went gladly. Broley paid him $100 a day, plus out-of-pocket expenses. Broley was on the Buffalo assignment for three years, and even when Berg's own work on the project was done, he visited Broley frequently, for four or five days at a stretch.

Broley admired Berg for the reasons many men did, and also because Berg intrigued him. Broley came to see that Moe Berg "didn't commit to people. He didn't get involved. I don't think he got involved with me." Even so, Broley did achieve a frequency of contact with Berg that almost nobody else ever had. He gave Berg money, bought him drinks at Bill Donovan's old club in Buffalo, the Saturn, and at the Plaza Hotel's Oak Bar in Manhattan, and he watched him operate. Berg traveled "with a toothbrush and a lot of phone numbers," and when he arrived somewhere, he'd flip through the numbers, place a call, announce "I'm in town for the night," and just like that would come an invitation. "He'd be there for three weeks," says Broley. "People liked to take him home. He stayed in thousands of houses. He felt if he came to your house, he was giving you something. His company and conversation."

At lunch in New York with John Snyder, an old Princeton classmate, Berg met another Arthur D. Little employee, named Warren Berg. Warren Berg had been baseball captain at Harvard, where he also studied engineering. He was no relation to Berg, but his nickname had long been "Moe," and he was delighted to meet the real Moe. Soon enough, Warren Berg was getting telephone calls: "I'm in town," Moe Berg would say. "I'll see you at six." Warren Berg never knew how long Berg planned to stay, but he welcomed him. Berg was fun. Warren Berg would watch him open a book, read a page, hand the book to Warren, and repeat the entire page from memory. While he was in Boston, Berg liked to drop by Warren Berg's office. If some Japanese clients were walking down the hall, Berg might bound out of Warren Berg's office, and a moment later the Japanese were clapping him on his back. Another day, they attended the Harvard commencement exercises, where Berg translated the Latin oration line for line as it was spoken. An elderly Harvard man, seated in front of them, turned around after the orator and Berg were done and said, "Brilliant." Warren Berg tried to give Berg work, but, with one exception, Berg always refused. "He seemed to never want to get pinned down," says Warren Berg. "He liked to be free to roam around."

The exception came in the spring of 1962. Charles Finley, the iconoclastic owner of the Kansas City Athletics, had quarreled with civic leaders in Kansas City and was threatening to move his team to Texas, claiming that Kansas City couldn't support a major league baseball team. Joe Cronin, the American League president, was no great admirer of Finley's, and at Berg's suggestion, he commissioned Arthur D. Little to prepare a confidential study appraising the team and its prospects for profit in Missouri. ADL, in turn, asked Berg to be a part of the consulting team, and he agreed, for $100 a day and expenses, some $500 a day less than the usual ADL daily consulting fee. From May 30 to June 4, Berg was in Kansas City, talking with fans, ushers, cab drivers, and hotel clerks; afterward he dictated his findings into a short, somewhat chaotic memorandum, which was incorporated into the larger ADL report, which in turn helped the American League to decide to deny Finley's proposed move to Fort Worth, Texas.

Berg especially liked to visit the Warren Bergs when they moved from their home in Winchester to their rambling summer retreat on the seashore in Gloucester. Berg arrived with nothing but a toothbrush and a sheaf of newspapers, took several showers a day and washed out his nylon shirt every night—"he was an immaculate son of a gun," says Warren Berg—and stayed, as Warren Berg puts it, "a bit longer than expected." While Warren Berg was at work, Berg read or talked baseball with Warren's elderly father. Once he convinced Mrs. Berg to drive him to Rockport to visit his old friend John Kieran, now retired from the *New York Times* and writing books about natural history. At the end of the day, Warren picked him up and drove him back to Gloucester. That was the only time after the war that Berg saw Kieran. On other days, Warren Berg would return from the office and join Berg in lengthy walks along the beach, where they talked physics and baseball.

Berg could be brusque, which Warren Berg observed when a radio station telephoned him, trying to find Berg and explaining that it wanted him to appear on a World Series quiz program. When the message was passed along, Berg's response was "Tell them to go to hell." In 1964, the Warren Bergs were expecting a number of guests at Gloucester, who would fill all their spare bedrooms. He told Berg about the situation, and Berg left, looking displeased. Warren never saw him again.

MANCHESTER, NEW HAMPSHIRE

From Boston, Berg sometimes made short trips to other parts of New England. One summer evening he appeared in the offices of the Manchester, New Hampshire, *Union Leader* and *Sunday News.* The *Sunday News* sports editor, Leo Cloutier, introduced Berg around the newsroom, and one of the people who met Berg that night was a young reporter named James Freedman. Freedman, destined to become the president of Dartmouth College, was leaving journalism to enter law school that fall, and when Berg heard about this, he looked at Freedman and said, "The law is the art of fine distinctions." Then he walked away.

BALTIMORE, MARYLAND

The Japanese documentary filmmaker Jiro Hirano produced a brief television film about Berg in 1979. When Hirano came to the U.S. to interview some of Berg's Princeton classmates, most told him that Berg was the only person they knew at college who had no close friends. The closest, these men agreed, was Berg's teammate on the baseball team, Crossan Cooper. Hirano spoke to Cooper about Berg, and Cooper described Berg first as "a loner."

In May 1959, Cooper was living in Baltimore, and Berg went to visit him. On the way, Berg opened a notebook and wrote down an outline of his life. He listed Columbia law school, baseball in Japan with Babe Ruth, the party where Ruth had harassed the geisha girl, and his photographing episode on top of Saint Luke's Hospital. Then came South America, Amaldi, Ferri, Flute, Meitner, Donovan, Göttingen, Nuremberg, and AGARD. These were some of the signal moments in his life, and Berg could not have forgotten them. Why, he'd been to Europe with Von Karman less than a year before. Of course he hadn't forgotten them. He was living off them. Berg knew that people were willing to host him because he entertained them, and so now he was priming his material, deciding what to tell and what to leave out during a long evening of talk in which the subject would be himself.

Cooper was not the only beneficiary of such preparations. Berg's notebooks are teeming with these summaries, some more robust than others. In 1960, Berg met Ellery Huntington, who had helped recruit him for the OSS, for lunch, and in this notebook outline Berg reminded himself of his days on the Balkans desk and in Caserta, his work with Broley in Buffalo, his CIA assignment to turn up clues about Bruno Pontecorvo, and his meetings at Princeton cocktail parties with Johnny von Neumann. People always said that Berg wouldn't talk about himself, but the truth was that he longed to. He was just extremely selective about what he said and how he said it. Ever the good intelligence man, Berg also made notes following his meetings. When a lunch with a man named Reggie Taylor was done, Berg took the first opportunity to write down the names of Taylor's wife and children, the children's marital status, the maiden names of all the women at the table, and a salacious bit of gossip about a suicide that had apparently been discussed during the meal. After the first day of what turned out to be a lengthy stay at Cooper's house in Baltimore, Berg wrote down, "told Marnie story. Crossan wants to be trusted."

WASHINGTON, D.C.

The explanation for how a man who had very little money was able to travel frequently to Washington, D.C., by train was the usual one with Berg. He befriended people, and they were glad to do something for him. A man named Charlie ran the dining car on the Trenton to Washington train for twenty years, and Berg lit up the room for Charlie with conversation. The extended Berg family held annual gatherings in New Jersey, all of which Berg avoided like scrofula, just as he did all family functions, but when the son of another helpfully disposed Penn Central conductor, named John, was married, Berg was on hand for the evening. When John needed letters written for him, he dictated and Berg wrote. Berg made himself familiar with the schedules of conductors he knew, boarded those trains, and rode for nothing.

Once he got to Washington, Berg shifted abruptly from the gregarious entertainer to the man of mystery. Whenever he encountered people in Union Station or on the city streets who knew him, he brushed past them, without a glance. "It wasn't politic to recognize him," says his friend from the OSS, Margaret Feldman. Berg did this in cities besides Washington, of course, but his ostentatious displays of secrecy were perhaps the most poignant in Washington, for in Washington was the CIA, the one place where it could be confirmed for certain that Moe Berg was a secret agent no more.

For an accomplished man who was doing nothing and wished people to believe otherwise, spying was an ideal cover. Nobody could dispute it. For a private man who was loath to reveal anything about himself, spying was also an excellent means of warding off questions. Yet when Berg left the false impression that he worked for the CIA, it was not just a matter of petty dissembling calculated to save face and veil personality. It was also symptomatic of a man suffering a protracted bout of wishful thinking. "He missed it, sure," says Harry Broley. "He was made for it. The greatest high a guy like Moe could get." Much of the peculiar behavior that Moe Berg exhibited toward the end of his life was a consequence of being rejected by the work that he loved, not an uncommon reaction in the intelligence world, according to Charles McCarry, the former deep cover agent for the CIA. "My guess is that what Moe Berg found stressful was not being in the floating secret village," says McCarry. "There's something tremendously comforting about being in the floating secret village where everybody's secrets are known—they've been so thoroughly investigated. Of course not everything was known, but it seemed that way, and that was a liberating factor. This pro-

▼

duces a tremendous sense of camaraderie, and it lasts throughout life. I don't think anybody who has been in that sort of
world trusts any outsider the way he trusts other spies. The
relationship between agents is deeper than marriage. My
mother didn't know about me until I was exposed on the 'Today
Show.' She said, 'Thanks a lot, Charles.' "

Berg had no wife or child and maintained strained, distant
relationships with his brother and sister. There was no particular agent with whom he shared the close friendship McCarry
describes, but he was franker with people like Earl Brodie and
Howard Dix than he was with anyone else. The real truth,
however, was that he was married to the work. This being said,
it is true that, besides playing the intelligence operator in
Washington, Berg did once propose marriage to a woman
there. The woman was vivacious, had blue eyes and chestnut
hair, and, predictably enough, she was part of his intelligence
past.

If Berg rarely confided in men, he was even more skittish
around women. Some women found him very handsome.
Many others, like Anita Loos, the author of *Gentlemen Prefer
Blondes*, thought his manners debonair and his store of arcane
knowledge impressive. More still were fascinated by the life
he described to them over a well-chosen bottle of wine. There
are many photographs of Berg seated with attractive women
at restaurant tables. Estella Huni told her son, Paul, that, although Berg liked to have his picture taken with pretty young
faces, it was just for show. Nothing was happening. Even if
no relationship was developing, Berg does seem to have
been quite experienced—and somewhat crude—in the art
of seduction. "Nobody knew what he was doing with
women, but he'd always end up with them," says the New
York talent manager Murray Goodman. "He had a quaint way.
He always told them how beautiful they were, and they believed him." One of Goodman's clients, Berg's old baseball
traveling buddy Al Schacht, took a dimmer view. "Never

let him near your wife," said Schacht. It was good advice.

In the late 1950s, the *New York Herald-Tribune* sportswriter Caswell Adams suffered a bad stroke, and was hospitalized on Long Island. Adams was a lively man, and he and Berg were friends. They attended boxing matches together in New York and met up in bars with other sportswriters, like Jimmy Cannon and Damon Runyon. It was a casual acquaintance, like the ones Berg had with many New York sportswriters, and he and Adams could in no way be described as close friends. So Adams's wife, Mary, was taken aback when the most frequent visitor at Caswell Adams's sickbed besides his own children and herself was none other than Moe Berg. Besides the strange act of regularly attending a man he didn't know very well, Berg's behavior was odd for two other reasons. The stroke had left Adams incapable of communication. In a year he uttered only one word—"goddammit"—and he was paralyzed except for the feeble use of an arm. One of Adams's son's girlfriends surveyed the situation and asked Mary Adams, "Mrs. Adams, have you any proof that Moe Berg knew your husband before he got sick?"

Why was Berg there? One answer is that there was something about human crises that appealed to a prurient side of Berg. His notebooks are full of information about friends' divorces, and Berg could sometimes be talked into investigating women whose husbands hoped to divorce them. When people like Diane Roberts, whose lover had died in Washington, or Marjory Sanger, on the verge of divorce in Cambridge, were vulnerable, he liked to see, and to know the details. Perhaps it felt like intelligence work, knowing something you weren't supposed to know. It's also possible that a man whose life has gone awry achieves comfort from assisting people in worse straits than he is. Another motive was lust. Berg fancied Mary Adams.

After some time, Adams was moved from the hospital to a rehabilitation center, where Berg kept up his hectic visiting schedule. One night, instead of going home, he asked Mary Adams if he could stay at the Adams home on Long Island. They got back, and she sat down on a living room couch and began weeping. Berg opened a book and read to her until she calmed down and fell asleep on the couch. She awakened there to find Berg beside her. He had not removed his clothes, yet he was exposed. She pushed him away and headed for the telephone. Berg looked terrified. "What are you going to do?" he asked. "I don't *know*," she said severely. She did nothing. There was a reconciliation, and his visits continued.

Several months after his stroke, Caswell Adams was moved again, from the rehabilitation center to a nursing home in Westchester County. One day Berg telephoned and invited Mary out on a date, and she accepted. She was taking classes at the New School for Social Research in Manhattan, and suggested that Berg meet her there. He said he would prefer to meet her in the middle of a block, a short walk from the school. She agreed, though she wondered why on earth he couldn't just go to the lobby. It was a clear night, and Mary drove a convertible, so as they headed out to Long Island, Berg unraveled the stars for her. At the house, Mary put on some opera music, which Berg thought was silly and said so. Then he moved toward her. "He knew what he was doing," Mary says. "I'll tell you one of his predilections. The floor." Afterward, she offered to try to find Berg a toothbrush. He stopped her. "Oh, no. I always carry one," he said. They saw a little more of each other. Once, when they were riding together on an uptown bus in Manhattan, Mary turned to say something to Berg, and he was gone. Another time, he offered to take her out to dinner, met her, and began walking. Fifty blocks later they were at Lü-chow's. Mary thought he was broke and ordered the cheapest thing on the menu. After a handful of encounters, it was over. "Lord knows why I was attracted to him," Mary says. "He just was charming."

Caswell Adams died in 1957. Some five hundred people attended his funeral, but Moe Berg was not one of them.

IN 1963, JUNE McElroy, a former CIA analyst, was introduced to Berg in Washington by a mutual friend, a Connecticut congressman. Instead of maintaining his usual Washington digs, at the swank Mayflower, Berg was staying at a third-rate establishment on Eye Street when McElroy met him. He looked third rate himself. Berg was now sixty-one years old, with a large umbilical hernia—an intestinal protrusion in the area of the belly button—bulging within a rumpled pair of gray suit pants, and spots spattered down the front of his white shirt. Still, McElroy found him "charming, effervescent, and very interesting. He was a genuine raconteur. He held everyone's attention." She also thought Berg was handsome, and the next time he was in Washington and called to ask her out, she was pleased. McElroy invited him over to dinner, and they talked.

Berg told her war stories, and even CIA stories, leaving her with the firm impression that he still worked for the Agency. About other aspects of his past, he said nothing. "He preferred to be the mystery man," she says. She thought Berg was being modest, and was not unintrigued. McElroy had an eight-year-old daughter, and Berg entertained her, too, telling her about rabbits. Over the next three years, McElroy and Berg saw each other occasionally, with Berg telephoning when he came to Washington and McElroy always responding with a dinner invitation.

One day in 1966, Berg was in Washington, and McElroy made dinner, put her daughter to bed, and began washing the dishes. Berg was standing with her and asked, "Do you ever miss being married?" She laughed and deflected the question, but she wondered about it. Was he making a pass at her? McElroy might not have minded if Berg had been, yet he'd never expressed any romantic interest in her before, and she was certain the question was to another purpose, one born not of lascivious intent but of a wanton curiosity.

The moment passed, and a little while later Berg excused himself. After ten minutes McElroy noticed that he was still gone. That was a long time to be in the bathroom. When she looked down the hall, she saw that her daughter's door was shut tight. The door was never closed at night. As McElroy approached, she heard giggling. She opened the door to find Berg sitting beside her daughter on the bed. "What's going on in here?" asked McElroy. "He's tickling me," her daughter said. McElroy didn't know what to think. The closed door frightened her. "Moe," she said, "I'd better take you back to the hotel." Berg's manner didn't change perceptibly. She drove him where he asked to go, to the Mayflower this time, dropped him off, and never saw him again. She did hear from him once, though. Or her daughter did. One day a package arrived, postmarked from Africa. Inside was an American Barbie doll.

McElroy doesn't think that Berg had done anything improper to her daughter. He had not had the time, and her daughter says that all he did was tickle her. Nonetheless, it was strange behavior, just as it was odd that he made Susie Makrauer break away in fear from his embrace and then chased her into her father's bedroom; and it was also peculiar that at a small party in Princeton, he walked up behind an attractive young woman, who was married, and hugged her in a way that she found objectionable. Irene Goudsmit, the wife of Berg's friend Sam, says, "If I'd met him without my husband I'd have been extremely cautious. I don't know why. Instinctively." Around some women, Berg seemed not quite in control of himself. Blue-eyed Clare Hall would come to a similar conclusion.

CLARE HALL MET Berg in London in 1944, when he offered her a ride in his chauffeur-driven sedan from a party at Soames House. In 1947, Hall quit her job at the CIA and married a physics professor from the University of Illinois. By December 1949, she and her husband had separated. Hall was back from Illinois, alone in Washington with a young child and working at the Pentagon, when she received a telephone call from Moe Berg. She had not told Berg about the separation, but somehow he had heard about it and now was asking what her plans were for the holidays. He said he didn't want her to be alone on Christmas. She told him that she had plans and that she was fine. That was the only time she remembers him calling long distance. In 1950 she was divorced, and in 1951 she began dating Berg. Sort of.

Hall thought Berg "a handsome lad, rugged, not pretty," and they got along very well. They talked "about everything under the sun," except, of course, Berg. "He talked about himself constantly, but he never spoke of his early life," she says. Hall "knew" Berg was working for the CIA, but he never directly said that he was. They would go to dinner, sometimes out in Maryland, and then sit around for hours afterward, lingering over coffee. Berg's favorite word was "marvelous," and Hall says that he was constantly looking at things and saying "Isn't that marvelous," in his low, nasal voice. At a restaurant with a picture of Adam and Eve behind the bar, they noticed that the artist had given both Adam and Eve belly buttons and wondered about this, since Eve was supposed to have come from Adam's rib. At a Japanese restaurant in New York, Hall admired a sake pitcher with a bird on top that let out a whistle when you poured the hot rice wine. She tried to buy one of the pitchers, but Berg stymied the purchase, saying, "No, no, no. I'll get you one sometime." He never did. Although Berg always paid for dinner and the baby-sitter, in twelve years of dating he never once bought Hall flowers or a present.

Nor did he ever do anything more than kiss Hall good night. If Berg asked for more, she declined, saying she still felt numb from the failure of her marriage. He always said he understood. When he came to Washington, Berg would telephone Hall, never giving her any advance notice. They saw each other perhaps seven times a year this way and exchanged letters, Hall writing to him at the Parker House in Boston. She doesn't know whether Berg was dating anyone else. She thinks he must have been.

Both were fond of Poe's poetry, and several times, at Hall's suggestion, they went to the Adams Memorial, an eerie spot in Rock Creek Cemetery that seemed appropriate to the macabre poet, and recited "Annabel Lee" and some of Poe's other poems together. The Adams Memorial is a Saint-Gaudens statue commissioned by the historian Henry Adams in memory of his wife. The androgynous statue is enclosed in a holly grove, which makes it a secluded, romantic spot. Saint-Gaudens's son once said that his father had intended his ambiguous figure "to ask a question, but not to give an answer." It was there, one day in 1954, with a gentle snow falling, that Berg turned to Hall and asked her a rather unambiguous question. "When are we going to get married?" he said. She was dumbfounded. Eventually she gathered herself and they talked about it. Hall didn't trust her judgment after the first marriage, and said she didn't want to marry a second time. Berg was understanding, and never brought the subject up again. "When he proposed to me, I took it seriously," she says. "I don't think I would have considered marrying him. I think he wanted children. I think he wanted a son."

In 1962, Clare Hall changed her mind and married Paul Smith. Berg still took her to lunch when he came to Washington, and sometimes he even went to dinner with Clare and Paul. He liked Paul, and would talk with him about used-book stores around the country. In the mid-1960s, after a lunch at the Mayflower, Berg said casually to Clare, "Come up to my room." She went upstairs with him, and the conversation continued for a while. Then Berg suddenly began undressing. By the time he'd finished, Clare was out the door and gone. "He never said what his intentions were," she says. "I thought they were obvious. I haven't the vaguest idea why it happened."

When Paul heard about this, he was upset, but eventually he got over it too, and the Smiths continued to meet Berg for lunches and dinners whenever he was in Washington. The last they saw of him in Washington was in the late 1960s, when they dropped him off at a cheap rooming house, out near the highway in southwestern Washington.

WASHINGTON IS A big city, and it pulsed with people Berg knew, from President Kennedy—slightly—to his old wartime boss, Bob Furman. For some men, life during peacetime can never equal their memories of war, but Furman, the man whom Sam Goudsmit dubbed "the Mysterious Major," was eager to put the war behind him and get on with establishing his building business. Between 1947 and 1949, Furman was sharing a large house in Georgetown with a few other young bachelors when Moe Berg arrived, unannounced, for a visit. Furman knew what it was like to walk through life crammed full of secrets and terrified that one might leak. The habits of war stayed with him into private life and, for a time, even the thought of talking about his work on the Manhattan Project made him ill. Even so, Furman found Berg's methods of comportment astonishing. "All of a sudden he was at the door," says Furman. "We had a nice time, talked, and all of a sudden he was gone, disappeared. I never knew where he lived or where he went." And he never saw Berg again.

One reason that Berg kept people like Furman from knowing very much about himself was his penchant for what Clare Hall calls "compartmentalizing his friends." Hall had met H. P. Robertson during the war, when Berg did, and liked him very much. Yet, when Robertson and Berg were in Washington at the same time and Hall would propose that they all go out together, Berg's response would be curt. "No," he'd say. "I'll see him tomorrow."

On his own, Berg saw all kinds of people, and liked nothing better than lunching with men of influence. He filled his note-

books with references to General Groves, and meeting Groves
for a meal at the Mayflower Hotel found Berg purring happily
as he dispensed stories and dined on Groves's honeyed words.
"If it wasn't for you," Groves said, "we'd have wasted a lot of
time and money on the German heavy water." In New York,
they once attended a baseball game at Yankee Stadium, where
Berg introduced Groves to Casey Stengel. In a photograph of
the three men, Berg looks blissfully happy, and he was. He
enjoyed serving as the conduit, bringing together interesting
men who had stories to tell, and then sitting back and watching
them talk to each other.

Most of the time, though, Berg was doing the performing.
In Washington, his stage of choice was Duke Zeibert's bar and
restaurant in downtown Washington. Duke's was noisy and
well lit, with photographs on the walls, and a man could find
company there from noon to closing. There were times in the
1950s and 1960s when Berg was there every day. He'd talk
for hours with the bartender and the regulars on their stools,
making one drink last the whole day. Skilled in the art of
beverage nursing, Berg was even better with food. Through
years of afternoons, he never once ordered a thing to eat.

One day at Duke's in the mid-1960s, Berg was introduced
to Joseph Crowley, a former CIA officer now working at a
brokerage house. Crowley strolled up to the bar to find Berg
in the midst of telling a story about Walter Johnson, the Washington Senators pitcher from early in the century who had been
known as "the Big Train" for the speed of his fastball. Crowley
could see that Berg had told the story many times before. "It
was late one afternoon and Johnson was pitching," Berg was
saying. "The umpire said 'Strike!' and Johnson yelled back, 'I
haven't thrown it yet.' " Crowley looked over Berg's shabby
clothes and decided that Berg looked like "a déclassé semi-
narian." When Berg's joke was done, everyone laughed, and
Crowley introduced himself to Berg. They talked, and Crowley
invited Berg to his home on Wisconsin Avenue for dinner, the

first of four times that Berg would eat supper with the Crowleys. Crowley wasn't impressed with Berg so much as he was intrigued. The truth was that Berg annoyed him. " 'Somebody recommended he see me because I'd read a book or two' is the sort of thing he'd say," says Crowley. Crowley found Berg's dinner table conversation "desultory." It was the same fraying potpourri he shared with most people, and the repetition must have showed. He told a few baseball stories, there was an occasional foray into linguistics, a bit about Lise Meitner, a modest aside that it was because of him that the U.S. could put aside its fears of a German bomb program, and a not so subtle allusion to the CIA, which Crowley assumed Berg was working for. "He husbanded his material very carefully," says Crowley. "There were no coherent or sustained accounts of anything. He was free form, and anything I can think of that he said was more or less designed to impress. I don't think he was interested in most people except as they were interested in him." Berg never told Crowley when he was coming to Washington or where he stayed when he was in town. He simply called and accepted dinner invitations. On one of the visits, Crowley decided that Berg was not very brave. Crowley's eight-year-old daughter showed Berg her pet gerbil, and Berg recoiled in fear and wouldn't go near the cage. "He was really spooked," says Crowley.

The better Crowley got to know Berg, the less he liked him. It was Crowley's opinion that carrying around foreign-language newspapers was an affectation designed to announce Berg's language skills, and he thought Berg's habit of reading ten American papers a day was a sad waste of time. Mostly, though, Crowley was irritated by Berg because he "found him completely lacking in an aesthetic. He had no wonder of the world. I'd say most of his charge came from being a character. A unique folk hero. There he is moving through Horace, Ovid, and Virgil, but he was one of the guys in whom an education as an aesthetic experience was wasted. He might as well have

▼

gone to drafting school." There are risks to living an uncon-
ventional life and there are lessons in it. Here it is a simple
one. Nobody, not even Moe Berg, could charm everybody.

William Klein's first meeting with Moe Berg was as casual as
their friendship was complex. Sam Faerberg, a friend of Klein's
who also knew Berg, introduced Berg to Klein across a cup of
coffee in the mid-1950s. A year went by, and then Klein received a telephone call from Berg. Klein was a peppy man, an
amateur astronomer interested in Greek and Latin etymology,
books, stamps, and coins, and gradually Berg became interested in him. By the end of the decade they were spending a
lot of time together.

Klein's job required him to meet with people at their homes
and offices. He would report to his own office in Jersey City,
plot the day's appointments, and then look out the window.
The neighborhood had been completely razed for rebuilding
projects, and so, for blocks, all Klein could see was vacant lots
squared by streets and a man in a gray suit, pacing up and
down through the eerie maze. It was Berg, waiting for Klein
to pick him up. For when Klein set out on the day's round of
appointments, Berg liked to go riding with him.

Day after day Berg appeared. Eventually a White Castle
hamburger restaurant was built across from Klein's office, so
Berg could stop walking and read the paper while he waited
for Klein. Klein would slide into the booth, across the table
from Berg, and order. Berg always ordered exactly what Klein
did, and during a dozen years of hamburgers, Berg offered to
pay only once. He pulled a one-dollar bill from his wallet and
extended it. The bill was yellow. Klein told him to put it away,
and another afternoon of driving began.

Instinctively, Klein knew how to get along with Berg. Berg
didn't want Klein to introduce him to other people. "Willie,

don't mix," he said, and Klein never did. Klein also never asked him about his private life, and never brought up baseball. Early on, Klein *had* asked him something personal and Berg had said, "Mustn't ask." After that, Klein displayed no curiosity. It wasn't easy, because Berg all but courted demands for explanation. Once they stopped into a coffee shop in Newark, and Klein spotted Jackie Robinson. He told Berg, who walked over to Robinson, stood behind Robinson, and whispered into his ear for a few seconds. Robinson never looked up or said anything. Berg came back over to Klein, and they left the restaurant. "He never said a thing about it," says Klein. "I never asked him about it. I think he liked that. I learned how to keep my mouth shut."

Klein found that if he waited long enough, sometimes the answers to his questions revealed themselves. One day, Berg told Klein that Ted Lyons had given him some land and they were looking for oil. Klein didn't say a thing. A year later, Berg suddenly said, "They didn't find any oil." Berg clearly enjoyed tempting his friend's curiosity, as he cultivated questions about himself from everyone he knew. "One day, out of nowhere, he said to me, 'No questions about Africa, Willie.' " No questions were offered and no explanations were ever given.

Klein once asked Berg, "Why me, Moe?" and Berg replied, "You are without guile, Willie," and that made sense. "I wish I had a million dollars, Willie," Berg once told him. "I could live the way I want to." Berg didn't have even a thousand dollars, but he did have Klein, who let Berg be and gave him whatever he seemed to need. If Berg wanted to sleep in the passenger seat, he was welcome to drowse as long as he liked. If he wanted to talk, Klein was an interesting man. If he wanted books, Klein knew every bookstore within a fifty-mile radius of Jersey City, and he took Berg to all of them and paid for what Berg selected. When Berg plainly needed a new gray suit, Klein took him to Brooks Brothers and bought him one. He made Berg feel utterly comfortable. He took Berg to dinner at the home of Helen's, his wife's, parents, and after a time Berg

▼

disappeared. Eventually Klein discovered him tucked into Helen's parents' bed. He'd taken a bath and was now fast asleep. Once Klein was holding a clipful of money that belonged to another man; Berg saw it, reached over, and helped himself to some. Klein didn't object.

For Klein, it was easy to indulge such a man. Berg added coriander to his life. Who else took him to a luncheonette just outside the Holland Tunnel, leading into Manhattan, and told the counterman the origins of words? Berg was interesting, he was fun to be with, and he was unpredictable. One day Berg said to Klein, "Willie, I have to go to Washington," and he was gone. Time went by, months, and then there was Berg, walking down a sidewalk with his collar up. "Moe!" said Klein.

"Willie," said Berg. "How are you? I'll see you tomorrow," and Klein had his partner back. Klein never quite knew what to make of Berg, and he didn't really try. He simply enjoyed him, and let him remain as opaque as the aphorism he was always offering to Klein. "There are no supermen, Willie," Berg would say, and Klein would nod without comment.

NEW YORK, NEW YORK

One summer day, Moe Berg took Harry Broley to a baseball game. They had passed through the turnstiles and begun to make their way through the crowd, up the runway toward their seats, when Berg said, "Stop!" He walked over to the wall at the side of the passageway, put his back to it, closed his eyes, and, speaking very softly, said, "Listen. Listen. There are no sounds in the world like these sounds. It's a symphony to me."

Berg also called baseball "my theater," and there are similarities. One of the pleasures of following baseball is that every day its characters participate in an unfolding narrative of events in which there are heroes, clowns, and villains, moments of comedy and tragedy, and plenty of time during the pauses between pitches for daydreaming. Yet, much as people may become absorbed in the fortunes of a team, baseball games are devoid of the hard consequences in life outside the foul lines. There is always a new game or a new season or a new second baseman. Except for those few men who play professional baseball, the game is ultimately only a diversion, and a diversion is what it was for Moe Berg, a man who badly needed one. Discussing baseball with a young sportswriter, Fred Down, Berg "said that he loved it," Down remembers. "There was nothing he enjoyed more. He said that 'some people like to swim, some people like to play cards, some like to watch the horses. My enjoyment is being with people and watching baseball.'" After the war, when he wasn't traveling at a dervish's pace from city to city, Berg spent the better part of spring, summer, and fall attending baseball games, mostly in New York. They brought him pleasure, muffled some of the disappointments that nagged at his later years, and gave him a place to go every day.

Following his retirement from baseball, Berg had been presented with a rectangle of plain metal not much larger than a credit card. On one side was engraved a lifetime pass to all American League ballparks, and the other entitled him to walk in, free of charge, to any National League stadium. This gave Berg dispensation to claim any unoccupied seat in any ballpark. Sometimes he would sit by himself in the stands and, purist that he was, send out bitter reproaches to infielders who failed to call for pop fly balls.

After the war, aside from chiding them from the stands, Berg avoided current players and stayed off the field itself. There were exceptions. In the 1956 old-timers game at Yankee Stadium, Berg batted fourth for one team, leading the *New York Times* to comment, "Moe Berg, playing shortstop and batting in the cleanup position, probably for the first time in his life caught Allie Reynolds unaware by blasting a mighty double to left." In 1963, Casey Stengel, the manager of those insuperable losers, the early New York Mets, asked Berg to address the team, and Berg drafted a long and tedious speech

▼

mainly about himself. As he rambled on about the Sorbonne, Nelson Rockefeller, Bill Donovan, Japan, and John Kieran, "the great sports columnist for the *New York Times* who wrote about me every rainy day," the bewildered young Mets looked at their shoes. None of them seem to remember it. "As far as I am concerned, Moe Berg was a mythical figure," says Larry Bearnarth, a pitcher on the team.

The fact was that most baseball professionals had never fathomed Moe Berg. Berg once took Harry Broley with him to meet Joe McCarthy, who had managed the great Yankee teams of the 1930s that starred Babe Ruth and Lou Gehrig. They ate sandwiches, and McCarthy and Berg talked about old times. Listening to it all, Broley was saddened. "It was clear McCarthy didn't see him as a player," he says. "He saw him as a character." Berg knew that and he hated it. He was always extravagantly grateful when men with long memories reflected upon the promising catcher he'd been before injuring his knee in 1929. After he hurt the knee, Berg's position in baseball had evolved from "the coming catcher" into a man whose very presence on a major league roster was regarded skeptically by some of his peers. To journalists, however, he had been something higher. They had lionized him, made him into a legendary figure—not just an amusing reserve ballplayer but the polyglot catcher and esteemed ballpark muse, Professor Berg. It was only natural that Berg would now gravitate toward the press. After all, in a time when some people were whispering that he was a bum, in the press box Berg was still one of a kind.

He was the only former ballplayer to arrive regularly in the Yankee Stadium, Ebbets Field, Polo Grounds, and, later, Shea Stadium press boxes with a copy of the *Times Literary Supplement* under his arm. Sometimes he stayed for only a moment. "You'd be at a game," says *New York Times* columnist Dave Anderson, "and all of a sudden he'd be behind you in the press box wearing a dark suit, dark tie, and white shirt. You'd look up again an inning later, and he'd be gone." Just as often, though, Berg would watch the entire game intently, talking over everything that happened on the field with the journalists in a restrained, sage fashion. He was especially hard on catchers. Some of the baseball writers would want to ask Berg about himself, but they never did. Sitting with Berg made Seymour Siwoff of the Elias Sports Bureau "feel sort of romantic. I'd want to know, 'Where do you live? What do you do?' but this man created an aura which told us, 'Don't ask me about anything but baseball.' And he knew baseball. God, he knew baseball." Ira Berkow once asked Berg if he'd ever published anything. "Only a treatise on Sanskrit" was the answer. Later Berkow happened upon the *Atlantic Monthly* article and the next time he saw Berg, he confronted him. "You caught me, Ira," said Berg.

After the game, while the journalists typed their stories, Berg read the *Manchester Guardian* or completed the *New York Times* crossword puzzle. Everyone knew, as Detroit Tigers radio broadcaster Ernie Harwell says, that "he had to read a virginal paper." When the stories were filed, he joined the writers in the press hospitality room, helping himself to the traditional spread of free food and drinks laid out on platters. Wherever Berg sat, the table filled quickly with the wizened aristocrats of the New York press box, Frank Graham, Red Smith, Jimmy Cannon, Arthur Daley, and Leonard Koppett. Baseball executives would stop by and ask Berg how to say "ball one" and "strike two" in different languages, and he would tell them. Sometimes, when he thought nobody was looking, he'd stuff a couple of sandwiches for later into his coat pockets. He might then head for the hotel room of one of the journalists in from out of town to cover the visiting team. Men would check into their rooms to discover Berg in the bathtub; he'd wangled a key from the front desk to get an early start on his soaking. Later, when the journalists assembled again to take on the town, Berg was with them. At the end, Berg's society came mostly from baseball.

In the 1950s, when the Dodgers still played at Ebbets Field,

Berg would go out to Brooklyn to see them with a man named Bruce Jacobs, who wrote for 25-cent sports magazines. Jacobs's office was in the Empire State Building, in Manhattan, and Berg would pick him up. From there, the two would walk downtown to City Hall, cross the Brooklyn Bridge, and stride out Flatbush Avenue to Ebbets Field, a distance of about ten miles.

Harry Grayson didn't walk anywhere if he could help it, and usually he could help it. Grayson, the white-haired sports editor of Newspaper Enterprise Association (NEA), did everything with a certain swashbuckling style, and walking was not stylish, especially with a hangover. The NEA offices were on Eighth Avenue in midtown Manhattan, an area that was as snarled with traffic in the early 1950s as it is now. More days than not, Grayson would arrive for work in the late morning and park his car right in front of the building, which was illegal. A policeman would notice the violation and write Grayson a ticket; when Grayson discovered it, he would scrawl "deceased" across the ticket and send it in unpaid. During the day, Berg liked to stop in at the NEA offices and talk with Grayson and the other resident NEA sportswriters, like Jimmy Breslin, Murray Olderman, Dave Burgin, and, later, Sandy Padwe and Ira Berkow. Olderman considered Berg to be "a well-dressed man of leisure," and was suspicious of him. Olderman had been an intelligence officer during the war and spoke several foreign languages. He tried to get Berg to speak with him in French or German, but Berg always demurred, just as he did when the subject of his intelligence work arose.

Grayson and Breslin were less skeptical. "Always remember," Grayson once advised a young reporter, "when you freeload, bitch. You maintain dignity." Grayson was a master of badinage, a loud-talking storyteller positive in everything he said who drooled slightly when he smiled, a former dentist who asked bartenders around the city to pour his whiskey into one of the dentists' paper rinsing cups he carried with him, and a shameless filch of a journalist who amiably pumped other writers for their stories, his inevitable cigar bobbing up and down at the side of his mouth. Grayson roamed Manhattan with an entourage that included a tough guy from the Bronx named Tony, a horseplayer named Andy, and Moe Berg. "Moe seemed the last guy to mix in that company, but he fit right in," says Olderman.

Come 7:00 PM, the ball games over, the stories filed, the press table cleared, Grayson, Breslin, and the rest headed for drops like 468 Eighth Avenue, a seedy modern horror show of a bar, where Berg spoke with the busboys in Greek; Joe Braun's Palace on Forty-fifth Street, an ugly little dive full of prominent theater people who wanted to talk sports with Moe Berg; the Pen and Pencil; Al Schacht's; and the most famous of all sporting life watering holes, Toots Shor's. These were good places to be broke. "He never paid a bill," says Breslin. "After work, anything could happen. Who the hell watched or paid attention? Christ, I never had any money either. There'd be thirty guys drinking and some rich guy picking up the check."

Night after night Berg would be right there with everyone, standing up straight with his wonderful posture, nursing a beer or a Bloody Mary, taking it all in. "I'd see him," says Frank Slocum. "He'd be talking at the bar in Shor's to some woman. She'd turn around to light a cigarette, turn back, and he'd be gone. A little bit frustrating Morris was!" Occasionally Berg brought along some friends. He'd have been out to the nuclear research laboratories in Brookhaven, Long Island, to visit Sam Goudsmit, and now was returning to New York with an entourage of his own, a group of young physicists eager to raise Cain and meet women. The scientists and the sportswriters were not always compatible. "He loved the scientists at Brookhaven," says Breslin. "Brookhaven scientists, sexual degenerates, gigolos, nuts, I don't know who they were."

At the end of the evening, Berg specialized in finding free places to stay for the night. He might go home with Grayson and stay at his house. "Grayson loved anybody to come home with him to take the heat off the wife," says Breslin. When the golf promoter Fred Corcoran was in town, he shared his hotel room with Berg, and the bathroom with Berg's rinsed-out white nylon shirt. In 1951, Corcoran was married in Saint Patrick's Cathedral. "How's the arm, Moe?" asked Cardinal Spellman as he walked by. When the Corcorans left for their honeymoon in Canada, Berg went with them. "Fred didn't want to turn him down," says Corcoran's wife, Nancy. "What he was doing was always a big mystery. I would say that my husband was one of his best friends, but he never told him anything about his private life."

One miserable, snowy winter night, Berg was leaving Toots Shor's at the same time as another reticent sort, Joe DiMaggio. Berg said he was on his way to New Jersey to sleep at his sister's. DiMaggio thought that was a long way to go and felt sorry for him. "Why don't you spend the night with me," he said. They walked through the snow together to DiMaggio's suite at the Madison Hotel. Berg stayed for six weeks. "All he had was what was on his back, and all his shaving stuff and a toothbrush," says DiMaggio. "We talked about what happened in the general day, baseball, things of that nature. His private life wasn't any of my business."

A pair of bachelors—Milton Richman, who covered the Mets for UPI, and his brother, Arthur, a baseball reporter for the *Daily Mirror*—also liked hosting Berg, and so did their mother, who made huge breakfasts that Berg enjoyed immensely. "We were Mama's boys and he loved my Mama," says Arthur. "When he came into your house, it was like he belonged there." Sometimes after a ball game, Arthur would take Berg out to dinner. He wouldn't let Berg pay. "I looked upon him as a member of my family," he says. "I wouldn't let my brother pay, why should Moe pay?"

Of all Berg hosts, for length of service, none rivaled the Chicago baseball writer Jerome Holtzman. Berg and Holtzman met at the Polo Grounds in the late 1950s and enjoyed a pleasant conversation. Holtzman was covering the Cubs at the time, and when the team was next in New York to play the Giants, Berg telephoned Holtzman at his hotel room and asked if he could share it with him. Holtzman said that was fine, and from then on, whenever he was in New York, and sometimes when he was in Boston, Baltimore, Philadelphia, or Washington, Holtzman asked for twin beds, one for himself, and one for Moe Berg. "He knew my schedule," says Holtzman. "I'd no sooner get to my room when the call would come from downstairs." Berg would arrive with his ditty bag, excuse himself, and take a bath. Later, Berg would carry Holtzman's briefcase and they would travel to the ballpark together on the subway. Berg would usually take a seat beside Holtzman in the press box. After the game, when Holtzman's story was finished, they'd take the subway back to midtown Manhattan. "Never walk in the middle of a crowd," Berg would always admonish Holtzman. "A crowd can turn ugly." Every night in New York they shared a snack at the Stage Delicatessen. Berg followed Holtzman's lead. If Holtzman ordered a fried bologna and egg sandwich, that is what Berg ate too. After two years of this, Holtzman said, "Moe, I need some money." Berg's wallet was out in a flash, and he handed Holtzman $200. When they got back to the room, Berg washed his underwear and shirt and took another bath. Sometimes he even left games early to go back to the hotel and bathe. The nomadic life of the baseball beat writer wore on Holtzman, and having Berg around comforted his loneliness. He says that Berg saw him as "a nice young man he could do business with who might want the company. I didn't want to stay three days alone. I was also delighted when he left." After Berg's final bath, the two men would stay awake at night talking, with Berg telling Holtzman stories about the OSS and the countesses he'd known. Holtzman says Berg was a real ladies' man, though he never saw him with a woman.

After the talking subsided, Holtzman would lie in bed, thinking about his companion. "I never thought he was a big spy," says Holtzman, who also believes that Berg "was not an intellectual. The only book I ever saw him with was a Sanskrit dictionary he was having rebound. I don't think he liked intellectuals. He preferred baseball players." Old baseball players such as Joe Cronin, Joe DiMaggio, Heinie Manush, and Tommy Thomas he liked especially. One of the reasons Berg enjoyed baseball was that he never saw the game change very much. Change, the passage of time, was difficult for him. Once in the hotel lobby, Holtzman asked Berg if he'd like to meet some of the Cubs players. "Hell, no," said Berg. "They think it all began with them." Holtzman says that "he didn't ever want anybody to say, Who is that guy?" Berg had similar distaste for many young sportswriters, or "chipmunks," as he called them. He resented modern journalistic innovations, such as interviews with the manager in his office after games. To Berg, the thought of people questioning John McGraw or Connie Mack about strategy was as unthinkable as women attending Princeton. The younger reporters, in turn, were baffled by Berg. They wondered what he did with his time, snickered that he was "a freeloader," and behind his back referred to him as "the world's greatest guest." About that, Holtzman was more circumspect. "People used to call him Mysterious Moe," he says. "I told him after five years, 'Moe, the only mystery about you is that you don't work, and nobody knows it.' Moe said, 'These people travel an hour to work, wasting their lives.' He didn't want to waste his life like these people, scurrying to and from trains every day. He lived his life the way he wanted. He didn't see any need to be working like that. He beat the game."

In the morning, Berg was up by 7:00 AM, hours before Holtzman. He'd have "a coffee," as he put it in his European way, and read the newspapers. At a prearranged time, Holtzman would get a wake-up telephone call from Berg. Holtzman liked to swim laps at the New York Athletic Club during the day before leaving for the ballpark. Berg would lounge at the poolside with a towel circling his waist and another one wrapped like a turban around his head, looking, to Holtzman, "like a

Roman senator." Above Berg's waist towel was a grotesque umbilical hernia. Holtzman never said anything about it, but other people urged Berg to go to a veterans' hospital and have the hernia treated. He refused, saying that he wouldn't let the army do anything for him.

Holtzman spent fifteen or twenty nights a year for a dozen years in hotels with Berg, hosted Berg once at his home outside Chicago, and never told a soul. "He showed different people different faces," says Holtzman. "He was a man of many sides. I knew one of them."

After he left Holtzman's room or, indeed, anybody's room, Berg would prowl about the city before going to the ballpark. He might poke around used-book stalls in Greenwich Village or a coin shop downtown on Nassau Street. He attended meetings of learned societies like the Linguistic Society of America, where he was a member of long standing, the American Physical Society, or the American Philosophical Society when he was in Philadelphia. He was also always game to spend a few hours with the aeronautical engineers from Brooklyn Polytechnic Institute or New York University he met through Antonio Ferri.

Berg did his best to keep up with the men he'd met during the war. He sent Nelson Rockefeller postcards with Latin American motifs, and liked to telephone him. Berg was in Toots Shor's with Jimmy Breslin on the day in 1958 when Rockefeller was elected governor of New York. Berg went over to a telephone booth, leaving the door open so Breslin could hear the conversation. He dialed a number, waited a moment, and then said, "Hello, Nelson! This is Morris. How are you? Congratulations." Whenever Rockefeller met up with Berg in public, either at a Dartmouth football game or on the streets of New York, he was affectionate with Berg, greeting him warmly and saying that if he were ever elected president, Berg would be his secretary of state. In 1954, Rockefeller gave Berg some work to do with one of his business concerns, but it didn't last long. Mostly, he was distant with Berg. Rockefeller's secretaries didn't always put Berg's telephone calls through—they tried to satisfy Berg with tidbits of news about the governor— and after Berg died, when Rockefeller was asked to serve on a committee charged with organizing a Moe Berg Memorial Scholarship, one of his assistants wrote and signed a letter for him, declining.

Berg also made strenuous efforts to stay in touch with some of the men he'd met through the OSS, by sending postcards and paying visits, often to people who barely knew him. Henry Ringling North would take Berg to sweat in the Turkish baths at the Yale Club, where he wondered about Berg's hernia. Henry Hyde, whom Berg had met at the OSS bureau in Algiers, says he was baffled when Berg telephoned him to schedule dinners with Hyde and his wife. "He seemed like a lonely man living a vagabond's life," says Hyde. "I can't imagine why else he'd come to dinner. I didn't know him well. I never knew where he lived." North and Hyde were wealthy men, but Berg never asked them for money, and he didn't take much of their time, either. "Easy man to entertain," says Hyde. "He didn't stay long."

No summer went by without Berg disappearing from New York for his forays to Boston, Washington, Paris, Cuba, and the rest. He'd send back an occasional postcard that gave no hint of what he was doing. And then, one day, he was standing at the bar at Shor's again, raising a Bloody Mary. "I'd say, 'What were you doing?' " says Breslin, "and he'd say, 'Now, James!' "

Wherever he went, Berg did his best to arrange matters so that he was free for the World Series and then, later, the divisional playoffs, too. The excitement of big games, packed ballparks, and excellent baseball was pure pleasure to him. Berg sat in the press box with Breslin during the fifth game of the 1956 World Series, watching the Yankees player Don Larsen make chattel of the Brooklyn Dodgers batters. By the sixth inning, when Larsen still had not permitted a Dodger baserunner, the possibility of pitching perfection loomed and the press box at Yankee Stadium grew tense. "Don't worry," Berg told Breslin. "He's strong enough to keep it going." And he did.

At the 1967 World Series, in Boston, a Boston pediatric surgeon, Hardy Hendron, was sitting in the Fenway Park press box, occupying his seat courtesy of a Boston journalist whose son Hendron had operated on. On Hendron's left was a dignified man who asked him what paper he wrote for. Hendron explained, and Moe Berg introduced himself, saying, "I'm a phony too." Hendron knew very little about baseball, and so they had a lively conversation through the game, with Hendron asking questions and Berg offering explanations. He predicted what pitches the St. Louis and Boston pitchers were going to throw, and he was always right. Afterward, as they walked out of the park together, Hendron noticed that everyone from the hotdog vendors to well-dressed Bostonians seemed to know Berg. Hendron was curious. He wanted to know more. There was a dinner party that night at his home in Brookline, and he asked Berg if he'd like to come. Berg said he would. Little did Hendron know that he was bringing into his home a man whose social skills at such occasions were unparalleled.

It was a varied assortment of people who came to Hendron's that night. There was an Italian industrialist from Milan, a French surgeon from Marseilles, and a surgeon from Tennessee. Berg spoke with the man from Milan and his wife in Italian, and conversed in French with the Marseilles doctor. There were some brass rubbings in the Hendrons' living room. Berg looked them over and casually translated their Latin inscriptions. At dinner, Hendron asked Berg how he'd been able to predict pitches so uncannily at the ball game that afternoon. Berg said it was because he'd been a professional catcher. Then he added, "Of course, professionals can be wrong. For example, you doctors sometimes operate for acute appendicitis and find that instead the diagnosis is a problem with Meckel's diverticulum." The surgeons nearly fell off their chairs. After dinner, Berg cornered the doctor from Tennessee and asked

▼

him if pediatric surgeons knew how to repair umbilical hernias, and was told that it was a routine operation.

Two months later, Berg appeared unannounced at Hendron's office at Massachusetts General Hospital, and when Hendron arrived for work, there was Berg, waiting for him and reading the *New York Times*. Berg said that he had been bothered by a hernia at his navel since he was a ballplayer in the 1930s. He'd kept it in a truss for thirty years, but thought that now was a good time to get rid of it. Hendron had a look. The hernia was as big as a grapefruit. In mid-December he removed it for Berg, free of charge.

After that, Berg would surface from time to time, arriving without warning, quietly seating himself outside Hendron's office and reading a newspaper. Hendron would discover him there and invite him to stay at the house in Brookline, and Berg always accepted. Berg slept in a bedroom above the one Hendron shared with his wife, and sometimes during the night, after everyone had gone to bed, Hendron would be awakened by a loud thump on the ceiling above his bed. Rushing upstairs, he would find that Berg had fallen out of bed. Older people sometimes grow confused during the night when they are away from home, and begin to grope around, trying to remember where they are. This is known colloquially as sundowner's syndrome, and the well-traveled Moe Berg, now in his late sixties, suffered from it in spades.

During the day, however, Berg was the picture of lucidity. Hendron never learned what Berg was doing, but Berg gave him the impression that he was working for the CIA. In 1969 he disappeared for several months and returned to say that he'd been involved in a deal that sent one hundred American military helicopters to Israel. (This was probably true, although what role Berg played in the arms shipment, and whom he was representing, is unclear from Berg's notes. Most likely, he found the job through his friends in the aerospace industry and worked in some form as a liaison. A persistent Berg family rumor was that Berg had met Golda Meir, and if he did, this is likely to be when it happened.) Berg also filled Hendron in on all the usual details from his life—the Japan photography expedition, Scherrer, Einstein, and Groves. He also did something that was very unusual for Berg: he brought Hendron a gift. In April 1968, Berg presented Hendron with a French manual for a young surgeon, which had been published in Paris in 1770. Berg said to Hendron that he'd found the book several years before and had been keeping it ever since, knowing that someday he would find someone who would think it a treasure.

NEWARK, NEW JERSEY

Two of the people who did the most for Berg in the years after he came home from the war were his brother and sister. Berg lived on Roseville Avenue in Newark with Dr. Sam from 1947 to 1964. Then, when his brother threw him out, Berg moved the half dozen blocks to Ethel's huge stucco mansion, on North Sixth Street, for the last few years of his life. Both Dr. Sam and Ethel were energetic professionals and devoted patrons of their communities. They gave generously to their baby brother as well, but neither of them was easy for him to live with, and they wore on him as he wore on them. The very complicated Moe Berg had a pair of very complicated siblings, who hated each other with such enduring passion that although they lived within a few blocks of each other, they did not speak for thirty years.

Dr. Sam—his preference for this appellation was unmistakable—attended New York University and then Bellevue Medical College, graduating in 1921. After a brief stint at a New York City contagious diseases hospital, he interned at Newark City Hospital, where he met his hero, the famous pathologist and medical examiner Dr. Harrison Martland. Martland made pioneering discoveries about the occupational hazards of working with radioactive materials, by studying a high incidence of "jaw rot" (cancer) in a group of women factory workers who painted radium on watch dials to make them visible in the dark. Martland found that the women were moistening their paint-brush tips to a fine point with their lips, and he proved that radium was gradually poisoning the women. This made him something of a medical celebrity, landing him in the pages of *Life* magazine. Martland's popular renown increased when he titled a paper describing a series of investigations into the cerebral effects of continual blows to the head among boxers "Punch Drunk," instantly whisking the phrase out of the gym and into the medical lexicon. The moon-faced Martland was a gruff, hardworking physician, and gruff, hardworking Dr. Sam admired almost everything about him, right down to the painting of a spectacular French nude that Martland kept in his office to inspire male patients he was treating for impotence.

In 1934, Dr. Sam became an assistant pathologist at Newark City Hospital, under Martland. During the war, the military sent Dr. Sam to the Pacific for three years, beginning in 1942, and then to Waltham (Massachusetts) General Hospital for 1946. After his release from service, he scampered back to Newark City Hospital.

For years after Martland's death in 1954, Dr. Sam would weep when he began to talk about him, and late in his life, he wrote a biography of Martland which he published at his own expense. Martland, however, does not appear to have been so moved by Dr. Sam and did not advance his career when he could have. "There was a great deal of hero worship there," says Dr. William Sharpe. "Sam always admired him because he thought Martland wasn't an anti-Semite. He'd given him a job. Martland, in fact, was an anti-Semite and this told me something about Sam; he was not very perceptive."

Besides his work as a pathologist, from the outset of his medical career in 1924, Dr. Sam also maintained a thriving family practice, out of his home. He took the unusual measure of converting his kitchen into a laboratory, which meant that he conducted blood and bone marrow tests in the same room where he cooked dreadful Spanish omelettes every morning.

Like his brother, Dr. Sam owed his greatest moments of professional fulfillment to the atomic bomb. He was establishing an army blood bank in the Philippines on September 2, 1945, when he was sent by General Douglas MacArthur to Nagasaki, where he spent eight weeks in a converted public schoolhouse, examining burn and radiation fallout victims. Rather than finding anything wrenching or morbid about this experience, Dr. Sam was exhilarated—a typical reaction from a man who was fascinated by illness. His letters informing friends or relatives of the deaths of other friends or relatives are blizzards of medical jargon and as impersonal and devoid of sympathy as a pathology report. Dr. Sam could be a cold and inept human being. His cousin Elizabeth Shames once found blood in her urine and, worried, she brought Dr. Sam a sample. "What do you want me to do, Elizabeth, drink it?" he asked. He was also sometimes cruel. At the funeral for his cousin Frances Book Kashdan's husband, Dr. Sam turned to his cousin, who was standing with her mother and her sister, all three of them now widows and said, "You Book women certainly can't hang on to your husbands, can you?" At family dinners he specialized in reducing his niece Frances Book to tears. "I was frightened of Sam," she says. "He was the stern doctor in the family."

Dr. Sam's sense of decorum was as eccentric as it was ramrod absolute. For twenty-five years he regularly borrowed books from Charles Cummings, a Newark librarian, and eventually willed everything he owned to the library, but he never let Cummings call him by his first name. He pursued an acquaintance with his brother's friend the scientist Sam Goudsmit. After one of their telephone conversations, Dr. Sam wrote "Dear Dr. Goudsmit" the following mea culpa. "Several months ago, while talking to you on the phone, I inadvertently called you Mister. I realized the error at once, but was too astonished to apologize at the time. Perhaps ashamed would be a better term, if you know what I mean. But I just have to clear my conscience. Although it was an innocent lapse of mind, I nevertheless offer my apology and hope you accept it in good grace. I have the greatest respect for you."

But this stiff and snappish man had another face to him. "You'd think at first he was a tough, hard-bitten person," says Charles Cummings. "He was also very kind and generous, a side he didn't always want people to see." As a young and middle-aged doctor, Dr. Sam squired several different Newark City Hospital nurses about Newark. He never married any of them, but he was a loyal and supportive friend right through their dotage, making his money and medical skills freely available to them and to their families. His cousin Elizabeth Shames thinks that all these relationships were platonic, and Barbara Irwin, a Newark librarian who knew Dr. Sam well, has the impression that "it was almost as if Newark City Hospital took the place of a warm family for him."

There was something austere about Dr. Sam. When he contributed a "Timely Medical Topics" column to the *Newark Evening News*, he wrote it anonymously. Toward the end of his life, he walked around Newark with a camera, systematically, lot by lot, with a tax map, taking thousands of photographs of streets and houses, to record the vanishing city of his childhood. Cummings called him the Samuel Pepys of Newark. "That's stupid," Dr. Sam would bark, but he loved it.

DR. SAM DID not, on the balance, enjoy the seventeen years he lived with his brother, Moe, in the trim house on Roseville Avenue, but they had some pleasant times together. On their happiest days, Berg awakened first. Wearing a rubber suit, he went for a run through Branch Brook Park and then walked from Roseville, on the outskirts of Newark, to a newsstand at Broad and Market streets, in the heart of the city, where he bought two copies of the *New York Times*. He passed by the house to give Dr. Sam his *Times*, and then Berg read his paper while drinking several cups of coffee at a drugstore or a lunch counter. In nice weather, Berg would sometimes spend an entire day seated on a bench in Branch Brook Park, reading newspapers. On weekends, Dr. Sam might go on outings with him. Both liked distance walking and, side by side, they covered many paved miles of Newark and Manhattan. Once they took a walking vacation alongside the Erie Canal. In Manhattan, they might turn off the sidewalk into bookstores. Berg always preferred owning books to borrowing them from the library, and Dr. Sam indulged him. Each would choose five or ten volumes; Dr. Sam paid for them, and had them sent to Newark. When Dr. Sam came upon Lord Macaulay's bon mot "I would rather be a poor man in a garret with plenty of books than a king who did not love reading," he copied it onto a piece of cardboard and hung it in Berg's room. He did his best to overlook his brother's habit of underscoring almost every line in almost every book he read with a thick dark pencil.

Berg could be thoughtful too. Dr. Sam liked to bathe before going to bed, and often fell asleep in the tepid water. Terrified that he would drown, Berg checked on his brother every few minutes, and buttonholed several of Dr. Sam's friends and colleagues, beseeching them to convince his brother that he should take shorter baths. On a trip to Atlanta, Berg was browsing in a used-book shop when he came upon a copy of William Beaumont's seminal 1833 text, *Experiments and Observations on the Gastric Juice and the Physiology of Digestion.* Here seemed to be a treasure. Berg later told Dr. Sam what happened next. "As Moe told it to me, he acted very nonchalant, picked up two other nondescript books, and asked the dealer how much he wanted for the three. A buck. Actually, the book is so damaged as to be worthless, except to me."

As children in Newark they had largely gone their separate ways, but as adults, in Manhattan, they pranked together. Sam would point at the top of a tall building and Berg would say, "Oh, yes, I see him." As a crowd assembled, the Berg brothers would slip off to the side and giggle at all the dupes craning their necks for a look at nothing.

Berg was always pumping Dr. Sam for information and reading his anatomy books and medical journals. Dr. Sam saw that Berg could talk about anything from physics to geology to semantics, or he could hold forth on the origin, development, and essential characteristics of Siamese cats, as he did one day when they met a woman who owned one. Dr. Sam found that unusual things were always happening with Berg. Another time, they were riding in a taxi up Fifth Avenue when Dr. Sam noticed Berg staring fixedly out the window. Dr. Sam looked that way himself and saw a striking woman's face staring at his brother from a taxi one lane over. At the first stop light, Berg got out of his cab, opened the door to the woman's cab, climbed in, and drove off with her. Later, when Dr. Sam asked him about it, Berg said he had never seen the woman before.

When Dr. Sam went out with women, he would sometimes ask his date to find one for Berg. Then the foursome would set out for restaurants as far away as Long Island. Dr. Sam dated a nurse named Margaret McNamara for many years, Berg occasionally went out with the middle McNamara sister, and as for Nettie, the youngest and still a schoolgirl, Berg taught her how to swim at a public pool. It seemed to some of the women who dated them in pairs that the Berg brothers got along famously.

Berg did not find dates for his brother. Dr. Sam had sensed the sort of company Berg kept when Chico Marx joined them for dinner in California during the war, and although Berg once offhandedly offered to introduce Dr. Sam to Albert Einstein, he generally maintained a policy of keeping his brother and his friends separate. An exception was the famous Broadway restaurateur Leo Lindy. For their mother's seventieth birthday, the brothers took Rose Berg to Lindy's, where birthdays were a specialty. A cheesecake decorated with lighted sparklers was always carried out by a waiter while the other waiters led a rousing chorus of "Happy Birthday." All this happened on Rose Berg's birthday party too, except that when the cake appeared, it had an escort—Leo Lindy. Setting down four glasses on the table, Lindy opened a bottle of wine, poured it himself, and toasted Rose. Dr. Sam picked up the check for the birthday party, just as he paid for his brother's clothes, food, travel, and books. There was no question about that. Dr. Sam knew his brother was penniless. What he didn't know was why.

On January 6, 1957, Rose Berg's health was obviously failing as she went to bed. Her two sons spent the night taking turns sharing her bed. The next morning, she was dead. Dr. Sam described it as a peaceful death.

By the late 1950s, Dr. Sam had begun to notice stranger things. There were periods when Berg didn't like to leave the house. Wearing a faded black kimono, with nothing on underneath it, he lolled in the one armchair he kept free of clutter, reading and napping. He didn't take most telephone calls or reply to most letters, and he took pains to avoid people. On days when he did dress and go outside, Berg walked the Newark streets aimlessly, with a glazed, distracted look. As often as not, people who said hello to him were ignored. He took to carrying an umbrella on sunny days.

Berg had always read several afternoon newspapers, besides the morning *Times*, and although he was still buying them all, these days he was not reading them. Drowsiness would overcome him, his head would sag, and the paper drifted to the floor. The unread papers began to accumulate, but Berg would not hear of throwing any of them away. They were alive. "I'll get to them" was the terse reply when Dr. Sam complained about the accumulation. Like the dust in Miss Havisham's manse, yellowed stacks of newspapers and piles of pencil-ravaged books stole over every available surface—tables, chairs, corners, and couches. Eventually Dr. Sam was forced to do his evening leisure reading in his office waiting room, which had a separate entrance, off the front hall, from the rest of the house. In the living room, the peripatetic Moe Berg had become sedentary.

Dr. Sam could have responded to such aberrant behavior by sending Berg for a psychiatric evaluation. He did not. He had Berg's blood tested for syphilis, and after the results came back negative, he made no further medical inquiries. He knew that his brother was acquainted with Albert Einstein, and later explained that nobody who could keep up conversations with Einstein could be experiencing the dulled faculties Dr. Sam associated with psychosis. But schizoid personalities are capable of periods of remarkable lucidity. Perhaps Dr. Sam did nothing because he was simply overwhelmed. If he was, that was understandable. The situation called for unusual sympathy from a man whose faculties of compassion had already been mightily extended. For Sam Berg, such sympathy was impossible, because roiling in his gut was an ambivalence about his strange and brilliant brother that had begun in childhood. As he watched his home disappear under layers of newsprint, powerful tension crackled inside him, and so did spite.

It could not have been easy to be Moe Berg's brother. Not only was Berg good at a great many things, he was famous for being good at a great many things. Dr. Sam, predictably enough, was jealous. He had been since boyhood. "I was the favorite of both my father and mother," Dr. Sam liked to tell people. Not quite. He was the model Berg child, but not the favorite, and he knew it. What was never clear to him was how that could be.

Sam had been a sober, easily bullied little boy. He studied hard, and he became the kind of professional his father said he prized. Yet his parents didn't seem to notice. They were always preoccupied with Sam's little brother. First it was the astounding news that Berg was the rare Jew going to one of the most prestigious colleges in the world. "What the hell are

you doing in Princeton?" was Dr. Sam's response when Berg
told him about it.

In March of Berg's freshman year at Princeton, he wrote
"A Sonnet on Becoming Eighteen." It was a light bit of verse,
full of references to "happy times at school," and Berg sent
his brother a copy. Dr. Sam responded with hostility. "That
sonnet . . . that you wrote was mistitled; it should have been
entitled "A Sonnet on Becoming Crazy," he began. "It is
doomed to become popular with idiots and others whose minds
run in the same channels as yours." He proceeded through a
six-page letter to refer to Berg as "dysphasiatic," "hallucina-
tory," "absolutely hopeless," and concluded with a satire of
Berg's sonnet, which reads in part: "When I reflect upon my
saphead days / I think of wasted years I spent at school, / How
teacher worked like hell to teach a fool . . ." He was always
bitter, terribly so.

After Princeton came baseball. Bernard Berg didn't talk
about his son the doctor, he complained about his son the
"sport." And Rose Berg? In Dr. Sam's words, "She exulted in
Moe being a ballplayer." Observing this, Dr. Sam took it upon
himself to join forces with his father in trying to hector Berg
into giving up baseball and becoming a lawyer. After the baseball crisis came one over women, or rather, one woman. While
the Berg family was dividing itself on the issue of Berg's romance with Estella Huni, Dr. Sam was falling in love with her.
In 1944, he sent her a deluge of postcards while Berg ignored
her. "I would have married her at the snap of a finger," he
once told Goudsmit. He was kidding himself. Estella had eyes
only for Berg. She visited Dr. Sam in Newark shortly after the
war to ask about Berg, and Dr. Sam told her "to have nothing
to do with him."

After Berg's death, when people came to ask Dr. Sam about
him, they were greeted by a painfully conflicted man. Sometimes he spoke with admiration for his brother, referring to
him as "a cultivated, diversified man of letters." Moments later
he would be reviling him as a "fitzgo," which, he said, meant

"a young fellow, well educated, very polite, kind and courteous, but who prefers to be a bum." Or he might explain to strangers that his brother had been "a mutation." Dr. Sam also took to seeding conversations about his brother with descriptions of his own accomplishments. To hear him tell it, he could run faster and walk longer distances than Berg, the athlete, could, and was much more of a war hero besides. He referred to his Nagasaki assignment as "the most important military medical assignment of the century" in his letters.

Dr. Sam went to lengths to befriend his brother's friends Sam Goudsmit and Earl Brodie, and although the catalyst for all conversations was the amazing behavior of Berg, Dr. Sam always brought matters around to himself. He sent Brodie Newark newspaper articles he'd written about himself, and made him a present of a cup and saucer he'd carried home from Nagasaki. With that went a note. "This cup and saucer," he wrote, "I assure you, is of extreme historic importance. When you see fit to dispose of them, I suggest you offer them to a major museum in your area."

Estella Huni may not have sensed the jealousy that ate at Dr. Sam, but a lot of other people did, and one of them, of course, was Berg himself. His response to a brother who admired and envied him was to punish him with silent contempt. "We were close in many ways, but not to the extent of sharing personal or intimate matters," wrote Dr. Sam after his brother's death. Dr. Sam lived with his brother for close to two decades, and Berg never told him anything about what he had done during the war or for the CIA. Dr. Sam eventually learned about Heisenberg and the rest by reading a story in the *Newark Evening News*. When Dr. Sam ventured a question that touched on something Berg didn't want to talk about, he put a finger to his lips and refused him with a sibilant hushing noise. It all left Dr. Sam bursting with questions. Why did Berg wear those clothes every day, why didn't he get a job, what did he do all day? Berg came and left the Roseville Avenue house as he pleased, sometimes leaving for an afternoon, sometimes for a month, and what happened to him after his thick black shoes touched the sidewalk, he wasn't saying. Like everyone else, Dr. Sam learned not to ask, but it rankled. Everyone else wasn't supporting Berg.

For a while their relationship was amicable enough, but gradually essential differences of personality polarized the household. During the 1956 presidential election, when Dr. Sam announced that he was voting for Eisenhower, Berg, who adored Adlai Stevenson, was appalled. Dr. Sam, in turn, was irritated by the telephone messages he was constantly scribbling down for Berg and thoroughly disgusted by his brother's slovenly domestic habits. Dr. Sam liked to keep up respectable appearances before his patients, and he found the possibility that a full waiting room might be treated to the sight of his scantily clad younger brother unnerving. In the late 1950s, with Berg increasingly uncouth and Dr. Sam ever more perturbed, they stopped speaking to each other. If they had to communicate, they left written messages on the newel post at the bottom of the banister. Berg, who was never emotional in public, sometimes referred to Dr. Sam as "that son of a bitch."

Yet, like Dr. Sam, Berg had a strict, somewhat skewed sense of fraternal protocol. In 1958, Dr. Sam suffered a severe heart attack, and was hospitalized. The next day, Berg arrived at the Clara Maass Medical Center. He wanted to know everything. What did the cardiogram show? What was his brother's blood count? What was the sedimentation rate? What did the cardiac enzymes show? "It was like talking to another specialist, not just a general practitioner," remembers Dr. Murray Strober, Dr. Sam's physician. Dr. Sam was in the hospital for more than three weeks. Berg made a vigil of his brother's illness, sleeping in a lounge at the end of a hall near Dr. Sam's room for all but two of those nights. Dr. Strober visited Dr. Sam each morning at 8:00 AM, and afterward, there would be Berg, wielding a *New York Times* and questions about "how my brother is doing." On the two nights Berg slept elsewhere, he called the hospital early the next morning for a report. Yet, never once during this time did he enter Dr. Sam's room or make any attempt to talk with him.

Berg stayed at Dr. Sam's house in Newark because it was free and convenient, and because at times he must have tired of scavenging for lodgings. Sam's house became his security residence. That never meant he liked it. Liked it? He hated it, hated living with his brother, hated Newark, hated the whole thing. But there was another advantage to compensate for the unpleasant aspects of life with Dr. Sam. Berg didn't feel he had to impress anyone.

BEFORE THE WAR, Berg had been a remote but reasonably good-natured relative. His cousin Frances Book hadn't seen him in years when she bumped into him on a Newark sidewalk in 1941. "Oh! My! How you've grown," he said with a huge smile, before telling her how glad he was to see her. A few months later, after Bernard's death, when the family was sitting shivah, Berg looked over at Frances and said he didn't like to see her there with a long face and began to tell her jokes. "He was such a warm, friendly, jolly person," she says. "I really loved him."

After the war he was different. Elizabeth Shames, Berg's cousin, came upon him by chance at the airport shuttle bus stop across the street from Grand Central Station in 1948. At the sight of her, Berg's eyes narrowed to slits and began darting from side to side. He got up, tucked a wad of newspapers under his arm, and looked at her, eyes flicking back and forth. Other people, in Newark, found him suspicious. For a time in 1948 or 1949, Berg would walk into Baker's Pharmacy every morning after his jog, drink eight cups of coffee in an hour, read the newspaper, and cut out articles he wanted to save. If anyone asked him what he was cutting out, he'd hiss at them, "No questions." Generally he rejected conversations, but if he did begin to say something and someone else offered a thought,

Berg would fold up his newspaper and leave. Joseph Brodsky, who worked at the store, once asked him why. "I want full attention" was Berg's reply. "If you interrupt me, you aren't paying full attention." One day, something was said to him— it was never clear what—and Berg got up, said, "I'll never be in this store again," and left for good. "When he walked out of the store, you'd think he disappeared into space," says Brodsky.

He did the same thing at Gruning's, a Newark luncheonette popular for its fresh ice cream. Berg began to go to Gruning's every night he was in Newark. There were booths at Gruning's, but Berg always sat at the counter, looking, with his hat on, like one of the lonely men in Edward Hopper's *Nighthawks*. He would read a book or a newspaper and sometimes consent to conversation, while a counterman named Mike poured him cup after cup of free coffee. Berg told Mike that he had done important things during World War II. One day someone asked Berg if he'd really played baseball with Babe Ruth. "Of all the things I have done, that was probably the least important," he replied.

Another person who met Berg at Gruning's was a Barringer High School English and foreign languages teacher, Julius Kritzer. "He was like my guru," says Kritzer. "Every day at the counter we'd discuss language and linguistics. Berg would sketch things on napkins." They also did crossword puzzles together. Once when the *New York Times* was on strike, Berg arrived at Gruning's with the puzzle from *Corriere d'Italia* and polished it off over his cup of coffee.

After two years at Gruning's, a new counterman, who hadn't been briefed on the situation, asked Berg to pay for his coffee. He got up, left, and never came back.

It was more difficult to walk away from Dr. Sam's house, so Berg stayed. With Dr. Sam, it was that ramrod sense of decorum that kept him host to his brother long after he'd tired of his company. So strong was Dr. Sam's sense of fraternal duty that, on several occasions, he paid his brother's debts without telling him he was doing so. When he heard that Berg owed people money, Dr. Sam would make inquiries and write a check on the spot. In one case, he sent $1,000 to a widow whose husband had loaned Berg money years earlier. The woman had two children in college, and wrote to tell Dr. Sam, "This is a tremendously fine thing that you want to do." There may have been more to it. Dr. Sam liked to tell people about Berg's woes, and didn't hide the fact that he was paying his debts. The spectacle of Berg, who was good at so many things, now falling apart may not have been entirely disagreeable to Dr. Sam. He'd always felt he was a better man than his brother. The forlorn figure asleep in the living room was the evidence.

By 1964, Dr. Sam had reached his limit, and he asked Berg to leave. Berg would not. Dr. Sam's lawyer, who had been at Columbia with Berg, sent Berg two letters of eviction, to no effect. Next, Dr. Sam threatened to make his intentions public, and in mid-June, Berg informed his brother that he had been in touch with their sister, Ethel, who was glad to accommodate him. On June 15, Berg handed Dr. Sam a piece of paper listing the whereabouts of his newspapers, books, personal papers, and clothes—as if Dr. Sam didn't know where it all was already—and he left. Two days later, Dr. Sam called over to Ethel's to forward a message to Berg from a friend, and Ethel's sharp voice asked, "What would Moe be doing here?" When Dr. Sam explained that Berg had told him he was moving to Ethel's, Ethel said she knew nothing about it and hung up. Dr. Sam began sobbing. It was only by chance, a month later, when he encountered someone who had spoken with Berg on the telephone, that Dr. Sam was sure that Berg was alive. Eventually Berg did turn up at Ethel's, but it took him awhile to get there.

In the meantime, Dr. Sam and Sam Goudsmit did their best to trace the vanished Berg. Of all Berg's friends, it was Goudsmit, the former detective student and sometime spy, who tried the hardest to keep up with Berg. From the late 1940s, Goudsmit was writing Berg letters at Dr. Sam's house that began "Where are you hiding?" and concluded with "Please, please, please, respond—react—write—phone—cable or 'say it with flowers.' "

When Berg disappeared from Dr. Sam's house, Goudsmit began to write letters to people, asking if they'd seen Berg. He wrote to Ted Lyons in early August 1964, and Lyons wrote him back to say that he had received a telephone call from Berg a month earlier, but had no idea where he was. Goudsmit followed up leads in Boston. He placed a cryptogram in the *New York Herald Tribune* that read "Moe Berg how are you," and when he spotted Berg being interviewed during a baseball telecast, Goudsmit called the studio. All was fruitless. Goudsmit kept Dr. Sam apprised of his efforts, and Dr. Sam wrote him back with his worries. "Twenty years ago I thought he was eccentric. Now I am frightened." By July 1965, a year after Berg had left, Dr. Sam had decided that "the fact that he willfully shuts himself off completely from his personal world indicates some measure of non-sanity."

Berg, meanwhile, may have been enjoying the anxiety he was causing in Brookhaven and on Roseville Avenue. He met a physicist he knew in Boston, and asked the physicist not to tell Goudsmit where he was. In October, he attended the 1965 World Series in Los Angeles, and visited William Fowler at Cal Tech. Goudsmit heard about the visit and dashed off a note to Fowler, and Fowler wrote back to say that he found himself "in a somewhat embarrassing situation. Moe gave us his address but specifically asked that we not tell anyone else." Fowler said that he had told Berg about Goudsmit's concern, and was willing to forward mail from Goudsmit to Berg. Goudsmit asked one of his government friends to look into the matter for him, and was assured that Berg was fine. From the Treasury Department, Dr. Sam learned that Berg had done some work for Arthur D. Little in Cambridge. By 1967, Dr. Sam had been out of touch with his brother for three years.

No later than 1966, Berg's security residence was a few blocks from Roseville Avenue, in the large stucco mansion on North Sixth Street where the eccentric spinster Ethel Berg lived. Berg had been installed at Ethel's for months, perhaps even years, before Dr. Sam could be sure that he was safe. Dr. Sam's response was to hire a small truck. After four round trips, fifty boxes of Berg's books were piled on Ethel's porch. And then, after twenty years of fretting about him almost daily, Dr. Sam washed his hands of his younger brother.

That was fine with Ethel. It's entirely possible that Berg *had* been at her house that day in 1964 when Dr. Sam called to pass along a message, and had misled Dr. Sam to make him suffer. Since 1934, Ethel and Dr. Sam had had nothing to say to each other. It's unclear what induced such a terrible breach between a brother and a sister, but it's certain that Ethel felt that Sam had done something so monstrous that nothing she did in return could equal it. She hated Sam with such fervor that she could barely utter his name. If she did speak of him, everything she said was pure vitriol. After Bernard's death, when Rose chose to move into Sam's house rather than Ethel's, Ethel was enraged. She would hold it against both of them for the rest of their lives. Dr. Sam was "a social misfit since childhood," who "practically ruined my mother's life." Dr. Sam was not given to ranting in kind about his sister. He praised her teaching skills—she grudgingly admitted that he was "a very good medical man"—was at pains to explain to other people that she had been a paranoid schizophrenic since age twenty, and made it his policy to defer to her rather than provoke her. The Berg family, and its various tendrils and offshoots—the Greenbergs, the Reichs, the Ginsbergs (the poet Allen Ginsberg and Moe Berg were distant relations)—had large family gatherings in Newark hotels or, in summertime, on the New Jersey shore and in Far Rockaway, Queens. When the reunions were organized, Ethel always responded first. If she was going, Dr. Sam did not. If she had other plans, Dr. Sam would attend. As for Berg, he was always aloof. Everyone would whisper hopefully, "Is Moe coming?" But he never did. After Berg died, Dr. Sam cooperated with three Massachusetts journalists on a book about his brother's life. When she heard about Dr. Sam's role in the project, Ethel promised to sue if her name appeared anywhere in the book. The writers obliged her, with the result that *Moe Berg: Athlete, Scholar, Spy* betrays no clue that Moe Berg had a sister. Meanwhile, at her own expense, Ethel assembled and published *My Brother Morris Berg: The Real Moe*, less a biography than an annotated collection of Berg's letters and memorabilia. Dr. Sam Berg's name appears on none of its 360 pages.

As a child, Ethel Berg liked to sing and to dance, had theatrical ambitions, and went to Vienna to study piano. But though she had a pure soprano voice and a pretty face, with attractive waves of dusky blond hair and blue eyes, she made her way through life as neither an actress nor a musician. Instead, as her father preferred, she became a kindergarten teacher, and a superb one. Ethel loved children, and they liked right back this thin, spry young woman who sometimes rollerskated down the hallways in the First Avenue School. In time, Ethel became a master teacher to apprentice kindergarten instructors, and had three assistants working for her.

Teaching was a well-chosen profession for Ethel Berg, both because she was good at it, and because it left her afternoons and summers free for her other interests. She made an annual trip to Vienna for many years, and then later visited her parents' old villages in Ukraine and toured the western United States. In New York City, she attended operas and frequented expensive restaurants. She collected expensive china, flatwear, dolls, Baccarat crystal and antique furniture—including a baby

▼

grand piano—and supported a number of charities, including one that benefited Israel and one that assisted American Indians. For a woman with expensive tastes who was interested in the arts, she was an unaccountably poor dresser. Her clothes might be well tailored, but nothing ever matched, and she looked to many people like a vagrant. On one of her trips to Vienna, she had met a young chemist and fallen in love with him. He gave her a ring with her initials on it and asked her to marry him. She helped him to immigrate to the United States, and for a while they were lovers. Eventually, he married someone else. She never quite got over it. From then on, she spurned all men, turning her attentions outside her work to two passions: her garden and her younger brother.

It was a garden like no other in Newark or, indeed, in all the Garden State. There were peppers of every color, carrots, zucchini, squashes, and strawberries and raspberries so sweet that when she brought a few pints of them to the chef at the Four Seasons in Manhattan, he would send out word that Miss Berg and her dining partner were the guests of the Four Seasons. There were flowers and a yellow dogwood, and fruit trees thriving in Ethel Berg's garden that botanists swore could not grow in New Jersey soil. Once a Rutgers University professor came to see for himself and left, shaking his head. Ethel was forever rushing out of her kitchen, apron flapping, to rake and prune. Her secret was a stable of police horses, two blocks from her house. Buckets of horse manure produced earth of uncommon richness.

If she was deft and gentle with plants and children, with adults Ethel Berg was strident and domineering. To some of her youngest relatives, she could play the doting cosmopolitan. Her cousin Frank Niceberg, as a little boy, went all over New York with Ethel, inspecting parks, museums, aquariums, and monuments. He saw more in a day with Ethel than in a week with anybody else. She walked quickly, spoke quickly, and angered quickly too. Her conversation usually fit into the simple rubric of commands: "you ought to; you should; you must;

do it." Many people found her inflexible—a harridan who was impossible to get along with. Anybody who did not agree with her was dismissed fiercely as "a liar." In Newark, people crossed the street to avoid her. Ethel's cousin Frances Book had buckteeth as a girl, and Ethel—a grown woman at the time—ridiculed her unmercifully for the imperfection, making faces and taunting her. When Frances was ten, Ethel dropped her at a downtown theater and told her to find her way home. Frances got lost, and was finally brought home by some firemen, whereupon Ethel gave her a tonguelashing. Frances's sister, Elizabeth, on the other hand, became Ethel's protégée. Ethel took her to fancy restaurants in Manhattan, and sent her to investigate and report back with all the details when Dr. Sam bought a house on Roseville Avenue.

As she grew older, Ethel became increasingly eccentric. She developed a terrible fear of childbirth and did not hesitate to hurl calumnies at pregnant women. "Isn't that awful," she'd say loudly. She endured thunderstorms by hiding under a bed, quivering. At night she suffered from insomnia, and to pass the time, she'd walk through her house blindfolded in the dark, so as to know her way around in case she went blind. When Elizabeth's daughter Barbara came from Melrose, Massachusetts, to visit Ethel for a week in Newark, Elizabeth called up Ethel after a few days and Ethel announced that Elizabeth needn't bother picking Barbara up—she was keeping her. Elizabeth's husband, Joe Shames, took the telephone out of his wife's hand and told Ethel that he'd be in Newark at 1:00 P.M. the next day to pick up Barbara. Barbara didn't like to visit Newark after that.

Ethel had much in common with Berg. Both walked quickly, had their own ideas about clothes, and demanded the full attention of the person they were speaking with—hurrying out the door and sometimes even severing the relationship permanently if they didn't get it. Moe and Ethel Berg also possessed an uncanny ability to get other people to give them things for nothing. Craig Miller and his father cut Ethel's lawn, fixed and carried things for her whenever she asked, and did the heavy work in her garden, all without remuneration of any sort. "We just did it," says Craig Miller. "I rebuilt her carriage house for her. You just did things for her." As she grew old, Ethel became known as a witch to the children in her neighborhood—a reputation she did not discourage by rushing out onto the porch and cackling at them. "Rahhh," she would scream. "I'm a witch." The family joke during the Newark riots in the 1960s was that Ethel's house was the safest place in the city, since everyone was afraid to go near it. For all this, Ethel appears to have shared one more thing with Berg: she was lonely. Once Craig Miller's mother, Dorothy, invited Ethel over for Christmas dinner. She came, sang carols with the Millers, and then broke down. "This is the best Christmas I've ever had," she said. In the Millers' guest book she wrote, "If you want to enjoy life, come here."

The Millers owned a drugstore in Roseville, and one day Ethel came into the store beaming. "Moe's coming to live with me," she said. Berg was one of the few people who wasn't cowed by his sister, but living with her wore on him. She built him shelves for all his books, provided his newspapers, a sun porch to read them on, and a dresser to stuff full of the ones he wanted to save. She cooked him lavish meals, made from the produce in her garden. But Ethel's prize niece, Elizabeth Shames, says, "If you allowed Ethel to do things for you, you virtually could not move without her permission." A woman like that sharing a house with a thoroughly independent man like Berg made for plenty of unhappiness.

If there were bucolic trappings now to Berg's new life in Newark, he brought with him to Ethel's some of the same eccentricities he'd revealed to his brother. He shunned people. When family members or the Millers came to visit, he left the house through the back door to avoid them or slipped upstairs to his room. To letters and invitations he offered no response. When telephone calls came to the house, Ethel would answer and Berg would hiss with alarm, "Mention the name!" until she did. He read dozens of books simultaneously, switching frantically from one to the next, and lining them all with stroke after stroke of lead pencil.

In 1966, when Elizabeth Shames arrived from Portland, Maine, Berg emerged from behind the Florentine glass front door to swing her around in greeting, just as he always had in the old days. He kissed her cheek, and while he did, Shames noticed a massive lump bulging at his navel. They went into the kitchen, and Ethel prepared a wonderful dinner, with Berg in rare form, telling stories. He talked about the Nuremberg trials, and about Heisenberg, completely relaxed, eyes flashing. "Elizabeth," he said, "do you like all this crap?" Then he asked her if she'd like to meet Anita Loos. All of a sudden Berg and Shames realized that Ethel was missing. It was spring, but it was cold and wet outside, and Shames found Ethel furiously pulling weeds in her garden. "He doesn't ask me to meet Anita Loos," she said. "He doesn't ask me to go anywhere." That stopped the storytelling.

After that, the only person anyone in Newark ever saw Berg with was his friend Takizo Matsumoto, the Japanese English professor he'd met in Tokyo. The two were inseparable for the duration of Matsumoto's visit. Ethel found the friendship disturbing. Why it upset her, she wouldn't say, but she told the Millers that it did.

Otherwise, when anybody saw him in Newark, Berg was always alone. His fine black hair had gone gray now. He was thick at the middle, and his skin was creased and sagging. He was an old man and vulnerable to criminals, who mugged him during his walks. Newark, too, was decaying. Interstate 280 had cut through Roseville, and helped its decline from a prosperous neighborhood to a dangerous slum where trash filled the streets and some families gave their homes away as they fled to the suburbs. Berg, who never learned to drive, was trapped in a peculiar home in a city that no longer resembled the one where everyone knew the famous Moe Berg. And so, as he had in the seventeen years he lived with Dr. Sam, Berg did his best to stay away. He went to ball games in New York, and he sat with New Jersey sportswriters through entire programs of horse races, never once placing a bet. He went to Boston, where Dr. Hendron removed his hernia, and on to Washington to see Clare Smith and Joe Crowley and, in 1971, to perform consulting services for a man who was seeking to purchase the Washington Senators from the team's owner, Bob Short. He gave legal advice to friends. Jerry Holtzman's room was always available to him, and Berg never missed a World Series. He killed time and kept moving. For a man nearing seventy, he moved pretty well.

The writer and editor Ray Robinson, who had known Berg since 1951, was working for *Good Housekeeping* magazine in the late 1960s when, on his way out to lunch, he came upon Berg at Fifty-seventh Street and Eighth Avenue in Manhattan. "Would you like to join me?" asked Berg, and Robinson said he would. Berg had walked up from Twentieth Street and now, with Robinson in tow, he went farther north. Block after block they went at a brisk pace, with Berg telling stories the whole way about Bobo Newsom, once a pitcher for the Red Sox, who, Berg said, phoned in bets from the bull pen after asking Berg's advice on where to lay his money. Sixty blocks later at Columbia, Berg finally slowed down and ducked into a scruffy luncheonette full of students. Robinson bought lunch for the sixty-seven-year-old five-mile walker, and Berg told war stories.

In 1967, Berg met Sayre Ross, the owner of a small Manhattan publishing firm, in the office of a mutual friend who was a lawyer. They left at the same time, and Berg walked Ross back to his own office on Park Avenue. It was a new office, and Berg admired it. The next day, when Ross arrived for work at 8:45 AM, Berg was waiting for him with seven newspapers under his arm. Setting them down on a table in a neat pile, Berg said, "Look, I don't want anybody to touch it." During the next three years, nobody in Ross's office ever touched Berg's stacks. Berg became a regular, sitting around the office every day, flirting with Ross's secretaries and reading the courtesy copies of books Ross got him from other publishers. Soon Ross could count 120 books piled beside the stacks of newspapers.

Ross was intrigued. "It was better than reading books to listen to him," he says. "He was a great storyteller. He was an embellisher, and who the hell wasn't. His language was a weapon of description. He colored it because people were interested." Berg became Ross's nearly constant companion. Everywhere Ross went, Berg wanted to go. They had long lunches together, and long walks afterward. Like everyone else who played such a role in Berg's life, Ross delighted in the singular experiences a man had when he was out on the town with Moe Berg. One morning, Berg walked into the office with Nelson Rockefeller and introduced him to Ross. Rockefeller gave them a ride to Toots Shor's in his limousine, they took a table, and in walked four Japanese men. "Let's have a little fun, Sayre," said Berg. "When I put up one finger, it's laugh. When I put up two, it's stop laughing." Berg began speaking in Japanese to Ross, mentioning Babe Ruth. Every few seconds he'd hold up a finger and Ross would laugh. The Japanese were astonished. Finally they interrupted, there were introductions, and, it turned out, they were businessmen working for Shell Oil. "Are you going to see the chairman of the board?" Berg asked. They were. "You tell him Moe Berg says hello," said Berg, writing down his name in Japanese.

It was obvious to Ross that Berg was broke and was miserable living at Ethel's, and so Ross began to take care of Berg. Some nights, Berg would sleep on the office daybed. On others, he would check into the Biltmore or the Roosevelt hotel, and have the bills sent to Ross. The hotels Berg selected were always those frequented by professional baseball teams, and Berg was careful to get Ross discounted baseball rates. Ross worried about him on weekends, and always gave Berg $50 on Friday. When Berg walked into the office one day, with his white shirt gone gray, Ross took him to Brooks Brothers and bought him a fresh one. When his pants began to fray, it was back to Brooks Brothers, where, Ross noticed, Berg had a hernia at his midsection that was so large he couldn't cross his legs. Berg never asked Ross for anything. Ross gave instinctively and freely. He thought Berg was "a little pathetic" and wondered why none of Berg's many friends gave him a job. The answer would have been that traveling the town with Ross was as much of a job as Berg wanted in New York.

In exchange for Ross's gifts, Berg provided him with information. If Ross wanted to contact Casey Stengel or Joe DiMaggio or the president of Chrysler, Berg knew the number and was willing to call. "Hello," he'd say, "tell him it's Moe Berg." And, says Ross, everyone spoke with Berg. "I enjoyed his intellect and his truthfulness," says Ross. "He refused to take money unless he could in some way offer recompense." Once Berg agreed to go with Ross to see the editor in chief of Doubleday Books, Kenneth McCormick, to begin work on Berg's autobiography. They met, and McCormick, who had long wanted to meet Berg, was ecstatic. A contract was arranged. They met again in the Doubleday reception room, to go out for lunch together. A junior editor stopped by to say hello and, thinking this was Moe of television's comic "The Three Stooges," he greeted him as such. "Let's get the hell out of here," Berg said to Ross, his face white with rage. A moment later, he was gone, and so was the book contract. Ross thinks that Berg reacted so strongly as a means of getting himself out of an obligation he never intended to fulfill.

Now and again Berg did offer Ross some respite from his visits. In November 1971, Berg was in a coffee shop on L Street in Washington around the corner from the Mayflower Hotel. At an adjoining table, Mary Barcella, twenty-two, a newly married recent graduate of Vanderbilt University and now working as a research assistant for a Washington labor union, was having lunch with some college friends. Barcella had studied linguistics at Vanderbilt, as had one of her friends, and they were discussing symbolic logic when the elderly gentleman seated at the next table cleared his throat. "May I join you?" he asked, and then proceeded to explain during the ensuing conversation that he'd persuaded Princeton to create a linguistics department.

Barcella encountered Berg a few more times at the coffee shop. He told her that he'd been a baseball player with the Red Sox and the Senators, that he'd attended Columbia law school, and that now he came to Washington regularly to do consulting work for the defense contractor Fairchild Industries.

A few weeks later, Barcella's father-in-law, Ernest Barcella, learned about her new acquaintance. Ernest had once been a sportswriter for the *Boston Globe*. He knew all about Berg and demanded that Barcella introduce him. She arranged a lunch where Berg and Ernest Barcella spent a vibrant two hours. Then Ernest had to leave for his office, and Berg said he would walk Mary back to work. As they turned down the sidewalk, Berg looked at her and said, "Mary, I love you," in a tone of voice that, she says, "was not very grandfatherly." She was stunned. "I thought he was very handsome," she says. "He was tall and not stooped. He had these killer eyebrows, and he was very much a gentleman. I did think he was attractive. He certainly looked his age, but he was aging well. He was still masculine and courtly." Barcella was still happily married, however, and so she never went back to the coffee shop. On Valentine's Day she received a card signed "By another M.B.," but she never saw Berg again.

Ross did. But by 1972, his business was flourishing. He had less time for Berg, and found the large fractions of the day that Berg demanded of him for conversation a burden he couldn't afford. When Ross decided to move to a larger office space, it was Berg's turn to frown. "He didn't like the idea of my becoming any bigger than I was," says Ross. "He wanted to be together and small. I think he felt because we were so busy, I didn't have time to listen." One day that spring of 1972,

▼

Berg vanished from Ross's office without a word. Ross never heard from him again—the usual story with Berg. Except that this time he really had disappeared. Berg was dead.

In late May 1972, Berg fell out of bed, bashing his torso into the corner of a night table. It was a painful experience, but he was, by now, stoically accepting the consequences of sundowner's syndrome. When Ethel asked him if he'd like to see a doctor, he declined. But he couldn't eat, and after four or five days of fluids, on May 27 Ethel telephoned Murray Strober, the doctor who had treated Dr. Sam in 1958, and said that Berg was requesting that he be his doctor. Strober checked Berg into Clara Maass Medical Center in Belleville, New Jersey, and recorded his symptoms. Berg felt anemic. He said he'd swallowed some bad fish and couldn't eat. Berg also mentioned vague abdominal pain and told the doctors that he'd fallen out of bed. There were black and blue marks on his face and abdomen. Strober listened and said to Berg that he might be suffering from diverticulitis. "Just a minute," said Berg. "That's derived from the Latin 'diverticulum' and the plural 'diverticula.'" Strober asked a young nurse to make a cardiogram. The nurse was wearing a name plate that said "Hippos," and when Berg saw that, he said, "You're Greek, aren't you, Miss Hippos?" She said she was. Berg then guessed that her ancestors came from Thessaly, and Miss Hippos was stunned. He was right. "How did you know that?" she wanted to know. "'Hippos' is Greek for horse," said Berg, "and Thessaly was the province in ancient Greece where people raised horses. If you are Greek and your name is Hippos, you must have come from Thessaly."

By the end of the day Strober still hadn't decided what was wrong with Berg. Two other doctors, including a urologist, were called in to examine him, but it was not until his blood count dropped that it was clear that what was ailing Moe Berg was neither bad fish nor a bad fall. It was a bad heart. Berg was suffering from an abdominal aortic aneurism, and he was bleeding to death. On May 29, 1972, he asked a nurse, "How are the Mets doing today?" and died before she could answer. It was baseball to the last.

BERG LEFT NO estate of any sort, but he did leave two distraught siblings. Both were furious with Berg's doctors for not saving him. Dr. Sam was on a train tour of England and Scotland when his brother became ill and died. When he learned what had happened, he stopped talking with one of the doctors who had treated Berg and confided to colleagues that he felt he should have been home to help save his brother. As for Ethel, she swore to people in Roseville that Berg had been poisoned, contributing to rumors that drifted around New Jersey that someone in the espionage trade had "done Berg in." Ethel was ever after nearly hysterical on the subject of her younger brother. Mostly she referred to him with close to mystical hyperbole, though she did confide to a Newark librarian that she disliked Berg because he used her. Ethel wrote crazed letters to everyone from John Kieran to the CIA, beseeching all for information about her brother. One letter to Kieran arrived written on a spool of paper that measured eight feet when he unwound it.

Berg's ashes were buried in a cemetery outside Newark, and Sam visited the plot to pay his respects every year on March 2, Berg's birthday. In 1986, Ethel Berg was discovered unconscious in her home. Dr. Sam visited her faithfully. Shortly before Ethel died the next year at age eighty-seven, Dr. Sam learned that, in 1974, Ethel had dug up Berg's urn and taken it with her to Israel. In Jerusalem, she asked a rabbi she'd met in New Jersey to help her arrange a burial, but he refused, explaining that cremation was against Orthodox ritual. When Ethel requested that the rabbi select an appropriate site for her younger brother's ashes, he pointed to a hill overlooking Jerusalem, which is known as Mount Scopus, and mentioned a grove of trees on top, not far from the campus of the Hebrew University. For years, Dr. Sam tried to learn where the grave was located so that Berg could be brought home and buried with his family, but the rabbi could not tell him. Dr. Sam died in 1992 at the age of ninety-two, so the final mystery of Moe Berg's inscrutable life is that nobody knows where he is.

CHAPTER 14

The Secret Life
of Moe Berg

After rousting Earl Brodie from the cigar shop at the Mayflower Hotel for a long walk through Washington late one night in 1949, Moe Berg told him about the brutal subtext of his Zurich meeting with Werner Heisenberg. And although he had not intended to do so, Berg betrayed another of his secrets to Brodie that evening. This second revelation came in the form of a question that was so unexpected and so painfully direct that for a brief moment it dissolved the patina of mystery beneath which Berg obscured himself. The two men had been walking for several miles at a rapid pace when Berg suddenly stopped dead under a street lamp, swiveled a face taut with anxiety and tension toward Brodie, and asked "Earl, did Colonel Dix like me?" Brodie was startled. "I had no idea whether Dix liked Moe," he says, "but I said that Dix indeed liked him very much. Any other reply would have devastated him."

▼

After meeting Berg in Washington in 1943, Howard Dix and his wife, Bertha, spent many pleasant evenings getting to know him. While Berg was working for him in Europe, Dix sent a faithful stream of messages filled with affection, praise, and encouragement. In New York, after the war, he had accompanied Berg to baseball games and lectures, and had traded news and gossip with him. Dix's loyalty to Berg was so great that Dix's superiors concluded that Dix had let "personal irons" interfere with his work as an administrator. Many of the irons were one man, Moe Berg. Dix had also allowed himself to spend chunks of time over the course of a year laboring on draft after draft of a letter recommending Berg for the Medal of Freedom. In some ways, Dix was like everybody else. What he knew of Berg was what Berg had told him, and Dix believed all of it. "Well, young fellow," Dix once said to Brodie, "when you invade Japan, you'll be doing it on the basis of pictures Moe took." Dix more than liked Berg. He admired him, bragged about him, and indulged him with a jocose, grandfatherly affection.

Berg would have had to be blind to doubt Dix's feeling for him, and in a way he was. He was blind to himself. Berg spent a lifetime crafting a brilliant persona that fascinated almost everyone who brushed close to him. But all that effort seemed only to reinforce Berg's conviction that he was nothing but a fake. Berg questioned Howard Dix's affection in the same way that he was skeptical of all people who claimed they liked him. Berg knew better. What they admired was the carefully orchestrated collection of set pieces he presented as himself. The real Moe Berg, he implied, was less impressive, which anyone would eventually see if he gave them the chance. He never did. To avoid exposure as a charlatan, Berg lived a bedouin life, ever on the move, always avoiding sustained relationships where people might get a clear look at him. And he was equally determined to skirt situations where he might be forced to consider himself. Berg suffered from an insecurity so severe that at times it debilitated him completely. More often, his lack of self-esteem banished all tranquillity from his life.

Berg's transition from a man who was unusually private to an obsessively secretive loner came during the war, when secrecy was his job. Berg liked secret work, and he liked the secret world. "There is a comfort to the secret world," says an American intelligence community psychiatrist. "One of the great stresses of undercover work is the inability to say what you are doing. You must take pleasure and gratification in that." With Dix and Donovan feeding him a rich diet of praise, Berg could do so. The trouble began when the CIA excluded him from the secret world. True spies can always live without recognition. Berg could not. Inside the secret world, Berg asked for reassurance from his superiors. In from the cold, he found he needed it more than ever. For some men, imposed secrecy becomes so ingrained that the habit carries over into civilian life. That wasn't what happened to Moe Berg. With Berg, the secrecy was worn self-consciously, like a thick topcoat, with a finger to his lips in place of a silk scarf at his throat.

In the press box one day, Bob Broeg told Berg, "You'd make a great spy—you know, you're the man who knew too much." Berg smiled at that. Broeg was thinking what Berg wanted him to think. Moe Berg lived a secret life because, as a matter of pride, he wanted to maintain the illusion that he was still an intelligence agent, and because it was a convenient way of avoiding things that caused him pain. The secrecy allowed Berg to say as much as he wanted to and no more. If an uncomfortable subject arose, the finger went to his lips. He could never be found out, his measure could never be taken.

As a baseball player, he avoided competition. In 1924, Berg had delayed his passage back from Europe when he needed to impress the Brooklyn Dodgers with sharp play if he wished to remain in the major leagues. Then, in 1926, he had gone to law school when there was a chance at winning the job as starting shortstop for the Chicago White Sox. Later, with the

Senators and Red Sox, he made it clear to his teammates that his ambition was to be on the team, not to play. It was Berg's policy to make himself unique, so that comparisons were impossible. In baseball, he was not first a player but an intellectual, and so he told his teammates and the press about Japan, linguistics, and the stars. Only outside baseball was he a ballplayer, one who sketched diamond diagrams for Paul Scherrer, told William Donovan's entourage about the exploits of Tyrus Raymond Cobb, talked about the Pirates with William Fowler, the Nobel Laureate, and the Phillies with the learned astronomer I. M. Levitt. On the radio program "Information, Please!" he refused to discuss the law, probably fearing exposure as a lawyer who didn't know his field. Now, after the war, nobody knew what he was doing, which kept Berg sealed from failure. Perhaps one reason he was comfortable when other people were in crises is that there was no competition, and his generosity and composure were so obviously appreciated. It's also possible that people talked with him so easily because he was restrained. There was no aura of competition. For a man with so many qualifications, people found him remarkably unthreatening.

That Moe Berg was secretive did not mean that he refused to say anything about himself. When he got back from the war, there came a gradual shift in Berg, from living to talking about living. He became a troubadour, telling and retelling the story of his life. He told it in bars and he told it in parlors, he told it in restaurants, he told it on walks through parks, and he told it while riding in cars. The audience did not seem to matter. Berg's standard repertoire of events began with his years at Princeton, moved on to Columbia law school and the Sorbonne, skipped his career as a baseball player except to mention the fleeting moment early in the 1929 baseball season when he was outhitting Lou Gehrig and Babe Ruth, and always contained a detailed account of his second trip to Japan, where he nosed about Tokyo with Babe Ruth and took illicit photographs from the top of Saint Luke's Hospital. Then it was on to the war, Rockefeller, Amaldi, Wick, Groves, Heisenberg, Meitner, and Von Karman. It was a wonderful oral history except for two flaws. It was highly selective and highly embellished.

Berg never discussed in detail his religion, his childhood, or his family, and he told nobody about Estella Huni or Clare Hall Smith. His time at New York University and his delayed graduation from Columbia law school remained secrets, as did the real reasons he "broke" with the CIA. When Berg wanted something to remain secret, no pincer in the world could pull it from him. His superiors at the Office of the Coordinator of Inter-American Affairs felt that they never learned exactly what Berg had done for them. Later, the CIA had the same frustrating problem with him.

What Berg did share with people was calculated to impress them, and usually it did. Berg implied that he had gone to the top of Saint Luke's Hospital at the behest of the U.S. government, and that the photographs he took there were used to plan the Doolittle raids. Fabulous stories, which became famous and oft-repeated, except that neither was true. He let people believe that he was a fluent speaker of a dozen languages and that he learned to speak Japanese in the course of a boat trip across the Pacific. Not true either. Berg sometimes said that he'd arrived in Rome by submarine, that he'd had love affairs with countesses all over Europe, and for years he implied that he was working as a deep cover agent for the CIA. All of this was altered or fabricated history.

Why did he do this? The answer is that although other people might have been impressed with the truth about Moe Berg, he was not. In 1945, when Whitney Shepardson requested that Berg write down an account of his war service so that the U.S. government would be aware of the OSS's valuable contributions to the war effort, Berg could not do it. Beginning in 1958, Berg tried many times to make a written record of his life, and he always failed. He began it on hotel stationery and on plain white paper, on notepads and on scraps of nap-

kins, but inevitably, after two pages or twenty, the prose slack-
ened into outlines, which dwindled to notes and soon sputtered
to a complete stop. Berg's ready public explanation for his
failure to write about himself would have been that he was a
spy and couldn't reveal what was classified, but that was an
excuse. There was no need to keep military secrets from Shepardson or Groves. Berg's real reason was that the story didn't
please him. Seated at a formica diner table stained with coffee
mug rings, telling five people about himself, Berg the storyteller
embellished freely and no harm was done. Alone at his desk,
Berg could gloss over and manipulate things no longer; he
worried that the life he saw unfolding on those pages was a
failed life. He never said what he really thought of himself,
but his actions suggest that he saw Moe Berg as a mediocre
ballplayer, a scholar only within the unlearned community of
baseball, and an intelligence agent whose work had come to
nothing. There was no bomb, and the CIA didn't want him.

The older Berg got and the further removed he was from
his glory days in baseball and the OSS, the more his need for
recognition grew. He could not tolerate interruptions, and he
stalked out of the room if they occurred. He courted praise
and he devoured it. He became lonely and compulsive, filling
notebook after notebook with copious lists of his friends, frantic
outlines of his life, conversational fragments like "Charlie:
'Moe Berg is a great guy' " and notations like "I was on TV
for quite a while before game Sunday with Lindsey Nelson,
top Mets announcer." Berg rarely shared his emotions with
other people, but in his notebooks he would write, as though
confessing something horrible, "M.B. embarrassed." He sent
himself postcards, and saved everything, cards and letters,
ticket stubs, press badges, Japanese hotel bills, German telephone books, restaurant menus, European train schedules, old
passports, and clippings from newspapers. They were all touch-
stones, and he went back to them as he went back to the few
central events in his life, over and again, needing to see them
and to talk about them, to feel that they mattered. One trinket

that was not in the collection of this man who saved everything was the Medal of Freedom, which might have served as an obvious ratification of his abilities. Why Berg refused it is, like so much else, unresolved, but one possibility is that he felt he did not deserve it.

An American intelligence community psychiatrist who is familiar with Berg's classified intelligence files, which include agent evaluations, says that "one thing in his files that was on some level traumatic for him was his concern about the permanence of CIA because OSS went away. That OSS disappeared fed his insecurity about performance. It doesn't exist anymore—does that mean it had no value?" Receiving the brush-off from the CIA might have angered another man, but Moe Berg avoided confrontation here just as he had with Dom DiMaggio in Florida, with Dr. Sam in Newark, and with Milton Kahn over Novelart. When he gave people legal advice and they did not offer to pay him for it, Berg did not request a fee or even ask to be reimbursed for his expenses. Instead, he wrote down on a piece of paper, "Those who behave this way must live with themselves. When I have to ask it is too late." Then he filed the piece of paper away. Always, instead of making an angry outburst, he kept his turbulent feelings to himself and walked away with them.

Berg's personal uncertainties were the most obvious in the way he resisted close bonds with other people. He was a wonder at meeting people and thoroughly unsuccessful at sustaining relationships with them. When things began to get close, he disappeared. Berg need not have been lonely. Many people would have thrilled to become his intimate, but such friendships were impossible for him. So was love. Save his romance with Estella Huni, Berg's known relationships with women were superficial and confused. He had sex, but only with Estella did it deepen into lasting affection, and then he let her go too.

This skittish behavior led people to wonder about him. Although Berg told the *New York Times* sportswriter Arthur Daley that he wished he had children, many people who knew him speculated that he was homosexual. There is no evidence that Berg was ever in a gay relationship, but there was plenty of gossip implying that he was. Some players on the Boston Red Sox saw an eccentric bachelor and they were suspicious. "He was always a guy to put his arm around you and give you a hug," says Bobby Doerr. "Once in a while he'd say, 'Just a little feel.' He did that with a lot of guys. Some took offense and would give him a shove or a little jab. You wondered a little bit, but you knew he was fooling around with women." Jack Wilson, Berg's friend from the bull pen, says, "Some guys thought he was queer. Guys from other teams would say, 'You've got a queer bastard.' He never made a pass at me or Jimmie Foxx, and he had all the chances in the world. I'll be damned if I believe it." Berg did make ambiguous friendships. On one of his visits to London, he met an Englishman and walked around the city with him. Two months after their meeting, the Englishman wrote Berg a letter, asking for money. Early in the letter, the man says, "I am 'He' who showed you around London the night you were here. I was to have seen you the next morning to have wished you 'God Speed' from Southampton. Would to God I had taken your advice and stayed the night with you." Who knows what it meant? To Irene Goudsmit, wife of Berg's friend Sam Goudsmit, "Moe seemed to have no leanings toward either men or women." Says Irene, "My husband always said that nothing could ever be determined about Moe's predilections." There were rumors in H. P. Robertson's family that Berg was amorously drawn to Robertson's son, Duncan, but Duncan, now a doctor, doesn't think so. "I think he was in the closet and he didn't know it," he says. "I don't think he was a practicing homosexual. I think he was attracted to people, period. I don't think he was more attracted to females than males. I don't think he knew his identity." What Moe Berg did not know, nobody else could either.

BERG'S PERIPATETIC EXISTENCE may have seemed to most people to be a hard way to live, but for him it was comfortable. By keeping on the move he didn't need to look at himself; he avoided work; he avoided competition; he avoided expectations. Yet much of Berg's behavior toward the end of his life went beyond eccentricity and became worrisome. Somewhere along the way Berg had become what Philip Larkin calls "one of those old-type *natural* fouled-up guys." His increasing obsessions with newspapers, umbrellas, and baths, his irritation at hearing the sound of his name in public, his refusal to take Newark buses because someone might discover him, the antipathy toward doctors that led him to walk around for years with a bulging hernia, these all sometimes interfered with Berg's ability to live a full life. His strange behavior with young girls and with Clare Hall Smith in her hotel room suggests that he was not always in control of himself. Dr. William Morgan, a clinical psychologist who assessed intelligence officers for the OSS and the CIA and is familiar with Berg's life, says, "It seems to me that as he got older, his personality constricted and he became more and more schizoid. For a schizoid person, think of a ball of yarn: 90 percent is tightly woven, 10 percent is loose. Berg is a complex personality. Within himself he may have been well integrated. He made sense to himself. I think some personalities cannot be explained, the more gifted and talented they are. I think Moe was in that range." The sources of a man's agonies are not easily sifted, and we cannot know what stones in Berg's nature conspired to trip up a person of such promise. One thing, however, is certain: it could not have helped him to be Bernard Berg's son.

BERNARD BERG KNEW only one way to work, and that was constantly. He made no time for vacations, holidays, or respite,

and seemed to his children to live in his white pharmacist's
coat. In 1942, the year he died, he was still working the same
long hours. Only late in the evening did he relax. After hanging
up the white coat and hiding away the day's receipts, before
retiring Bernard liked to read books of philosophy and politics
in French, Italian, Spanish, and English. When Bernard wrote
prescriptions, he did so in English, but Yiddish was the language of his imagination, and it was in bright, florid Yiddish
that he wrote a novella. The story of Yerachmiel the cantor is
a romance, and as far as anyone knows, it is the only story
Bernard ever wrote.

Bernard dedicated the story to his sister-in-law Bessie and
his brother-in-law Benny, and it begins in the homespun fashion of one of Old Peter's Russian tales: "Bessie and Benny, I
am going to write a story for you." Yerachmiel is a poor cantor
with a limpid singing voice who lives in a Ukrainian village.
His life is unfulfilled, largely because of his arranged marriage
to a woman who stutters and will not permit her husband to
see her naked. Near the modest home that the expressive and
passionate Yerachmiel shares with his tongue-tied, frigid wife
is a large house recently purchased by a wealthy Englishman.
One day, as Yerachmiel is walking past the Englishman's
house, he hears the strains of someone playing classical music
on the piano. To this point Yerachmiel has known only li-
turgical music. He is transfixed. Night after night Yerachmiel
returns to stand in the shadows outside the Englishman's
house, listening to wonderful sonatas. In time he learns that
the pianist is the Englishman's daughter, they meet, and Yerachmiel falls in love with her and she with him. Alas, he is
married. What to do? The conflict seems resolved when the
Englishman and his daughter move away, but then one day
the daughter passes through town and decides to attend one
of Yerachmiel's services. As she enters the temple, Yerachmiel
is in the full flight of song. When he sees her, he is overcome.
He stops singing and drops dead on the spot.

Yerachmiel has the misfortune to live in a rigid society,

which pulls the spirit out of a man by forcing him to submit to life as convention arranges it. That Bernard Berg, who abandoned life in a Ukrainian Jewish village for a secular existence in Newark, wrote such a story is ironic, because when his own son made choices that ran contrary to what Bernard had arranged for him, Bernard reacted with fury and derision. In fiction, he was a romantic. In life, he was no better than a small-minded small-town moralist who decrees with a frown that anyone indiscreet enough to flout convention must be punished.

Bernard Berg could be very gracious, greeting his nieces and nephews with chocolate bars when they came to visit him. At the Sunday family gatherings he and Rose sometimes hosted, the food was plentiful but the levity more sparse, because, whenever Bernard was in the room, challenges were always in the offing. "I always thought that the standard of behavior in Newark was very high," says Elizabeth Shames. "A lot of my cousins didn't want to go there. The table was very beautiful. They'd always seat me next to Moe and my sister next to Sam, and Sam would look at her and he might say something or not and she'd start to cry. Moe would be piling things on my plate. Creamed onions, sweet potatoes, pickles, pickled beets, it was all gorgeous. Moe was warm. My aunt was warm. My uncle was reserved but very passionate. I felt when he embraced me it was with longing fervor.

"Picture Dr. Albert Schweitzer," she continues, "that's what my uncle Bernard looked like and sounded like. He was soft spoken, and he spoke with deep care. I always felt a sadness in my uncle Bernard. It was almost as if a lot of people had disappointed him, but he understood. I think of him as a man of enormous wisdom and great compassion."

Bernard raised his children to revere him, and so they did, with an intensity that bordered on idolatry. Ethel Berg's voice was at its most frenzied pitch when she described her father as not just a pharmacist but "a healer." After Bernard died, Ethel told anyone who would listen, "My father was a genius."

Dr. Sam was not given to such rapture about anything, but here he was in agreement with his sister. Portraits of his father and mother dominated the wall in Dr. Sam's living room, and, like Ethel, Dr. Sam seems never to have questioned anything about his parents. There is no record of any Berg, Moe Berg included, ever publicly speaking in anything but respectful terms about Bernard Berg. Not that there weren't tempting opportunities. There was, for example, Bernard Berg's unusual method of banking. If he wished to deposit $60, he sent one child to the bank cashier with sixty one-dollar bills, instructing the child to exchange the ones for six tens and bring them home. The next child was given the tens and told to return with three twenty-dollar bills. And then, only on the third trip, might the $60 be deposited. Habits like this Berg blithely ascribed to his father's "idiosyncratic European behavior." Because the Berg children were so scrupulously loyal to their father, most of what went on in the apartment upstairs from the pharmacy never left the apartment. But enough seeped out to make it clear that Moe Berg and his father did clash, and painfully. The issue was always the same—what a young man should do with his life.

A great many Jewish American immigrant parents of Bernard Berg's generation pushed their children into professions. Most sincerely believed that work as a doctor or lawyer would guarantee their children an easier life than theirs had been. There were other motivations. Some first-generation Jewish immigrants sought to transcend their own sense of cultural inferiority vicariously, by elevating themselves, as Philip Roth says, "through the children—through us." Bernard Berg had made sacrifices for his family. He left behind the woman he loved in the Ukraine, came to a new country, learned a new language, and took on a new trade in middle age. Bernard positioned his children to have lives as well-educated professionals, and he expected them to become nothing less.

Sam became a doctor, and Ethel, who wanted to be an actress, submitted to her father's suggestion that she become a teacher and use her summer vacations to pursue dancing and music. Berg was the maverick. He read and he studied, but he also played games. Bernard could not understand his son's obsession with baseball.

Here Bernard's views dovetailed with those of many of his peers, including another Russian immigrant father, who addressed a baffled letter to Abraham Cahan, the daily advice columnist for the Yiddish-language newspaper *Jewish Daily Forward*. "It makes sense to teach a child to play dominoes or chess," the anonymous father wrote. "But what is the point of a crazy game like baseball? The children can get crippled. When I was a boy we played rabbit, chasing each other, hide and seek. Later we stopped. If a grown boy played rabbit in Russia, they would think he had lost his mind." Spoken and unspoken was the Jewish coda that games were for the *goyim*. Berg wasn't shirking his schoolwork for athletics. He was successful at both. Yet this was no conflict of reason but one of wills and mores, and so the pristine report cards and French medals Berg brought home from school did nothing to soften Bernard's firm opposition—no, revulsion—to baseball. By the time Berg had reached high school, Bernard's hostile feelings about baseball were well known around Roseville.

Berg was obviously the most gifted of Bernard's three children, and his every success encouraged him to stand his ground. But he wanted more than just to play. Berg was a young American boy excelling at the American game and, unlikely as it was that he would be able to, he wanted to share it with his father. He wanted his father to be impressed. Bernard, of course, was not in the least impressed, and felt baited by the constant mention. Baseball, a game he knew nothing about, became an affront to his stature. His other children submitted to their brilliant father, and this one would learn to bend too.

Early in Berg's freshman year at Princeton, Bernard was already writing him scathing letters, mocking the quality of the letters Berg sent him, rebuking his son for his lack of

▼

common sense, and faulting him for taking so many languages.
Berg replied with a six-page defense that begins by explaining,
"When I sit down to write, I do not attempt to write a literary
gem (as you would probably have me)." He informs his father
that although Addison, Cicero, and Pliny's epistolary master-
pieces were composed "not for the purpose of information to
a friend, but . . . for the purpose of publication, or as you would
probably put it, to appeal to the hoi polloi," their casual letters
made crude reading. As for the lack of common sense, says
Berg, "I never pretended to have any." Berg then defends his
interest in foreign languages, with the help of an extended
metaphor in which he explains that "having been acquainted
for more than five years [with] that beautiful creature known
as Latin," it is only natural to want to be introduced to Latin's
"offspring." As Berg warms to the battle, he grows snide. "I
surely cherish the possession of your ornate, loquacious, and
highly instructive epistle. . . . Therefore, dear father, I hope
that in the future, you will not be disappointed by my miscues
in grammar, logic etc., but in addition, you must not think that
I always am in earnest. This, I hope, explains my ignorance
and lack of common sense so profusely displayed in that letter.
I wish you would continue to pour out your consoling, fatherly
advice." Then Berg signs off, "Your dearer? son Moe." A postscript adds, "Princeton won today 34–0."

This letter is many things—petulant, witty, intelligent, overwrought, and calculated to remind Bernard how much his son
knows that he does not, but most obviously it is sad. For all
his spirit, when Berg sarcastically thanks his father for his
consoling advice, he sneers where he craves. And when Berg
passes along a football score, the postscript that must have
been a final galling affront to Bernard, it reads like a regret.
When Berg wonders if he is the dearer son, the gesture is
puckish and yet remarkably poignant, for he seems to have
been asking that all his life.

A few weeks later, Berg sent home brief word that he had
won the autumn baseball series and that he had been awarded

his "Princeton 1923 numerals," and received a "fine" Princeton letter sweater from Spalding. "How are you Pa?" he asks, before asking his father, "Write me a few more inspiring letters." Then this cheeky seventeen-year-old who has just breezed through his freshman uniform tests—"not very hard"—signs off as "The Bum."

The letter Berg sent home from Camp Wah-Kee-Nah, where he was a counselor in the summer of 1921, is preoccupied with informing his father how impressed everyone is with him. Bernard is told how "nice" it makes Berg feel to find that his work is "appreciated by the directors et al." The boys are described as jumping "with glee" to "play ball with me." In their own letters home, "all the kids tout me to the skies," so that "when the parents come to visit over a weekend they know me immediately." When Berg says he is happy because "it's what I like most of all, the open country air with unprejudiced boys for real companions and none of the stiff-collar conventions or proprieties of the city and especially because I'm getting paid for what is easy for me and appreciated by those above," he is comparing celebrity life at a boys' camp in New Hampshire both with his lonely existence as a reviled Jewish undergraduate at Princeton and with his plight as an unappreciated son.

Here were two men who each spoke many languages, but didn't understand each other. Back at Princeton as a junior that fall, Berg kept trying to share his enthusiasms with his father. In one letter he describes the fall class baseball championships and evaluates the prospects for Princeton's football team with a seasoned appraiser's eye—"Watch for the Chicago Princeton game here next week, a real intersectional match," he tells Bernard. In the winter, Berg closes a hastily scribbled account of himself with a brief musing on—who else?—his father. "I've got some good stuff for Pa to read when I get home," he says. "I just thought of it—Sam takes Pa's scientific mind, I his literary, Eth his instructive."

After Princeton, Berg consulted with a man his father's age

before deciding to sign a contract with the Brooklyn Dodgers. Bernard never went to a game. That winter, Berg attended the Sorbonne, and sent back letters alternately complaining about a father who was always working in "that damn white coat," chiding himself for being "lacking in filial devotion," and slipping into the caustic argot favored by Bernard to send him back ingratiating tidbits. "I told one of the history profs already that Papa could talk his customers to a standstill quicker than he could the pupils." After France came demotion to the minor leagues and the sudden decision—maybe Bernard was right —to enter law school. Most people regarded Berg's moonlighting with the law while simultaneously playing professional baseball as an extraordinary feat, and it was. But this was nothing that Berg hadn't always been doing, bifurcating his existence so he could accommodate his father while also accommodating himself.

Berg was on the road with the Chicago White Sox when he learned, from the results published in the May 9, 1929, *New York Times*, that he'd passed the New York bar exam. Immediately he telephoned his father with the news. "Pa," said Berg, "I passed the bar."

"You didn't have to call long distance," Bernard Berg told his son. "I read the papers," and he hung up.

That winter, during the baseball off-season, Berg began working for a prominent Wall Street firm, but he hated the work and soon gave it up. Bernard was disgusted and so was Dr. Sam, who ingratiated himself with his father by linking arms with him in opposition to Berg's baseball career. "Pa and I detested the baseball part of his life," said Dr. Sam. Standing in front of the drugstore with his father one day in the early 1930s, Dr. Sam remarked how nice it was that his brother was playing ball and making good money during the Depression, which left so many young Princeton graduates without work. Bernard snapped, "He's just a sport, he doesn't have a profession." Then he spat. Bernard habitually spat when baseball was mentioned.

Bernard Berg sent his son letters full of spleen. "There is nothing new here," he writes around 1930, describing a Depression-blasted Newark full of threatening weather, violent crime, and reeling drunks. Then he widens his lens in an extraordinary and uncontrolled screed that reads like a cross between Allen Ginsberg's *Howl* and the midnight rantings of a sidewalk lunatic. The state of the world is

a veritable chaos. The young generation running forward after bubbles taking them for realities, the old generation staring forward with disgust, afrighted and full of concern for their offsprings—and backward with regret, unable to retreat unwilling to advance, and made fools of. . . .

This is not pessimism—true conditions.

Political world corrupted, degenerated, perverted. In civil life money making, scheming, pleasure seeking, not for real well deserved recreation, but to get ones befogged brains drunk—to forget to bury the conscience. A great deal of base money making interpreted as "sport" is made by playing made to order, stuffed athletes in the human arena at the baseball diamond and other places like so many were pulled—jumping jacks, soon to be dropped with degenerated hearts, deformed, rough-necky, slangy, glorifying in their former performances with an obscure future, and the public hoodwinked, cheated with pockets inside out applauding, yelling getting crazy.

Such is life now. It is left for you, new generation, and educated to change systems. Would like to live and see how you will do it.

Berg, who was one of those "stuffed athletes" on the baseball diamond, must have read such a violent diatribe with horror. Or maybe just with resignation. He was used to them by then.

The battles with Berg wore on Bernard, too, of course, as did his son's increasingly prodigal behavior. Attempting to understand the latter, toward the end of his life, Bernard made

▼

self-conscious efforts to skirt conflict. He began a letter in 1937 cautiously, writing, "I do not want you to think I am abusing my authority as a parent to command or reprove—that age is long past between us." The problem was that on his most recent visit home, Berg had asked to borrow a thousand dollars, and the time before that, he had requested two hundred. Bernard says, "I care nothing about the money." But on Bernard's mind is not concerned sympathy for a son in trouble, but only Bernard's reputation. Bernard says he worries that Berg is either gambling, spending too much money on women, or giving handouts to needy friends. "After the example I have been setting to my children with my life it would be revolting to me and mama to think of you as a debauche," he says, before demanding an explanation. Berg is now in his mid-thirties, and Bernard says, "It hurts me to see the almost best part of your life's work dwindle away. I may be old fashion in many ways, but there ought to be a sound reason back of ultra modern ways." After cautioning Berg not to "get angry and upset," he makes it clear that Berg should feel contrition for putting his father through such duress. "And you must know," he says, "that parents misgivings about their children work overtime and act on the nerves and heartstrings like the tedious, enervating and devastating monotony of an even measured, ear splitting drip of drops of water on same spot same time and same noise. Be yourself your judge and ours and do not get angry."

From the time eight-year-old Moe Berg changed his name to Runt Wolfe to play for a Newark church league baseball team until his retirement as an active player with the Boston Red Sox thirty years later, he begged his father to come see him play baseball. Bernard Berg never did. "No matter how much I entreat the man, my father will not see me play," Berg once said. "Perhaps he's to be commended. He's a great man who sticks by his convictions." One of the pale ironies of Berg's life is that January 14, 1942, the day he finally retired from baseball to go to work for Nelson Rockefeller, was the day

Bernard Berg died. Baseball made Berg famous and respected throughout the country, but it left him a pariah in his father's home. The same happened when Berg shared a Manhattan apartment with Estella Huni. Whereas Rose, Ethel, and Sam Berg all visited Berg and the love of his life, Bernard refused to meet her. Berg's enthusiasms created a chasm between him and his father, because for Bernard they were the wrong enthusiasms. As for Berg, for all the bluster in his letters and the coltish independence of his actions, there was a part of him ever uncertain that Bernard Berg might not be right.

Fifteen months before Bernard died, Berg wrote to his father on his birthday from Washington, offering congratulations and conciliation. Berg told Bernard that he was "an oracle." He thanked him for imbuing them "with a firm grasp of the human side of life," and for giving all three children "a sense of values." Then Berg cut to the heart of the matter. "If ever there was any uneasiness," he said, "it was because we are all of us quick to react." He urged Bernard to have more fun, to relax. It was a nice gesture, and it must have made Bernard feel good. But if a father's aim is to raise children who themselves raise good citizens, he failed. None of the three Berg children ever married or had children. It's almost futile to begin to say why. Dr. Sam was the only Berg to discuss the situation. "I never got married, my sister never got married—the three of us stayed single," he once said. "Lack of sanity." For Berg, one other possible explanation looms obvious. Fatherhood was associated with disappointment.

IF HAVING A father who so bitterly disapproved of him was confusing for Berg, so was the experience of growing up with parents who told him he had no religion, only to discover, when he set foot outside his parents' house, that to other people he was a Jew. Your background mattered to many Americans, and some held Berg's creed against him. Either way Berg looked, he felt alienated. Who was right? His father, who told

▼

him to ignore Judaism and yet wrote in Yiddish and resisted changing his name as so many Jews did, or the bigots who saw that name, knew that Moe Berg was a Jew, and ostracized him because of it?

Bernard Berg had settled in Roseville because there weren't any Jews there, and here Berg followed his lead. He was always drawn to institutions—Princeton, Satterlee and Canfield, professional baseball, the OSS, and the CIA—where there were few if any Jews. When he fell in love, he fell in love with a Christian. Berg's desire was to avoid his Jewishness, to blend in. His persona as Professor Berg had everything to do with being baseball's lone intellectual and nothing to do with his existence as one of its only Jews. In the OSS, when people talked about Berg, they talked about baseball and they talked about books, but if he could help it, they never talked about him as one of the organization's few Jews.

For many minorities in America, athletics has been a means of achieving cultural parity, but Berg wanted no part of breaking bloodlines. Yet if Berg seemed to many people not to care at all about religion, it was an act. It's difficult to say how Judaism affected him spiritually, but socially it was a problem and a puzzle. Princeton told him quickly that, like it or not, he was different, and a kind of different that some people loathed. After Princeton, he was always conscious of his religion, and sometimes, usually among other Jews, he let show how much. Roman Catholics to him were "my R.C. friends," as in "Oh, if my R.C. friends could see me now!" He once explained that for him to say "Oh Jesus" was "not swearing, because I'm Jewish." When he badly wanted work from the CIA, he proposed a mission to Israel, insisting that "a Jew must do this." In 1956, Berg was invited to Howard Dix's funeral, but he did not attend. He may have wished to avoid his former OSS colleagues. When Bertha Dix arrived at home after the service, Berg was standing alone in front of her house. He offered his sympathies and wanted to know whether he could be of assistance in any way. She thanked him, said no, he couldn't, and then she asked Berg why he hadn't come to the funeral. "I would not have been welcome," said Berg. "I am a Jew." A man who says such things is a man who anticipates rejection and avoids it by calculating limits for himself beyond which he will not pass. He wasn't going to stay around long enough to give people a chance at rebuffing him because of what he was. One of the reasons Japan was "a page out of a dream" to Berg may have been that there all foreigners are the same—*gaijin*, outsiders.

THAT BERG GOT along badly with his intransigent father and was ambivalent about his religion are important clues in unlocking the mystery of Moe Berg, but they are no Rosebud. Berg sought to fashion a secret life for himself, and he was successful enough in doing so that there is much about him that will forever remain opaque. When he wanted company, Berg sought out people who refrained from asking him questions about himself. Some things Berg kept to himself, and other clues as to how a warm, enthusiastic child became such a haunted and inscrutable old man were as much a secret to him as to anybody else.

When A. J. A. Symons began to look into the life of the talented English writer and painter Frederick Rolfe (Baron Corvo), who died poor and broken in Venice, he found that he "could not banish from my mind the thought of that gifted and intellectual man dragged down by his kink of temperament to perish in shame, want and exile." There is a similar tendency among some people who saw the aging Berg to lament what he might have been. This seems misguided. Berg did a great deal with his life. He gained admission to two of the most rarefied clubs in the world—professional baseball and professional espionage—and for a brief time, his service in each compared favorably with anyone's. As a spy working in Europe for the OSS, Berg was at the center of the seminal event of his time, the building of an atomic bomb, and his performance was exemplary. Some of Berg's other accomplishments are a matter of degree. He was no scientist, but he learned more physics than most people. He was not formally a linguist, but he was a sensitive and appreciative student of languages, and knew a lot about them.

Most compelling, however, is the way he responded to life after the war. He might have lived as most men do, with a home, a family, a driver's license, and a profession. People were always trying to saddle him with work, and had he been inclined, he might well have enjoyed a brilliant career as a CIA agent, or a corporate lawyer, or in any number of other fields. Yet whatever quirks of constitution and spasms of uncertainty kept Berg far outside the world of biweekly paychecks, they also allowed him a crepuscular existence, which suited him. Berg molded himself into a character of fantastic complication who brought pleasure and fascination to nearly everyone he brushed against during his fitful movements around the world. In the end, there are few men who find ways to live original lives. Moe Berg did that.

A Note on the Sources

▼

Moe Berg, and also his brother and sister, died before I began writing about him, so I never spoke with any of them. As I hope this book makes clear, Berg was a willfully secretive man and he made it difficult for people who met him to learn very much about him. Yet, sometimes in spite of himself, Berg did leave behind abundant traces of his life.

I have chiefly relied upon interviews with and letters from people who either knew Berg or the Berg family, or who had information that figured into the narrative. Among the few hundred people interviewed for this book, some of them over several days, are the following: Heinz Albers, Kurt Alder, George Allen, Hubert Alyea, Ugo Amaldi, Dave Anderson, Roger Angell, Fred Armenti, Lee Arnold, Eldon Auker, Howard F. Baer, Mary Barcella, Joel Barr, Buzzy Bavasi, Jonathan Bayliss, Eleanor Berg, Irwin Berg, Ted Berg, Virginia Berg, Warren Berg, Boze Berger, Ira Berkow, Gilberto Bernardini,

Edward Bernstein, Richard Beth, Hans Bethe, Richard Bissell, Martin Bloom, Vera Boles, Russell Bowen, Horace Bresler, Jimmy Breslin, Earl D. Brodie, Joseph Brodsky, Bob Broeg, Harry Broley, John Buckley, Dave Burgin, Timothy Burke, Georg Busch, Paul Busse, Robert M. Callagy, Horace Calvert, Joe Cascarella, George Chaplin, Frances Chavis, Julia Child, Elsie Chmelnik, Fred Cifradella, Rhoda Clark, Ray Cline, Giuseppe Cocconi, William Colby, Robert Cole, Ken Coleman, Nancy Corcoran, Max Corvo, Mildred Cronin, Joseph Crowley, Charles Cummings, Christine Curtis, Anthony DelGaizo, Gene Desautels, Sal DiGerlando, Dominic DiMaggio, Joe DiMaggio, Joe Dobson, Bobby Doerr, Sid Dorfman, Fred Down, Mel Edelstein, Richard Edie, Carl Eifler, Edith Engel, Richard Evans, Clifton Fadiman, Markus Fierz, Gary Foster, Terry Curtis Fox, Mariette Fay, Margaret Feldman, Rick Ferrell, Renata Ferri, Robert Fish, William Fowler, Eugene Fubini, Robert Furman, Margaret Jennings Gahan, Joel Gaidemak, Denny Galehouse, Charlie Gehringer, Cliff Gelb, Dorrit Gloss, Ken Gloss, Stanley Goldberg, Murray Goodman, Bert Gordon, Irene Goudsmit, Stephen Jay Gould, William Greifinger, Wilma Grey, Calvin Griffith, Richard Gurner, Nettie Hafer, Barry Halper, Mel Harder, Charles Hardy, Lee Harrison, Ernie Harwell, Herb Hash, Yoshihisa Hayashi, Mary Hedges, Richard Helms, W. Hardy Hendron, Cyril Herrmann, Jerome Holtzman, Cordelia Hood, William Hood, William Horrigan, Lawrence R. Houston, Otto Huber, Willis Hudland, Jane Smith Hutton, Henry Hyde, Aldo Icardi, Masaru Ikei, Barbara S. Irwin, Jerry Izenberg, Donald Griffin, Louis Jacobson, Oscar Janiger, Martin Jassie, Geoffrey M. T. Jones, Ines Jucker, Steven Jurika, Paul Kahn, Monroe Karasik, Frances Book Kashdan, Sam Kashdan, Milton Katz, Helen Klein, William Klein, Willie Klein, Johann Kloimstein, Julius B. Kritzer, Mariette Kuper, John Lansdale, Max Lapides, Bud Leavitt, I. M. Levitt, Bernie Levy, Paul Libby, Robert Lindsay, Hannah Litzky, Ing Gianni Luzi, Alice Lyon, Elsie Lyon, Jane Lyons, Charles McCarry, Jimmy McDowell, June McElroy, Elizabeth

McIntosh, Lee MacPhail, Jr., Fred Makrauer, Jean Makrauer, Susan Makrauer, Abe Matlofsky, Heinrich Medicus, Ron Menchine, Larry Merchant, Craig Miller, Dorothy T. Miller, J. P. Miller, William Morgan, Philip Morrison, William Moskowitz, Edmund Mroz, Timothy Naftali, David Niceberg, Leo Nonnenkamp, Henry Ringling North, Lou Nucci, Eugenia O'Connor, Jim Ogle, Bruce Old, Murray Olderman, Charles O'Neill, Charles Owen, Victor Parsonett, Boris Pash, Eddie Popowski, Jack Porter, Shirley Povich, Thomas Powers, Edwin Putzell, Jacqueline Reifsnider, George Reynolds, Arthur Richman, Diane Roberts, Duncan Robertson, Ray Robinson, Harold Rosenthal, Larry Rosenthal, Sayre Ross, Giorgio Salvini, Grace Sandager, Marjory B. Sanger, Ted Sanger, Kazuo Sayama, Morris Schappes, Charles Segar, Pasquale Sforza, Denise Shames, Elizabeth Book Shames, Donald Shapiro, William Sharpe, John Shepardson, Allan Siegal, Morrie Siegel, Arnold Silverman, Seymour Siwoff, Frank Slocum, Clare Hall Smith, Richard F. S. Starr, Jack Steinberger, Murray Strober, George Sullivan, Ted Tannenbaum, Birdie Tebbets, Caroline Thomas, Margaret Thompson, Peter Tompkins, Cecil Travis, Thomas Troy, Marian Visich, Herman Waftler, Charlie Wagner, Claire Wagner, Robert Wallace, Arthur Weisman, Richard Weiss, Victor Weisskopf, Joe Wells, Billy Werber, John Wheeler, Vanna Wick, Arthur Wightman, Ted Williams, Jack Wilson, Harvey Yavener, Duke Zeibert, and Werner Zünti.

Moe Berg saved things, and so a great many of the papers, documents, menus, ticket stubs, draft cables, letters, and photographs he accumulated during his life still exist. Ethel Berg left a number of her brother's personal papers in the collection of the library at the Columbia University law school, New York, and in the Morris "Moe" Berg Special Collection of the New York Public Library. I am grateful to Whitney S. Bagnall at Columbia for her assistance. A number of private collectors and historians own Moe Berg materials, and several of them were kind enough to allow me access. Berg left a great deal of material at the house of his brother, Sam, and Sam Berg, in turn, presented much of it to Charles Owen, who has been researching Moe Berg longer than anyone else. Charles Owen shared a great many things with me—most crucially, his collection of Moe Berg's personal papers, notebooks, and photographs. I thank him for everything. Thomas Powers, the author of *Heisenberg's War: The Secret History of the German Bomb*, opened his compendious files to me. Lou Jacobson gave me the run of his collection of Berg materials, including the text of an interview he conducted with Dr. Samuel Berg. What the novelist Joel Barr had to show me made the trip to see him in Florida well worth it. Irwin Berg lent me some of his Berg material and much of his enthusiasm for the subject. Warren Berg, Renata Ferri, Terry Curtis Fox, Ed Goldman, William Horrigan, Aldo Icardi, and Dr. Murray Strober all sent me valuable material. Other useful research material was given to me by Captain John L. Bender, Paul Busse, Robert Fish, Dr. Hardy Hendron, Arnold Kramish, and Joseph M. Overfield.

The OSS papers are stored at the National Archives, Military Records Division, in Washington, D.C. I spent months there, tracking Berg's OSS career by picking through thousands of overstuffed boxes of old records and hundreds of spools of microfilm. The OSS records are only now beginning to be catalogued, and whatever gold I found in that unruly river of paper is because of the assistance I received from Larry MacDonald, Ed Reese, and especially the ever-patient, always-helpful John Taylor. People wishing to see the OSS and Manhattan Project documents relevant to Moe Berg's OSS career should consult Record Group 77, Entry 22; Record Group 226, Entries 88, 90, 92, 108, 108-B, 124, 134, 134-E, 137, 140, 146, 174, 190. Note that Record Group 226, Entry 140, Box 19, Folder 155 contains the Project Larson file and that the AZUSA file is contained in Record Group 226, Entry 134, Box 228. Record Group 165, Box 138 contains the Alsos Mission records, as does the Manhattan Engineer District records Entry 5, Box 64. (Some of the Berg portion of this material is also contained in Berg's declassified CIA file, which the CIA makes available to researchers upon request.) On microfilm, M-1108 and M-1109 are documents from the Alsos Mission, and M-1642 contains William Donovan's OSS Director's Files. In our separate lengthy investigations of this material, Tom Powers and I found a great deal of information about Berg's war. We both think that future research may well yield even more.

The other formal collections and archives I consulted include the American Institute of Physics Niels Bohr Library, College Park, Maryland, which owns many of the Samuel Goudsmit papers; the Biloxi (Mississippi) Public Library, where I thank Murella Hebert Powell; the Bobst Memorial Library, New York University, New York; the Bostonian Society; the Brooklyn Public Library; the California Institute of Technology archives in Pasadena; the Hoover Institution Library and archives in Palo Alto, California, which owns the Stanley Hornbeck papers, and where I thank Linda Bernard; the Japanese Baseball Hall of Fame Library in Tokyo, where I thank Miwako Atarashi; the Library of Congress, Washington, D.C., audio archives, where interested visitors can listen to the recordings of Moe Berg's appearances on the radio show "Information Please!"; the Library of Congress microfilm collection of American newspapers; the Lower East Side Tenement Museum in New York, where I thank Anita Jacobson; the Museum of Television and Radio, New York; the National Baseball Library in Cooperstown, New York, which has a file of newspaper articles about Moe Berg, and where I thank Bill Deane, Tom Heitz, and Pat Kelly; the NBC radio archives, which have partial transcripts of some of Berg's appearances on "Information, Please!", and where I thank Catherine Lim; the Newark (New Jersey) Public Library, which has many of the old *Newark News* articles about Berg, as well as some of Samuel Berg's papers and photographs, and where I thank Charles Cummings; the New Jersey Historical Society, where I thank Nancy Blankenhorn; the New York Public Library's copy of the U.S. patent registry and its microfilm collection of American newspapers; the *New York Times* library; the Princeton University Alumni Records office in Princeton, New Jersey, where I thank Rick Ryan; the Princeton University Office of Athletic Communications, where I thank Mark Panus and Chuck Sullivan; the Princeton University Archives, where I thank Ben Primer and Nanci Young; the Reading (Pennsylvania) Public Library; the Rockefeller Archives Center at Pocantico Hills, New York, where I thank Darwin Stapleton; the *Sports Illustrated* library, New York, where I thank Linda Wachtel; the Time & Life Library, which has a modest file of Berg-related clippings and memoranda; the United States Army Military History Institute in Carlisle, Pennsylvania, where I found relevant material in Boxes 78, 78-B, and 81-B of the William Donovan papers, and where I thank Richard Sommers; the United States Department of State Archives at the National Archives in Washington, where I thank Dane Hartgrove and Milton Gustofson; the United States National Personnel Records Center in St. Louis, Missouri; the University of Medicine and Dentistry of New Jersey's Samuel Berg special collection in Newark, where I thank Barbara S. Irwin.

The CIA and the FBI both released material to me after I placed requests for it under Freedom of Information and Privacy legislation. John H. Wright at the CIA and J. Kevin O'Brien at the F.B.I. were as helpful as they could be.

Without exception, the past and present CIA employees whom I spoke with went out of their way to do what they could for me. I am permitted to thank some of them by name: William Colby, Gary Foster, Richard Helms, Charles McCarry, and Moe Berg's great fan, the ebullient Linda McCarthy.

Two previous biographies of Berg have been published. The first was *Moe Berg: Athlete, Scholar, Spy*, written, with the cooperation of Berg's brother, Sam, by Louis Kaufman, Barbara Fitzgerald, and Tom Sewell. Ethel Berg, Moe's sister, did not cooperate with the authors of this book, threatened to sue if her name appeared in it, and wrote and published at her own expense *My Brother Morris Berg: The Real Moe*, a panegyrical response to it. Her book is, in fact, more of an annotated scrapbook than a biography. Both books contain much valuable material and also many factual inaccuracies. Thomas Powers's *Heisenberg's War: The Secret History of the German Bomb* contains a superb portrait of Berg's OSS career. Of the many newspaper articles written about Berg, I think the best are those written by Berg's friends Ira Berkow, "The Catcher Was Highly Mysterious," *New York Times*, December 14, 1989, and Jerome Holtzman, "A Great Companion," *Sporting News*, June 24, 1972. John Kieran's witty columns, published during the 1930s and early 1940s in the *New York Times*, are indispensable reading for Berg aficionados.

In 1979, the Japanese television company NHK produced *The Spy Who Loved Japan*, a mid-length documentary film about Berg made by the famous reporter Jiro Hirano and the director Yoshihisa Hayashi. Hirano went on to publish *The Spy Who Loved Japan*, a book about his experiences while making the film.

In 1992, NBC presented a brief, seven-minute film about Berg entitled *To Catch a Spy*, which was produced by Ann Kemp and reported by Stan Bernard.

In May 1992, I received a brief note postmarked Newark, which reads: "I knew Ethel Berg well, for many years. I have a few interesting stories to tell. Her brother Moe Berg used to hide in a room built by my father, so I am told. My father knows much but may be somewhat tight lipped." It was signed only Michele, with a telephone number that has been disconnected, and with no return address. While such an experience was fully in keeping with Berg, most of the other letter writers I heard from were less elusive. Among the many people from whom I received helpful correspondence are the following: Heinz Albers, George R. Allen, Ugo Amaldi, Roger Angell, Miwako Atarashi, Samuel D. Atkins, Joel Barr, J. Paul Barringer, Jonathan Bayliss, John L. Bender, Irwin M. Berg, Edward Bernstein, Felix Boehm, Horace J. Bresler, Earl D. Brodie, Alyn Brodsky, Ethan Casey, Thomas T. Chappell, Frances Chichowski, Michael Choukas, Jr., Paul A. Ciccone,

Sheldon Cohen, Josephine Colluci, Joe Crowley, Charles F. Cummings, Robert B. Daroff, Stephen R. Dujack, Melvin Edelstein, Richard A. Evans, Mariette Fay, Margaret Feldman, Renata Ferri, James O. Freedman, Fumihiro Fujisawa, Margaret Jennings Gahan, C. V. Garnett, Allen Ginsberg, Irene B. Goudsmit, Stephen Jay Gould, A. J. Greenberg, Donald W. Griffin, Fritz Gygi, John R. Hall, Barry Halper, Bill Hannis, Lee Harrison, John Healy, Mary Hedges, Jiro Hirano, Fred H. Hitchcock, Jr., Lawrence R. Houston, Aldo Icardi, Masaru Ikei, Barbara S. Irwin, Louis Jacobson, Lyall E. Johnson, David Kahn, Monroe Karasik, Esther M. Kelser, Daniel J. Kevles, Paul J. Kiell, Margaret F. Kieran, Lyman Kirkpatrick, Arnold Kramish, Bernie Levy, Robert Lindsay, Hannah Litzky, Cecil B. Lyon, Jane I. Lyons, Linda McCarthy, June P. McElroy, Elizabeth McIntosh, Jean Makrauer, Mario Marti, Arnie Matanky, Abe Matlo, Ron Menchine, Chris Mohr, William J. Morgan, Bingham Morris, William Moskowitz, Timothy Naftali, Klara Nil-Walti, Lou Nucci, Eugenia O'Connor, Charles O'Neill, Ellen O'Neill, Joseph M. Overfield, Carmel Pallante, Victor Parsonnet, Jonathan S. Reed, George Reynolds, Richard Rhodes, Lawrence Ritter, Rodman C. Rockefeller, Lester Rodney, Philip Roth, Marjory B. Sanger, Kazuo Sayama, Morris U. Schappes, Norman Seidelman, Elizabeth Shames, Melville D. Shapiro, William D. Sharpe, David Shulman, Uriel Simri, Russell Sinoway, Seymour Siwoff, Clare H. Smith, John Snell, Murray Strober, Ted Tannenbaum, John Vernon, Robert T. Wallace, and Carl Friedrich von Weizsäcker.

Some of these letters were prompted by author's queries that appeared in *Jewish Currents*, the *New York Review of Books*, the *New York Times Book Review*, the *Newark Star Ledger*, and the *Washington Post*.

In Tokyo, Japan, I thank Miwako Atarashi of the Japanese Baseball Hall of Fame Library, Fumihiro "Fu-Chan" Fujisawa, Yoshihisa Hyashi, Kathleen Kouril, Takenori Seki, the director of the Publications Section at Saint Luke's Hospital, and Yasuaki Suda, sports editor of the Mainichi newspapers. I am also grateful to my friend Michie Yamakawa, who generously helped me to translate Japanese documents, including those written by Moe Berg, when I returned to New York. In Italy, I thank George Armstrong of Rome; Gilberto Bernardini of La Romala, Florence; Giorgio Salvini of the Accademia de Lincei in Rome; and Vanna Wick of Torino. My friend Nicholas Weinstock accompanied me on this trip and served as an impeccable translator.

In Switzerland, I am grateful to Heinz Albers of Zurich; Ugo Amaldi of the European Center for Nuclear Research (CERN) in Geneva; Johann Kloimstein, the head waiter at the Kronenhalle in Zurich; Ines Jucker of Bern; Jurg O. Lang of the Swiss Technical University (ETH) in Zurich; and Mario Marti of the Bern City Archives.

The following people also assisted my research: Anthony Cave Brown, who is William Donovan's biographer; Joseph Capobianco of Columbia University; Patricia DeJohn of New York University; Helena Foley of Barnard College; Patty Frank, who helped me with the title; Larry Freundlich; Carol Gluck of Columbia University; Stanley Goldberg, who is at work on a biography of General Leslie Groves; Joe Goldstein, who risked the wrath of Joe DiMaggio by putting me in touch with him; Geoffrey M. T. Jones, head of the Veterans of OSS, who accepted my many telephone calls with grace and good humor; Joan Karasik; Ann Kemp of NBC; Dana Kull, who made complex legal matters clear; Peter Kurth told me about Anastasia; Sylvia Pelikan of Hopkins School; Thomas Pinney of Pomona College; Doug Salas, who eased my computer woes; Paul A. Samuelson, who put me in touch with Philip Morrison at MIT; the OSS historian Richard Harris Smith; John Henry Williams, who made it possible to interview his father, Ted Williams; the Yale intelligence historian Robin Winks, who gave me good advice in the early going; and the Harvard historian John Womack, who told me how to learn more about Latin America in 1943.

At *Sports Illustrated*, I thank the two fine managing editors I have worked for there, Mark Mulvoy and John Papanek; Myra Gelband, who asked me to write about Moe Berg; and Rob Fleder, Chris Hunt, Stella Kramer, and Stefanie Scheer, for their help with "Scholar, Lawyer, Catcher, Spy," a piece I wrote about Moe Berg for the magazine's March 23, 1992, issue. Amy Nutt answered a few late questions with aplomb.

Stuart Krichevsky, of Sterling Lord Literistic in New York, is a terrific agent.

At Pantheon, I want to thank Claudine O'Hearn and Alan Turkus. I can't say how glad I am that Dan Frank is my editor. No one could have been kinder or more helpful.

A number of friends accompanied me through this book, offering encouragement, criticism, and lodging in their homes when I came to town to conduct research. I want to thank Patrick Bennett, Ira Berkow, Rebecca Brian, Ted Conover, Sally Dawidoff, Frank Deford, Rachel Dretzin, Sue Halpern, Annette Hamburger, Laura Hilgers, Michael T. Kaufman, Adam Kolker, Mike Lindsay, Leila Luce, Sarah Lyall, Greg Lyss, Austin Murphy, George Packer, Sara Rimer, the Weinstock family, Jonathan Wiener, Jamie Wright, and Ginger Young. Charles Siebert listened in his cheerful way to everything I read aloud to him and responded with wonderful suggestions. When Tom Powers said "I'll help you in any way I can," he couldn't have known what he was getting himself into, but he was good as his word, which anyone who knows him realizes is always the case.

This book is dedicated to my mother, Heidi Gerschenkron Dawidoff, and to my grandmother Rebecca Dawidoff Rolland, cherished friends and beloved relations. As I wrote about Moe Berg, I thought often of two deceased members of my family, my grandfathers. Like Bernard Berg, Ted Dawidoff worked long hours in his pharmacy so that his children might try something else if they wished to. Grandpa Ted died before I was born, but everyone I know who met him says the same thing —that he was a bright, generous, and gentle man. Alexander Gerschenkron really did understand all those languages sportswriters said Moe Berg could speak. Russian-born, Grandpa Vati embraced this, his adopted country, where he taught his students at Harvard and everyone else who knew him so very much. One of the many things he taught me was to like baseball.

Notes

▼

Prologue. Who Was Moe Berg?

4. "When Linda McCarthy": Interview with Linda McCarthy, Langley, Virginia.

5. "Allan Siegal is": Interview with Allan Siegal by telephone.

5. "The offending sentences": *New York Times*, February 28, 1993.

6. "Charles Owen is": Interview with Charles Owen, Washington, D.C.

7. "during his sophomore": Interview with Lou Jacobson, Princeton, New Jersey.

8. "Moe Berg was a": Interview with George R. Allen by telephone.

8. "he had slept in": "The Strange Story of Moe Berg, Athlete, Scholar, Spy," by George R. Allen. A talk given at the annual J. William White Dinner of the Franklin Inn Club, Philadelphia, January 17, 1991, p. 2.

8. "Irwin Berg is": Interview with Irwin Berg, New York.

Chapter 1. The Public Berg: Professor Moe

11. "For Kieran earned": See Jerome Holtzman, ed., *No Cheering in the Press Box*," pp. 34–46. Interview with Margaret Ford Kieran by telephone, and correspondence from Margaret Ford Kieran.

12. "most erudite sports writer": Damon Runyon, *New York Journal-American*, October 27, 1936.

12. "Kieran produced": John Kieran, "An Obscure Baseball Item," *New York Times*, December 8, 1938. My collection of Kieran clippings comes from the *New York Times* library. Kieran wrote many, many more Berg-related columns for the *New York Times* than I can discuss here, and readers who seek them out will not be disappointed. Some of my other favorites are "Barrister Berg Examines a Witness," June 16, 1931; "A Baseball Barrage," February 7, 1936; "Night Life in the Big Leagues," February 14, 1940; and "Rain-Maker for Rent," September 17, 1942.

12. "In a January": John Kieran, "When the Bookworm Returned," *New York Times*, January 27, 1938.

13. "The mysterious Berg": See Ring Lardner, *You Know Me, Al.*

13. "For a 1937": John Kieran, "What a Catcher Thinks About," *New York Times*, September 13, 1937.

14. "Berg is even": John Kieran, "It Must Be Catching," *New York Times*, January 31, 1939.

15. "The volume was": This clipping has no byline, and was given to me by Joel Barr. I have a surfeit of clips of the Professor Berg genre. Some others are "Dr. Berg, Backstop," from May 1940, *American Mercury*; "He Can Talk Baseball in Ten Languages," from *Baseball* magazine; and "Professor Berg Inspects Fenway," by John Drohan, January 30, 1940. Many of these clips come from private collections, including Moe Berg's, and are missing bylines and publication information.

15. "Movius Berg": John Drohan, *Boston Traveler*, May 23, 1935.

16. "Berg spent his": Frank Yeutter, *Philadelphia Bulletin*, December 17, 1938.

17. "In a column": Joe Williams, *New York World Telegram*. Please note that a great many newspaper articles about Berg were saved by Berg himself. They were clipped in such a way that often complete identification for purposes of attribution is impossible.

18. "Cajoling the": Francis Stann, *Washington Star*.

18. "When, for instance": United Press International, *Newark News*, May 22, 1966.

Chapter 2. Youth: Runt Wolfe

19. "When Bernard Berg": Interviews with Irwin Berg in New York and Elizabeth Shames in Portland, Maine, informed this discussion of Berg's youth.

20. "In New York": Looking through period photographs of the neighborhood that are in the collection of the New York Public Library informed the discussion of Ludlow Street.

20. "When Rose joined": Samuel Berg letter of January 4, 1979, and Bernard Berg's *Newark News* obituary, January 14, 1942.

20. "Once he was": Interviews with Irwin Berg, New York; Elizabeth Shames, Portland, Maine; and Eugenia O'Connor by telephone informed this discussion of Bernard Berg's feelings about religion.

21. Discussion of Moe Berg's early life informed by Samuel Berg papers and *My Brother Morris Berg*, by Ethel Berg.

21. "The city of Newark": Frank John Urquhart, *A History of the City of Newark, New Jersey*, p. 830.

21. "Between 1870 and": Newark Board of Trade, *Newark, the City of Industry*, p. 15.

21. "to marvel in": Urquhart, p. 825.

21. "The Germans and": Ibid., pp. 827–30. See also Philip Roth, "The Man in the Middle," *New York Times*, October 12, 1992.

22. "Here the natives": Newark Board of Trade, p. 18.

22. "Antebellum Newark": Urquhart, p. 827. See also Barbara Cunningham, ed., *The New Jersey Ethnic Experience*,

pp. 304–8; John T. Cunningham, *Newark*, pp. 201–84; and Arnold S. Rice, ed., *Newark*, pp. 86–92.

22. "It was also a": Barbara Cunningham, p. 244.

22. Description of Berg's Newark was informed by Sam Berg's papers and by telephone interviews with Eugenia O'Connor and Robert Wallace.

24. "The report cards": Robert Slater, *Great Jews in Sports*, pp. 31–34.

24. "He tried": Sam Berg, January 4, 1979.

25. "Moe usually": Ibid.

25. "The famous old": Ibid.

25. "His father, who": Interview by telephone with William Moskowitz.

25. "A coal chute": Ethel Berg, p. 8.

26. "In an article": *Newark Eagle*, month and day illegible, 1918.

27. "Moe saw": Interview by telephone with Hannah Litzky.

27. "There were no": Sam Berg papers.

27. "Following his father": Sam Berg to Elizabeth Shames, December 21, 1985.

27. "We did not": Sam Berg to Louis Jacobson, May 14, 1989.

27. "Moe Berg generally made": Unidentified (publication illegible) clipping provided to me by Louis Jacobson.

Other valuable sources of information for this chapter were interviews with Charles Cummings, Newark; Margaret Gahan by telephone; Helen and William Klein, New York; Craig and Dorothy Miller, Cranford, N.J.; Charles Owen, Washington, D.C.; Ted Sanger, Cambridge, Massachusetts; Clare Hall Smith, Washington, D.C.

Chapter 3. The Stiff Collar

28. "It was a": *Nassau Herald*, 1923, p. 32.

29. "Yet when Jimmy": Interview with Jimmy Breslin, New York.

29. "The shortstop on": Princeton transcript courtesy of Lou Jacobson.

29. "After graduating from": Interview with Patricia DeJohn, New York University.

29. "The isolation and": Especially helpful to me in writing about Berg's Princeton were Donald Griffin and Howard F. Baer and information provided by Rick Ryan of the alumni office.

30. "I'd say he": From Jiro Hirano et al., *The Spy Who Loved Japan.*

30. "Howard Baer, a": Interview by telephone with Howard F. Baer.

30. "After graduation, when": Lou Jacobson's interview with Donald Griffin, Princeton, New Jersey.

30. "lazy and good looking": Arthur Mizener, *The Far Side of Paradise*, pp. 34 and 38.

30. "Berg's situation was": Ernest Hemingway, *The Sun Also Rises*, p. 4.

30. "No one had": Hemingway, p. 4.

31. "Berg *was* the": Louis Kaufman et al., *Moe Berg*, p. 49; interview with Elizabeth Shames; Ethel Berg, p. 14. See also "Princeton Sting to Jews Is Gone," *The Jewish Week–American Examiner*, December 3, 1978.

31. "He was not": Donald Griffin interview.

32. "He didn't enroll": Moe Berg, October 17, 1921.

32. "As a junior": Moe Berg, undated letter.

32. "I am a great": Ibid.

32. "I'm feeling fine": Moe Berg, October 17, 1921.

32. "Berg's letters home": Moe Berg, undated letter, and ibid.

33. "Bill 'Boileryard' Clarke": Super sports feature on Bill Clarke, Princeton athletic files, February 17, 1957.

33. "wearing snowshoes": Madeleine Blais, unidentified news article from Princeton alumni files.

33. "Grimes returned to": Donald Honig, *A Donald Honig Reader*, p. 588.

34. "When an opposing runner": Kaufman, p. 46.

34. "To him baseball": Berg uses these terms in a speech

▼

he gave at Meiji University in Tokyo, Japan, in November 1934. Text courtesy of Lou Jacobson.

34. "Like Cohn, Berg": Hemingway, p. 3.

34. "During vacations": Kaufman, p. 42.

34. "Berg wrote to his": Moe Berg, July 26, 1921.

35. "Happy as he": Interview with Monroe Karasik, Chevy Chase, Maryland.

35. "Berg to Pass": *Newark News*, June 16, 1923.

35. "He'd been voted": *Nassau Herald*, 1923, pp. 387–402.

36. "The next day": Edmund Robbins to Moe Berg, June 27, 1923.

36. "The modern languages department": Interviews with Ted Sanger and Robert Wallace.

36. "New York City had": Ron Berler, "Let's Hear It for the Rabbi of Swat," *Sports Illustrated*, October 21, 1991.

37. "The shrewd manager": Ibid.

37. "Berg was hesitant": Arthur Daley, *New York Times*, June 1, 1972.

37. "The check they": Unidentified clipping from the Moe Berg papers.

Other valuable sources of information for this chapter were interviews with Richard Edie by telephone; Larry Merchant by telephone; and Richard F. S. Starr by telephone.

Chapter 4. Robin in Paris

39. "On June 27": *Brooklyn Daily Eagle*, June 27, 1923, p. 1; *Brooklyn Citizen*, June 27, 1923, p. 1.

40. "Moe Berg Impresses": *Brooklyn Daily Eagle* and *Brooklyn Citizen*, June 28, 1923.

40. "In assessing Berg": *Brooklyn Daily Eagle*, June 28, 1923.

40. "to accumulate jack": Ibid.

40. "He has noted": *Newark News*, June 28, 1923.

41. "On July 27": *Jewish Tribune*, July 27, 1923.

41. "McGraw revealed": Ibid.

41. "The truth of it": In September, McGraw's quest fi-

nally ended in Hutchinson, Kansas, where one Mose Solomon was discovered thriving in the local outfield. The son of a Columbus, Ohio, Jewish junk dealer, Solomon was a short, thick-waisted outfielder who had pounded out 49 home runs that summer for the Class C Hutchinson Wheat Shockers. Local fans said that Solomon couldn't catch a cold, much less a baseball, but McGraw put him on a train to New York anyway. With much fanfare, he introduced Solomon to the press as "The Rabbi of Swat," and then quietly sat him down on the Giants bench, where he languished. Solomon was inundated with dinner invitations from prominent New York Jewish families, but he batted only eight times in the major leagues.

41. "Although Brooklyn was": Samuel P. Abelow, *A History of Brooklyn Jewry*, p. 13.

41. "With Brooklyn wallowing": Sam Berg to Lou Jacobson; Shames interview; interview by telephone with Charlie Segar.

42. "The poor throwing": *Brooklyn Eagle*, August 17, 1923.

42. "Language study was": Berg to George Weinstock, December 10, 1923.

43. "Within a week": Berg, November 5, 1923.

43. "Just to walk": Ibid.

43. "I go in like": Berg, December 2, 1923.

43. "No matter how national": Berg, December 8, 1923.

43. "John McGraw said": Berg, December 2, 1923.

44. "They charged him": Berg, January 17, 1924. See also Charles Alexander, *John McGraw*, p. 253.

44. "McGraw asked Berg": Berg, January 17, 1924.

44. "Who ever heard": *Newark News*, December 28, 1923.

44. "For the 32 francs": Berg, December 2, 1923.

44. "I don't let": Ibid.

44. "I'll tell the professor": Berg, December 9, 1923.

44. "Naturally the ideal": Berg, December 8, 1923.

44. "No matter how well": Berg, January 17, 1924.

45. "nickel-squeezers": Berg, December 8, 1923.

45. "dirty faces": Berg, December 2, 1923.

45. "there'd be a riot": Berg, January 17, 1924.

45. "The women have": Berg, December 10, 1923.

45. "The French musical": Berg, December 8, 1923.
45. "I have been accosted": Ibid.
46. "a flock of": Berg, December 15, 1923.
46. "Well, pretty soon": Berg, January 17, 1923.

Other valuable information for this chapter was provided to me in an interview with William Klein, New York, and in Berg's notes in the Moe Berg papers.

Chapter 5. Good Field, No Hit

47. "Joe Cascarella was": Interview by telephone with Joe Cascarella.
48. "In 1933, Roberts was": Interview by telephone with Diane Roberts.
48. "As Berg sailed home": *Newark News*, undated 1924 clipping from Berg papers.
49. "His tardy appearance": See 1924 issues of the *Minneapolis Morning Tribune* for Millers information.
49. "Perverts, Berg called": Berg, undated letter.
50. "the 1924 Mud Hens": See 1924 issues of the *Toledo News Bee* for Mud Hens information.
50. "*The Affirmative Particles*": *Romanic Review*, vol. 16, no. 2 (April–June 1925), p. 191.
51. "the Great Moe": *Newark News*, May 12, 1925.
51. "a revelation": Ibid.
51. "the whole show": *Reading Eagle*, May 22, 1925.
51. "the brilliant young": *Reading Eagle*, May 24, 1925.
51. "has been pickling": *Reading Eagle*, July 22, 1925.
51. "a disastrous afternoon": *Reading Eagle*, June 11, 1925.
51. "the best double-play artists": *Reading Eagle*, July 18, 1925.
52. "This was such an unusual": *Newark News*, August 10, 1925.
52. "They took him more": Ibid., February 20, 1926, and April 3, 1926.
52. "And what would I": Ibid., April 12, 1939.
53. "Berg 'was intent,' ": *Chicago Tribune*, March 6, 1926.

53. "I have always considered": Ethel Berg, p. 31.

53. "lost because of": *Chicago Tribune*, September 5, 1926.

54. "Moe Berg isn't much": *Chicago Tribune*, clipping date illegible, 1926; and *Boston Evening Globe*, July 9, 1937.

54. "My Dear Young Man": Ethel Berg, p. 29.

54. "A player reporting": Ibid., p. 30.

54. "Up in New York": From Spink, "Three and One," *Sporting News*, November 16, 1939.

55. " 'Moe,' he said once": *Sporting News*, June 17, 1972.

55. "A few days after": There are many accounts of this famous story. Using those from the *Chicago Tribune*, August 6, 1927; *Sporting News*, November 16, 1939; *Washington Post*, March 13, 1932; and Kaufman, p. 62, I pieced together the correct sequence of events.

56. "kindly deliver the body": Kaufman, p. 62.

56. "With Philadelphia, Bruggy": *Chicago Tribune*, August 9, 1927.

56. "He went forward": Ted Lyons to Charles Owen.

57. "The distinguished Corean": *Chicago Tribune*, August 9, 1927.

57. "He also amused himself": *Chicago Daily News*, September 7, 1927.

57. "Part of Berg's": The best account of the early days of baseball remains Lawrence Ritter's *The Glory of Their Times*.

58. "There had been": Joseph Overfield is the world's George Davis authority. See his "The Other George Davis," in the 1989 *Baseball Research Journal*, pp. 33–35. I also interviewed Overfield by telephone.

58. "a full-time lawyer": Davis worked as a lawyer for more than forty years, and he loathed his work. Astronomy is what interested him. His library contained a powerful telescope and a collection of 1,500 astronomy texts in French, Sanskrit, Greek, Latin, Arabic, Persian, and German. He never claimed fluency in these languages, but taught himself to read them well enough so that he could understand the books. In his spare time he lectured on astronomy at the University of Buffalo, was a member of the American and Royal Astronomical

▼

societies, published articles, and began a two-volume history of constellations. In 1960, Davis finally retired as a lawyer and set out to finish his book. He never did. Five months later, after a stock market slump cost him a large sum of money, he hanged himself.

58. "On February 15": Ethel Berg, p. 31.

59. "Afterward, he took": *Newark News*, February 1928; otherwise undated clipping.

59. "By May, the team": *Chicago Tribune*, May 12, 1928.

60. "Berg speaks from": Ibid., September 29, 1928.

60. "For many, the National": Interviews by telephone with Horace Bresler and Stephen Jay Gould; letters from Gould, Lester Rodney, and Melville Shapiro; and Peter Levine's book *Ellis Island to Ebbets Field* were all especially helpful in constructing this section.

60. "The paleontologist": Telephone interviews with Bresler and Gould.

61. "I've done nothing": *New York World Telegram*, March 11, 1940; *Newark Star Eagle*, March 20, 1939; and Tommy Thomas interview in the Japanese film *The Spy Who Loved Japan*.

61. "The same year": Levine, pp. 112–16.

61. "In seventh place": *Chicago Tribune*, June 6, 1929.

62. "There was, as John": Quoted in an otherwise unidentified article by Harry T. Brundidge, in Berg's National Baseball Library file.

62. "The first announced": *Chicago Tribune*, July 30, 1929. See also Shires file in the National Baseball Library.

63. "After that, Thomas": *The Spy Who Loved Japan*.

63. "Eight days later": *Chicago Tribune*, September 16, 1929, and June 17, 1930. See also the National Baseball Library file.

63. "While across town": *Chicago Tribune*, September 17, 1929.

63. "He could make": *The Spy Who Loved Japan*. Fred J. Bendel column, *Newark News*, October 11, 1929.

63. "In New York": *Newark News*, undated spring 1930 dispatch.

64. "Berg smiled, turned": Interview with Charles Owen, Washington, D.C.
64. "many baseball players": Interview with Shirley Povich, Washington, D.C.

Chapter 6. You Never Knew He Was Around

66. "On May 2": *Chicago Tribune*, May 2, 1930.
66. "The nuns gathered": Kaufman, p. 73.
67. "The itinerary included": Ibid., and Ethel Berg, pp. 83–84.
67. "Only in October": Ralph Kelly's April 16, 1931, article on the subject in an unidentified Cleveland newspaper makes it clear that Berg went to Satterlee and Canfield after he'd both graduated and passed the bar. It is, of course, possible that Berg misled Kelly. Bob Callagy of the firm was helpful to me in the construction of this section.
68. "In April 1931": Ralph Kelly, April 16, 1931.
68. "Thereupon he": Gerry Moore, unidentified clipping from Berg file. See also Murray Strober's medical history, May 27, 1972.
68. "Berg had one hit": Interview with June McElroy, Washington, D.C.
68. "It was a thoroughly": Interview with Willis Hudlin by telephone.
69. "After luring Berg": Interview with Larry Rosenthal, Boston.
69. " 'Moe,' Wagner told him": Interview with Charlie Wagner by telephone.
69. "As to why": Interview with Jimmy Breslin, New York.
69. "When he'd finished": Interview with Boze Berger by telephone.
70. "The train would pull": Interview with Monroe Karasik, Washington, D.C.; Ted Williams, Boston; and Edward Bernstein, Boston.
70. "No, Al": Interview with Bernie Levy by telephone.

70. "In one trunk": Interview with Mildred Cronin by telephone.

71. "You never saw": Interview with Shirley Povich, Washington, D.C.

71. "The game ended": Interviews with Billy Werber and Jack Wilson by telephone.

72. "The Indians gave": *Washington Post*, March 10, 1932.

72. "That said, Povich": Morrie Siegel interview by telephone.

72. "On March 13": *Washington Post*, March 14, 1932.

73. "I wish less attention": *American Mercury*, May 1940.

73. "Too much has": F. C. Lane, in *Baseball Magazine*, unidentified clipping from Berg's National Baseball Library file.

73. "I don't suppose": Ethel Berg, p. 36.

73. "The minute he learned": Unidentified clipping from Berg file.

74. "You kept me": This letter appears in Ethel Berg, p. 308.

74. "I was fascinated": Interview with Shirley Povich, Washington, D.C.

75. "I would say that": *American Mercury*, May 1940.

Chapter 7. Strange Foreigner with Camera

76. "A few occasions": An interview with Professor Masaru Ikei in New York was helpful in constructing this section, as was his manuscript "Double Play: Baseball in U.S.– Japanese Relations."

78. "By the time": Berg letter, October 11, 1932.

78. "They tell me": Ibid.

78. "Berg spent a": Ethel Berg and *Newark News*, April 12, 1939.

78. "On October 20": Berg kept a great deal of information about his trips to Japan in his boxes. His brother and sister sent that material to the Columbia law school library,

New York Public Library, Newark Public Library, and Charles Owen.

79. "I have never": Berg letter, November 9, 1932.

79. "He slept on a": Berg letter, November 26, 1932.

79. "You must inhale": Berg letter, November 9, 1932.

79. "He even made": Arthur Daley, *New York Times*, December 2, 1964.

79. "He also attended": Hirano, *The Spy Who Loved Japan*, p. 253.

80. "She refused, telling": Interview with William Klein, New York.

80. "Berg was intrigued": Spink, *Sporting News*, November 16, 1939.

80. "Matsumoto helped him": Berg letters, November 9 and 26, 1932.

80. "Don't fear—safe": Berg letter, November 26, 1932.

80. "He toured Shanghai": Ethel Berg, p. 137; and Berg letter, December 31, 1932.

80. "After a day": Ibid. and Spink.

81. "I am always": Berg letter, December 31, 1932.

81. "I have decided": Ibid.

81. "It was clear": Hirano, p. 125.

81. "Instead, by February": *Biloxi Daily Herald*, February 27, 1933.

81. "a rather poignant example": *Washington Post*, March 7, 1933.

82. "Japan was the": Hirano film *The Spy Who Loved Japan*.

82. "As a rule": Frank Young, *Who's Who in Major League Baseball*, 1933, p. 76.

82. "Alice's mad chess game": Correspondence from Melville D. Shapiro. See *The Annotated Alice*, edited by Martin Gardner, p. 172, for chess-game details.

82. "During spring training": Francis Stann, *Washington Star*, November 16, 1955.

83. "Berg didn't play": Kaufman, p. 95.

84. "He was studying all": Interview with Cecil Travis by telephone.

84. "One day, instead": Interview with Marjory Sanger, Winter Park, Florida.

85. "Another person who": Interview with Frank Slocum by telephone.

86. "On July 25": *Washington Post*, July 26, 1943.

86. "The Cleveland manager": *Jewish Independent*, Cleveland, September 14, 1934.

86. "He has performed": Ibid.

87. "His performance on": "The Most Exciting Game," by John Kieran, *This Week*, April 24, 1960, p. 2.

87. "By 1934, Japan": Reischauer, "What Went Wrong?" in Morely, *Dilemmas of Growth*, p. 496.

88. "In particular, there": War Department memo, July 27, 1933, in the Department of State Far Eastern Affairs Division archive at the National Archives.

88. "To Japanese eyes": See especially *Osaka Jiji Shimpo*, July–September 1934; *Japan Chronicle*, July–September 1934; *Kokumin Shimbun*, July–September 1934; and *Japan Times*, July–September 1934.

88. "They come ostensibly": *Tokyo Nichi Nichi*, July 20, 1934.

88. "Despite the utmost": *Japan Chronicle*, September 29, 1934.

88. "An American entomologist": American consulate memo from Richard F. Boyce to Cordell Hull, August 6, 1934.

89. "He liked to dance": Kaufman, p. 12, and interview with Jane Lyons, Baltimore.

89. "With Moe it became": Interview with Jane Lyons, Baltimore.

89. "I wanted to be": Interview with Joe Cascarella by telephone.

89. "After two weeks of": Hirano, pp. 54–55.

90. "That was two weeks": Bus Saidt, *Trenton Times*, July 1972, and interview with Harvey Yavener by telephone.

90. "Ruth arrived to": *Osaka Mainichi*, November 3, 1934.

90. "Everybody wanted to see": *Japan Times*, November 3, 1934.

90. "The next time": Interview with Cliff Gelb by telephone.

91. "But Berg was": Charles Owen owns this film footage, some of which appears in the Japanese NHK production *The Spy Who Loved Japan.*

91. "The Americans played": It was Lefty O'Doul who suggested that the Tokyo team call itself the Giants.

91. "One fan walked": Berg file and *Spalding Baseball Guide*, 1935.

92. "In February, Shoriki": Kaufman, p. 87.

92. "He's more a scholar": *Baseball News of Osaka*, November 25, 1934.

92. "You have done us": Text courtesy of Lou Jacobson.

93. "Berg may have heard": Interview with Masaru Ikei, New York.

94. "Entering the hospital": Berg told a great many people this story. Chapter 1 of Kaufman is the best written account. A written description by Berg is included in a letter he wrote to Theodore Von Karman in the summer of 1958. Also, interviews with Elsie Lyon, Hancock, New Hampshire; and Bob Broeg by telephone. See also Hirano, for a more skeptical presentation.

95. "Berg had been riding": *Osaka Mainichi*, February 5, 1935.

96. "In Manchouli he": Interview with Clare Hall Smith, Washington, D.C.

96. "I was young then": Bus Saidt, *Trenton Times*, July 1972.

96. "Berg told John": Kieran, *New York Times*, January 22, 1935, and July 5, 1935. See also Saidt; Henry P. Edwards, American League press release, January 23, 1938; and interview with William Klein, New York.

Other valuable information for the Japan section of this chapter was provided to me in interviews with General Jimmy Doolittle by telephone; Margaret Feldman by telephone; Charlie Gehringer by telephone; Ken Gloss, Boston; Dr. Hardy Hendron, Boston; Jane Smith Hutton by telephone; Steve Jurika by telephone; Esther Kelser by telephone; Charles Owen,

Washington, D.C.; Jacqueline Reifsnider by telephone; Grace
Sandager by telephone; and in a letter from John Snell, of the
Honolulu Advertiser.

Chapter 8. Mr. Berg, You've Been Brilliant

98. "In December, Griffith": *Newark Star Eagle*, incompletely identified clipping from Powers Berg file, October 1934.

98. "On April 11": *Boston Evening Transcript*, April 17, 1935.

98. "Cronin asked him": Larry Merchant, "Moe Berg" and "More on Moe," *New York Post*, June 6 and June 7, 1972.

98. "Joe Cronin liked": Interview with Ted Williams, Boston.

99. "Boston pitchers like": Interview with Jack Wilson by telephone.

99. "He didn't care": Interview with Gene Desautels by telephone.

99. "He was a fine catcher": Interview with Billy Werber by telephone.

100. "Joe Cronin's locker": Interview with Rick Ferrell by telephone.

100. "Isn't this wonderful": "In the Dugout with Rumill," clipping, otherwise unidentified, from Berg file.

100. "In this way": Interview with Leo Nonnenkamp by telephone.

101. "In the bull pen": Interview with Jack Wilson by telephone.

101. "After one game Al Schacht": Schacht, *Clowning Through Baseball*, p. 161.

101. "Moe was really something": *Sporting News* Berg obituary, June 17, 1972.

101. "I was warming up": *Boston Globe*, October 12, 1967.

102. "Berg even put in": *Boston American*, September 7, 1935.

102. "The Red Sox traveled": Interviews with Billy Werber and Joe Dobson by telephone.

103. "I remember one": Interview with Eldon Auker by telephone.

103. "Quite a few of us": Interview with Jack Wilson by telephone.

103. "Once in a while": Interview with Bobby Doerr by telephone.

104. "For all his color": Interview with Charlie Wagner by telephone.

104. "Berg and Wagner also": Interview with Boze Berger by telephone.

104. "None of us": Interview with Billy Werber by telephone.

104. "Tom Daly and I": Interview with Jack Wilson by telephone.

105. " 'Secret,' Williams called Berg": Interview with Ted Williams, Boston.

105. "Whenever possible, he": Sam Berg file.

106. "It all looked": Interview with Arthur Weisman, Boston.

106. "We were friends": Interview with Larry Rosenthal, Boston.

106. "Bernstein had the same": Interview with Edward Bernstein by telephone.

106. "For at least part": Interview with Denny Galehouse.

106. "Berg helped Takizo": Letter from Masumoto, February 17, 1937; Cappy Harada, "Bridge over the Pacific Ocean," from Japanese Baseball Hall of Fame collection; and Charles Owen collection.

107. "Marjory Bartlett of Baltimore": Interview with Marjory Sanger, Winter Park, Florida.

107. "Margaret Ford had": Interview with Margaret Ford Kieran by telephone and correspondence.

108. "With the Red Sox": Ethel Berg, p. 151; and undated Princeton University Department of Public Information press release.

108. "Greek classes": Arthur Sampson column, *New York Herald Tribune*, February 16, 1939.

108. "St. Louis could mean": John Kieran, *New York Times*, January 28, 1935.

▼

108. "He once went from Washington": Kaufman, p. 110.

109. "One day in the": Interview with I. M. Levitt, Philadelphia.

110. "match races were a prime": Nicholas Dawidoff, "Meet George Case," *Sports Illustrated*, October 6, 1986.

110. "Others were plain bizarre": Ritter, pp. 195–97.

110. "He was well known": *Boston Post*, September 21 and 23, 1935; Merchant, "Moe Berg" and "More on Moe," *New York Post*, June 6 and June 7, 1972; and interview with Frank Slocum by telephone.

111. "He boasted that": *Time* magazine, interoffice memo proposing Berg story, February 3, 1942.

111. "When the footage": Interview with Margaret Jennings Gahan by telephone.

111. "Two years earlier": Ethel Berg, pp. 112–13; Berg file; and Kaufman, p. 234.

112. "Ratner filed a story": *Newark News*, January 21, 1943.

112. "Down in Washington": *Boston Globe*, July 9, 1937.

112. "an excellent example": *Boston Post*, March 6, 1938.

113. "Truth or Consequences": John Dunning, *Tune in Yesterday*, pp. 303–5; Harrison Summers, *Radio Programs Carried on National Networks, 1926–1956*; Frank Buxton and Bill Owen, *Radio's Golden Age*, pp. 168–69. I listened to "Information, Please!" tapes in the Museum of Television and Radio in New York and at the Library of Congress audio archive in Washington, D.C. Berg's three appearances were on February 21, 1939; October 17, 1939; and November 21, 1939. Those three recordings are not available at the Museum of Television and Radio. I transcribed them by hand at the Library of Congress.

114. "As the train pulled": Arthur Sampson, *New York Herald Tribune*, February 16, 1939.

114. "Edith Engel interviewed": Interview with Edith Engel by telephone.

115. "Other people thought so": Ethel Berg, p. 121.

115. "Berg replied": Taylor Spink, *Sporting News*, November 16, 1939.

115. "Kenesaw Mountain Landis": *Trentonian*, July 9, 1971. I think it's likely that Berg embellished this story.

116. "To a legal mind": "Information, Please!", November 21, 1939.

116. "He was not": Interview with Clifton Fadiman by telephone.

117. "Many immigrant Jewish": Roth, "The Man in the Middle," *New York Times*, October 12, 1992.

117. "That made baseball acceptable": Roger Angell, "Three for the Tigers," in *Five Seasons: A Baseball Companion*, pp. 96–122; *Jewish Daily Forward*, June 21, 1991; and correspondence from Lester Rodney, June 24, 1992, informed this section.

117. "Hank Greenberg, by": Interview with Don Shapiro by telephone.

118. "Harry Danning, a": Interview with Harry Danning by telephone.

118. "Yet to close friends": Berkow and Greenberg, *The Story of My Life*; and interview with Ira Berkow, New York.

118. "a dirty kike": Sam Berg, August 17, 1989.

118. "Most of the Red Sox": Interviews with Eldon Auker and Joe Dobson by telephone.

118. "Jack Wilson, who": Interview with Jack Wilson by telephone.

119. "Players could be": Interview with Billy Werber by telephone.

119. "Pitcher Herb Hash": Interview with Herb Hash by telephone.

119. "I think he liked": Interview with Ted Williams, Boston.

119. "does everyone still": Kaufman, p. 118.

120. "The linguistic Moe Berg": *Boston Globe*, February 2, 1940.

120. "At spring training": *Boston Post*, March 11 and 12, 1940.

120. "DiMaggio found Berg": Interview with Dominic DiMaggio by telephone.

120. "Although he claimed": Office of Administrative Service investigation report, November 12, 1942.

121. "In a Cuban restaurant": Interview with Charles O'Neill by telephone.

121. "On the boat": Interviews with Bobby Doerr by telephone and Charles Owen, Washington, D.C.

121. "Except to give": Joe Cronin letter to Charles Owen.

121. "The Red Sox had": Kaufman, p. 110; Merchant, "Moe Berg" and "More on Moe," *New York Post*, June 6 and June 7, 1972.

121. "Berg did some composing": Edward Weeks to Berg, May 12, 1941.

122. "Pitchers and Catchers": "Pitchers and Catchers" is reprinted in *The Armchair Book of Baseball*, edited by John Thorn, pp. 35–45.

122. "Good fielding and pitching": Ibid., p. 35.

122. "to fool the hitter": Ibid., p. 38.

123. "Judges, if you": Ibid., p. 43.

123. " 'The catcher,' says Berg": Ibid., p. 44.

123. "The physical requirements": Ibid.

123. "Finally, displaying grace": Ibid., p. 45.

123. "I seek no other man's": Kaufman, pp. 247–48.

124. "Sam Berg, who despaired": Sam Berg letter, December 31, 1978.

124. "Another time Sam said": Nicholas Dawidoff, *Sports Illustrated*, March 23, 1992.

Chapter 9. Southern Junket

127. "As things turned out": William Casey, *The Secret War Against Hitler*, pp. 10–11. Note that R. Harris Smith says that the OSS did operate secretly in Latin America; see Smith, *OSS*, p. 20.

127. "Montaigne said a": Ethel Berg, p. 138.

128. "Europe is in flames": *New York Times*, June 1, 1972.

128. "In November Berg": Ethel Berg, pp. 163–65; and Kaufman, p. 136.

128. "By Berg's account": Joe Fitzgerald, *Keene Sentinel*, October 12, 1967.

128. "Berg's angst": Translation of document by Michie Yamakawa. Document courtesy of Lou Jacobson.

129. "Initially the idea": Document courtesy of Lou Jacobson.

129. "They would not": FBI file.

129. "Jerry Nason, describing": *Boston Evening Globe*, January 15, 1942.

130. "Berg himself was": *Newark News*, January 16, 1942.

130. "*Time* and *Newsweek*": The publication date for both magazines was January 26, 1942.

130. "What's the past participle": Interview with Charles O'Neill by telephone.

131. "I never had a friend": Hilton, p. 19.

132. "Free food was sent": This discussion of the OIAA was informed by interviews with Charles O'Neill and Rhoda Clark by telephone; OIAA memo, July 16, 1941; the journal Berg prepared for Nelson Rockefeller to describe his Latin American trip, which is in the Berg file, Rockefeller archives; *Life* magazine profile of Rockefeller, April 27, 1942; David Bradley, *Journal of a Johnny-Come-Lately*; and Kaufman. Berg's reports to Rockefeller appear in Ethel Berg and in the Rockefeller archives.

133. "The speech, of course": Kaufman reprints the whole thing, pp. 141–46.

133. "In a meeting": FBI file.

133. "On July 11": Letter to Berg, July 11, 1942; and Ethel Berg, p. 169.

134. "On July 17": A. Seymour Houghton to Berg, July 17, 1942.

134. "A week after that": Berg, undated letter to his mother, saved by Ethel Berg.

134. "On the thirtieth": Berg to Ethel Berg, July 30, 1942.

135. "for the surprise": Interview with James Doolittle by telephone.

135. "Beginning in 1939": Interview with Steven Jurika by telephone; Ted W. Lawson, *Thirty Seconds over Tokyo*, p. 37; Carroll V. Glines, *Doolittle's Tokyo Raiders*, pp. 84–86, 176.

135. "In 1944, when": Glines, p. 86.

135. "plenty of published sources": Interview with Professor Carol Gluck by telephone.

135. "Jurika himself had": Glines, p. 84.

135. "almost certainly apocryphal": I say "apocryphal" because Jurika, who spent eighteen days on the Hornet, planning the raids and briefing the pilots, never saw the films and neither did Doolittle. One of Doolittle's pilots, Royden Stark, when shown copies of Berg's films by a Japanese NHK journalist, said he had never seen them before. There is no evidence that Berg in 1934 was involved in secret government service in any of the State Department, Naval Intelligence, or OSS records that I have reviewed. Most obviously, it would have been impossible for the Berg films to be used by pilots charged with bombing Tokyo, since those raids took place months before Berg screened his films for military officers.

136. "Always a mysterious bird": John Kieran, *New York Times*, August 20, 1942.

137. "one day he did": See Walter Winchell's name card in the Morris "Moe" Berg Collection of the New York Public Library.

137. "Berg's enthusiasm": *Time* magazine interoffice memo, November 5, 1942.

137. "He stayed a week": Journal to Rockefeller, March 29, 1943, p. 1.

137. "To get to": Ibid., p. 2.

138. "He bought all": *Time* memo, November 5, 1942.

138. "Man without woman": Journal to Rockefeller, March 29, 1943, p. 5.

138. "venereal Utopia": Ibid., p. 6.

138. "from our 'bad' boys": Ibid.

138. "Nobody has been accepted": Berg to Ethel and Rose Berg, September 14, 1942.

139. "So it was": Leslie B. Rout and John F. Bratzel, *The Shadow War*, p. 202.

139. "He was also treated": Journal to Rockefeller, March 29, 1943, p. 13.

139. "In Natal, Berg": Donald Griffin to Lou Jacobson.

139. "Elsewhere about town": Journal to Rockefeller, March 29, 1943, p. 16.

▼

140. "Bounding about town": Ibid., p. 21.

140. "Berg couldn't do that": Ibid.

140. "There isn't much": John Clark to Ethel Berg, November 5, 1942.

140. "By this time": Hilton, pp. 231–35.

140. "Still, it was": Ibid., p. 24.

141. "In January": Journal to Rockefeller, February 27, 1943, p. 4.

141. "In all my visits": Ibid., p. 7.

142. " 'At times,' admitted": Berg to Rockefeller, April 10, 1943.

142. "Instead, four days": Rockefeller to Berg, April 14, 1943. Appears in Ethel Berg, p. 183.

142. "Clark, writing to": Bradley, p. 129.

142. "There wasn't the fear": Interview with Charles O'Neill by telephone.

143. "Or maybe he wasn't": Much information about Estella Huni comes from interviews with Paul Kahn, New York; Christine Curtis, by telephone; and from Estella's papers, which Paul Kahn generously shared with me. Charles Owen owns copies of Estella's letters to Berg during the war.

144. "*Madama Butterfly*": Interview with Harry Broley, Washington, D.C.

144. "She also taught him": Interview with William Klein, New York.

145. "Another time he wrote": Reference to it in Estella Huni to Moe Berg, June 9, 1944.

145. "Ethel was jealous": Interview with Elizabeth Shames, Portland, Maine.

145. "He referred to his": Sam Berg to Samuel Goudsmit, July 23, 1964.

145. "In early May": Estella Huni to Moe Berg, May 7, 1944.

145. "Three weeks after": May 25, 1944.

145. "In mid-June": June 19, 1944.

145. "I look best": July 1, 1944.

145. "When he did": July 10, 1944.

146. "Years later she": Interview with Paul Kahn, New York.

146. "In many ways": Interview with Christine Curtis by telephone.

Chapter 10. Remus Heads for Rome

147. "They charged": Richard Dunlop, *Donovan*, p. 97; Stanley Lovell, *Of Spies and Stratagems*, p. 197; Thomas Powers, *Heisenberg's War*, p. 224.

147. "During prohibition in": Anthony Cave Brown, *The Last Hero*, pp. 73–88; Dunlop, pp. 148–51.

148. "He wanted the OSS": R. H. Smith, p. 35.

148. "He was a rather small": Interview with Julia Child by telephone.

148. "He didn't really try": Lovell, p. 177.

148. "For my activities": Ibid., p. 7.

149. "Donovan would have": Interview with Monroe Karasik, Washington, D.C.

149. "He was too talented": Anthony Cave Brown, pp. 102–16.

150. "I can vouch": Ellery Huntington to R. Davis Halliwell, June 4, 1943. OSS file.

150. "What the hell": Sam Berg to Lou Jacobson.

150. "Sam hadn't known": Berg to the family, June 9, 1943.

150. "It most definitely": Ethel Berg, p. 147.

151. "Berg delighted in": Interviews with Jimmy Breslin, New York; Joseph Crowley, Washington, D.C.; Rick Ferrell by telephone; Ken Gloss, Boston; and Harvey Yavener by telephone.

151. "Yet, when in": Interview with Irene Goudsmit by telephone; and interview with Max Corvo, Cromwell, Connecticut.

151. "He had a nice": Interview with Edwin Putzell by telephone.

152. "During his life": See Spink, *Sporting News*, November 16, 1939; and Berg personal notes on the subject.

152. "He listened and": Sam Goudsmit to Ethel Berg, June 21, 1976.

152. "The next day": Halliwell OSS memo, July 17, 1943, CIA file.

152. "It is evident": Ibid.

153. "By August 2": Berg CIA file.

153. "Finally, it was 'believed'": CIA file.

153. "Recruits were sometimes": Information for this section comes from Dunlop, pp. 381–82; Corey Ford, *Donovan of OSS*, p. 138; Henry A. Murray et al., *Assessment of Men*, pp. 25–100; interview with Earl Brodie, San Francisco; interview with William Horrigan, Tequesta, Florida; interview with William Morgan, Washington, D.C.; interview with Ed Mroz by telephone; interview with Edwin Putzell by telephone.

153. "This capture-the-flag": Phillip Knightley, *The Second Oldest Profession*, p. 226.

154. "One OSS man": Interview with Edwin Putzell by telephone.

154. "A forged piece": Bradley F. Smith, *The Shadow Warriors*, p. 208.

154. "Perhaps because this": Interview with Edwin Putzell by telephone.

154. "In Washington, Berg": R. H. Smith, pp. 129–32, 142–44, 152–53, 158–60; Berg undated notes to himself; Berg file, October 13, 1943.

155. "He resorted to": Interview with Margaret Feldman by telephone.

155. "OSS travel orders": Casey, p. 16.

155. " 'Be careful,' he warned": Interview with Aldo Icardi, Winter Park, Florida.

155. "Berg had lunch": Interview with William Horrigan, Tequesta, Florida.

155. "Toward the end": Outline from Thomas Powers's Berg file.

156. "I didn't need": Interview with William Horrigan, Tequesta, Florida.

156. "Just before Christmas": Richard Rhodes, *The Making of the Atomic Bomb*, p. 253.

156. "She wrote Hahn back": Ibid.

156. "Gazing out his": Ibid., p. 275.

157. "Heisenberg had been": Samuel Goudsmit to Sam Berg, April 11, 1973.

157. "See Fermi, see Heisenberg": Ugo Fano to Tom Powers, September 18, 1993.

157. "as the Dutch-born": Samuel A. Goudsmit, *Alsos*, pp. 3–4.

157. "Worse, they were sure": Thomas Powers, *Heisenberg's War*, p. 66.

157. "Instead, Szilard badgered": Powers, *Heisenberg's War*, p. 64; and Rhodes, pp. 305–9.

158. "Fritz Reiche, who": Powers, *Heisenberg's War*, p. 107.

158. "Eugene Wigner heard": Interview with Arthur Wightman by telephone; Wigner, *The Recollections of Eugene P. Wigner*, pp. 240–42.

158. "Physicists in the U.S.": Interview with Arthur Wightman by telephone.

158. "Certain the U.S. program": Daniel Lang, "A Farewell to String and Sealing Wax," November 7, 1953, p. 47.

158. "many sleepless nights": Rhodes, p. 356.

159. "Groves was a tendentious": Powers, *Heisenberg's War*, p. 177, and Rhodes, p. 425.

159. "I detested General Groves": Interview with Philip Morrison, Cambridge, Massachusetts.

159. "It took Groves": Interview with Hans Bethe by telephone.

159. "Bohr's inference from": David Irving, *The German Atomic Bomb*, p. 49.

160. "The nuclear age was": Interview with Robert Furman, Washington, D.C.; and Powers, *Heisenberg's War*, p. 217.

160. "In July 1943": Interview with John Lansdale, Washington, D.C.

160. "The ten-man Alsos Mission": Interview with Robert Furman, Washington, D.C.

160. "One day when the general": Interview with John Lansdale, Washington, D.C.

161. "Trying to learn about": Luis Alvarez, a physicist working for Enrico Fermi at the Metallurgical Laboratory in Chicago, designed a scrubber for Groves that could detect the residue of radioactive gases lingering in the air above the Ger-

man nuclear reactor that produced them. Alvarez's machine sensed nothing suspicious over Germany. Probably the fault of the machine, was the pessimists' reaction. Philip Morrison, also at the Met Lab, and Karl Cohen, a young chemist working under Harold Urey at Columbia, were asked to analyze hundreds of recent German scientific periodicals. It all seemed banal; the Germans appeared not to be very far along in their nuclear research. A decoy to deflect attention from the atomic work at hand, Morrison and Cohen decided. Morrison tested water drawn from German rivers, examined the luminous dials on the instrument panels of downed Messerschmitts, and interviewed German scientist prisoners of war. But every tactile piece of evidence indicated that the Germans were doing nothing unusual with their uranium, which American investigators explained as more subterfuge. How could they not? To accept the evidence was to accept that the best physicists in the world were not preparing an atomic bomb for delivery to Adolf Hitler. It was too much to concede, and so the intelligence gathering continued. It was work designed to drive one mad.

161. "Better, then, to supply": A document dated May 16, 1958, in the Berg FBI file says that the OSS knew about the Manhattan Project in November 1942.

161. "After creating": Interview with Horace Calvert by telephone.

161. "In late 1943": OSS Larson file.

161. "What most people": Ibid., December 27, 1943; and Powers, *Heisenberg's War*, p. 292.

161. "Soon thereafter": Berg personal papers, March 12, 1964.

162. "In conversation he": Interview with Earl Brodie, San Francisco.

162. "They can take us": Berg personal papers, August 4, 1968.

162. "Find out what": Ibid., March 12, 1964.

162. "Most of the talk was": Ibid.

162. "You've got a good spy": Interview with Robert Furman, Washington, D.C.

162. "On December 22": *Washington Post*, December 22, 1943.

163. "Three New York papers": *New York Daily News, New York Herald Tribune, New York World Telegram*, all December 31, 1943.

163. "And in an article": *Newsweek*, December 13, 1943.

163. "Before Pash left": Boris Pash, *The Alsos Mission*, p. 10.

163. "Berg and Horrigan": Berg CIA file.

163. "At first, Berg": Ibid.

164. "William Fowler, a": Interview with William Fowler by telephone.

164. "Among the people": OSRD document courtesy of William Horrigan.

164. "Fubini on the other hand": Interview with Eugene Fubini by telephone.

164. "Toward the end": Berg CIA file.

164. "Suits had received": Guy Suits to Heinz Albers, May 1, 1990.

165. "Back in Washington": Berg OSS file.

165. "The New Year arrived": Powers, *Heisenberg's War*, p. 299.

165. "In this conclusion": Manhattan Engineering Project (MEP) document, December 22, 1943.

165. "The Germans were": Ibid., January 2, 1944.

166. "Four days later": *Tonawanda Daily Press* (in MEP file), January 6, 1944.

166. "Furman's feeling was": Interview with Robert Furman, Washington, D.C.

166. "Besides, the last": Interview with Philip Morrison, Cambridge, Massachusetts.

166. "In late January": Interview with William Horrigan, Tequesta, Florida.

166. "Boris Pash knew": Pash, pp. 21–31; and Powers, *Heisenberg's War*, pp. 298–303.

166. "Elsewhere, there was": Powers, *Heisenberg's War*, pp. 211–13; and Rhodes, pp. 512–17.

167. "Heisenberg would be": OSS document from Thomas Powers, February 27, 1944.

167. "In March, Shaheen": CIA file.

167. "Feldman, who worked": Interview with Margaret Feldman by telephone and correspondence.

167. "Moe was a guy": Interview with Earl Brodie in San Francisco.

167. "He'd never been": Requests made, for example, April 7 and 13, 1944, CIA file; and Powers, *Heisenberg's War*, p. 294.

167. "And then, when all seemed": Berg personal notes.

168. "In February, the": Powers, *Heisenberg's War*, p. 337.

168. "Last, he requested": Berg personal papers.

168. "Heisenberg, for example": Ibid.

168. "On May 4": Berg CIA file; and Powers, *Heisenberg's War*, p. 297.

168. "The general couldn't": More likely, Donovan just liked the idea of talking with such a compelling, secretive fellow. The OSS people who met Berg uniformly describe him as the most enigmatic person they ever met. Why should the director, who loved enigmas, be any different?

Chapter 11. A Perfect Spy

169. "Boarding the airplane": Powers, *Heisenberg's War*, pp. 298–99.

170. "Malcolm Muggeridge described": Malcolm Muggeridge, *Chronicles of Wasted Time*, p. 447. In an *Esquire* magazine article, Muggeridge wrote this phrase a bit differently: ". . . arriving like jeunes filles en fleur straight from a finishing school, all fresh and innocent, to start work in our frowsy old intelligence brothel." See Knightley, p. 228.

170. "On May 11": OSS file, May 11, 1944.

171. "More useful was": Powers, *Heisenberg's War*, p. 306.

171. "In the U.S.": Interview with Hubert Alyea by telephone.

171. "Now he was working": *Physics Today*, vol. 14, no. 11 (November 1961), p. 90; and interview with Hubert Alyea by telephone.

171. "Robertson was a": Interviews with Hubert Alyea by

telephone; Richard Beth by telephone; and George Reynolds, Princeton. And Robertson to Berg, October 14, 1947.

171. "He resurfaced": Interview with Geoffrey Jones, New York.

172. "A Sergeant E. G. Pothblum": Berg CIA file.

172. "On May 29": From Turkey, Berg could logically have been on his way to Yugoslavia, perhaps to see Tito, although it seems somewhat doubtful the Russians would have permitted it. Still, in his notebooks Berg writes that on June 4, Tito was being brought in by Russians from Yugoslavia. On June 1, in Naples, Berg definitely received a letter of introduction to John Peters Esq. in Istanbul, which means that at one point he was convinced he was headed that way. Whatever the explanation, Berg never went to Turkey. Berg letter to the family, September 20, 1944.

173. "In the event that": Berg OSS file, June 5, 1944.

173. "Berg may not": Interview with Earl Brodie, San Francisco.

173. "On June 1": Berg OSS file.

173. "Three days later": Berg to his mother, June 29, 1944.

173. "After Berg showed": Berg personal notebook entry, December 1, 1965.

173. "Then a command car": Berg to his mother, June 29, 1944.

173. "On June 6": Edoardo Amaldi told Thomas Powers that he met Berg on the fifth; Amaldi's son, Ugo, told me the same; and Stanley Lovell cites the fifth in a memo on the subject; but Berg's letter home says he arrived in Rome on the eighth. Since Rome was liberated on the fifth, and the liberation celebration took place on the sixth, and since the trip from Naples that Berg describes takes four hours, not three days, from Naples, I think he arrived in Rome on June 6.

173. "Berg checked into": Berg to his mother, June 29, 1944; and Powers, *Heisenberg's War*, p. 306.

173. "For all that trouble": Gian Carlo Wick to Thomas Powers, March 7, 1989.

174. "Amaldi told him": Interview with Ugo Amaldi, Geneva, Switzerland; Pash, p. 31; and Powers, *Heisenberg's War*, p. 305.

174. "Though he detested": Ginestra Amaldi, who communicated with me through her son Ugo.

174. "The son of a": Interview with Jack Steinberger, Geneva, Switzerland; Rhodes, p. 208; and Carlo Rubbia et al., *Edoardo Amaldi*, p. 3.

174. "Their collaboration had lasted": Interview with Giuseppe Cocconi, Geneva, Switzerland.

174. "for the others": Rhodes, p. 241; and Rubbia, p. 3.

174. "At a clandestine": Rubia, p. 6.

174. "From September 1943": Amaldi to Berg, June 10, 1944. Document from Powers file.

174. "When a second": Interview with Ugo Amaldi, Geneva, Switzerland, and correspondence.

175. "That evening": Pash, pp. 31–32; and interview with Boris Pash by telephone.

176. "Something happened": Interview with Ugo Amaldi, Geneva, Switzerland.

177. "A hearty meal": Interview with Ugo Amaldi, Geneva, Switzerland, and correspondence.

177. "Amaldi, Berg reported": Berg OSS file, June 10, 1944; handwritten copy courtesy of Thomas Powers.

177. "During these early days": Interview with Jack Steinberger, Geneva, Switzerland; and with Vanna Wick, Torino, Italy. Also, Valentine E. Telegdi, Gian Carlo Wick appreciation, *The Independent* (London), May 9, 1992.

178. "Once a week": Powers, *Heisenberg's War*, p. 164.

178. "Berg took Wick": Interview with Vanna Wick, Torrino, Italy.

179. "Wick was, says": Interview with Jack Steinberger, Geneva, Switzerland.

179. "Wick had last seen": Wick to Thomas Powers, 1990 interview.

179. "Wick said he missed": Berg to Dix, June 10, 1944; Berg notes September 6, 1962; and Powers, *Heisenberg's War*, p. 308.

179. "Berg arranged, through": Thomas Powers gave me a copy of the postcard.

180. "And Wick knew more": Wick to Thomas Powers, March 7, 1989.

▼

180. "In his cable": OSS file, June 18, 1944; and Powers, *Heisenberg's War*, p. 308.

180. "the answer came from": Berg to his mother, June 29, 1944.

181. "The old religious city": Interview with Aldo Icardi, Winter Park, Florida.

181. "Berg kept in touch": Berg notes, June 13, 1966.

181. "Traveling to the": Interview with Philip Morrison, Cambridge, Massachusetts. There is no paper record of Berg's trip to the Met Lab, and I think it's possible that someone in the U.S. gave Berg the journal, and that Berg visited Morrison in late April or in the first two days of May, before he left for Europe.

182. "Berg enthusiastically": OSS cable, June 20, 1944.

182. "These sources were": See, for example, Shaheen file of January 7, 1944.

182. "In addition to": OSS cables June 19, 23, 25, 27, 1944.

182. "If documents required": Ibid., July 5, 1944.

182. "Berg's pouches went": See cable from John Teeter thanking Berg, July 18, 1944.

183. "Soon notes of appreciation": Ibid.; and J. C. Hunsaker to Stanley Lovell, July 21, 1944.

183. "Lovell and Donovan": Lovell, July 19, 1944; Donovan, July 21, 1944.

183. "Rome wasn't all work": Interview with Aldo Icardi, Maitland, Florida; Berg to his mother, June 29, 1944.

183. "the evenings were cool": Berg to his mother, June 29, 1944.

184. "Sometimes during the day": Aldo Icardi to Charles Owen.

184. "Robert Furman came to": Interview with Robert Furman, Washington, D.C.

184. "Furman left Rome": Powers, *Heisenberg's War*, p. 311.

184. "Furman also made sure": Ibid.

184. "Florence was still": Interview with Max Corvo, Cromwell, Connecticut.

184. "As they drove north": Max Corvo, *The O.S.S. in Italy, 1942–1945*, pp. 172–73.

185. "There he began": Interview with Martin Bloom by telephone; interview with Paul Libby by telephone; and James R. Hansen, *Engineer in Charge*, pp. 311–24.

185. "Three days after": Berg accounts August 4, 1944, and September 6, 1944, OSS file.

185. "Then, one step": Interview with Renata Ferri, Huntington, New York; and Vladimir Peniakoff, *Popski's Private Army*, pp. 319–31.

185. "Rumors of the bandit": Interview with Renata Ferri, Huntington, New York.

186. "In June, Berg": Interview with Renata Ferri, Huntington, New York; and interview with Paul Libby by telephone.

186. "When Ferri got back": Interview with Paul Libby by telephone; and OSS file, July 25, 1944.

186. "On July 25": Furman to Berg, July 25, 1944.

186. "This was just": OSS file, July 25 and 27, and August 1 and 2, 1944.

186. "Ferri and Berg": Interview with Renata Ferri, Huntington, New York.

186. "There were also accounts": OSS file, August 4, 1944.

187. "On August 10": OSS file, August 15, 1944.

187. "He hung a": Interview with Aldo Icardi, Winter Park, Florida; and Terry Curtis Fox to Thomas Powers.

187. "By August 20": Kaufman, pp. 183–87.

188. "Shell and sniper fire": Corvo, p. 188.

188. "He spoke with the owner": Interview with Dr. Ing Gianni Luzi, Florence, Italy.

188. "the company produced range": OSS file, August 21, 1944.

188. "Furman's gaze meanwhile": Powers, *Heisenberg's War*, p. 313.

188. "There were other plans": OSS cables, August 21, 22, 1944; and Powers, *Heisenberg's War*, p. 313.

188. "As far as": OSS cable, August 22, 1944.

188. "By the time": OSS cable, August 25, 1944.

189. "By this time": Powers, *Heisenberg's War*, p. 314.

189. "Martin Chittick": OSS cable, August 30, 1944.

189. "On September 6": OSS cable, September 6, 1944.

189. "As for Moe": CIA file.

189. "A few days after": Berg to his family, September 20, 1944.

190. "Finn named Helvi": Michael Burke, *Outrageous Good Fortune*, p. 120; interview with Henry Ringling North, Maison de Beauregard, Switzerland.

190. "In London, Berg": Interview with Clare Hall Smith, Washington, D.C.

190. "With H. P. Robertson": Interview with John Wheeler, Princeton.

190. "The OSS European Headquarters": Interview with Horace Calvert by telephone.

191. "Estella was also": OSS cable, September 28, 1944.

191. "The first involved": R. H. Smith, p. 243.

191. "I have to confess": Interview with Hans Bethe by telephone.

192. "Kidnapping and murder": Interview with Hans Bethe by telephone; and Powers, *Heisenberg's War*, pp. 190–92.

192. "It was probably": Powers, *Heisenberg's War*, p. 257.

192. "In January 1944": Furman interview with Morrison, January 12, 1944, R. G. 77, entry 22, Box 170.

192. "Carl Eifler never": Interview with Carl Eifler by telephone. Also Brown, pp. 412–16; R. Dunlop, pp. 327, 381, 421–25; Powers, *Heisenberg's War*, pp. 260–69; Bradley Smith, pp. 131–32; R. Harris Smith, pp. 246–48; and Barbara Tuchman, *Stillwell and the American Experience in China, 1941–1945*, p. 340.

193. "A German scientist": Powers, *Heisenberg's War*, p. 265.

193. "Eifler doesn't like": Interview with Carl Eifler by telephone.

193. "They would fly": Powers, *Heisenberg's War*, p. 265.

194. "Stanley Lovell supplied": Ibid., p. 312; and interview with Carl Eifler by telephone.

194. "By the autumn": Goudsmit, p. 69; interview with Thomas Powers, South Royalton, Vermont; and Irving, p. 224.

194. "In his autobiography": Leslie R. Groves, *Now It Can Be Told*, p. 217.

194. "Groves's account": See OSS document, November

10, 1944, from Donovan, which says, "We recognize Furman's chief Groves as only office of active control for AZUSA." AZUSA file.

195. "Berg soon complained": OSS cable, January 3, 1945.

195. "If Marsching seems": OSS cable, November 23, 1944; and Powers, *Heisenberg's War*, p. 389.

195. "With Marsching gone": Carlisle, Pennsylvania, military collection document, November 6, 1944.

195. "Brodie was on": Interview with Earl Brodie, San Francisco.

196. "Chittick hadn't yet arrived": Interview with Ed Mroz by telephone; and Powers, *Heisenberg's War*, p. 389.

196. "The professor's files": Robert Jungk, *Brighter Than a Thousand Suns*, p. 164; and Goudsmit, pp. 69–71.

197. "On one letterhead": Goudsmit, p. 69.

197. " 'No, no,' he": Pash, pp. 68–71.

197. "Germany had no": Goudsmit, p. 71.

197. "Immediately he was": Groves, p. 218.

197. "A bit of digging": Powers, *Heisenberg's War*, p. 377.

198. "As a young man": Interview with Heinz Albers, Georg Busch, and Herman Waftler, Zurich, Switzerland.

198. "During the war": Interview with Thomas Powers, South Royalton, Vermont.

198. "With this in mind": Dulles cable, September 12, 1944, OSS file.

198. "Nazi spies were": Interview with Heinrich Medicus by telephone.

198. "After Dulles warned": OSS document, November 15, 1944.

198. "The choice for": OSS document, November 20, 1944.

198. "Berg's annual salary": OSS documents, November 15 and 28, 1944.

199. "On December 8": Interview with Bud Leavitt by telephone.

199. "Goudsmit was fascinated": Goudsmit to Ethel Berg, June 21, 1976.

199. "That fellow Goudsmit": Daniel Lang, "A Farewell to String and Sealing Wax," *New Yorker*, November 14, 1953, p. 59.

199. "Goudsmit was particularly": Interview with Stanley Goldberg, Washington, D.C.

199. "In March 1943": Goudsmit, p. 47.

199. "As for his": David Cassidy, *Uncertainty*, p. 485.

200. "That may explain": There are other possibilities. Goudsmit's postwar memoirs become, at times, almost fustian in their scorn for the Germans. But at the Ritz, without the benefit of hindsight and Hiroshima, he may still have had more doubts then about what the skilled German physicists were doing in Hechingen than he was later willing to admit. Either way, it didn't matter. Goudsmit's job was to pass along orders from Groves, and Groves wasn't yet convinced of anything.

200. "Nothing spelled out": Berg notes, September 6, 1962; and Powers, *Heisenberg's War*, p. 392.

200. "Toward the end": Interview with Ken Gloss, Boston.

201. "It was nearing": Interview with Earl Brodie, San Francisco. Berg told a briefer version of the story to Harvey Yavener and Bus Saidt (interview with Yavener by telephone) and to Elizabeth Shames (interview, Portland, Maine).

201. "The last person": Interview with Horace Calvert by telephone.

202. "In Rome, liberation": Studi E Fonti Per La Storia Dell'Universita Di Roma/Registo Delle Lauree Honoris Causa Dal 1944 AL 1985/Jole Vernacchia-Galli, p. 18. Translation by Renata Ferri.

202. "They say that": Ibid.

202. "When Moe Berg": Interview with Ken Gloss, Boston; interview with Elizabeth Shames, Portland, Maine.

202. "To support this": Interview with Bernie Levy by telephone; interview with Ted Sanger, Cambridge, Massachusetts.

203. "By various accounts": Groves, pp. 216–17. Interviews with Heinz Albers, Zurich, Switzerland; Willie Klein, New York; and Edwin Putzell by telephone.

203. "Berg arrived for Heisenberg's": Berg's detailed written account courtesy of Thomas Powers; Powers, *Heisenberg's War*, pp. 397–400. Interviews with Markus Fierz by telephone; Herman Waftler, Zurich, Switzerland; and Werner Zünti by telephone. All of them attended the meeting.

205. "very interesting because": Interview with Herman Waftler, Zurich, Switzerland.

205. "The pistol stayed": Tablets were standard issue for such work. Berg told Elizabeth Shames that he carried one.

205. "There was plenty": Berg draft cable courtesy of Thomas Powers. See also Powers, *Heisenberg's War*, p. 401.

206. "I am working": Werner Zünti to Heinz Albers.

206. "We assumed that": Interview with Werner Zunti by telephone.

206. "I am not": Powers, *Heisenberg's War*, p. 402.

206. "When Gregor Wentzel": This is often quoted. See Cassidy, p. 493; Goudsmit, p. 114; and Powers, *Heisenberg's War*, p. 402.

206. "This was one": Powers, *Heisenberg's War*, p. 403.

207. "Berg asked more": Ibid. Note that Elisabeth Heisenberg's memoir of her husband says, "A young man whom he had noticed throughout the evening and whom he found exceptionally agreeable accompanied him back to his hotel. On their way the conversation was relaxed and animated." E. Heisenberg, *Inner Exile*, p. 97. Her manuscript is rife with errors, so I tend to doubt this account.

207. "I have no doubt": Interview with Philip Morrison, Cambridge, Massachusetts.

207. "It is our hope": Dix to Berg, December 22, 1944.

208. "There were several reasons": Interview with Ines Jucker, Bern, Switzerland.

208. "secretive and ebullient": Interview with Herman Waftler, Zurich, Switzerland.

208. "Berg took a room": Interview with Ines Jucker, Bern, Switzerland.

209. "Between 1915 and 1919": All this information was gathered during a visit to this beautiful restaurant.

209. "Scherrer was a teacher": Interview with Herman Waftler, Zurich, Switzerland.

209. "My explanation": Document courtesy of Charles Owen.

209. "On other days": OSS cables, December 30 and 31, 1944.

▼

209. "The OSS had": Dix to Berg, January 5, 1945.

210. "Bushie": Interview with Ines Jucker, Bern, Switzerland.

210. "In Belgium": Calvert to Furman, January 15, 1945.

210. "The Scherrers thought": Interview with Ines Jucker, Bern, Switzerland.

210. "Such strange things": Interviews with Heinz Albers, Georg Busch, and Herman Waftler, Zurich, Switzerland; Ines Jucker, Bern, Switzerland; Kurt Alder, Werner Bantle, Markus Fierz, Heinrich Medicus by telephone; and Ina Scherrer to Ethel Berg, undated.

211. "We never saw": Interview with Ines Jucker, Bern, Switzerland.

211. "Dulles had slipped": Bradley F. Smith, pp. 189–93, 222–26; Corey Ford, pp. 285–89; and R. Harris Smith, pp. 211, 267–68.

212. "Bern was even quieter": Interview with William Hood, New York.

212. "American legation": Mary Bancroft, *Autobiography of a Spy*, p. 134.

212. "Dulles liked calm": OSS cable, September 12, 1944.

212. "Twenty-four Dufourstrasse": Bradley, pp. 149–50; and interview with William Hood, New York.

213. "I remember I": Interview with William Hood, New York.

213. "The Germans, for": Interview with William Hood, New York; Bancroft, p. 182; Bradley, p. 149.

213. "Berg ate alone": Interviews with Edwin Putzell and Duncan Robertson by telephone.

213. "At night, Berg": Interviews with William Hood, New York; and Cordelia Hood, Edwin Putzell, and Robert Wallace by telephone.

213. "If Berg was": Rhodri Jeffreys-Jones, *The CIA and American Democracy*; and Leonard Mosely, *Dulles*, pp. 73–74, 92–94, 299–301.

214. "Moe was secretive": Interview with Edwin Putzell by telephone.

214. "There were a lot": Interview with Cordelia Hood by telephone.

214. "Confidentially, he is": Dulles cable to Donovan, March 25, 1945.

214. "Donovan's approach": Interview with Edwin Putzell by telephone.

215. "Scherrer wanted badly": OSS cable, March 19, 1945.

215. "This is very": Separate OSS cable, March 19, 1945.

215. "Nothing doing": OSS cable, March 20, 1945.

215. "Please trust my": OSS cable, March 23, 1945.

216. "A few days later": Powers, *Heisenberg's War*, p. 390; OSS cable, April 20, 1945; and Sam Berg's schedule written by hand given to me by Tom Powers.

216. "And what I was doing": Berg notebook, December 1, 1965.

216. "At the famous": Interview with Robert Furman, Washington, D.C.

217. "In Hechingen": Goudsmit, p. 108.

217. "It was so obvious": Ibid., p. 106.

In the winter of 1944, the ETH was full of rumors that an atomic bomb was possible, and Scherrer, more than anyone else, must have realized both its inevitability and the divisive impact it would have on scientific politics. Scherrer had worked closely with Heisenberg on S-matrix theory, and he had also anticipated fission before Hahn's and Meitner's discovery. For a physicist, he was a shrewd and political man. His enemies whispered that he was "jealous like an old wife," and made up a slogan about him: "Only Scherrer is allowed to speak."

Enthusiasm is one thing, risking your life is another. Many Swiss scientists hated Hitler, and it's impossible to say what drove Scherrer to move beyond silent protest and make himself available to an American intelligence organization. "We were all against the Nazis," says Herman Waftler, exaggerating somewhat. "Nobody knew Professor Scherrer was more than anyone else."

Chapter 12. Always Good Company

219. "On May 2": OSS cable, May 2, 1945.

219. "Berg's itinerary was": OSS cable, May 4, 1945.

▼

219. "One of the reasons": Interview with Milton Katz by telephone.

219. "Berg went along": Interview with Monroe Karasik, Chevy Chase, Maryland.

219. "In London": OSS cable, May 24, 1945.

219. "Scherrer would be": OSS cable, May 19, 1945.

219. "John Kieran turned": Interview with Monroe Karasik, Chevy Chase, Maryland.

220. "And your name is": Interviews with Monroe Karasik, Chevy Chase, Maryland; and Edwin Putzell by telephone. Berg told a different version to Margaret Feldman, but Karasik was there.

220. "On May 30": OSS cable, May 30, 1945.

220. "Groves placed": OSS cables, June 5 and 6, 1945.

220. "Back in London": CIA file.

221. "She had fits": Meitner to Otto Hahn, June 27, 1945.

221. "Dr. Berg was": Meitner to Scherrer, June 26, 1945.

221. "Berg would see": Berg notes, September 6, 1962.

221. "I feel that": Meitner to Otto Hahn, June 27, 1945.

222. "Otto Hahn was not": Powers, *Heisenberg's War*, p. 428.

222. "Eventually the letter": Berg notes, September 6, 1962.

222. "On June 30": OSS cable, June 30, 1945.

223. "It was hoped": CIA file.

223. "he and Scherrer": OSS cable, July 26, 1945.

223. "Berg suggested that": OSS cable, July 31, 1945.

223. "They traveled using": OSS cable, July 21, 1945.

223. "He invited Scherrer": Kaufman, p. 217.

223. "At Washington's Griffith": Interview with Rick Ferrell by telephone.

223. "Berg was reluctant": Kaufman, p. 217.

223. "He passed one": Interview with Margaret Feldman by telephone and correspondence.

225. "We are entitled": Shepardson to Berg, August 9, 1945.

225. "With the Manhattan": OSS document, September 14, 1945; and interview with Heinz Albers, Zurich, Switzerland.

225. "It would wind up": OSS cable, September 19, 1945.

225. "At the same time": Berg file, September 23, 1945.

226. "As for Berg": Dix to Berg, October 1, 1945.

226. "In a third": Dix to Berg, October 9, 1945.

227. "Warner thought this": Joe Mooney, "Profiles," *Seattle Post Intelligencer*, October 21, 1976.

227. "If the offer": Interview with Horace Calvert by telephone; and Kaufman, pp. 222–23.

227. "Came November": Berg kept the ticket stub; CIA file.

227. "In early January": CIA file.

227. "Meitner had been": Meitner to Max Planck, January 1, 1946.

228. "Why didn't the": Berg notes on the meeting dated January 9, 1946, given to me by Thomas Powers.

228. "he talked about her": Harvey Yavener (interview by telephone) and Joe Crowley (interview in Washington, D.C.) are two.

229. "Rather, they sent him": SSU documents, February 15 and 26, 1946.

229. "Two days after": Dexter Masters and Katharine Way, *One World or None*, Introduction, p. x.

230. "Then Berg checked": Dix to Colonel Quinn, September 30, 1946; Kaufman, pp. 226–27; interview with Thomas Powers, South Royalton, Vermont. Charles Owen showed me the Bohr-inscribed book.

230. "Skinner recommended": SSU document, February 14, 1946.

230. "He always liked": Interview with Lyall Johnson by telephone and correspondence.

231. "Mr. Berg has": SSU memo, March 6, 1946.

231. "Lieutenant Colonel Skinner argued": SSU memo, March 12, 1946.

231. "I have no concern": SSU memo, March 20, 1946.

231. "The Dutch, for": Berg cable, May 24, 1946.

231. "At Nuremberg": SSU cable, July 2, 1946.

232. "You are ordered": Quinn to Berg, CIA file; interview with Larry Houston by telephone.

232. "In one draft": Dix draft, September 30, 1946.

▼

233. "In a position": CIA file; a copy was also supplied to me by Arnold Kramish.

233. "On December 2": CIA file, December 2, 1946.

233. "Houston remembers that": Interview with Larry Houston by telephone; SSU document, January 30, 1947 (CIA file).

233. "Houston got back": CIA file.

233. "In April": Documents of April 2 and 8, 1947, CIA file.

234. "Everyone I knew": Interview with Larry Houston by telephone.

234. "the most dangerous": Masters and Way, p. 59.

234. "In notes he": Courtesy of Charles Owen.

Chapter 13. A Life Without Calendar

238. "A moment later": Terry Hauser to Ira Berkow.

238. "the partnership did well": Novelart documents, Berg file.

238. "When Berg left": Kaufman, p. 234.

238. "The government proceeded": FBI file. Note that in New York State, bankruptcy records are destroyed after ten years.

239. "Ted Lyons, the": *Newark News*, November 27, 1946.

239. "Berg paid $500": FBI file.

240. "He appears to be": Ibid.

240. "According to Ethel": Ethel Berg to Sam Goudsmit, May 11, 1973.

240. "Of the 13,000": Interview with Thomas Troy by telephone.

240. "You can't get": Berg notebook entry, November 14, 1951.

240. "Must learn to": Ibid., November 20, 1951.

240. "He holed up": Interview with Charles Owen, Washington, D.C. Owen owns the text of Berg's proposal describing a new Eastern European policy for the CIA.

241. "A Jew must": Berg notebook entry, November 27, 1951.

241. "Did any mail come": Sam Berg notes, March 10, 1979.

241. "Or, as Richard Helms": Interview with Richard Helms, Washington, D.C.

241. "far more regulations": General Walter Bedell Smith, DCI from 1950 to 1953, was a flinty man with a reverence for organization. The transition to what might be called a corporate approach to American intelligence occurred years beyond Smith, but "Beedle's" imprimatur at CIA was to infuse the Agency with a taste for discipline.

241. "Station chiefs, for": Interview with William Hood, New York.

242. "American intelligence began to": Rhodes, p. 568.

242. "In Washington, in 1952": Thomas Powers, *The Man Who Kept the Secrets*, p. 68.

242. "On February 5, 1950": Berg FBI file.

243. "It was eventually revealed": Bertrand Goldschmidt, *Atomic Rivals*, p. 349; Alan Moorehead, *The Traitors*; and Pontecorvo's obituary in the *New York Times*, September 28, 1993, were all useful in constructing this section.

243. "Berg was given a fat": CIA anonymous sources who worked directly with him or who are familiar with Berg's operations file. Much of this section of the text relies on interviews with past and present CIA employees who choose to remain anonymous. This is the case with all further CIA material in the text, unless otherwise noted. Also, Edoardo Amaldi told Thomas Powers about Berg and Pontecorvo.

243. "to interview Anna Anderson": Berg told June McElroy, among others, this story. Interview with June McElroy, Washington, D.C.

244. "No one is to disturb": Interview with Timothy Burke by telephone.

244. "For the maid": Kaufman, p. 243.

244. "The maid did not": Interview with Timothy Burke by telephone.

244. "He always wore": Hirano, p. 183.

244. "Timmy told her husband": Interview with Timothy Burke by telephone.

246. "He once explained to Sam": Goudsmit to Irwin Berg. Interview with Irwin Berg, New York.

246. "Berg told Ted Sanger": Interview with Ted Sanger, Cambridge, Massachusetts.

246. "Dulles was a big": Interview with William Hood, New York.

247. "A Berg who is": Interview with Richard Helms, Washington, D.C.

247. "The goal of the craft": Interview with Charles McCarry by telephone.

247. "Moe was an amateur": Interview with Monroe Karasik, Chevy Chase, Maryland.

247. "Every success he had": Interview with Harry Broley, Washington D.C.

248. "As always, fluid": Berg notebook entry, December 1954.

248. "It wouldn't become me": Berg to Russell Gray, November 1959.

248. "Like George Orwell": George Orwell, *Down and Out in Paris and London*, p. 20.

249. "I do not know": Dix to Earl Brodie. Interview with Earl Brodie, San Francisco.

249. "Each time he went": Interview with Duncan Robertson by telephone.

250. "drop small hints": Interview with Mariette Fay by telephone.

250. "He was evasive": Interview with Duncan Robertson by telephone.

250. "he didn't look Japanese": Interview with Mariette Fay by telephone.

250. "curve ball curves": Interview with Duncan Robertson by telephone.

250. "Princeton parties": Interview with Arthur Wightman by telephone.

250. "Pocket Books published": Edward Weeks, editor, *The Pocket Atlantic*.

251. "That was Kieran's version": Interview with Margaret Ford Kieran by telephone and correspondence.

251. "Mr. Berg, you teach": Ira Berkow (Newspaper Enterprise Association), *Ann Arbor News*, June 18, 1972.

251. "After the Robertsons": Interview with Jean Makrauer by telephone.

251. "While he was sitting": Interview with Richard Edie by telephone.

251. "transcribed twenty-seven pages": Berg notebook entry, November 7, 1958.

251. "My God, Sam": Sam Berg, December 12, 1978.

251. "At one of them": Interview with Robert Wallace by telephone and correspondence.

252. "On Saturdays": Interview with Harvey Yavener by telephone.

252. "He'd appear and disappear": Interview with Harvey Yavener by telephone.

252. "Nobody knows": Interview with Morrie Siegel by telephone.

253. "already disappeared": Interviews with Ted Berg, October 19, 1992; and with Virginia Berg, October 15, 1992, both by telephone.

253. "When Berg telephoned": Interview with I. M. Levitt, Philadelphia.

253. "an oil deal": Berg, undated 1954 notebook entry; interview with Horace Calvert by telephone.

254. "stainless steel": Berg notebook entry, October 1955.

255. "according to his brother": Sam Berg to Sam Goudsmit.

255. "A few months after": Interview with Earl Brodie, San Francisco.

255. "H. P. Robertson was": Interview with Mariette Fay by telephone.

256. "a very smart man": Interview with William Fowler by telephone.

257. "through Antonio Ferri": Interviews with Renata Ferri, Huntington, New York, and with W. R. Sears by telephone were helpful in constructing this section.

▼

257. "Budapest-born Von Karman": Theodore Von Karman and Lee Edson, *The Wind and Beyond*, pp. 246–48.

257. "Jewish bachelor": Interview with Lee Arnold by telephone.

257. "Japanese mispronunciations": Interview with W. R. Sears by telephone; and W. R. Sears, undated letter to the *Princeton Alumni Weekly*, from Princeton University alumni files.

258. "Von Karman's brother": Ethel Berg, p. 266; and interview with Lee Arnold by telephone.

258. "Berg's government employment form": Morris Berg Office of Personnel Management file.

258. "My new career": Berg notebook entry, June 12, 1958.

258. "The assignment": Kaufman, p. 244, says that Berg was working with scientists and military personnel to decide NATO's missile launching base sites. I think it unlikely that Berg had expertise in this area.

258. "He nosed around Europe": Berg AGARD notes, undated, from Powers's Berg file.

259. "In late June": Ibid.

259. "In Zurich": Berg, undated notebook entry.

259. "Bastard—black marketeer": Berg notebooks, July 1958.

259. "Alice was at": Berg notebooks, undated.

259. "I was able to": Berg notes to Dr. Von Karman.

260. "sixty-three of them": Berg notebook entries, August 5, 1958, and April 23, 1960.

260. "I don't know why": Interview with Eugene Fubini by telephone.

260. "Fidel Neroes": Berg to Sam Goudsmit, undated.

261. "Silverman never knew": Interview with Arnold Silverman, Boston.

262. "He talked about himself": Interview with Dorrit Gloss, Boston.

262. "as a small token": George Gloss to Berg, April 26, 1965; Ethel Berg, p. 285.

263. "He used my stand": Interview with Larry Rosenthal, Boston.

263. "thirteen-century French": Interview with Ted Sanger, Cambridge, Massachusetts.

263. "waiters at the Ritz": Interview with Jean Makrauer by telephone.

263. "Cronin was the": Interview with Warren Berg, Boston.

263. "At a coffee shop": Interview with Richard Gurner by telephone.

264. "I'll do that": Interview with Jean Makrauer by telephone.

264. "Susie had an upsetting": Interview with Susie Makrauer by telephone.

264. "He'd give me": Interview with Fred Makrauer by telephone.

264. "It was at the Parker House": This section is based on interviews with Marjory B. Sanger, Winter Park, Florida; Ted Sanger, Cambridge, Massachusetts; Harry Broley, Washington, D.C.; and Berg's notebook entries on the subject.

271. "pillar to post": Interview with Ted Sanger, Cambridge, Massachusetts.

271. "Ted and Marnie affair": Berg notebook entry, May 1, 1959.

272. "Moe had a kind of": Interview with Harry Broley, Washington, D.C.

272. "four or five days": Interview with Harry Broley, Washington, D.C.; and Berg's Arthur D. Little file.

273. "Berg had been baseball": Interview with Warren Berg, Boston.

273. "confidential study": Arthur D. Little documents, May 25, June 29, and July 18, 1962.

274. "From May 30": Berg's report, dated June 5, 1962.

274. "That was the only time": John Kieran to Asa Bushnell, December 1, 1972.

275. "*Sunday News* sports editor": Correspondence with James Freedman.

275. "When Hirano came": Hirano, p. 115.

275. "Berg knew that": Berg notebook entry, May 6, 1959.

▼

276. "Berg's notebooks are": Ibid., February 29, 1960.

276. "When a lunch with": Ibid., April 1960.

276. "After the first day": Ibid., May 6, 1959; and interview with Robert Wallace by telephone.

276. "A man named Charlie": Interview with Fred Armenti by telephone.

276. "Penn Central conductor": Bus Saidt to Ethel Berg; and Ethel Berg, p. 308.

277. "Berg made himself": Interview with Jerome Holtzman by telephone.

277. "brushed past them": Interview with Margaret Feldman by telephone and correspondence.

277. "He missed it": Interview with Harry Broley, Washington, D.C.

277. "floating secret village": Interview with Charles McCarry by telephone. McCarry now writes former CIA director Richard Helms's favorite spy novels, the Paul Christopher thrillers..

278. "Estella Huni told": Interview with Paul Kahn, New York.

278. "Nobody knew": Interview with Murray Goodman by telephone.

278. "Never let him near": Interview with Jimmy Breslin, New York.

279. "In the late 1950s": Interview with Mary Hedges, in East Hampton, New York, and by telephone and correspondence.

279. "Berg's behavior was odd": In the next room, recovering from an automobile accident, was the Dodgers catcher Roy Campanalla. Mary Adams says Berg never went in to say hello. Instead, he sat beside Caswell Adams.

279. "His notebooks are full": Berg notebooks, late 1950s and May 1960.

281. "In 1963, June McElroy": Interview with June McElroy, Washington, D.C., and correspondence.

282. "He's tickling me": Ibid. Interview with Joseph Crowley, Washington, D.C.; interview with Alexandra Gelmi by telephone.

282. "Clare Hall met": Interview with Clare Hall Smith, Washington, D.C., and correspondence.

285. "Washington is a": Ibid.

285. "For some men": Interview with Robert Furman, Washington, D.C.; interview with Thomas Powers, South Royalton, Vermont.

285. "compartmentalizing his friends": Interview with Clare Hall Smith, Washington, D.C.

285. "He filled his notebooks": Berg notebooks, entry for September 10, 1959, for example.

286. "If it wasn't for": Interview with Harry Broley, New York.

286. "In New York": Groves to Berg, October 1959.

286. "Through years of afternoons": Interview with Harry Broley, Washington, D.C.; interview with Duke Zeibert, Washington, D.C.

286. "One day at Duke's": Interview with Joseph Crowley, Washington, D.C.

288. "William Klein's first": Interview with William and Helen Klein, New York.

290. "One summer day": Interview with Harry Broley, New York.

291. "Discussing baseball with": Interview with Fred Down by telephone.

291. "sit by himself": Interview with Jimmy Breslin, New York.

291. "1956 old-timers game": *New York Times*, August 26, 1956.

291. "In 1963, Casey Stengel": Berg's "Notes for Mets," May 28, 1963, courtesy Charles Owen.

292. "The fact was that": Interview with Harry Broley, Washington, D.C.

292. "He was always": Hy Goldberg, *Newark Evening News*, undated clipping from Berg file.

292. "He was the only former ballplayer": Interview with Roger Angell by telephone and correspondence.

292. "You'd be at a": Interview with Dave Anderson by telephone.

292. "Just as often": Jerome Holtzman, "A Great Companion," *Sporting News*, June 24, 1972.

293. "Sitting with Berg": Interview with Seymour Siwoff by telephone.

293. "You caught me": Interview with Ira Berkow, New York.

293. "After the game": Interview with Ira Berkow, New York; interview with Harold Rosenthal by telephone.

293. "Everyone knew": Interview with Ernie Harwell by telephone.

293. "When the stories were filed": Holtzman, *A Great Companion*, p. 164.

293. "Baseball executives": Interview with Buzzy Bavasi by telephone.

293. "stuff a couple of sandwiches": Interview with Larry Merchant by telephone.

293. "Men would check": Interview with Larry Merchant by telephone; interview with Bob Broeg by telephone.

293. "In the 1950s": Interview with Harold Rosenthal by telephone.

294. "A policeman would notice": Interview with David Burgin by telephone.

294. "He tried to get": Interview with Murray Olderman by telephone.

294. " 'Always remember,' Grayson": Interview with Ira Berkow, New York.

294. "Grayson was a master": Interviews with Jimmy Breslin, New York; and Shirley Povich, Washington, D.C.

295. "Moe seemed the last": Interview with Murray Olderman by telephone.

295. "He never paid a bill": Interview with Jimmy Breslin, New York.

295. "He'd be talking": Interview with Frank Slocum by telephone.

295. "The scientists": Interview with Jimmy Breslin, New York.

296. "How's the arm": Interview with Jimmy Breslin, New York.

296. "Fred didn't want": Interview with Nancy Corcoran by telephone.

296. "Why don't you spend": Interview with Joe DiMaggio by telephone.

296. "A pair of bachelors": Interview with Arthur Richman by telephone.

296. "Of all Berg hosts": Information for this section comes from Jerome Holtzman's article about Berg, "A Great Companion," *Sporting News*, June 24, 1972, and several interviews with Holtzman by telephone.

298. "the world's greatest guest": Interview with Lee MacPhail, Delray Beach, Florida.

299. "coin shop": David Shulman correspondence.

299. "He was also always": Interview with Lee Arnold by telephone.

299. "He sent Nelson": Rockefeller archives.

299. "Berg was in Toots Shor's": Interview with Jimmy Breslin, New York.

299. "In 1954, Rockefeller": Berg notebooks, 1954; interview with Charles Owen, Washington, D.C.

299. "Rockefeller's secretaries": April 27, 1966, memo to Nelson Rockefeller.

300. "one of his assistants wrote": letter, March 8, 1973, Rockefeller file.

300. "Berg also made strenuous": Interview with Henry Ringling North, Beguins, Switzerland.

300. "Henry Hyde, whom Berg": Interview with Henry Hyde, New York.

300. "No summer went by": Interview with Jimmy Breslin, New York.

300. "By the sixth": Interview with Jimmy Breslin, New York.

301. "At the 1967 World Series": The source for this section is an interview with Dr. Hardy Hendron, Boston.

304. "The moon-faced Martland": Samuel Berg, *Harrison Stanford Martland.*

304. "In 1934, Dr. Sam": Sam Berg's résumé.

304. "Dr. Sam would weep": Interview with Barbara S. Irwin, Newark.

304. "hero worship": Interview with William Sharpe, New York. Further information about Sam Berg comes from in-

▼

terviews with William Greifinger by telephone; Charles Owen, Washington, D.C.; and Murray Strober, Nutley, New Jersey.

305. "an army blood bank": Sam Berg file; Berg, *Harrison Stanford Martland*; Guy Savino, "Disrupted Lives to Help War Effort" and "Fate Links Newarkers, Bomb," *Newark Evening News*, December 7 and December 8, 1966; and interview with Earl Brodie, San Francisco.

305. "You Book women": Interview with Elizabeth Shames, Portland, Maine.

305. "I was frightened": Interview with Frances Book Kashdan by telephone.

305. "For twenty-five years": Interview with Charles Cummings, Newark.

305. "Several months ago": Sam Berg to Sam Goudsmit, December 4, 1951.

306. "You'd think at first": Interview with Charles Cummings, Newark.

306. "As a young": Interviews with Elsie Chmelnik, Nettie Hafer, and William Greifinger by telephone.

306. "it was almost": Interview with Barbara S. Irwin, Newark.

306. "Timely Medical Topics": University of Medicine and Dentistry of New Jersey file.

306. "That's stupid": Interview with Charles Cummings, Newark.

306. "Wearing a rubber suit": Interviews with Richard Evans, Margaret Jennings Gahan, Nettie Hafer, and John P. Healy by telephone.

307. "Berg would sometimes spend": Interview with Robert Cole by telephone.

307. "I would rather be": Sam Berg notes, December 31, 1978. See also G. O. Trevelyan, *Life and Letters of Macaulay* (London, 1876), vol. 1, pp. 203–4.

307. "Terrified that he": Sam Berg, "Recollections About Moe Jotted Down Now and Then," undated.

307. "A buck": Ibid.

307. "As children": Sam Berg notes, March 10, 1979.

308. "Berg was always pumping": Sam Berg, "Recollections."

308. "Dr. Sam found": Ibid.

308. "Siamese cats": Sam Berg notes, January 4, 1979.

308. "At the first stop light": Ibid., January 2, 1979.

308. "When Dr. Sam went out": Interviews with Elsie Chmelnik and Nettie Hafer by telephone.

308. "Dr. Sam dated": Interviews with Elsie Chmelnik and Nettie Hafer.

308. "An exception was": Sam Berg notes, March 10, 1979.

309. "On days when he": Sam Berg to Charles Owen, July 17, 1983.

310. "In the living room": Sam Berg, "Some Thoughts About Brother Moe," a speech given at Princeton University, June 3, 1988.

310. "tested for syphilis": Sam Berg to Charles Owen, July 17, 1983.

310. "He knew that": Sam Berg, speech at Princeton University.

310. "I was the favorite": Sam Berg notes, January 4, 1979.

310. "What the hell": Ibid., May 14, 1989.

311. "That sonnet": Undated letter from Sam to Moe Berg. Courtesy of Irvin Berg.

311. "She exulted in": Sam Berg notes, January 2, 1979.

311. "Observing this": Ibid., March 2, 1979.

311. "I would have married her": Sam Berg to Sam Goudsmit, July 23, 1964.

311. "She visited Dr. Sam": Ibid.

311. "After Berg's death": Sam Berg notes, December 31, 1978.

311. "Moments later": Ibid.

312. "a mutation": Ibid., March 2, 1979.

312. "To hear him tell": Ibid., May 4, 1979; and Princeton speech.

312. "the most important": Sam Berg notes, December 31, 1978.

312. "I assure you": Sam Berg to Earl Brodie, March 17, 1985.

312. "Estella Huni may": Others I interviewed who describe Sam's feelings of jealousy are Yoshihisa Hyashi, William Klein, Ted Sanger, Elizabeth Shames, and William Sharpe.

312. "We were close": Sam Berg, Princeton speech.

312. "When Dr. Sam ventured": Sam Berg to Lou Jacobson.

313. "Dr. Sam, in turn": Berg notebook entry, February 18, 1960.

313. "Berg, who was never": Interview with William Klein, New York.

313. "Yet, like Dr. Sam": Sam Berg says 1958 in his notes; Murray Strober, his doctor, says it happened in 1959.

313. "Yet, never once": Interview with Dr. Murray Strober, Nutley, New Jersey.

314. "He was such a warm": Interview with Frances Book Kashdan by telephone.

314. "After the war": Interview with Denise Shames, Portland, Maine.

314. "If anyone asked": Interview with Joseph Brodsky by telephone.

315. "at Gruning's": Interview with Richard Evans by telephone.

316. "owed people money": Sam Goudsmit to Sam Berg, August 20, 1964; Sam Berg to Emily Hughes, August 21, 1964; Emily Hughes to Sam Berg, August 26, 1964; interview with Ted Sanger, Cambridge, Massachusetts.

316. "Dr. Sam liked to": See, for example, his Princeton speech.

316. "Dr. Sam had reached": Sam Berg to Sam Goudsmit, June 17, 1964.

316. "It was only by chance": Ibid., July 23, 1964.

317. "Please, please, please": Sam Goudsmit to Berg, October 17, 1949.

317. "He wrote to": Sam Berg to Ted Lyons, August 7, 1964. Reply is August 14, 1964.

317. "Goudsmit followed up": *New York Herald Tribune*, June 27, 1965.

317. "Twenty years ago": Sam Berg to Sam Goudsmit, undated letter, probably January 1965.

317. "By July 1965": Sam Berg to Sam Goudsmit, July 4, 1965.

317. "He met a physicist": Sam Goudsmit to Ethel Berg, May 10, 1973.

317. "he attended the 1965 World Series": *Los Angeles Times*, October 3, 1965.

317. "Goudsmit heard about": William Fowler to Sam Goudsmit, January 6, 1966.

317. "Goudsmit asked one": Sam Goudsmit to Ethel Berg, April 11, 1973.

318. "By 1967": Sam Berg to Sam Goudsmit, March 7, 1967.

318. "No later than 1966": Ethel Berg to Sam Goudsmit, May 11, 1973.

318. "Since 1934, Ethel": Interview with Elizabeth Shames, Portland, Maine.

318. "social misfit": Ethel Berg to Sam Goudsmit, June 27, 1976.

318. "Dr. Sam was not": Ibid.; and Sam Berg notes, July 21, 1989, courtesy of Charles Owen.

319. "When the reunions": Interviews with Sam Kashdan by telephone; and Elizabeth Shames, Portland, Maine.

319. "Everyone would whisper": Interviews with Sam Kashdan and Hannah Litzky by telephone; interview with Elizabeth Shames, Portland, Maine, and correspondence with Litzky and Shames.

319. "a superb one": Interviews with Margaret Jennings Gahan and Hannah Litzky by telephone.

319. "In time, Ethel": Ethel Berg notes; and Sam Berg notes, July 21, 1989.

320. "Her clothes might be": Biographical information about Ethel Berg comes mainly from interviews with Craig and Dorothy Miller, Cranford, New Jersey; Frances Chavis by telephone; and Elizabeth Shames, Portland, Maine.

320. "She never quite": Interview with Elizabeth Shames, Portland, Maine.

321. "a liar": Sam Berg notes, July 21, 1989.

321. "Ethel's cousin": Interview with Frances Book Kashdan by telephone.

▼

321. "all the details": Interview with Elizabeth Shames, Portland, Maine.

321. "a terrible fear": Interview with Elizabeth Shames, Portland, Maine.

321. "Elizabeth's husband, Joe": Interview with Elizabeth Shames, Portland, Maine.

322. "I rebuilt her carriage house": Interview with Craig Miller, Cranford, New Jersey.

322. "If you allowed Ethel": Interview with Elizabeth Shames, Portland, Maine.

322. "When family members": Interview with Elizabeth Shames, Portland, Maine; interview with Craig and Dorothy Miller, Cranford, New Jersey; and interview with Claire Wagner by telephone.

323. "That stopped the storytelling": Interview with Elizabeth Shames, Portland, Maine.

323. "After that": Interview with Craig and Dorothy Miller, Cranford, New Jersey.

323. "in a city that no longer": Interview with Craig and Dorothy Miller, Cranford, New Jersey; interview with Charles Cummings, Newark.

324. "horse races": Undated clipping from Berg's *Newark News* file at the Newark Public Library.

324. "to purchase the Washington Senators": Summary of meetings, July 29 and 30, 1971, Berg file.

324. "The writer and editor": Interview with Ray Robinson by telephone.

324. "In 1967, Berg met": Information for this section comes from an interview with Sayre Ross, New York.

327. "not very grandfatherly": Interview with Mary Barcella by telephone.

328. "He said he'd swallowed": Dr. Murray Strober's patient history, May 27, 1972. Provided to me by Dr. Strober.

329. "On May 29, 1972": Death-scene information comes from interviews with Dr. Anthony DelGaizo and Dr. Martin Jassie by telephone; and Dr. Murray Strober, Nutley, New Jersey. See also Sam Berg, "Recollections," and his notes, March 10, 1979.

329. "Dr. Sam was": Princeton speech.

329. "When he learned what": Interview with William Greifinger; and S. Goldhaber to Sam Berg, March 8, 1987.

329. "As for Ethel": Interviews with Margaret Jennings Gahan and Eugenia O'Connor by telephone.

329. "Mostly she referred": Interview with Frances Chavis by telephone.

329. "One letter to Kieran": John Kieran to Asa Bushnell, December 1, 1972; and Ethel Berg to the CIA, May 28, 1975.

329. "Berg's ashes": Sam Berg notes, May 14, 1989, and July 21, 1989; Sam Berg to Charles Owen, January 7, 1987; S. Goldhaber to Sam Berg, March 8, 1987; S. Goldhaber to Ethel Berg, May 29, 1977.

Chapter 14. The Secret Life of Moe Berg

331. "Earl, did Colonel Dix": Interview with Earl Brodie, San Francisco.

332. "After meeting Berg": Bertha Dix to Berg, January 18, 1957.

332. "Dix's superiors concluded": April 30, 1948, CIA memo.

332. "Well, young fellow": Interview with Earl Brodie, San Francisco.

333. "In the press box": Interview with Bob Broeg by telephone.

334. "the fleeting moment early in 1929": Berg notes, June 23, 1966.

335. "His superiors at": Interview with Charles O'Neill by telephone.

335. "He began it on": Some of Berg's most interesting outlines are dated September 7, 1958; September 10, 1959; September 6, 1962; March 12, 1964; June 13, 1966; August 4, 1968; August 18, 1968; March 9, 1970.

336. "Moe Berg is a": Undated notebook entry.

336. "I was on TV": Ethel Berg, p. 300.

336. "M. B. embarrassed": Berg notebook entry, February 18, 1960.

336. "He sent himself": Ethel Berg, p. 262.

337. "Those who behave": Ethel Berg, p. 242.

338. "He was always a guy": Interview with Bobby Doerr by telephone.

338. "Jack Wilson": Interview with Jack Wilson by telephone.

338. "Berg did make ambiguous": Undated, anonymous letter from Berg file.

338. "Moe seemed to have no leanings": Interview with Irene Goudsmit by telephone.

338. "There were rumors": Interview with Duncan Robertson by telephone.

339. "old-type *natural*": Philip Larkin, *Collected Poems*, p. 170.

339. "He made sense": Interview with William Morgan, Washington, D.C.

339. "Bernard Berg knew only one": A copy of the novella manuscript was provided to me by Elizabeth Shames. She also gave me Anne Levy's translation of it.

341. "chocolate bars": Interview with Frances Book Kashdan by telephone.

341. "I always thought": Interview with Elizabeth Shames, Portland, Maine.

341. "a healer": Interview with Craig and Dorothy Miller, Cranford, New Jersey; and Ethel Berg to Aldo Icardi, January 14, 1985.

342. "unusual method of banking": Interview with Harry Broley, Washington, D.C.

342. "through the children": Philip Roth, "The Man in the Middle," *New York Times*, October 12, 1992. A letter I received from Lester Rodney was also especially helpful to my understanding of Jewish codes at the time.

343. "Bernard's hostile feelings": Interview with William Moskowitz by telephone and correspondence.

343. "Early in Berg's": Berg to his father, October 18, 1919.

344. "A few weeks later": Undated letter, fall 1919, from Berg to his father.

345. "Camp Wah-Kee-Nah": Berg to his father, July 26, 1921.

345. "Watch for the Chicago": Berg to his father, October 17, 1921.

345. "I've got some": Berg to his father, undated letter, Berg's junior year.

345. "After Princeton": Letters from France, December 2 and 8, 1923.

346. "I passed the bar": Berkow (Newspaper Enterprise Association), *Ann Arbor News*, June 18, 1972.

346. "Pa and I detested": Ibid.

346. "He's just a sport": Sam Berg notes, December 28, 1978, and January 2, 1979.

347. "There is nothing new": Bernard Berg to Berg, undated letter except for "Tuesday." Ethel Berg, who scribbled notes on it in the margin, guesses that her father wrote it in 1930.

348. "He began a letter": Bernard Berg to Berg, March 25, 1937.

348. "No matter how much": Kaufman, p. 111.

349. "on his birthday": Berg to his father, August 9, 1940.

349. "I never got married": Sam Berg notes, December 28, 1978.

350. "my R. C. friends": Interview with William Klein, New York.

350. "He once explained": Interview with Jonathan Bayliss by telephone and correspondence.

350. "Berg was invited": Interview with Earl Brodie, San Francisco.

351. "Baron Corvo": A. J. A. Symons, *The Quest for Corvo*, p. 28.

Selected Bibliography

▼

Abelow, Samuel P. *A History of Brooklyn Jewry.* Brooklyn, N.Y.: Scheba Publishing Co., 1937.

Alexander, Charles. *John McGraw.* New York: Penguin Books, 1988.

Allen, George R. "The Strange Story of Moe Berg, Athlete, Scholar, Spy." Philadelphia: Keepsake of a talk given at the Annual J. William White Dinner of the Franklin Inn Club, January 17, 1991.

Angell, Roger. *Five Seasons: A Baseball Companion.* New York: Simon and Schuster, 1972.

Bancroft, Mary. *Autobiography of a Spy.* New York: William Morrow and Co., 1983.

Bar-Zohar, Michel. *The Hunt for German Scientists, 1944–1960.* New York: Hawthorn Books, 1967.

Berg, Ethel. *My Brother Morris Berg: The Real Moe.* Privately published by the author in Newark, N.J., 1976.

Berg, Samuel, M.D. *Harrison Stanford Martland, M.D.: The*

Story of a Physician, a Hospital, an Era. New York: Vantage Press, 1978.

Bishop, Gordon. *Greater Newark: A Microcosm of America*. Chatsworth, Calif.: Windsor Publications, 1989.

Bradley, David. *Journey of a Johnny-Come-Lately*. Hanover, N.H.: Dartmouth Publications, 1957.

Brown, Anthony Cave. *The Last Hero: Wild Bill Donovan*. New York: Times Books, 1982.

Burke, Michael. *Outrageous Good Fortune*. Boston: Little, Brown, 1984.

Buxton, Frank, and Bill Owen. *Radio's Golden Age*. New York: Easton Valley Press, 1966.

Casey, William. *The Secret War Against Hitler*. Washington, D.C.: Regnery Gateway, 1988.

Cassidy, David. *Uncertainty: The Life and Science of Werner Heisenberg*. New York: W. H. Freeman, 1992.

Conover, Ted. *Rolling Nowhere*. New York: Penguin Books, 1984.

Corvo, Max. *The O.S.S. in Italy, 1942–1945*. Westport, Conn.: Praeger, 1990.

Creamer, Robert W. *Babe*. New York: Simon and Schuster, 1974.

Crowley, James B. *Japan's Quest for Autonomy: National Security and Foreign Policy, 1930–1938*. Princeton, N.J.: Princeton University Press, 1966.

Cunningham, Barbara, editor. *The New Jersey Ethnic Experience*. Union City, N.J.: William H. Wise and Company, 1977.

Cunningham, John T. *Newark*. Newark: New Jersey Historical Society, 1966 (revised, expanded edition, 1988).

Dulles, Allen W., editor. *The Craft of Intelligence*. Westport, Conn.: Greenwood Press, 1977.

Dunlop, Richard. *Donovan: America's Master Spy*. New York: Rand McNally and Company, 1982.

Dunning, John. *Tune in Yesterday: The Ultimate Encyclopedia of Old-Time Radio, 1925–1976*. Englewood Cliffs, N.J.: Prentice-Hall, 1976.

Einstein, Charles, editor. *The Fireside Book of Baseball*. New

York: Simon and Schuster, 4th edition, 1987. Jerome Holtzman's memoir of Berg, "A Great Companion," begins on p. 163.

Ford, Corey. *Donovan of OSS*. Boston: Little, Brown. 1970.

Foster, John B., editor. *Spalding's Official 1935 Baseball Guide*. New York: American Sports Publishing Company, 1935.

Frye, Alton. *Nazi Germany and the American Hemisphere, 1933–1941*. New Haven, Conn.: Yale University Press, 1967.

Gleick, James. *Genius: The Life and Science of Richard Feynman*. New York: Pantheon Books, 1992.

Glines, Carroll V. *Doolittle's Tokyo Raiders*. Princeton, N.J.: D. Van Nostrand and Company, 1964.

Goldschmidt, Bertrand. *Atomic Rivals*. New Brunswick, N.J.: Rutgers University Press, 1990.

Goudsmit, Samuel A. *Alsos*. New York: Henry Schuman, 1947.

Greenberg, Hank. *The Story of My Life*. New York: Times Books, 1989.

Groves, Leslie. *Now It Can Be Told*. New York: Harper and Brothers, 1962.

Hansen, James R. *Engineer in Charge: A History of the Langley Aeronautical Laboratory, 1917–1958*. Washington, D.C.: NASA, 1987.

Heisenberg, Elisabeth. *Inner Exile: Recollections of a Life with Werner Heisenberg*. Boston: C. Morris Birkhauser, 1984.

Hemingway, Ernest. *The Sun Also Rises*. New York: Charles Scribner's Sons, 1954.

Hersh, Burton. *The Old Boys: The American Elite and the Origins of the CIA*. New York: Charles Scribner's Sons, 1992.

Hilton, Stanley E. *Hitler's Secret War in South America, 1939–1945*. Baton Rouge: Louisiana State University Press, 1981.

Hirano, Jiro, Yoshihisa Hayashi, et al. *The Spy Who Loved Japan*. Tokyo: NHK, 1979.

Holtzman, Jerome, editor. *No Cheering in the Press Box*. New York: Holt, Rinehart and Winston, 1973.

Honig, Donald. *A Donald Honig Reader*. New York: Simon and Schuster, 1988.

Irving, David. *The German Atomic Bomb*. New York: Simon and Schuster, 1967.

Jeffreys-Jones, Rhodri. *The CIA and American Democracy.* New Haven, Conn.: Yale University Press, 1989.

Jungk, Robert. *Brighter Than a Thousand Suns.* New York: Harcourt, Brace, 1956.

Kaufman, Louis, Barbara Fitzgerald, and Tom Sewell. *Moe Berg: Athlete, Scholar, Spy.* Boston: Little, Brown, 1974.

Knightley, Phillip. *The Second Oldest Profession: Spies and Spying in the Twentieth Century.* New York: W. W. Norton and Company, 1987.

Kramish, Arnold. *The Griffin: The Greatest Untold Espionage Story of World War II.* Boston: Houghton Mifflin, 1986.

Kurth, Peter. *Anastasia: The Riddle of Anna Anderson.* Boston: Little, Brown, 1983.

Lardner, Ring. *You Know Me, Al.* New York: Vintage Books, 1984.

Larkin, Philip. *Collected Poems.* New York: Farrar, Straus and Giroux, 1989.

Lawson, Captain Ted W. *Thirty Seconds over Tokyo,* New York: Random House, 1943.

Leitch, Alexander. *A Princeton Companion.* Princeton, N.J.: Princeton University Press, 1978.

Levine, Peter. *Ellis Island to Ebbets Field: Sport and the American Jewish Experience.* New York: Oxford University Press, 1992.

Loos, Anita. *Cast of Thousands.* New York: Grosset and Dunlap, 1977.

Lovell, Stanley. *Of Spies and Stratagems.* Englewood Cliffs, N.J.: Prentice-Hall, 1963.

Masters, Dexter, and Katharine Way, editors. *One World or None.* New York: McGraw Hill, 1946.

Mizener, Arthur. *The Far Side of Paradise.* Boston: Houghton Mifflin, 1949.

Montague, Ludwell Lee. *General Walter Bedell Smith As Director of Central Intelligence.* University Park: Pennsylvania State University Press, 1992.

Moorehead, Alan. *The Traitors.* New York: Harper and Row, 1963.

Morely, James William, editor. *Dilemmas of Growth.* Princeton, N.J.: Princeton University Press, 1971. This volume contains "What Went Wrong?" by Edwin O. Reischauer.

Mosely, Leonard. *Dulles.* New York: Dial Press, 1978.

Moss, Norman. *Klaus Fuchs: The Man Who Stole the Bomb.* London: Grafton Books, 1987.

Muggeridge, Malcolm. *Chronicles of Wasted Time.* Washington, D.C.: Regnery Gateway, 1972.

Murray, Henry A., et al. (OSS Assessment Staff). *Assessment of Men.* New York: Rinehart and Company, 1978.

Newark Board of Trade. *Newark, the City of Industry: Facts and Figures Concerning the Metropolis of New Jersey.* Newark: Newark Board of Trade, 1912.

Orwell, George. *Down and Out in Paris and London.* New York: Harcourt, Brace, Jovanovich, 1961.

Pash, Boris. *The Alsos Mission.* New York: Award House, 1969.

Peniakoff, Vladimir. *Popski's Private Army.* New York: Thomas Y. Crowell Company, 1950.

Powers, Thomas. *Heisenberg's War: The Secret History of the German Bomb.* New York: Alfred A. Knopf, 1993.

———. *The Man Who Kept the Secrets: Richard Helms and the CIA.* New York: Alfred A. Knopf, 1987.

Ranelagh, John. *The Agency: The Rise and Decline of the CIA.* New York: Simon and Schuster, 1986.

Reichler, Joseph L. *The Baseball Encyclopedia.* New York: Macmillan, 1985.

Rhodes, Richard. *The Making of the Atomic Bomb.* New York: Simon and Schuster, 1988.

Ribalow, Harold U. *The Jew in American Sports.* New York: Bloch Publishing Company, 1955.

Rice, Arnold S., editor. *Newark: Chronological and Documentary History, 1666–1970.* Dobbs Ferry, N.Y.: Oceana Publications, 1977.

Ritter, Lawrence S. *The Glory of Their Times: The Story of the Early Days of Baseball, Told by the Men Who Played It.* New York: Vintage Books, 1985 (expanded version).

Roth, Philip. *Patrimony.* New York: Touchstone, 1991.

Rout, Leslie B., and John F. Bratzel. *The Shadow War: German Espionage and U.S. Counterespionage in Latin America Dur-*

ing World War II. Frederick, Md.: University Publications of America, 1986.

Rubbia, Carlo, et al. *Edoardo Amaldi, scienziato e cittadino d'Europa.* Milan: Leonardo Periodici, 1992. I also used an article-length English-language summary of this, entitled "Edoardo Amaldi, Scientific Statesman." Geneva: CERN, 1991.

Schacht, Al. *Clowning Through Baseball.* New York: A. S. Barnes and Company, 1941.

Slater, Robert. *Great Jews in Sports*, Middle Village, N.Y.: Jonathan David, 1983.

Smith, Bradley F. *The Shadow Warriors: OSS and the Origins of the CIA.* New York: Basic Books, 1983.

Smith, R. Harris. *OSS: The Secret History of America's First Central Intelligence Agency.* Berkeley: University of California Press, 1972.

Summers, Harrison B. *Radio Programs Carried on National Networks, 1926–1956.* Columbus: Ohio State University, 1958.

Susskind, Charles. *Dictionary of Scientific Biography.* New York: Charles Scribner's Sons, 1973.

Symons, A.J.A. *The Quest for Corvo: An Experiment in Biography.* New York: Penguin Books, 1986.

Thorn, John, editor. *The Armchair Book of Baseball.* New York: Charles Scribner's Sons, 1985. Contains Berg's "Pitchers and Catchers."

Thorn, John, and Pete Palmer, editors. *Total Baseball.* New York: Warner Books, 1989.

Tuchman, Barbara. *Stilwell and the American Experience in China, 1941–1945.* New York: Macmillan, 1970.

Urquhart, Frank J. *A History of the City of Newark, New Jersey.* New York: Lewis Historical Publishing Company, 1913.

———. *A Short History of Newark.* Newark: Baker Printing Company, 1953.

Von Karman, Theodore, and Lee Edson. *The Wind and Beyond: Theodore Von Karman, Pioneer in Aviation and Pathfinder in Space.* Boston: Little, Brown, 1967.

Weeks, Edward, editor. *The Pocket Atlantic.* New York: Pocket Books, 1946. Contains Berg's "Pitchers and Catchers."

Wigner, Eugene P. *The Recollections of Eugene P. Wigner.* New York: Plenum Press, 1992.

Winks, Robin W. *Cloak and Gown: Scholars in the Secret War.* New York: William Morrow, 1987.

Young, A. Morgan. *Imperial Japan, 1926–1938.* New York: William Morrow and Company, 1938.

Index

▼

▼

▼

ABOUT THE AUTHOR

Nicholas Dawidoff graduated from Harvard and spent a year in Asia as a Henry Luce Scholar. He has written for *Sports Illustrated*, *The New Republic*, *The New York Times Magazine*, *The New Yorker*, and *The American Scholar*. He lives in New York. This is his first book.